THE *Gardiners* OF MASSACHUSETTS

Revisiting New England: The New Regionalism

SERIES EDITORS

Siobhan Senier   *University of New Hampshire*

Darren Ranco   *Dartmouth College*

Adam Sweeting   *Boston University*

David H. Watters   *University of New Hampshire*

This series presents fresh discussions of the distinctiveness of New England culture. The editors seek manuscripts examining the history of New England regionalism; the way its culture came to represent American national culture as a whole; the interaction between that "official" New England culture and the people who lived in the region; and local, subregional, or even biographical subjects as microcosms that explicitly open up and consider larger issues. The series welcomes new theoretical and historical perspectives and is designed to cross disciplinary boundaries and appeal to a wide audience.

Richard Archer, *Fissures in the Rock: New England in the Seventeenth Century*

Judith Bookbinder, *Boston Modern: Figurative Expressionism as Alternative Modernism*

Donna M. Cassidy, *Marsden Hartley: Race, Region, and Nation*

Joseph A. Conforti, editor, *Creating Portland: History and Place in Northern New England*

Nancy L. Gallagher, *Breeding Better Vermonters: The Eugenics Project in Vermont*

Sidney V. James, *The Colonial Metamorphoses in Rhode Island: A Study of Institutions in Change*

Maureen Elgersman Lee, *Black Bangor: African Americans in a Maine Community, 1880–1950*

Christopher J. Lenney, *Sightseeking: Clues to the Landscape History of New England*

Donald W. Linebaugh, *The Man Who Found Thoreau: Roland W. Robbins and the Rise of Historical Archaeology in America*

Pauleena MacDougall, *The Penobscot Dance of Resistance: Tradition in the History of a People*

T. A. Milford, *The Gardiners of Massachusetts: Provincial Ambition and the British-American Career*

Diana Muir, *Reflections in Bullough's Pond: Economy and Ecosystem in New England*

James C. O'Connell, *Becoming Cape Cod: Creating a Seaside Resort*

Priscilla Paton, *Abandoned New England: Landscape in the Works of Homer, Frost, Hopper, Wyeth, and Bishop*

Jennifer C. Post, *Music in Rural New England Family and Community Life, 1870–1940*

David L. Richards, *Poland Spring: A Tale of the Gilded Age, 1860–1900*

Mark J. Sammons and Valerie Cunningham, *Black Portsmouth: Three Centuries of African-American Heritage*

Adam Sweeting, *Beneath the Second Sun: A Cultural History of Indian Summer*

THE
Gardiners
OF MASSACHUSETTS

Provincial Ambition and the British-American Career

T. A. Milford

University of New Hampshire Press
Durham, New Hampshire

PUBLISHED BY UNIVERSITY PRESS OF NEW ENGLAND
HANOVER AND LONDON

University of New Hampshire Press
Published by University Press of New England,
One Court Street, Lebanon, NH 03766
www.upne.com
© 2005 University of New Hampshire Press
Printed in the United States of America

5 4 3 2 1

Library of Congress Cataloging-in-Publication Data
Milford, T. A., 1970–
The Gardiners of Massachusetts : provincial ambition and the British-American career / T.A. Milford.
    p.   cm. — (Revisiting New England)
Includes bibliographical references and index.
ISBN-10: 1–58465–503–8 (cloth : alk. paper)
ISBN-13: 978–1–58465–503–9 (cloth : alk. paper)
ISBN-10: 1–58465–504–6 (pbk. : alk. paper)
ISBN-13: 978–1–58465–504–6 (pbk. : alk. paper)
1. Gardiner, Silvester, 1708–1786. 2. Gardiner, John, 1737–1793.
3. Gardiner, John Sylvester John, 1765–1830.
4. British Americans—Massachusetts—Boston—Biography.
5. Colonists—Massachusetts—Boston—Biography.
6. Ambition—Case studies. 7. Boston (Mass.)—Biography.
8. Boston (Mass.)—Politics and government—1775–1865.
9. Boston (Mass.)—Social conditions. 10. Boston (Mass.)—
Intellectual life. I. Title. II. Series.
F73.9.B7M55 2005
974.4'03'0922—dc22   2005009923

to W.R.M.

and to the memory of

W.D.M.

I profess to write the history of a man placed in the middle rank of life; of one whose vices and virtues were open to the eye of the most undiscerning spectator; who was placed in public view without power to repress censure or command adulation; who had too much merit not to become remarkable, yet too much folly to arrive at greatness. I attempt the character of one who was just such a man as probably you or I may be; but with this difference, that he never . . . formed a wish which he did not take pains to divulge.

—Oliver Goldsmith,
The Life of Richard Nash, Esq.
(1762)

No advantages in this world are pure and unmixed.

—David Hume,
"Of the Rise and Progress of the Arts and Sciences"
(1742)

CONTENTS

ACKNOWLEDGMENTS

Portions of "The Independent Province" appeared in the *New England Quarterly*, and portions of "Letters and Distinction" appeared in *Anglican and Episcopal History.* I thank these journals for allowing the republication of this material.

Had the late Alan Heimert not been such a determined advocate of early national literature, I would never have met the Gardiners. If David Hall hadn't given me enough rope, I would never have written about them. And if Bernard Bailyn hadn't signed off on such an odd piece of work, I'd still be in Widener Library. Thank you all.

Thanks are also due to Robert H. Gardiner, Phyllis Gardiner, Rhys Gardiner, and Susie Burke, who tolerated or even approved of my snooping into their ancestors' affairs. I was aided in this enterprise by Danny Smith. C. M. Wigan treated me to lunch at his club and entrusted me with his family's papers. Andrew J. O'Shaughnessy showed me the way to St. Kitts.

Eliga Gould, Sheila Skemp, and Lisa McFarlane read this book in manuscript; their comments have been of great help to me. Phyllis Deutsch and Ann Brash, my editors, have been supportive throughout. Dan Hulsebosch has been the best kind of friend and counsellor, but he'll understand if I thank Liza Velazquez last, for being the bestest friend of all.

THE *Gardiners* OF MASSACHUSETTS

Prospect

In January of 1792 John Gardiner stood among his peers in the Massachusetts House of Representatives and declared the virtues of the theater. His aim was to convince his listeners that the commonwealth's ban on theatrical performances was an obstacle to growth. He spoke at great length and tested, no doubt, the patience of the assembly—though the greater part of it would prove sympathetic to his cause. Gardiner was a pest. He had made trouble wherever his career had taken him: London, Wales, the West Indies, Boston. The last was the town of his nativity and childhood, but many of its residents, when faced with a now older Gardiner whipping along his chariot team of hobby-horses (the theater, the arrogance of the bar, the separation of Maine), concluded that he was half a foreigner, and driven by displaced priorities. He belonged to a different place and a different time, to Georgian England before the war, and before the breaking of Britain's first empire.

We can only guess how he looked to his audience. Some critics wrote that excess had inflamed his countenance, but ruddy features—however hard won—could have been found all around the room. There is a portrait of Gardiner, painted by John Singleton Copley.[1] By the date of Gardiner's theater speech, it was almost twenty-five years old, but it is suggestive nonetheless. The face is unprepossessing. Though he is just past his thirtieth year, his chin has receded into a pillow of fat. The jawless neckline reminds one of Lord North, whose dumpling head sat atop King George's government for most of the Revolutionary crisis. But whereas North's pudginess was absolute, encompassing every corner of his face, Gardiner's long nose and prim mouth have an almost effeminate delicacy. The eyes are widely spaced but hint at a playful intelligence. One cannot help but think that the sitter is an interesting yet not entirely serious person.

The contrast with his father's portrait—one of Copley's master-pieces—could not be more striking.[2] Silvester Gardiner's likeness has a palpable gravitas, a bourgeois majesty. He needs no props other than the chair on which he sits. His son, on the other hand, leans forward over a table and two of his books. One finger points toward and beyond the picture frame's edge. John's portrait is therefore the more superfi-cially dynamic, but one gets the sense that Silvester has already gone some great distance and arrived at that happy point from which move-ment is unnecessary and unwanted (though only four years after his sitting the Revolution would force Silvester's exile). His success has benefited his son—John's clothes and demeanor reveal this—but we are not sure that the son will multiply the father's gifts. In any case, the younger Gardiner is determined to make his own way in the world. His books are not the playthings of leisure but symbols of the knowl-edge he has accumulated and is now applying to improve himself and—again the pointing finger—others.

When he sat for Copley, John Gardiner was approaching middle age.[3] He had some good years behind him, but he had not yet made his fortune. He was, in fact, on his way to the sugar-rich West Indies hoping to do just that. The cares and occasional disappointments of adulthood were visible in the wrinkles under his eyes. His gray wig aged him as well; already he seemed a man not quite of his own time. By late middle age, he found that this judgment still stuck to him. He had returned to New England, but his post-Revolutionary career was fired by the now antique enthusiasms of 1760s London. And when he wasn't reminding everyone of his service to the radical John Wilkes or quoting the poetry of Wilkes's Falstaffian sidekick, Charles Churchill, Gardiner's mind and tongue raced into the future. Reform was his message: reforming his church to free it of bigotry and nonsense; reforming his profession, the law, to save it from an exclusiveness that bred resentment rather than respect; reforming the culture of his town and commonwealth, to push them along the path of progress. Other Bostonians found him to be a bit much, an odd combination of the old and the new. And Gardiner's manner was indeed eccentric, even offputting. He was, however, oddly in step with the tendencies of the period. Many of his reforms confirmed or anticipated early national developments, and these developments, though gauged to the needs of a newly independent nation, took their original strength from the bonds that once held Britain and America together.

For most of the eighteenth century, America's break with Great Britain could not have been comfortably predicted. To the contrary, several circumstances hinted at a further and deeper intermingling of destinies. Americans conformed, with ever increasing willingness and vigor, to English norms and expectations, and many thought that the empire would provide the natural ends or extensions to their careers. British provincials—Scot and Yankee, Antiguan and Liverpudlian—assumed that their stature in the English-speaking world and in its capital, London, depended on the empire's growth and continued success. Atlantic commerce advanced a wider British culture and encouraged a cosmopolitan state of mind friendly to imperial projects.[4]

Nevertheless, a revolution was in the offing—and for good reasons. While they shared a common language and a common history, Americans and metropolitan Britons misunderstood each other in political matters, and these misunderstandings were, by the late stages of the imperial crisis, dangerously extravagant. The course of constitutional history since the 1680s had not prepared British parliamentarians to stomach a confederative, compromised sovereignty, but that is exactly what most colonial politicians expected of them. Americans were at first too sanguine about their relationship with the British nation, and, when government policy told a different tale, they grasped at an explanation adequate to their disappointment. The complex of sentiments we call "republicanism" was an artifact of Atlantic civilization, but it was also the means by which the empire's integrity was deranged and finally broken.[5]

Yet living and working within the empire had trained British Americans in other ideologies and habits of mind, and these endured into the national era even if they had not been as forthrightly employed in the Revolution's service as republican or "country" rhetoric had been. Take liberalism, for example. The American Revolution was once understood as a liberal event, as a chapter of Whiggish scripture in which John Locke played patron saint. Then, as is well known, a closer look at the sources determined that much of the Revolution's intellectual superstructure was *il*liberal: the needs of the community were often favored over the individual's; progress took a back seat to nostalgia; rustic verities trumped urban sophistication.[6] This new political history unintentionally complemented the social history that came into its own at around the same time: a history that rediscovered village America. Americans, it seemed, were slow to join the modern world, and liberalism could wait until after the Revolution.

As of the writing of this book, our understanding of Anglophone society has evolved considerably. Republican moralism was a real phenomenon—and its effect on American history should not be minimized—but the piety entailed imposture. Republicanism might well have been a stalking horse that obscured the very modern desires (and, with them, regrets) of American provincials. Most of these people—and certainly the merchants, planters, and professionals who led the Revolutionary movement—were deeply implicated in the exchanges, consumption patterns, and vicarious anxieties and attainments of an expanding market economy. As liberalism describes and mythologizes the priorities of such economies, we are not surprised to find liberal ideologies once again accorded respect by historians of the period.

Their accounts honor the era's dominant economic trends and the intellectual temperament that accompanied them, but the emphasis is still firmly on national and political outcomes. One of the most seasoned observers of eighteenth-century British America notes that its people wanted to be as British as roast beef but felt excluded from the homeland's increasingly robust nationalism. This exclusion forced Americans, as well as the Irish rebels of the day, to construct their nationalisms around liberal and universal notions of natural right.[7] Given what happened in 1776, there is little to be gained from ignoring this national story. It is what people want to hear, and it has within it a truth that is no less fundamental for being obvious: the Revolution wrought a great change in the lives of Americans and in the history of the world. The danger is that we miss the continuities that yoked early national America to its immediate colonial past. To privilege the political history of Patriots and Founders is just, but to privilege it absolutely is misleading, for not everything changed as dramatically as America's political constitution. To put it another way: the politicians of the early republic confronted a new set of problems—problems raised by the fact of American independence—but they did so with social, cultural, and intellectual equipment demanded by their country's imperial engagements.

Historians of Great Britain in the eighteenth century are increasingly respectful of the nascent middle classes and the influence they exerted. High politics was an aristocratic affair, but—in other endeavors, and in the political substrate—merchants, lawyers, doctors, master craftsmen, and their literary sons and brothers became important molders of opinion and taste. Their rise was hastened by the expansion of empire but then stymied somewhat by the new challenges facing the British state after the American Revolution. Britain would rally around its aristocratic and military core, even as it acknowledged the necessity of a flexible approach to imperial government. The nation accelerated its extraordinary commercial drive, but its commercial people, the middle classes, had to attach themselves to the traditional elite if they wanted to become truly powerful.[8]

This branch of social history, the story of the frustrated fortunate, deserves more attention from students of British America. In America there was less to prevent men of that type from realizing their ambitions socially and politically. Some very suggestive material is well worn—Washington's pique at being refused a regular officer's commission; the bad blood, seasoned with the hot envy of near equals, that set Adamses and Otises against the Hutchinsons and their kin—but these and similar anecdotes have not been connected to the liberalism that was and still is the natural ideology of able and prosperous climbers.[9] This book makes those connections and thereby more firmly links the British Atlantic experience to the intellectual history of the late colonial and early national periods. Other historians have explained how provincial elites—enjoying some power, but never enough—were inclined to identify their ambitions with the common good.[10] Liberalism thus became a language of political aspiration as well as an apology for success. And imperial engagement brought, to provincials in particular, increased opportunities and increased exposure to risk. A British officer in America had hard coin in his purse—a rare treat for colonial shopkeepers—but his troops might bring disease and disorder. English luxuries beckoned. An accelerated commerce meant increased litigation. Who would manage these risks and profit by them? Merchants, lawyers, and doctors, in the main, and we should not be surprised therefore that many of them adopted a liberal stance (tolerating freedom and risk for the sake of profit and cultural improvement) when addressing public controversies.

Professionals were the most learned and articulate of Americans, and as such they were more likely to be familiar and comfortable with the progressive literature of political economy generated within the British Empire, most notably in Scotland. Professionals and merchants performed intermediary and transactional functions that made them more aware of imperial standards and space, for ideas and markets alike operated across great distances and followed maps on which the metropolis and other important ports-of-call were clearly marked. Cosmopolitanism, and a sophisticated ethic of troubleshooting, became more pronounced behaviors among Americans active in early national political and cultural debates, because they had been bent to these orientations by the imperial environment and their vocational experience within it.

◂§ · §▸

What follows is a story of ambition, a native human quality that, to be sure, has not gone unnoticed in studies of the Revolution and its aftermath. Creole elites resented any attempt to check their political gains or reduce their already considerable authority. They especially resented the irregular nature of imperial patronage, whereby unproven or unloved men were catapulted into positions of seemingly extraordinary influence. Many patriots fought not to destroy privilege but to insure that its disposition agreed with local realities.[11] All this is known and is instructive; the challenge is not to counter these claims so much as to turn them on their heads. Ambition does not just explain events; it *is* the event, a long event spanning the Revolutionary troubles and linking the young nation to the old empire.

For a century, at least, the ambitions of merchants, lawyers, and other middling persons had been gathering historical momentum. This was first and foremost an economic process, tied to the growth and sophistication of trading and financial arrangements, but it also compelled the attention of intellectuals, who welcomed advances in knowledge and a higher regard for the knowledgeable. Middling hopes and middling pride found their spokesmen in the commonwealth tradition, in Augustan periodicals, in Benjamin Franklin's homely wisdoms, and in the seminal analytical works of Scottish thinkers. Adam Smith, David Hume, and their compatriots described a modernity that had ambition at its creative center and a liberal perspective that encompassed the opportunities of empire.[12] This perspective would color American politics and society after the imperial crisis was resolved. Indeed, liberalism emerged as a viable political program in America much sooner than was possible in Britain, where aristocratic grandees continued to enjoy the primacy. American merchants and professionals were truly in the ascendant, but their sense of fitness, their pretensions to elite status, drew on a characteristically provincial compound of energy and insecurity.

The Gardiners of Massachusetts

Persons from what Hume called the "middle station of life" were, in social terms, the least stationary of ranks.[13] This is not an immediately obvious point. The body of people that stretched from the top of the artisanal order through the more prosperous burgher classes and into the lower echelons of the gentry was, from one angle, the very trunk of modern society. These people feared loss more acutely for their experience of gain; they understood the value of stability. On the other hand, the most effective revolutions began among men and women, who were otherwise the most solid of citizens. And one need not dwell on uncivil political episodes in order to gauge the dynamic qualities of the middling sort. Restlessness characterized their economic activities, and it was at the bottom of the long revolution of manners—bloodless by design, if not in fact—that transformed the West into a bourgeois civilization: clean, rich, democratic, and nervous. Merchants and especially professionals also promulgated ostensibly universal standards of conduct and judgment, which eased communication and aided the rational pursuit of goals.

Like their fellows in England or Flanders, eighteenth-century Americans of the "middle station" saw themselves as intermediaries, but they eventually faced a challenge particular to their case. The imperial crisis disrupted commerce, communications, and the relations of province and metropolis—areas of endeavor at which merchants and professionals were adept. To be sure, many of these men profited by the crisis and welcomed its result, but all such men, whatever their politics, had to foreshorten their perspective, which hitherto was drawn along the extensive lines projected by the British Empire. Yes, a continent—and with it Jefferson's "empire of liberty"—was at their feet, but their reorientation was difficult nonetheless. In the new state of affairs, Americans could prosecute their claims to authority, but they could not forget that these claims were nurtured under an older and, in some ways, grander dispensation.

A study of ambitions must put men before ideas, and so this one shall do. Three men from Massachusetts interest us particularly: Silvester Gardiner, his son, John, and John's own son, the improbably named John Sylvester John (J. S. J., hereafter). Each Gardiner was born into the first British Empire and adjusted, with varying success, to its retrenchment. There is nothing extraordinary about this fact; one might invoke a host of threesomes that shared in this accident of fate. Nor should one, to take a different approach, offer the Gardiners up as representative Americans of their era. Their personalities were excessive, their backgrounds a shade too colorful, and their experiences unusually broad. Yet it is exactly this breadth that recommends them to the historian. Their stories are entangled with many others, and the range of their careers demonstrates the limits and opportunities of provincial life in late-eighteenth-century British America.

Even on a strictly American scale of importance, the Gardiners and most of their associates were men of the second rank. They were not Founders, and they do not immediately command our consideration, as men like Washington, Jefferson, and Hamilton do. They were, nevertheless, influential people: notable in their professions and active in politics and society. Such people might not tell us much about statesmanship, but they do tell us about the behavior of America's political class, the larger body of men from which its statesmen emerged. This class was not defined by the franchise, which was too broad to provide proper definition; instead, its members were distinguished by their public credit. They had the wherewithal to be a part of civic culture, and they engaged in its debates. This smaller group of participants remains an unwieldy subject for quantitative analysis, and, in any case, statistics cannot adequately register changes in outlook and attitude. Continuities are more evasive still, especially when the constitutional innovations of the Revolutionary era encourage us to see changes everywhere and in everything. A fine-grained inquiry, which focuses on a few men from successive generations of one family, is a much more sensitive gauge.

It must be stressed that what follows is less a family history than a generational one. Without granting the "generation" any universal value as a concept, one can and should describe how, for example, two similar persons or cohorts can seem very different because they come of age thirty years apart. A family history is something else entirely. It assumes that consanguinity and shared experience create a discrete environment, and it tends to approach the family as an institution, which, in the upper social strata, is productive of other institutions: schools, museums, and other semiprivate endowments. In America, the so-called "Boston Brahmins" have inspired the best histories of this kind.[14] Importantly, theirs is a nineteenth-century story. The progenitors of the Brahmin class turned to industrial enterprise and its charitable adjuncts in order to escape the insecurity of eighteenth-century mercantile wealth. Silvester, John, and J. S. J. Gardiner belong to the earlier, less confident period. While some of their projects anticipated the firmer developments to come, these men made their way in the world by mediating between various commercial interests, political formations, and bodies of knowledge. For them, the problems of empire were problems of social as well as political identity.

◆§ · §◆

Silvester Gardiner, who established the family's fortunes in Boston, almost thoughtlessly expected Britain's ambitions to accord with his. He was a dedicated Anglican and, when the time came, an unrepentant if unhappy Loyalist. His allegiances, however, must be situated within a larger pattern of development. His initial rise to prominence as a colonial surgeon was pegged to a burgeoning respect for professional training and practice. He acquired this training in Britain and advertised its superiority upon returning to Massachusetts. His medical work led to other, more lucrative ventures. Gardiner was a giant in the drugs trade; by his efforts, Europe's finest patent medicines reached the far corners of New England's backcountry. In one especially spacious corner, in what is now the state of Maine, he made his deepest mark. At a time when land speculation was the common passion of American men on the make, Silvester Gardiner was a leader of the Kennebeck Company, an aggressive project that, for better or worse, brought civilization to the northern woods. More to the point, it served the interests of its partners and of an expanding empire.

At the end of the Revolution, when Silvester Gardiner's vast landholdings were in jeopardy, his son returned to his native New England after a long and eventful absence. This book is a study of three careers, but John Gardiner's engrosses its attention. His career is the most sensational and varied of the three, but it is also, at first glance, the most resistant to analysis. He was almost too rubbery a character, too ready to change as chance demanded. But, as he in fact argued, his elasticity was his strength, and it recommends the strength of his example. He was fully at ease within the empire. When he sought to better his position in the provinces, he relied on his knowledge of imperial administration and on his connections at Whitehall and Westminster. At the same time, he held that many durable structures of government and jurisprudence tended to arrest social progress and the advancement of society's best men. His liberalism always engaged his opportunities, and he left the empire in the same spirit by which he had honored it.

He was, furthermore, making good on the promise of his education and early training. John Gardiner attended university in Glasgow, when the Scottish Enlightenment had nearly achieved its mature brilliance. Adam Smith, the most influential expositor of liberal political economy, was one of his professors. After taking his degree, and after a brief apprenticeship in a Boston law office, Gardiner moved to London and to its Inns of Court, where he continued his legal studies in the distinctly unrigorous fashion of the day. This education was as social as it was scholastic, and the young American fell in with Wilkes, one of the great Georgian libertines. As a newly minted barrister, Gardiner helped to defend Wilkes and his cronies when their public insolence provoked the Crown's fury. From these experiences and associations he absorbed several lessons. He adopted a raucous and ideological style of dissent. He learned to decry Scots, even as he expressed their wisdoms. And, finally, he learned that versatility was a most modern and practical virtue.

This last lesson was reinforced by Gardiner's legal practice, which demanded that he seek clients and causes in far-flung parts of Britain's empire. For several years, he lived in Wales, England's oldest province. He then moved on to St. Kitts, in the West Indies, where sugar wealth floated many new fortunes. Lawyers, along with merchants, had the most to gain by extensive travel. They depended on local clients, but it was their business to integrate smaller concerns into larger. The commodities or problems of one place assumed more value when linked to transatlantic markets or schemes of thought. The common law was one such scheme. It was a powerful binding agent, but it also supplied the text of rebellion. Provincial lawyers were pulled in two directions. While they increasingly sought preferment within the empire, they were, at the critical juncture, the best advocates and representatives of the discontented creole elite. Gardiner, in his Caribbean period, was a zealous supporter of parliamentary supremacy, but upon returning to Massachusetts in 1783 he became a convincing patriot.

His homecoming, after nearly a lifetime abroad, was not as momentous as it might seem: he was simply moving back to the province of his birth. Despite the break with Britain, it was a province still; even men and women much less traveled than John Gardiner thought so. Postwar Boston saw a number of controversies that were arguments of scale. The inhabitants of town and commonwealth had to decide how far they would go in meeting the wider world: in welcoming foreign merchants and comedians, in recognizing the intellectual authority of lawyers, in imitating other cities, and in bowing to the sovereignty of the United States. Gardiner played a key role in these controversies, as did liberal ideas about the desires and distinctions that energized progressive societies, ideas that had been powerfully articulated by the Scottish writers. Liberalism's currency in America was not fixed to a post-Revolutionary economic transformation; instead, the liberal rhetoric that colored Boston's civic life in the early national period was the exercise of an imperial reflex.[15] Commercial and professional elites, long accustomed to mediating local and metropolitan concerns, had to come to terms with their own success. They were aspiring cosmopolites who had the run of a contracted field.

John's son, J. S. J., was too young to make a responsible decision about the Revolution, but he did, quite consciously, confront the issue of New England's continuing provincialism. Like his father and grandfather before him, this young Gardiner was a professional. Somewhat retrogressively, a cleric succeeded a lawyer and a doctor. And J. S. J. wasn't just a minister; he was an Episcopalian priest. This was in keeping with the family traditions, although John Gardiner made a show of rejecting the Trinitarian prayer book. J.S.J.'s career followed a narrower path than his father's had. He spent almost his entire adulthood in Boston, and he served the same church for over thirty years. His politics were Federalist, and, when Federalist prospects dimmed on the national stage, he became an even more rigid Yankee. His sympathies and fears are evident in his sermons and belletristic writings. These writings, along with his expertise in classical languages, won him a proud place among Boston's literati at the beginning of the nineteenth century. His circle, the immediate predecessors to Emerson's generation of writers, could be dismissed as a gang of crabbed and disappointed aesthetes. Emerson himself was of this opinion.[16] But letters offered more than consolation; to devotees, they outlined the expansive cultural horizon that Americans had first sighted with Britons' eyes.

These, then, are the Gardiners. They carve—it is hoped—a fascinating trajectory. Federalist followed Wilkite followed Tory, and, as we shall see, a disinheritance reflected the era's tumultuous politics. One Gardiner rejected Anglican orthodoxy; the next re-embraced it. And each was such a complete, even extreme, character: Silvester's loyalties to Crown and Church meshed so neatly; John played the ungovernable gadfly with such enthusiasm; and John Sylvester John loved order in language and in society. Yet these differences, here so boldly delineated, fade after closer inquiry, as do many of the partisan distinctions that mark our understanding of this period. Indeed, the Gardiners' story encourages us to look beyond party and the contested patriotisms of the Revolutionary age to find prominent men of means adopting a common idiom by which to explain their advantages.

Witness how, in 1792, John Gardiner asked his fellow legislators in the General Court of Massachusetts to repeal the commonwealth's longstanding ban on theatrical entertainments. "The dark, gloomy bigot must soon go off the stage of life," to be replaced, he said, by "a new set of Actors . . . of more liberal ideas, and of a more refined taste, formed to enjoy the polished refinements of social life."[17] Gardiner was saying two things at once. The improvement of society, as he saw it, was general and inevitable. It included everyone and every endeavor, over time. Still, some came to the process sooner than others—and with more to contribute. "Liberal ideas" had emerged, in part, to explain the agreement of general and particular interests. Liberal optimism had an edge, and later chapters will document that many Bostonians supported their claims to merit by speaking well of progress and luxury and self-interest.

Much is known about the impact of liberal ideas on American constitutional questions, but liberalism follows, and must be seen to follow, experience. The progressive sensibility at work in John Gardiner's speech and elsewhere in late-eighteenth-century Boston was more than the product of book learning; it evolved in response to political and social conditions. The Scots, after all, wrote about society to explain their place in Britain. Likewise, the anxieties of America's early national political class—and its argument that the competition of interests refined "the art of managing well"—recalled the behavior and strategies of aggressive provincials within the British Empire.[18]

Silvester

Interest and Empire

Silvester Gardiner made a convincing Tory. His enterprises benefited from a cozy relationship with the provincial authorities and required contacts at the imperial center. As a doctor, he serviced the Royal Navy. As a churchman, he sought to replicate England's ecclesiastical order in the new settlements. He was, however, no less of an American for having spent seven years in British exile. He was born in Rhode Island, and he was happy to return there after Independence. His response to the Revolution was not the consummate moment of his career. Gardiner's loyalty to the Crown indicates the strength of his imperial connections, but it also cramped his expansive style of business, a style that the empire had encouraged.

Moreover, Gardiner's mercantile and speculative endeavors were extensions of a professional career sprung from a life of imperial engagement and from the problems and opportunities associated with colonial America's own cultural, commercial, and political relations with Great Britain. American professional culture was not a product of empire—the history of social elaboration is too large to be contained by any national narrative, however ambitious—but that culture, in its infancy, owed much to an imperial frame of reference: to the diffusion of knowledge from centers of learning (such as the Scottish universities) into less sophisticated provinces, and to standard vocabularies (like that provided by the common law) that manufactured both a shared, transatlantic competence and the leverage by which local practitioners and their allies might pry themselves away from metropolitan authorities.

Doctors, lawyers, and clergy were also best equipped to meet and profit by many of the challenges of contact, exposure, and growth that characterized early modern society, challenges often introduced or deepened by the experience of empire (as was the case when Britain's imperial wars enriched some Americans, impoverished others, and accelerated the exposure of many to a range of social influences, from the manners of the British officer class to the diseases that followed the typical military camp). This professional equipment did not predispose its handlers to take one side or the other during the Revolutionary crisis. If anything, a professional education and career allowed one to identify with both sides. What is more interesting—though less obvious—than the political choices made by particular actors is the ethos that informed but ultimately transcended political action of all sorts.

Silvester Gardiner's loyalty is therefore less significant than the attitudes he assumed in common with latter-day political foes. These attitudes were, in the main, progressive and elitist. America's future development was urged, and, for most of the century, nearly everyone thought that this development would proceed within the British imperial tent. The wilderness would be settled and cultivated; a growing population, in both town and country, would itself grow rich and demand a broader selection of goods and services; knowledge would spread with wealth, though prosperity and sophistication and political capability would of course accumulate at the same end of the social spectrum. Progress would not be without pain, but education and experience prepared America's increasingly confident professionals to administer to these ills. They would help manage the stresses of growth and promote a level of social fitness that could tolerate the occasional disorder for the sake of persistent achievement. This attitude had its complement among merchants, who were accustomed to competition and risk. The line between professional and commercial activity was quite thin, and no one crossed it more readily than Silvester Gardiner, who folded the dividends of his expertise into the expansion of the Atlantic economy.

The man's accomplishments were unanticipated of the boy: Gardiner was not a likely child. His vigor stolen by poor health, he seemed ill-suited to the role of gentleman planter defined by his family's successes in the seventy years since they had settled in the Narragansett country of Rhode Island. The future would ridicule this estimate, but in the 1720s Gardiner entered his adolescence in need of a patron. How fortunate, then, that his family had joined others at St. Paul's Church in Kingstown to petition the bishop of London for a missionary. James MacSparran arrived in April of 1721; he would prove to be one of the most durable representatives of the Society for the Propagation of the Gospel in Foreign Parts (SPG).[1]

The SPG was born in a fit of turn-of-the-century Protestant activism and organizational spirit. The increasingly visible problems of England's swelling towns and cities—and of London, the "great wen," above all—provoked a fresh sortie from philanthropic societies and societies aiming to reform the manners of a wayward people. England's imperial commitments also became objects of ecclesiastical concern. Something had to be done, surely, about the unchurched (or underchurched) in the English dominions abroad. Certain Anglican divines contemplated the rollback of nonconformity there, as well as closer to home, but, in the earliest years of the eighteenth century, this theme was muted by the need for Protestants everywhere to unite in opposition to his most Catholic majesty, Louis XIV of France. The SPG, for example, reached out to Continental Protestants with discrepant theological leanings.[2]

On the other side of the Atlantic, New England ministers, like their counterparts in colonial politics, emerged from the seventeenth century with moderated principles and a compromised sovereignty. We are not surprised, then, to find Yankee clerics—Benjamin Colman was the acknowledged bellwether—seeking a rapprochement with the Church of England and its traditions. The ecumenical strain would never disappear entirely from the constitution of British Atlantic Christianity: it would color the forthrightly but diversely Protestant brand of cultural chauvinism that was, by another name, British patriotism, and it would inform the Wesleyan and other revivals of later decades. But ecumenism passed out of the ascendant in the Georgian era, when the Anglican Church—aware of its weakness—sought to improve its fortunes, often at the expense of other denominations. The SPG became the creature of this cause.[3]

Also worth noting, in this context, is the political union of England and Scotland and its ramifications for Anglican missionaries and others whose work was defined by the transatlantic environment. Finalized in 1707, a year before Silvester Gardiner's birth, the Union of Parliaments complicated the empire's religious identity: Scotland maintained a Presbyterian establishment. Anglican Scots who pursued a career in divinity were frequently constrained to pursue it far afield, outside of Scotland and, given the dearth of good livings in England, even beyond the British Isles. This was in step with imperial trends. The Union of Parliaments curtailed Scottish independence at the same time that the American colonies were being royalized or otherwise reigned in, but the empire gave scope to the ambitions of Scots and other provincial Britons, including the Americans.[4]

The example of James MacSparran is instructive. He was Scots-Irish, and he was graduated from the University of Glasgow as Scotland was bestirring itself from its late Stuart doldrums. Older, slower rhythms were disrupted; an impoverished pride was humbled but then put in loose harness and briskly exercised by an imperial project directed from England. Soon Glasgow and Edinburgh would harbor some of the empire's richest merchants as well as an admired intelligentsia that did much to universalize (and, by a stroke of subtle vengeance, de-anglicize) the meaning of progress. James MacSparran was a firm British chauvinist and empire-man, much like his friend and patron Francis Nicholson, the sometime governor or lieutenant governor of several North American provinces. MacSparran believed, for example, that American pretensions to learning and leadership were empty without British standards and education. He was a banner-bearer of the national church.[5]

In fact, his investment in England's church and in the Anglo-American empire far exceeded his respect for England itself. Well before the imperial crisis—which he did not live to see—he expressed his concerns about corruption and mismanagement at the empire's heart. He was wary about future *formal* extensions of imperial government (to his native Ireland, for instance).[6] In other words, he honored the empire for a regularity and civilizing influence that was less metropolitan than cosmopolitan. The agents of empire—men like himself, who articulated its priorities by word and deed—were more worthy and, ideally, more influential than the empire's distant and distracted ruling class.

Once settled in Rhode Island, MacSparran became a pillar of the community that had called him there, a community dominated by the Narragansett gentry. Theirs was a country of fine pacing horses and of broad fields worked by African slaves (MacSparran himself became an owner of slaves and a determined and often unwanted missionary to them). By marrying Hannah Gardiner, MacSparran formally allied his fortunes to that of the local squirearchy. But he was also a refining influence on that society. He played host to the Anglo-Irish prelate and philosopher George Berkeley, when Berkeley sought to transplant the best in learned culture to the poorer—but, when compared to Walpole's England, decidedly purer—soils of America. MacSparran sat for one of New England's first portrait painters—John Smibert, whom we shall meet again—and christened the most famous portraitist of the Founding Era: Gilbert Stuart. MacSparran was a teacher of the classics; one of his first students was Thomas Clap, a future president of Yale College.[7]

And consider MacSparran's influence on Silvester Gardiner, his young brother-in-law. MacSparran convinced him that his best chances lay elsewhere. He convinced Silvester's father, William Gardiner, to let the boy spend his patrimony on a medical education in Boston and, most decisively and expensively, abroad. The eighteenth century would see more and more young men of the farm—and especially younger sons—seek professional training.[8] The pattern would be repeated by Silvester Gardiner's children, again with the encouragement of the Reverend MacSparran. In one sense, he was the imported Anglican parson, an ornament of the provincial gentry; in another and more enduring sense, he was the vessel of an enterprising, progressive spirit that Gardiner and many others imbibed enthusiastically.

While France practiced the best surgery through the seventeenth century, the years of Gardiner's apprenticeship saw that distinction passing to Britain. Gardiner split the difference, learning his trade in the hospitals of London and Paris from 1727 to 1734. His stay in France, however much it advanced his technique, did not endure happily in the doctor's memory. To the end of his days, he remained an unabashed Gallophobe.[9] The case was different with England, and Gardiner was more than willing to advertise its influence. His chief teacher there was William Cheselden. This surgeon was quite a celebrity, having built his reputation on the popular *Anatomy* and pioneering work in the treatment of cataracts and bladderstones. One "Grateful Patient" set his thanks to verse in a *Gentleman's Magazine* of 1732: "And above all the race of men / I bless my God for Cheselden." Another poet, Alexander Pope, wrote that his innovations saved thousands of lives. Isaac Newton and Queen Caroline sought out his care.[10]

Instructed by this and other, less famous, mentors, Gardiner was ready to launch his Boston practice in 1734. From that year until his exile in 1776, he was among the two or three most important physicians in Massachusetts. Gardiner established his name in a number of ways. During a visit to Boston in the early thirties, he married Anne Gibbins, the daughter of John Gibbins, a wealthy doctor under whom Gardiner had studied as a teen and with whom he would serve as a vestryman at King's Chapel.[11] Gardiner also made common cause with other physicians in securing the boundaries and prerogatives of their profession. Scottish doctors, many armed with Edinburgh degrees, were emigrating to America, where they found a ready market for their expertise. By 1736, Gardiner had joined William Douglass, one of the most prominent of these Scots, to form the Medical Society of Boston. This group published a manifesto of sorts in the *Boston Weekly News-Letter*, which called for the regulation of all of the province's doctors by a board to be certified by the General Court. These measures would, the authors hoped, suppress the practice of "Shoemakers, Weavers and Almanack-makers, with their virtuous Consorts," who had strayed from "the proper Business of their Lives." Douglass and Gardiner made much of their British training, and their attempts to define and so elevate the doctor's place in America were consciously attached to the advances won by British civilization.[12]

A Medical Society notice of 1741 is illustrative. Denouncing the "quackish" views of some advertisers, the notice offered a demonstration of real ability. A boy of six years was painfully afflicted by a bladderstone, and his prospects had narrowed to death or surgery. Luckily, the surgeon was Silvester Gardiner, who was educated—the article notes—on the other side of the Atlantic. Cutting "according to Mr. Cheselden's late Improvement of the lateral [as opposed to the suprapubic] way," he quickly removed the offending deposit in full view of the Medical Society and "others without reserve." The dimensions of the stone (one and a half inches at its shortest diameter) were described in detail, as was the boy's complete recovery.[13] No homespun remedies here, just good science updated from across the sea: Dr. Gardiner was at your service.

Gardiner attracted more than his share of patients over the years, but surgery alone was too uncertain to support the fortune and position he would come to enjoy. Even in his area of expertise, the lithotomy, Gardiner's efforts did not always meet with success. When one Amos Turner died a year after Gardiner removed a stone from his bladder, his heirs declined to pay for the operation. They had some cause, for an autopsy revealed more stones that the doctor had apparently missed. Exhibiting the litigious nature that, for the next fifty years, would occupy lawyers from rude frontier courthouses to the halls of the Privy Council, Gardiner sued for his fees and for the damage to his name.[14] In another instance, the diary of one of his students, William Jepson, offers dry commentary on the vagaries of medical practice. Jepson noted in June of 1753 that Gardiner went to Marblehead to see a Robert Lee about his stone. An entry five days later mentions Lee's burial.[15]

Jepson's account is not always so dire, or even so medical. Indeed, what impresses the reader of his diary is the range of activity in his master's world. While Gardiner's practice took him far from Boston—to attend a patient in Connecticut, for instance—the doctor stretched his talents and enterprises even further, in mercantile pursuits. His ships ferried cargo to Newfoundland and to the Maine settlements, where his hired men built mills and storehouses. His correspondence shuttled back and forth between Boston and London. Jepson, the doctor's apprentice, recorded these events as faithfully as he did visitations to the sick. And for good reason: Jepson was entering Gardiner's commercial orbit and would remain there for nearly two decades. Their partnership was not limited to any one trade, but drugs were their bread and butter.[16]

Silvester Gardiner was the leading apothecary in colonial New England. He probably opened his shop, at the sign of "the Unicorn and Mortar," soon after settling in Boston in the mid-thirties. In time, no other dealer could provide as many products and in such variety. When confiscated by the Continental Army in 1776, his stock and equipment filled twenty wagons. While we cannot be sure what his income was, there is no doubt that his take from the drug trade far outstripped what he made in fees. One informed guess is that his earnings were seven times that of the average doctor.[17] We shall soon discuss to what uses he put his money. Of more interest here is how the conduct of his trade measured the gauge of his ambition.

He was not content to practice within the ring of his acquaintances, carrying from house to familiar house his secret knowledge and a small bag of goods. His profession and his business must be considered of a piece. As has been seen already, his expertise had metropolitan origins. He was similarly connected by the traffic in drugs. Much of it passed through London, and, like all apothecaries, Gardiner sold patent medications from England such as Bateman's elixir and Goodfrey's "British oyl." His advertisements appealed to merchants and captains responsible for outfitting ocean vessels. His medicine chests were, he wrote, exactly like those provided to the Royal Navy at home. Gardiner also acted as agent to London druggists who were trying to collect their American debts.[18]

He was both a manager and a satellite of the Atlantic mercantile system. Gardiner profited from the very extensiveness of trade within the empire, but, as much as possible, he made that empire his own. He consigned his drugs to other doctors and apothecaries and thus became their chief creditor. He underwrote the practices of men such as Donald Cummings, a Scot and former surgeon in the British Army who had settled in far eastern Massachusetts (that is, Maine). William Jepson handled his master's affairs in Hartford. Elsewhere in Connecticut, Gardiner sued an indebted physician and, upon a favorable judgment, lent the money locally at a high rate of interest. His lawyer in this matter was William Samuel Johnson, the son of the first president of King's College and himself a future president of the same school, after it was rechristened "Columbia." In the years to come, the younger Johnson would compete with Gardiner's son for imperial office. Such were the associations and obligations encompassed by the doctor's career.[19]

Like many rich men and women, Gardiner lent his considerable resources to large projects of public concern. Tellingly, his first benefactions along the medical line actively supported the imperial presence. During King George's War, he built a hospital on Boston Common for the sick and wounded in His Majesty's Fleet. During the French and Indian War, he offered to build, at his own expense, an inoculating hospital to combat the smallpox. His broadside advertising the offer demonstrates a sensitivity to the fears surrounding the disease and its controversial treatment. He emphasized that the hospital was to go up in a part of town from which the contagion could not easily spread. Furthermore, a high fence would surround the offending infirmary.[20]

For all these assurances, however, apology was not Gardiner's business. His broadside resembled a lecture more than a solicitation. The doctor reminded the public of the damage, human and economic, caused by the disease. Backed by statistical data, he explained how inoculation effectively decreased the number of smallpox deaths even as it artificially stimulated infection. Nor did Gardiner omit a schedule of costs for the services available; his charity had uses as well as limits. In this case, the citizens of Boston were not buying. After a long debate, the town meeting rejected his offer. Years later, during the incipient epidemic of 1764, the governor and council brooked no reluctance, and Gardiner, with a number of his colleagues, established an inoculating hospital at Point Shirley in Chelsea.[21]

The recollections of George Robert Twelves Hewes, the elfin cobbler of the Boston waterfront and a Tea Party Mohawk, offer us another glimpse of Silvester the medical practitioner. In 1765, with the smallpox threatening, Hewes was inoculated by Dr. Gardiner (*gratis*, one suspects, given the patient's poverty). The sufferer was confined to lodging and enjoined against eating, as the ordeal was best passed on an empty stomach. Hewes, however, had other ideas: he filched a joint of roast veal, dipped it in melted butter, and, after the feast, took to bed a happier man. But within hours, his guts were on fire, and the doctor was again called. Gardiner was merciless: "You will be cold coffee, Hewes, in twelve hours from this; and remember it's no fault of mine." Poor Hewes, in pain, but always too proud to do exactly as he was told, asked for—and, with Gardiner's exasperated consent, was given—a mug of flip. Perhaps this was meant as a last morbid toast; perhaps Hewes was reciting, in a lived vernacular, the lesson of inoculation—a little wrong can turn larger wrongs aright—in any case, Hewes survived the night, to his relief and to the doctor's amusement.[22]

In the 1760s and during other moments of acute crisis, Gardiner and his peers in the medical community treated Boston's poor for free. This was altruism; it was also sound policy for public health. The Point Shirley hospital was, however, a private enterprise first and foremost. Only the well-to-do could afford to repair to such an institution. The fee for treatment was high, and the opportunity cost in time and wages lost to confinement was much higher.[23] The hospital administered to the commonweal, in the sense that the remedy on offer was one that would work for all but the unlucky. It was a remedy that all would do well to seek, because it worked better than the alternatives and was an education in what the best medical science could accomplish. The business of inoculation was therefore very modern: its claims encompassed everyone but its efforts focused on the elite who ran the business and consumed its product.

Most of Gardiner's partners in the hospital venture were doctors like himself, but two were already his partners in the enterprise of settling the eastern wilderness of Maine: James Pitts and John Hancock.[24] Hancock's fame needs no embellishment here, but it might be worthwhile to consider the contemporary ambivalence of his celebrity. He inherited great wealth, and it was his wealth that gave him standing in town and later in provincial and continental politics. He cut, then, a curious figure; he was a kind of macaroni tribune, who raised the mob even as his investments made him the associate of those men the mob would scourge. His generosity won him votes, but he was no less generous with himself. His often incapacitating gout was blamed on early and promiscuous visits to the punchbowl.[25]

There was another lesson to be learned from Hancock's illness. The gout frustrated the straightforward moral admonitions it seemed to invite. Some of Hancock's coevals viewed it as a "good and useful disease," a "white devil" that forestalled more destructive maladies. It was the byproduct of excess and of luxury, it could not be cured, it brought pain; yet the dangers of gout were to be borne nobly, as the disease signified the resilient strength won through rich and varied experience. It was a sign of what the Georgians called "bottom." As we shall see, the politics of gout were akin to the politics of Federalist reform.[26] Both were rooted in a knowing, almost cynical realism. Both chided but ultimately respected appetite and ambition. Hancock, later an opponent of Federalism, operated successfully in the same climate of opinion that fostered Hamilton's and Madison's masterly qualifications. The inoculation controversy likewise: progress went hand in hand with peril, just as the future Patriot, John Hancock, worked shoulder to shoulder with his business partner and fellow advocate of inoculation, Silvester Gardiner, the future Tory.

◆ᢌ · ᢙ◆

As a young doctor, Gardiner had pegged his rise to the standards of his profession and their conformity with British expectations. His career mirrored colonial developments, which in many ways drew America nearer to Britain in the eighteenth century. Gardiner became an investor in the schemes and structures of progress. The inoculating hospital was one example of his patronage. Another was the linen manufacturing scheme of the early 1750s. Its sponsors wanted to establish a trade complementary to metropolitan interests and, more urgently, to put the town into good working order. Implicated in this effort were the ideas, then current, of what constituted a good society and of how successful persons within it were to behave.

Many writers on both sides of the Atlantic were occupied in the observation and, in most cases, furtherance of new manners and a new respectability. Commerce was not vulgar, its advocates argued, but quite the contrary: commercial activity produced true gentlemen and savvy leaders. The nobleman in search of glory or safe in his sense of place had little use for politeness. Courtesy was predicated on an uncertain market of opinion, wherein relative unknowns could inflate their value by persuasion or wit. Outside the courts and salons, where influence was increasingly an accountable stock, merchants and professionals learned complaisance in order to win custom and credit. The early eighteenth century saw the British middle classes beginning to demand a level of respect commensurate with their economic weight. The old dignities and honors became unreliable markers of station, or, more to the point, the undisciplined use of words like "esquire" or "gentleman" accurately suggested the breadth of change and the truth of social mobility.[27]

The chief spokesmen for middling virtues and middling gentility were among the most widely read authors in the Anglophone world: Daniel Defoe, Joseph Addison, and Richard Steele. To these writers, merchants were the most valuable subjects. They had accomplished what the sword and the gun had not yet done, in the years before Plassy and Quebec: the steady extension of British authority. Addison and Steele's *Spectator* delighted in the Royal Exchange and in seeing there "a Body of Men thriving in their own private Fortunes, and at the same time promoting the Publick Stock."[28] When Steele launched a new essay series, *The Guardian*, in 1713, he promised to write for the benefit of mechanics and traders, ladies and gentlemen, and he noted that the "unjust Application of the Advantages of Breeding and Fortune is the Source of all Calamity both Publick and Private." Steele also admitted that he wrote to satisfy his passion for fame, but then, "it is no great matter to the Publick what is the Incentive which makes Men bestow time in their Service, provided there be any thing useful in what they produce."[29]

The ninth *Guardian* explained what kind of usefulness was best for Britain. The essay told of one Mr. Charwell, a City merchant, who, finding himself able to leave behind the town and its business, purchased a nobleman's country estate. Charwell was not about to rest on his laurels, however, and he immediately determined to run his estate with the same "exact Oeconomy" that ruled his mercantile affairs. The property was in need of improvement; his few tenants were near beggary. He saw that what his piece of country lacked was a market that would encourage the consumption of local goods. Indeed, what the country lacked was a town, and Mr. Charwell set to building one. He was aided in this venture by an abundance of coal on his estate—already his blessed plot rumbled with extractive industry. Eventually, all was as Charwell, and Steele, had hoped. The countryside was populous and thriving. The tenantry had grown rich, and the happy owner looked forward to doubling the rents.[30]

This particular *Guardian* found an attentive reader in Sir Richard Cox, an Irish baronet who had come into a destitute estate. His personal interest in improving the land was compounded by his political interests. Cox was an Orange partisan. He fought at the Battle of the Boyne in 1690, and he was instrumental in extending William and Mary's Whig imperium throughout Ireland. His estate reforms were in tune with the commercial and Protestant spirit of the reconstituted monarchy. He had to turn his dependents into capable and prosperous subjects, but he could not effect this change by means offensive to Britain's economic priorities. Woolens, therefore, were out, and, in any case, that industry tended to debase the lowest rank of workers. Cox wanted his tenants to adopt diligent habits, but he also hoped that they might profit by their employments and so become reliable consumers as well as laborers.[31]

Cox's alternative was linen. He continued to rely on a putting-out system, whereby tasks and materials were distributed among many cottages, but no factory could have been more closely monitored. Cox kept a neatly columned tally for each weaver, and he hired a Quaker to inspect the shops and confirm the returns. A "Table of Honour" recorded superior output; Cox remarked that "this seeming trifle" did more to encourage his workers than any other, more costly, measure. The satisfaction of individual vanity was, it appeared, the key to happiness and excellence. Of course, Cox did not shrink from offering hard coin, and he awarded premiums to the best producers in several categories of effort.[32]

He also asked for as much or more than he gave. The manufacture of linen was a procedure of many steps, from the cultivation of flax to the spinning of yarn to the weaving of cloth. It engaged the whole community: men, women, and children. Cox made a point of publicly chastising idle boys and girls. Respites were few. "Numerous holidays," wrote the baronet, "are the Bane of all Industry, and the Ruin of every Country."[33] Luckily, the reformed religion had converted much of the calendar from red to black, and Cox did not hesitate to abridge the remaining legal holidays. He allowed but three at Christmas and two at Easter. May–day was the other exception, but Cox appropriated it for his own uses. It became a sort of labor festival, at which workers received their premiums and demonstrated their skills in spinning exhibitions. Cox's daughters also took part, to prove that only "good Spinners" achieved "the greatest Honour and Perfection of the Female Sex."[34]

In 1753, when Boston's "Society for encouraging Industry and employing the Poor" needed to drum up support for their linen manufacture, it staged a similar exhibition on the Common, where wealthy merchants' daughters joined trainees from the spinning schools in showcasing their craft. The society was familiar with Sir Richard Cox. It had republished the record of his project in 1750, when the Boston scheme was just getting off the ground. The society's steering committee, of which Silvester Gardiner was a member, referred to Cox and his success in their petitions to the provincial government. Merchant sponsors looked to Ireland as a model for New England. If linen had helped the Irish find their niche within the imperial economy, perhaps it could do the same for Massachusetts.[35]

More distressing than the imbalance of trade was Boston's particular economic weakness. The provincial militia had answered King George's call in the wars of the 1740s, and Yankees perished in great numbers in the assaults on Cartagena and Louisbourg. As Boston's men died, and as their families sank into penury, the town's tax burden swelled for those still able to pay. The early 1750s saw the Boston town meeting instruct its representatives in the colonial legislature to press for laws regulating the arrival of new inhabitants. Without the proper controls, such people might overburden the town's taxpayers and charities.[36] In these same years, resistance to an influx of "strangers" and other worries about the colony's ragged social fabric moved the legislature to ban theatrical entertainments in Massachusetts. Policies of this color represented a reaction to the dangers of imperial entanglement.

The linen manufacture would, it was hoped, alleviate the pressures of poverty while addressing, in a more constructive way, the limits and opportunities of commercial enterprise within the British Empire. Most of the work was suitable for the sort of people, women and children, who filled the poor rolls. Their labor would put food in their mouths, clothes on their backs, and money back in the pockets of the townspeople who were supporting them. Like England's workhouses, Boston's linen factory would gather the poor and instill in them the spirit of industry, but it would not affront their independence by compelling their labor or residence. A workhouse had opened on the Common in 1739, but very few unfortunates had sought resort there. The merchants behind the linen venture played on their fellow Bostonians' pride. Like the Irish Cox, and at the urging of another projector, Benjamin Franklin, the society offered prizes to its hardest workers.[37]

Not that the occasional harsh note was unheard of in the society's literature. Again like Cox, Boston's linen backers imagined a rather unforgiving program, even with its incentives. Samuel Cooper, in a sermon to the society, hoped that the town's children "may be trained up, not only to endure, but even to love a constant Employment." Charles Chauncy, in his sermon to the same body, quite agreed; he regretted that children had hitherto been suffered to play idly. The title of Chauncy's address is worth quoting: *The Idle-Poor secluded from the*

Bread of Charity by the Christian Law. And so is his text: "This we commanded you, that if any would not work, neither should he eat."[38]

Chauncy's sermon is a telling example of social articulation. While he asserted that his text did not apply equally to "Rich" and "Poor," he did not excuse privileged idleness or impute crassness to trade, writing, "We were made for Business." Inherited wealth was not, however, an evil; it was simply a store of labor and only by more labor "can it be improved to Advantage." In Chauncy's ideal world, the public good coalesced from the individual good, multiply pursued. Enterprising peoples, the improvers of arts and trade, were destined for greatness, and these improvements were inevitably the result of particular efforts. Chauncy used the language of "parts" and "systems." The arrangement of the former, however various, mattered little as long as the system they constituted was, in the final calculation, benevolent.[39]

Chauncy and the merchants to whom he preached were poised between distinctly opposed conceptions of society, but they were also deeply engaged by a moral philosophy that had already done much to accommodate the old social attitudes with the new. The linen manufacture's prospectus numbered among its goals the depression of the price of labor. Yes, the poor would be well fed and clothed, but the laboring classes in general would be less likely to escape their condition. On the other hand, the same literature appealed to the poorer citizen's desire for self-improvement and a better life. Chauncy often seemed to rely on notions of social organization akin to the "chain of being," whereby the order of the world depended on conformity to static ranks. But, as we have just seen, he also stressed that "Business" was a universal concern. He believed that stimulus was necessary to action and that excellence was proven rather than preordained.[40]

Society sorted itself into superiors and inferiors, but prior social identity, such as that provided by good birth, was not a decisive factor. To put it another way: Chauncy's sociology, as in the medieval or organic vision, was founded on inequality, but it respected process. He still naturalized differences, but these had to emerge from experience. Rather than advert to obvious social markers, Chauncy emphasized the "disparity of mental powers." He was developing an idea of intellectual merit, an idea attractive to the many arrivistes who filled the pews at First Church. Such people needed to justify their rise and feel entitled to their distinction.[41]

Moreover, the social vocabulary of the linen venture, while keyed to parochial concerns, did not originate in Boston.[42] Charles Chauncy,

Samuel Cooper, and undoubtedly many of their listeners were aware of a more general discussion of harmony and interest. The ministers' habitual use of words like "self-love" and "benevolence" are sure evidence of this. Lord Shaftesbury was well known in the colonies, and his special subject was the "Oeconomy" of existence and the delineation of its "parts." This philosophical earl was of an agreeable and optimistic temper, and he resolved the dilemma of public and private goods by tautology and sheer will: true self-interest was entirely salutory because it involved, at bottom, a love of the Whole. Dr. Bernard Mandeville gleefully took an opposite tack, though the result was much the same: an acceptance of commercial practice. Mandeville defined virtue so rigorously that he destroyed it and was left with nothing but vice from which to derive "publick benefits." Christendom rose in revolt against such a notion, but the much demonized Mandeville—whom Ben Franklin met in a London tavern and pronounced "a most facetious, entertaining companion"—could not be easily dismissed.[43]

His best critics came to regard virtue and vice a bit more circumspectly, or even, through a utilitarian lens, distantly. Bishop Butler offered that self-love and benevolence were perfectly coincident; in his view, the average human being did not sufficiently indulge either affection. Interestedness was simply not a proper index of moral quality. Butler also doubted that benevolent endeavors "will in particular instances produce an overbalance of happiness upon the whole, since so many and distant things must come into the account."[44] David Hume and his fellow Scots would refine this reasonable skepticism into a science. They dedicated themselves to the long view, to a detached, historical understanding of purportedly rational decisions and their unintended consequences. Their calibrations of public and private interests were famously acute, and their anatomy of the modern social order would instruct the children of Boston's colonial merchants.

With the linen scheme, those merchants certainly demonstrated the limits of benevolence. The material basis for such an enterprise was probably insufficient. Silvester Gardiner and his partners made the petitionary rounds, begging for money that would keep the factory open, and the General Court assented, after a fashion. It granted £1,500 to the manufacture but proposed to raise that sum by an excise on coaches and chaises. We can guess that this measure displeased Gardiner and company. They were the very people who owned such conveyances. Their industrial venture, which they began with the express purpose of lowering their own taxes, now exacerbated their complaint.

The province managed to collect only half of the allocated amount; in 1759, it foreclosed on the factory building. Sixty years later, another group of Boston merchants would finally make textiles pay. Their mills in Lowell and Lawrence hummed with the labor of industrious young women. Their wealth multiplied and purchased then what it never could in the eighteenth century: a secure status.[45]

◆§ · §◆

Silvester Gardiner and his fellow provincials could not and, wisely, did not commit to establishing a sizable manufacturing base. This is not to say, however, that their operations lacked scale. Maritime commerce spanned great distances. Another huge undertaking was settlement, as practiced by land speculators. Millions of acres of unimproved land came easily to investors with the right connections and a taste for risk; settlers made the property, and so the investment, worthwhile. Attracting and maintaining the type of settlers who equated the frontier with opportunity was one problem. Others included securing title to the land and defending it from rival claimants, foreign and domestic. The eastern marches of Massachusetts—what is now the state of Maine—were the scene of many such speculations, and Gardiner was a leader among the many men and women who tried to raise that raw country to productivity and multiply their own fortunes in the bargain.

The story of the Kennebeck Proprietors has been well told elsewhere.[46] In 1629, William Bradford and other leading Pilgrims petitioned the Council for New England that they be granted a patent to lands in the Kennebec River valley. The Pilgrims hoped the revenues from this property would erase the debts encumbering their infant settlements. They received a generous but vaguely conceived portion. For approximately fifty miles of the Kennebec, all the land within fifteen miles of each bank was theirs. The Pilgrims could do little with this gift, and, in 1661, they sold out to four Boston merchants for four hundred pounds. No serious efforts at improvement were made until 1749, when several heirs to the purchase met to revive their claims as the New Plymouth Company. While this name endured, the members became better known as the Kennebeck Proprietors after they incorporated in 1753.[47]

By that point, Gardiner was already deeply involved in the company's affairs. He quickly acquired two full shares (of twenty-four), and it was always his practice to attend personally to money matters.

Besides, there was so much to do; a man of Gardiner's industry naturally rose to the challenge. He became, in the words of another proprietor, the "mainspring" of the company. He was the company's moderator from 1764 until the Revolution. In December of 1751, at his first proprietors' meeting, he took the lead in planning the first large settlements in the Kennebec.[48]

Gardiner was fully aware that one had to give up something to get anything in return. The Kennebec region lacked infrastructure; the proprietors had to conjure it out of their purses. For example, the first settlements required all manner of goods that could only be shipped from Boston. Gardiner offered to build a sloop at his own expense and devote it to the Maine run. The company deeded him four hundred acres as a gratuity, but the real reward came from the practical monopoly on shipping, which he enjoyed for many years. Likewise, when a lesser proprietor could not build the sawmill and gristmill in the time allowed by the company, Gardiner bought the rights to the project for ten shillings. At tremendous cost to himself, he built the mills and earned the one thousand acres attached to the grant, plus the profits of the milling business.[49] Such was his normal mode of operation. His interests were caught up in the development of the province and, with it, the projection of imperial power.

The character of his relationship with Britain was never clearer than when war threatened in the mid-1750s. The proprietors relied on the royal governor, William Shirley, for protection against the French and their Indian allies. In return, the company offered logistical support in any campaign to the north. These were the beginnings of an affair that quickly progressed beyond a simple exchange of favors. In 1754, the proprietors renamed their main outpost, Fort Frankfort, in honor of the governor. When word came of taking the fight to the French, the company volunteered to build two forts further upriver, abrogating year-old promises to the Indians that white settlement would stop at the rechristened Fort Shirley. The proprietors, of course, had already surveyed phantom townships in the disputed area; the military adventure gave spine to these dreams. Besides, the garrisons at the new forts would be spending provincial money on company goods; it was a good investment from every angle. Fort Western and Fort Halifax went up in short order (the former was named for the governor's English relations). Shirley took possession long enough to see that the French had not showed. He then returned to Boston in triumph.[50]

The proprietors' ambitions coextended with the empire, and the chief men in the company were certainly grateful to the empire's representative. Silvester Gardiner put the matter rather blandly: "the Company thou't it for their Interest, that Governour Shirley should be interested in their patent."[51] And so several months after the northernmost fort was built, the company voted Shirley a full share. It should now come as no surprise that it was Gardiner who gave up one of his own shares to make this gift possible. Nor is it surprising that he was well compensated, in land grants, for his generosity. Shirley tried for a time to be the good partner. He secretly petitioned the Lords of Trade for a new charter that would legitimate the company's extravagant reading of the original grant. These efforts came to naught, and Shirley's usefulness expired in 1756, when the governor was recalled because of the early failures of the French and Indian War. His share fell into delinquency and passed back into the hands of the proprietors.[52]

Gardiner and company were not the complete masters of their domain. Despite their wealth and influence, they could not control the legal proceedings upon which their claim hinged. The proprietors caused a courthouse to be established in Pownalborough (named for Governor Shirley's successor, Thomas Pownall), in the heart of their territory. Finding that they could not reliably win judgments there, they litigated at further and further remove. For example, in an attempt to expand the original Plymouth patent to the sea, the proprietors sought the opinions of the king's chief law officers, including Attorney General William Murray, the future Lord Mansfield. Armed with these opinions, the company pressed its claims in several jurisdictions.[53]

Gardiner was at the center of this litigation when it came to a head in the 1760s. The company had allotted him twelve thousand acres in Georgetown, land that others already held through an Indian purchase. To establish his and the company's title, Gardiner pursued the matter in Pownalborough and then in the Massachusetts Superior Court. He and his compatriots almost expected to lose, but their eyes were on the Privy Council, where they planned to air an ultimate appeal. One of their number, Florentius Vassall, lived in London and looked after the company's interests there.[54] Being familiar with the exercise of power within the empire had its advantages, and the proprietors hoped to make use of the imperial trump in their speculation.

Nor did they neglect to bring their considerable resources to bear within the province. They hired the best lawyers, such as James Otis Jr., who briefly argued the Crown side in Vice-Admiralty before his rather more famous turn in the opposition. Otis remained on the company's payroll as the Stamp Act crisis worsened—and as he began to regret his part in precipitating it.[55] His Kennebeck masters may have even had a hand in the climactic event of that crisis, the sacking of Lieutenant Governor Thomas Hutchinson's house in Boston. Through his historical studies, Hutchinson had come into possession of maps and documents harmful to the company's cause. Certain proprietors, like John Hancock, had pull with the mob, and a delicious but unsubstantiated rumor has it that Hutchinson suffered more for his meddling in Maine affairs than for his offense to American liberties. Silvester Gardiner certainly respected the historical authorities. Two months before the Stamp Act riots, as he marshaled his evidence for the pending lawsuit, Gardiner made sure that William Bradford's account of Plymouth Plantation was close at hand.[56]

Gardiner was also ready to play the patriot when the legal process disappointed him. In 1767 a board of arbitrators found that he had unreasonably hounded one of his debtors. The wounded Gardiner took the affair to "the Public," printing his version of the case and a critique of the decision. According to this pamphlet, the doctor had been "stript of his freedom, the natural and inherent right of a freeborn citizen, the darling privilege of every Englishman to be tried by a jury of twelve honest men."[57] Gardiner's opponents repaid him in kind. The author of *A Strange Account of the Rising and Breaking of a Great Bubble*—who was, in all likelihood, the remunerated debtor—applauded the Sons of Liberty for resisting Parliament's "oppressive Acts" but wondered, "Have we not as much Reason to cry out of Oppression at Home?" He then catalogued the excesses of the Kennebeck Company and of Gardiner in particular.[58]

This imbroglio exposed both the extent and the limits of Gardiner's influence. The pamphlets describe an aggressive manager of people and properties. Gardiner owned the land, but he also delivered his tenants' provisions and shipped their lumber. He could demand signatures for friendly depositions, and, when such exhibits proved unconvincing, he upbraided the arbitrators for failing to understand standard mercantile practice. And there's the rub, of course: Gardiner's money and power did not guarantee him a favorable court decision; they guaranteed him, at best, a fairly comfortable existence. His critics might have called him a "lord," but this was a transparent sneer. Like his son after him, Gardiner was cast as "Don Quixot," full of "Brass and Arrogance," and consumed by "grand pursuits." He was a weighty character, but he rode on a cloud. His gains were always subject to reverse, and a great shock could bring him low.[59]

◁◦ · ◦▷

Understandably, Silvester Gardiner preferred a steady background to his speculative projects. The goals, standards, and traditions of the British Empire framed his field of gain. This pattern reveals itself in Gardiner's religious life as well. He was a very active member of the Church of England. This is not to suggest causation one way or the other; the issue is rather one of consistency. He was born an Anglican, and his dedication to the Church resembled his dedication to his work. This consistency goes a long way toward vindicating the exemplary role this essay has assigned to him. Silvester Gardiner was in no way an average man. His partners in the Kennebeck venture, future patriots like John Hancock and James Bowdoin, shared similar imperial habits of mind, but the thorough hold of those habits on Gardiner suggests how the colonial mind operated at one extremity.

Gardiner's church life folded easily into the rest of his experience. After the reconstruction of King's Chapel was completed in late 1754, he could sit in his pew along the center aisle and, with only a slight turn to the right, see his friend and co-conspirator William Shirley, who occupied the pew reserved for His Majesty's Governor.[60] A builder of mills and hospitals, Gardiner reprised a familiar role at King's Chapel. As the church was being rebuilt, Gardiner's responsibility was to oversee the delivery of stone. This material was a matter of great pride to the members, and it distinguished the chapel then as today (grey stone stands out in redbrick Boston). While the granite was quarried in Braintree, Gardiner and his fellows on the building committee sought the advice of experts in England. Likewise, when the organist was lured away by an offer from Jamaica, Gardiner was one of the members charged with asking Barlow Trecothick, owner of pew number one and the sometime Lord Mayor of London, to procure a replacement from the metropole.[61] The leading congregants of the chapel understood their provincial mission very broadly. In his church, as in everything he did, Gardiner was a leader. He was an almost continual presence on the vestry for the forty-odd years he lived in Boston. He served as warden—the chief layman and church administrator—for twice as many years as did any other man in the colonial period.[62]

A pillar of King's Chapel, Silvester Gardiner did not hesitate to imitate its good order in the conduct of his Maine enterprise. Alongside his mills and trading posts, he built churches and deeded the land for their support. In the late 1750s, Gardiner took an interest in Jacob Bailey, a recent Harvard graduate who had preached in a number of Congregational pulpits but was leaning to Anglicanism. After a quick trip to London, Bailey returned to New England in 1760 as a priest and missionary in the Society for the Propagation of the Gospel in Foreign Parts. His particular station was the Kennebec region, and his chief patron for the next fifteen years was Dr. Gardiner.[63] His aid would prove a mixed blessing.

Gardiner never backed away from his commitment to the Anglican Church in the east; indeed, his efforts were so vigorous as to threaten many settlers and colleagues. Gardiner granted the income of a large farm to the people of Pownalborough for Bailey's support. He solicited funds for a church and parsonage in the same village. Further to the north, in Gardinerstown, he offered on his own account to establish another priest with church and glebe lands.[64] These were not private endeavors. Gardiner understood the establishment of religion to be the business of the company. He wanted the other proprietors, many of them Congregationalists, to underwrite Bailey's mission by the donation of a glebe. He did not succeed until a poorly attended meeting of 1769, when Gardiner carried the Anglican cause with his absentee proxies.[65] This was a year after the *Liberty* riot, when the Boston mob swarmed the docks on behalf of Hancock, a Kennebeck proprietor whose imperial interests were not so neatly consonant as Gardiner's.

The following year brought the Boston Massacre, in which Gardiner played a very small and very nearly perilous part. A mob menaced a small troop of British soldiers with threats and (apparently rock-hard) snowballs and received in return a volley of musket fire. Among the fallen, most memorably, was the mulatto patriot Crispus Attucks. Dr. Gardiner was called to his side, at which point some soldiers took aim at him, his assistants, and his expiring or already expired patient. An order from the redcoats' commander, Captain Preston, stayed their hand and possibly prevented the death of a most loyal Bostonian.[66] Gardiner, of course, was not thinking about politics at that moment; he was doing his professional duty. His sometime lawyer, John Adams, demonstrated a similar ethic when he successfully defended Preston at trial, though Adams was also happy for the publicity.

The early 1770s saw Gardiner in his late prime, as yet undiminished by the crisis to come. The year of the Boston Massacre was the last full year he would spend with his wife of nearly four decades, Anne Gibbins Gardiner. She was by all accounts a suitable mate—tough on her husband's assistants, perhaps, but no tougher than he. She bore him eight children, six of whom survived her. William, the oldest, had high spirits, gentle manners, and little ability. After riding out the Revolution, he would die (and die a bachelor) in 1787 from an accidental overdose of laudanum. Of John, the second child and son, later chapters will have much to tell. Of the four Gardiner girls to reach adulthood—Anne, Hannah, Rebecca, and Abigail—Anne was initially fortune's favorite. She was the first Gardiner to have been painted by John Singleton Copley; the portrait marked her debut and her father's aggressive patronage. She married the second son of an earl, and the first son was sickly. Her hopes for entitlement were, however, never realized. Hannah made the best match, marrying into the Hallowells, a family aligned with the Gardiners by business, politics, and religion. Her son would become the master of Silvester's estates.[67]

Anne Gibbins Gardiner died in 1771. Her children were perhaps her major legacy, but she also left a long annotated list of family recipes that tells us at least as much about Boston society and its place in the Atlantic world as the remnants of her husband's medical career. The recipes demonstrate that Gardiner was attuned to the latest trends in cookery and to the print culture that accelerated those trends. The gallimaufries of the medieval kitchen—promiscuous casseroles of seemingly whatever came to hand: seasonal fruits, hardy root vegetables and hardier nuts, offal, and spice—were giving way to the relative simplicity and refinement of the modern table. A few antiques bless Mrs. Gardiner's list (one pie combined sweetbreads, cinnamon, bone marrow, and artichokes), but the majority were rather more up-to-date. Some were adapted from an English cookbook published in 1769, two years before Gardiner's death.[68]

Her collection of recipes was, therefore, an artifact of empire. The metropolitan style was dominant and reinforced by the American appetite for British books. But provincial tastes and commodities made their mark. Fish were abundant in the waters off Massachusetts and in Gardiner's recipes. Here and there are references to Indian meal and to other American foodstuffs that might be comfortably substituted for the staples of English cookery. And the conversation among England's provinces is recorded as well. The pickling techniques of West Indians come recommended, as do the "catchups" of India proper.[69]

One such ketchup had, according to Gardiner, a shelf life of twenty years (its ingredients included stale beer, anchovies, cloves, and mushrooms). If she laid down a jar in the 1760s, it outlasted its maker as well as the king's authority in Boston. But its survival would have depended not just on the careful preparations of mistress and servants; the grace of Gardiner's successor was also requisite. Silvester wasted no time in finding another wife; he married the widow Abigail Pickman Eppes in 1772. Family histories suggest that she was not well received; sources hint that she was responsible for her husband's Toryism and exile. It is unlikely that such help was needed. Dr. Gardiner, for his part, was very pleased by the new match. In the first year of their marriage, he had John Singleton Copley paint both of their portraits, probably in partial payment for land Copley purchased from Gardiner on what was later known as Beacon Hill.[70]

Silvester Gardiner, by Copley, is satisfaction and confidence incarnate. The body has pedestal poise; atop it is the doctor's magnificent block of a head, a thing of Jovian gravity, the face surprisingly benign. His wife's portrait has a different character. The fleshiness that commends Silvester's features is less welcome in Abigail, and Copley was not so shy or complaisant as to hide her double chins. He compensates, however, in the beauty of her dress and accessories. Hair and robe are strung with pearls. The style is that of *turquerie*, an Oriental mimicry fashionable among the British upper classes and the Americans who followed their lead.[71]

When the Revolution finally came, Dr. Gardiner and many of his associates suffered for the thoroughness with which they had bound their fortunes to Britain. Jacob Bailey remained at his post well into the war years, faithfully saying prayers for the king when other Anglicans had stopped. Harassment and poverty eventually drove him to Nova Scotia. Many other Loyalists departed in the evacuation of Boston. Henry Caner, the rector of King's Chapel, took the communion plate with him. His chief parishioner, Silvester Gardiner, was unable to take much of anything. His drugs stayed behind, as did, of course, his houses and lands. After a brief stop in Halifax, Gardiner took up residence in New York, which was still safely British. He clung to the colonies as long as his diminished resources would allow. In November of 1778 he reluctantly sailed for Great Britain. He lived in Bristol and then, with more dedication, in Poole on the Dorset coast, though the business of exile—petition and complaint—occasionally brought him up to London.[72]

Exile was an unhappy experience for most Tories, whose loyalty did not render them any less American. The removal to Britain reduced the exiles, and they chafed at their contracted place. With credit no longer buoyed up by land and easy commerce, the network of bonded obligations underwent a nasty collapse. Fellow Tories turned on each other as they called in their debts.[73] And they viewed their great patron, the king, as the biggest debtor of all. American Loyalists pressed for state pensions. Gardiner saved his receipts from all manner of English transactions, from buying a wig to renting a townhouse. These would support his claims for compensation. Of the "Voluminous Accounts" Gardiner prepared in his attempts at redress, a son-in-law wrote, "his attention and clearness was almost beyond belief."[74] Such volume was to be expected when a lifetime's pursuits, stretching between continents and into the wilderness, were confined to a balance sheet.

Gardiner's memorial to the claims commission also spoke to the depth of his imperial attachments. In an account of services to the Crown, the doctor mentioned his care of the British casualties from Bunker Hill. He mentioned his enabling role in the establishment of Forts Halifax and Western. And his petition began with a tenuous but nonetheless extraordinary claim that extended to the roots of the first British Empire. During the Seven Years' War, as King George's men made their final push on French Canada, General Amherst sent a message, in triplicate, to his colleague Wolfe, who was then languishing below Quebec. Two of the messengers traveled a direct route along the St. Lawrence and were captured by Indians. The third went to Boston, where he sought out Gardiner's advice. Gardiner, finding the provincial government slow to help, took the matter in hand. He put the messenger on one of his ships and accompanied him to the Kennebec. There the doctor arranged for an experienced and well-supplied escort. Amherst's missive—which read, in part, "Now is the time!"—reached Wolfe just before his attempt on the Heights of Abraham. We cannot know if the letter encouraged the young general; perhaps it added to his desperation. Gardiner did not entertain any doubts. By his accounting, his quick action had won the war. He had done nothing less than facilitate British dominance of the continent.[75]

Even as he tallied his losses, Gardiner did not confine his imperial vision to the backward glance. Early in the war, he resurrected plans to establish a colonial episcopacy, a proposal that made its way, through

Henry Caner, to the bishop of London. As the war ended, he looked to improve what remained of British America. He had long been interested in settling the large expanse between the Penobscot River and Nova Scotia. Other Tory exiles adopted this scheme and, with military assistance, founded "New Ireland" in 1779. The colony was short lived, and Gardiner had the foresight not to involve himself. He instead concentrated on Newfoundland and, as he put it in his sixty-page prospectus, "the many advantages which will arise to this kingdom on colonizing that Island."[76]

Gardiner urged Britain to overcome its recent troubles and recover "its former splendor & Glory." In the place of thirteen loyal provinces now stood an "ambitious rival." If properly developed, Newfoundland could be the counterweight to American influence. Its fisheries were a proving ground for British sailors, but the government had not done enough to align the fishermen's interests with the nation's. The inhabitants of Newfoundland, actual and potential, deserved an "equal claim to the benefits of our constitution." Property would secure this claim. The promise of property, Gardiner knew, drove people to extreme measures. Fishermen turned backwoodsmen or even indentured themselves in the hope of one day owning a piece of America's abundance. An attractive Newfoundland settlement, offering easy land grants, would suck the fishing talent out of the States and divert immigrants who were otherwise bound for them.[77]

Clearly, Gardiner was trying to perfect the methods he had applied in the Kennebec. He recommended carefully plotted townships of eight miles square, subdivided into two-hundred-acre parcels. Glebe lands were set aside in each township; settling duties insured that the land's productivity would steadily increase. As in Maine, Gardiner seemed to notice every detail. He planned the Newfoundland project from his home in Poole; the port's merchants were prominent in the fisheries' supply trade. The author was privy to the most current intelligence on wages, catches, ship complements, population trends, and agricultural experiments. He even held forth on the proper way to kill a seal: by clubbing the nose rather than the skull. Gardiner's politics could sometimes get the better of his information. He argued, for example, that Newfoundland was not as frigid or as snowy as Massachusetts.[78]

Of course, Gardiner did not intend to settle in any of the Canadian provinces, no matter how tidy or warm they promised to be. His heart was still in New England. Throughout the war, he kept abreast of happenings in Massachusetts. In 1781, while living in Poole, Gardiner began to worry over the condition of his green damask window curtains, which he had left behind in Boston. He sent a key to a friend there, so he might rescue these draperies from their trunk and give them a good airing. That the doctor had held on to this key at all—and for so long—testifies to his almost unseemly tenacity.[79] So did his domestic affairs. His second wife, Abigail, died in 1780. Gardiner saw out the Revolution as a widower. But in 1784, he married again, this time to a woman almost forty years his junior. She was Catharine Goldthwaite, the daughter of Colonel Thomas Goldthwaite, the former commander of Fort Pownall in Maine. The associations might have embittered one less capable, but, with Catharine at his side, Gardiner plotted an end to exile.[80]

He apparently made a few bids to come back to Boston, but its patriots could not welcome such a recalcitrant neighbor. He informed his attorney, "if I should ever return . . . it will not be in a skulking manner," and his actions betrayed no signs of penitence. Thinking himself wrongly proscribed, Gardiner sent very specific instructions as to how his property might be saved and his debts collected. Among the items he had taken to England were his record books, and the doctor was prepared to call his delinquent tenants to account. Though an exile, Silvester Gardiner was still at the center of large plans. From New England, his Kennebeck partners sought his counsel on company matters, of which, his son wrote, "no one here knows half so much." His interests were too extensive to be ignored or—fortunate man—to be confiscated whole.[81]

The Gardiners arrived in Rhode Island in 1785. The doctor died there a year later, a man of mark and still a considerable landholder. In his honor, the merchant ships of Newport flew their colors at half-mast. The local paper lamented his losses in the "late civil war" but noted that Gardiner's vigor and perseverance had guaranteed to his posterity a sizable estate. His last will and testament is a fitting remnant of his controlling personality. Gardiner's houses and plots descended in varying portions to his many heirs. Money was set aside to complete St. Ann's Church in Gardinerstown. The parish was also to receive an annual sum of twenty pounds sterling. In the bequests to three of his daughters, Gardiner obliged them to make smaller contributions to the same church. St. Ann's, for its part, would allow the family to nominate its minister.[82] His death sealed the remarkable impression his life had made on Massachusetts and on the Episcopal Church. Despite its many setbacks, his career must be called a success.

And, for all its odd turnings, that career was historically significant. Silvester Gardiner's interest in frontier development was highly politicized, but it was, in retrospect, larger than the politics of the period: the process of development was a continuous and common enterprise that helped to spark the Revolution (as American settlers and speculators chafed at the restrictive policies of 1763), survived it, and gave the new nation its purpose and mission. The march of civilization, however, demanded more than the establishment of villages and farms in the once wild forests; it required as well the development of talent.

In both cases, the imperial environment conditioned the character of improvement but did not necessarily bind that which was improved. Land speculation in Maine and elsewhere remained a British-American enterprise (by any reasonable financial analysis) even as Maine became (fuzzy borders aside) a strictly American province. Legal action both protected and threatened Gardiner's legacy, even as lawyers—whose profession came of age politically during the late colonial era—took turns acting as the Revolution's chief provocateurs and its most articulate opponents. It is fitting, then, that one of Silvester's sons was a lawyer with Atlantic ambitions and a meddling concern for the lawyer's place in early national society. He did not share his father's politics, but he was following in his father's footsteps. Dr. Silvester Gardiner was in the vanguard of professional formation. His medical expertise established him as a man of means and underwrote his interest in real estate. This expertise had an imperial frame. But the process of professionalization, like the fate of his property, transcended its original background and lent its strength to the new empire that was born in 1783.

John

A Worldly Education

"Westward the Course of Empire takes its Way": so wrote George Berkeley, the Anglo-Irish philosopher and divine, as he contemplated his plans for America.[1] In the 1720s, Britain appeared to be courting its own ruin. The South Sea Bubble had burst, and what Berkeley called the "old English modesty" was evaporating apace. Worse still, vice brazenly passed for virtue. "Other nations have been wicked," he wrote, "but we are the first who have been wicked upon principle."[2] Berkeley deplored Bernard Mandeville's amoral logic. His projected college in Bermuda would look to other teachers, but his vision was progressive nonetheless. It pointed in two directions: with loathing, toward luxury, irresponsible enterprise, and overweening sophistication; with hope, toward learning and empire. Berkeley did not imagine that virtue demanded the sacrifice of refinement, of the arts, or of adventures overseas.

In the eighteenth century, much intellectual effort went into reconciling virtue and commerce, goodness and greatness. Berkeley's solution, the flight westward, was abortive. Rhode Island had the favor of his company for a few years while his Bermuda scheme fell apart. He sailed back to Britain, and many Americans followed, culturally if not physically. To them, progress led to the east, to the center of empire. Britain offered the best education, the most profitable connections in trade, and the closest acquaintance with the political structures that ruled America. But what Americans learned, in Britain or from other metropolitan contacts, did not always reinforce their links to the Crown and its governments. Bostonians reaching their prime in the turbulent period preceding the Revolution could not afford to invest their hopes as Silvester Gardiner had. The empire ceased to be a stable environment in which to realize their aspirations. Britain still had much to offer, but its increasingly disordered relationship with the colonies presented other, more promising opportunities to provincials on the rise, to persons like Williams Smibert.

Gardiner's acquaintanceship with the Smiberts almost certainly began with Williams's father, John. This Edinburgh native was Boston's first major portrait painter. After studying his craft in London and Florence, he practiced it for a time in the British capital before accompanying George Berkeley to Rhode Island in 1728. While in that colony, John Smibert was a visitor at the home of Hannah MacSparran, Silvester's older sister. Smibert would later paint her portrait and that of her husband, the Reverend James MacSparran. Smibert did not return to England with Berkeley but instead settled in Boston and married a doctor's daughter just a few years before Gardiner did.[3]

By the time of his death, in 1756, he had left quite a visible mark on Boston society. He designed Faneuil Hall, the center of the town's civic and commercial life, and Holden Chapel, still a colorful ornament to Harvard Yard. The list of men and women who sat for him is long and distinguished; it includes the venerable Judge Samuel Sewall, Benjamin Colman, the pastor of Brattle Street Church, and Henry Caner of King's Chapel. Smibert's compositions were formally, as well as historically, interesting. He painted a group portrait of the three young Olivers: Daniel, Peter, and Andrew. The first was already dead; the other two would become notorious members of the Thomas Hutchinson connection. An even younger subject was the nine-year-old James Bowdoin II, later Silvester Gardiner's partner in the Kennebeck Company and, later still, governor of Massachusetts during Shays's agrarian revolt. Smibert painted him as one ready for rustic adventure, armed with bow and arrow.[4]

While John Smibert's ambition demanded that he leave Edinburgh, his son's career was best served by returning there. Its university was one of the foremost institutions of medical learning in the West, and Williams Smibert was one of the first natives of Massachusetts to earn an Edinburgh M.D. He was acutely aware of the respect and advantages his degree might win. Might win, that is, if men such as Gardiner did not block his way. In a letter to a former classmate, John Morgan of Philadelphia, Smibert sourly remarked that their "Science," while obviously superior, did not guarantee their preeminence over a "retailer of drugs."[5] Smibert's characterization was inapt. Silvester Gardiner preceded him on the same path. Gardiner was a provincial who studied, though in the older clinical fashion, with some of the finest doctors in Europe. That

John

education was instrumental in his efforts to professionalize Boston's medical practice, efforts shared by provincial Scots. Smibert's anatomical and surgical knowledge may have been more advanced than Gardiner's, but his vocational development and bias were similar.

What would prove to be of more value than knowledge was a political dexterity not found in the older doctor. As Smibert put it to Morgan, "my being so connected with both parties renders it impolitic in me to declare my sentiments on one side or the other, [and] I therefore slide silently between them."[6] Such cunning might prove false if decisiveness were required, but, when the Revolution forced the issue, John Morgan was one who made the fortunate choice. As chief physician of the Continental Army, Morgan plundered Silvester Gardiner's drug store in 1776.[7] Gardiner resented this poor treatment, but he might have expected it as the natural course of events. He had, after all, raised an opportunist quite on the level with the Smiberts and the Morgans.

◆§ · §◆

John Gardiner was born in Boston in 1737. He entered the Latin School in 1744, where he probably met Williams Smibert, who had begun his courses the previous year. Even at this early stage, Gardiner's talents began to tell. One report suggests that the boy's memory was prodigious, although this estimate dates from the 1780s and might bear the impression made by a voluble adult.[8] He was also, like his father, a younger son. It made sense that, receiving less in land, he would have a better and more profitable education. In any case, young Gardiner showed enough promise to be packed off to Britain. In 1752, after a few more years of elementary schooling, he matriculated at the University of Glasgow. This was James MacSparran's alma mater, and the good minister appears to have been as influential in John's education as he had been in Silvester's. Much later in life, Gardiner complained to Samuel Adams that he had wanted to attend Harvard, but his father sent him abroad, having been "persuaded by a bigotted, Scots, episcopalian Priest."[9] The fifteen-year-old boy was of a different mind. He informed his rector, Henry Caner, that he was attending public worship in its familiar, Episcopal mode. Caner counselled prudence—a virtue at which Gardiner would sneer in the coming decades—and a firm resistance to the temptations, physical and spiritual, that afflicted university students.[10]

Glasgow held much to draw the eye. Its population doubled during the first half of the eighteenth century; when Gardiner resided there, it was a third again as large as his native Boston. Glasgow's Market Cross, the busiest part of town, was a various scene full of characters who might have intrigued a young American. Impoverished Highlanders walked next to merchant grandees cloaked in scarlet and brandishing gold-knobbed canes. The merchants' riches were newly won. Between the Union of Parliaments in 1707 and Gardiner's matriculation, Scottish tobacco imports increased fourteenfold, and Glaswegians handled the lion's share of this trade. The number of partners in the most lucrative firms was never large, but the infrastructural demands of the expansion succeeded in mobilizing the surplus capital of the region's nascent middle classes as well.[11]

The university reflected the mercantile aspect of the town. Many future merchants in the tobacco and West Indian trades attended the school. Glasgow's professors were more likely to be the sons of merchants and professionals than were their counterparts at Britain's other universities. In the 1740s, a quarter of the students came from commercial or industrial families, and this fraction was steadily increasing. Whatever their occupation, the fathers of these students must have recognized a good bargain in Glasgow. Lecture fees and the cost of maintenance were low, amounting to as little as five pounds a year.[12]

And what could students buy with their spare coin? Despite its bustling economy, the town was not as entertaining as it might have been. Theatrical companies did not find a regular home in Glasgow until the 1760s. In the fall of 1751, concertgoers who sat through the intervals were applauding a Mrs. Gorman, who, as her advertisement states, walked "the Stiff Rope, such as was never done in this City before."[13] The next year, townsfolk witnessed a more ambitious attempt at dramatic entertainment—and its spectacular ruin. A wooden theater went up near the cathedral. Well-known actors and actresses traveled to Glasgow so they might perform there, and the common as well as the fashionable turned out for their performances. Some of the richer patrons arrived at the theater borne aloft in sedan chairs. Soon, however, the evangelist and former player George Whitefield visited the town, and his inspirited listeners destroyed what they saw as the "Devil's Home."[14] John Gardiner, in or entering his first term at university, might very well have watched this debacle.

He and his fellows had other options. When, forty years later, Gardiner recommended the theater to a still skeptical Massachusetts, he recalled having frequented playhouses in various British cities, including Edinburgh. While the dramatic muse fell silent in Glasgow, she carried on in the old Scottish capital, where her reputation was better established and less sinister. During Gardiner's Scottish years, students on holiday from their lectures could visit Edinburgh's Canongate Hall and see Shakespeare's *King Lear* or *Macbeth*. Lighter fare was also on the schedule. Gardiner and the other Glaswegian boys could hardly have been expected to resist David Garrick's *Miss in Her Teens*.[15]

Glasgow's professors tried to rein in student extravagance. In October of 1752, a university committee unanimously agreed to implement a series of regulations. Students were not to wear lace or play billiards. They were not to join the Freemasons. They were prohibited from attending more than three concerts or balls a session. At least one member of this committee would not be remembered as an enemy to refinement and luxury. This was Adam Smith, who was in his second year on the faculty. Ten years later, Smith worked with the city's magistrates to prevent the erection of a playhouse in Glasgow. He would come to believe, if he did not already, that the theater improved a society, but his rather conservative approach to university government should warn the observer that the liberal could and did adopt stringent measures.[16]

Of course, Adam Smith the philosopher interests us more than does Adam Smith the administrator. John Gardiner was acquainted with both. If his future lifestyle and associations are any kind of guide, he would have bridled at the rules laid down by Smith and the rest of the Glasgow professoriate. On the other hand, when we review his mature utterances, we might suspect that the young Gardiner listened attentively to Smith's lectures. This he could have done at any time in his Glasgow days, as university professors lectured publicly as well as privately. Gardiner was obligated to study ethics in his second year, when that subject was in Smith's bailiwick as moral philosophy chair.[17]

These lessons in ethics were eventually published as the *Theory of Moral Sentiments*. Smith's students learned that the power of sympathy was beneficent not only as it reconciled one member of society to another within the pale of a common human sensibility but also because it put all persons on their guard. The sensitive watcher was, at the same time, the anxiously watched. This anxiety—personified as the "impartial spectator"—was fundamental to society; it moderated tempers and encouraged reliable patterns of behavior. The humor of Smith's political economy was already evident in this, an ostensibly gentler survey of moral capacities. His system of ethics operated according to the same clever and rather hardnosed accounting that character-ized *The Wealth of Nations:* particular inconveniences supported a gen-eral happiness.[18]

Such connections were probably clear to John Gardiner and his fel-low students. Smith's lectures on jurisprudence would have followed hard on his ethics, and these expositions on justice, revenue, and expe-diency were the germs of his later, more famous book. At the heart of the lectures was the historicism and respect for progress typical of eighteenth-century Scottish thought. This progress did not touch human nature so much as it transformed the structure of human soci-ety. Smith very consciously described and designed a jurisprudence for his age, which he understood to be the most advanced. It was an age of commerce, in which divisions of labor maximized production and made possible a rapid and voluminous exchange of commodities. He lectured on the political freedoms consequent to the extension of trade and the humbling of the feudal aristocracy. He traced the legal ramifi-cations of these changes and discussed those laws that fell short. An example—one upon which Gardiner would eventually act—was entail, which restrained heirs from dividing their estates and selling the par-cels. While these strictures could be evaded, Smith thought their very existence absurd. He argued that the value of land would increase if the property frequently changed hands. The laws of land tenure had to conform to the latest definitions of wealth; they had to partake fully of the commercial spirit.[19]

Change, in the gross, was for the better and proceeded in one direc-tion. Smith was quite confident about these propositions, but he was also honest enough to admit that the process had its bends and eddies. Some participants moved swiftly along the top while others were pushed below. This was one of history's bargains. Smith offered the ex-ample of the common laborer. The laborer's life in the middle of the eighteenth century was to be preferred over a chieftain's in ages past, but that same worker was hopelessly debased by the system that en-riched him.[20] The invisible hand had two sides. One scooped everybody into that happy situation wherein nearly every action contributed to the common good; the other was more discriminate and, with demean-ing slaps, herded the unfortunate to their places.

Early social science was a literate calculation of gains and losses, with the balance tipping steadily to society's credit. These calculations did not begin with the Scots, though they refined the method. Their in-tellectual genealogy is distinguished, with Machiavelli, Francis Bacon, and Montesquieu as forebears. To this last writer the Scots thought themselves particularly obliged. John Millar, another philosopher of civil society, wrote that Montesquieu was the Lord Bacon of his field and that Smith, Millar's teacher, was its Newton. Montesquieu connected private interests to the national interest, but he differed from the Scots in preferring high politics over the economy. The monarch's honor—rather than the country's opulence—united the body politic.[21]

Honor became less of a consideration as philosophers decided that avarice was the more useful quality. Developing alongside the study of politics was the study of passions. Because human beings were so abandonedly passionate, political theorists began to wonder how these instincts might be made to countervail each other. If encouraged, the relatively innocuous passions might ameliorate or prevent the damage that their dangerous cousins caused on irregular occasions, and to devastating effect. This line of inquiry, itself a companion to early modern economic growth, redeemed the value of greed. Once held to be the most contemptible of sins, greed became almost virtuous, exactly because it was petty. Its diffuse constancy was just what the eighteenth century needed in order to imagine a scientific politics.[22]

No one took up this project more candidly than did Bernard Mandeville. This Dutch-born Londoner's major work, *The Fable of the Bees*, first appeared in 1714. He described how "those very vices of every particular person by skilful management were made subservient to the grandeur and worldly happiness of the whole."[23] The skill that Mandeville celebrated is less memorable than the ironic liberality of his formula, but the real irony of unintended consequences was that they served the designs of an intellectual or knowledgeable elite. He credited "wary politicians" with the cleverness to govern by crossed appetites: "This was the statecraft, that maintain'd / The whole, of which each part complain'd: / This, as in music harmony, / Made jarrings in the main agree."[24] Of course, it was an unobtrusive statecraft, because it did not attempt to reform human nature and because it echoed strains of behavior evident within society. Mandeville wrote of citizens who "Convert to their own use the labour / Of their good-natur'd heedless neighbour." The industrious as well as the knavish turned this trick, as "All trades and places knew some cheat, / No calling was without deceit." Mandeville's first example was the law, whose practitioners would dominate America's political class by the end of the century. His second was the practice of medicine (Mandeville's own vocation: his specialty was the treatment of hysteria and hypochondria), and we would do well to remember how the early modern physician's often parlous attempts to restore the body's equilibrium mirrored the efforts of notable eighteenth-century politicians and political thinkers to achieve—by morally compromised means and judgments—the equipoise observed in the best constitutions.[25]

◄§ · §►

The genius of Bernard Mandeville was to discern the happy effects of contrary causes; the Scots extended this idea into a pattern of inquiry. Moral philosophy, sociology, political economy, history: every field of social thought assumed this perspective. According to David Hume, the historian had to understand and describe "the remote, and commonly faint and disfigured originals of the most finished and most noble institutions" and "the great mixture of accident, which commonly concurs with a small ingredient of wisdom and foresight, in erecting the complicated fabric of the most perfect government."[26] Hume's *History of England* set about to do exactly that. It suggested that the key event in Europe's emergence from its dark age was the serendipitous discovery of Justinian's *Pandects*. It demonstrated, by the case of Cromwell's Independents, how tolerance and reasonableness might follow in the fanatic's train.[27] Hume ascribed to the historical process a resilient, inhumane intelligence, but, as we shall see below, he did not dismiss the need for intelligent decision. His respect for accident was not an abdication of science. Rather, it indicated the scientist's taste for experiment and hypothesis. Hume was a careful registrar of inputs, but he privileged results and general inclinations, no matter the incongruity of their component data.

Progress took a definite shape. John Gardiner studied its outlines with Adam Smith, who, along with Anne-Robert-Jacques Turgot and the other physiocrats, developed a stadial theory of history.[28] Human societies passed through four socioeconomic stages: an age of hunters, of shepherds, of agriculture, and of commerce. Political customs conformed to the requirements of each era. For example, Smith explained how commerce degraded aristocratic influence. Whereas the medieval man spent any surplus on his retinue, the modern man could buy many more and different kinds of things. Service flowed through the market instead of the household; therefore, the political will of the rich acted at a much greater distance and was unlikely to inspire obedience.[29]

Like Smith, Hume knew that politics increasingly bowed to commercial imperatives. He wrote his *History*, in part, to demystify the nation's political legends. One especially sacred cow was the ancient constitution, under which the Angles and Saxons lived well and freely before the imposition of the Norman yoke. This was, for Hume, a Whiggish fancy. He discredited the Saxon past; its stability was a crippling stagnation. The nobles lacked the wherewithal and opportunity to burden their estates with debt for the sake of improvement; the commons, likewise, were financially unsophisticated and lacked the means to greater wealth. Thus the first rank of men were secure in their land, in their power, and in their poverty, while the generality had their poverty and little else.[30]

This situation changed as municipal corporations began to guard their own privileges. Their inhabitants withdrew from the feudal bonds. In time, the financial savvy of the cities would master the nation. By the Tudor period, landowners were keener to profit by their lands than to support tenants who were once necessary to castlebreaking and other military adventures. As the barons learned the ways of money, so too did they learn the habits of luxury that in turn dissipated their fortunes. The trades and the cities were the gainers. Mechanics and merchants lived by their own labor, and the aristocrats, wrote Hume, "retained only that moderate influence which customers have over tradesmen." The expansion of commerce and liberty were coincident and enabled the middling rank—always vague in composition but including master craftsmen, merchants, professionals, and even the lesser gentry—to become a considerable social force in Great Britain.[31]

Hume's *History* completed a motion of his thought that had begun in his pithy and accessible essays. These, like the *History* and unlike the dense philosophical treatises, were widely read in the British Atlantic world. They are a typically Scottish blend of caution and positive effort. He reminded his readers of the casual and imperfect origins of government. As Smith would in his Glasgow lectures, Hume disputed the truth of an original contract between rulers and ruled.[32] Rational consent, they thought, was a thin reed by which to hang government's grand and motley edifices.

But what Hume took from reason with one hand he gave back with the other, though slyly and under the table. These compensations bore Mandeville's mark; again and again, Hume's essays recommend the equivalent of "skilful management" to the politician who would govern well. "No advantages in this world are pure and unmixed," wrote

Hume; this apothegm conveyed the fundamental wisdom of his politics.[33] His good magistrates knew that they had to accommodate the interests of bad men and that vice was often its own "cure." The essay "Of Commerce" drives the point home:

> Sovereigns must take mankind as they find them . . . it is requisite to govern men by other passions, and animate them with a spirit of avarice and industry, art and luxury . . . The harmony of the whole is still supported; and the natural bent of the mind being more complied with, individuals, as well as the public, find their account in the observance of those maxims.[34]

This language would have been familiar to anyone who read Mandeville and, later in the century, to the close reader of James Madison's *Federalist* essays.[35]

Hume demanded a studied, even clever, approach to government. Fortunately, he found that if men and women never overcame their essential shortcomings, they at least improved in knowledge and in political acuity. He linked these improvements to the same process that enriched the nation, fostered liberty, and refined the manners of the people. The chief beneficiaries of this process were the middling ranks, but they also gave as good as they got. As merchants, tradesmen, and professionals acquired a larger share of property, they became the political ballast as well as the economic engine of their society. Inclined neither to submit nor to tyrannize, they promoted equality and reliability in the law.[36]

These were still unintended goods, the collateral benefits of a middling interest, but Hume went further and suggested that men of that sort were better citizens and governors because they had gained a superior perspective. They were able to see through particular interests to the general good. Hume understood knowledge to be another commodity. A commercial people were richer in everything, including knowledge. Improvements and inventions, the products of knowledge, had a considerable cash value. Knowledge, like money, circulated widely and rapidly.[37]

Knowledge of all sorts was therefore more available to every sort of person, but Hume emphasized that persons from the "middle station of life" were more likely to acquire a knowledge "of Men and Things" and the wisdom to direct them both. They were familiar with a broader range of experience, they retained the leisure necessary for learning and observation, and they were ambitious to learn more and do more.

Hume calculated that professionals, in particular, were refined and excellent spirits. "There are more natural Parts," he wrote, "and a stronger Genius requisite to make a good Lawyer or Physician, than to make a great Monarch."[38]

Certainly, Hume would not have extended to every wine trader or solicitor the ability to divine "the general course of things" from "the concurrence of a multitude of causes." Such "abstruse thinkers" were rare, but—lest his word "abstruse" put us on the wrong scent—they were also society's "most useful and variable" members. "General reasonings" and "universal propositions" were the "chief business" of philosophers and politicians and, Hume might have added, historians. He sketched these employments in the essay "Of Commerce" and aligned the versatility of the commercial and professional classes with the capacity for higher thought. He also identified his own intellectual project as another symptom of the improving age.[39]

◄❦ · ❦►

The adolescent John Gardiner could not have fully comprehended the developments astir in the Scotland of his university years. He had no way of knowing how far the country had come in the previous half century, and he was probably unaware that he was living in the midst of a cultural renaissance. But Glasgow was not wholly alien to his experience. John Gardiner was the native of an important provincial seaport. Boston had nothing to match the venerable grandeur of Glasgow's cathedral or the newly minted grandeur of its tobacco lords, but Gardiner, a quick youth as well as a typically plastic one, was surely not too out of sorts.

Only a very dull boy could have missed the fact that he was in the middle of something, and something rather exciting at that. Gardiner arrived in Scotland just a few years after Bonnie Prince Charlie's uprising. When he spied a raggedy Highlander skulking around the market in search of work or passage to America, he must have reflected on what he had heard of Culloden and the final bloody charge of the loyal clans.[40] He might have witnessed the pious mob's attack on the theater. And he must have been aware of the religious controversies that erupted as a vibrant Kirk confronted novel ideas and the inevitable challenges to its authority. The same year Gardiner left Scotland, Popular elements within the General Assembly prosecuted David Hume for heresy. He was not convicted.[41]

Scotland was finally settling into the role demanded of it by the Union of 1707. Scottish merchants could work within the pale of the English mercantile system; literally a world of opportunity was open to them. Glasgow's tobacco firms were among the first to seize this advantage. Moreover, Scots flourished within the empire exactly because they had lived so long without it. Talented Scots sought their educations and fortunes far from home. The country had longstanding ties to the continent, and these ties held fast even after the Union.[42]

Experiences such as these were at the root of what became known as the Scottish Enlightenment. Dugald Stewart, a Smith disciple and chief popularizer of the Enlightenment's philosophies, attributed "the sudden burst of genius" to the "constant influx of information and of liberality from abroad," and Stewart was simply repeating what his elders had taught him.[43] William Robertson, in "A View of the Progress of Society in Europe" (1769), described how the Crusades, "the effect of superstition and folly," nonetheless exposed Europeans to "the first gleams of light which tended to dispel barbarity and ignorance." Hume's *History*, as a part of its effort to sully the antique Saxon myth so precious to Whigs and many Tories, asserted that the Norman conquest introduced into an ignorant island "the rudiments of science and cultivation" in addition to the altogether less welcome habits of feudal bondage.[44]

Fundamentally, Stewart was quite right. Hume, Robertson, and the other Scots writers cheered cosmopolitan impulses at work in the past because they were similarly inclined. After 1707, Scotland lacked the central political institutions so invigorating to civil society. Scots could and did go to London, but their political futures in England were hardly assured. Almost by way of compensation, their histories and political economies imagined a different kind of citizenship. Their men of the "middle station" made the best citizens because they were citizens of the world, of a larger society connected by commercial transaction.[45]

Such men were closer to the realities of life. They combined the vigor of aspiration with the even temper of experience. They were better able to overcome their provincial attachments, but because their drive and cosmopolitanism began at home, in the provinces, they did not have to abandon these attachments entirely. Thus Hume, who loved Paris, admitted London's primacy, and despised Scotticisms in the English language, was also a proud Scot who praised the counterfeit minstrelsy of Ossian and damned the roast beef bigotries of English "Barbarians."[46]

The writers of the Scottish Enlightenment commented upon their own position in Britain and in the world. By necessity, theirs was also a commentary on work; one powerful—and personal—narrative was the rise of the professions. The opportunities for professional men increased with the advancement of freedom, knowledge, and enterprise. Society's progress, in other words, was the professional's gain. The law offered the best example. William Robertson noticed that, as European cities prospered and social intercourse intensified, the need for regulation became acute. The subordination of citizens to a system of law accompanied the refinement of manners. Systems demand specialists, and so did the developing legal regime. Most nobles, accustomed to ruling by force, were unwilling or unable to follow the taxing course of study that the law now required of its practitioners. Other men stepped into the gap. Robertson put their case best:

> An order of men to whom their fellow-citizens had daily recourse for advice, and to whom they looked up for decision in their most important concerns, naturally acquired consideration and influence in society . . . A new road was opened to wealth and eminence. The arts and virtues of peace were placed in their proper rank, and received their due recompence.[47]

While John Gardiner was familiar with this process and its theory, he need not have been in order to have recognized the promise in law. The possibilities could be seen and experienced firsthand. The lawyer's ascent started in Europe's middle ages, but, in British North America, he was just beginning to see his way clear to the top of society and politics as Gardiner came of age.

❧ · ☙

After taking his M.A. in 1755, Gardiner returned to Boston, where, for three years, he "sucked in the first rudiments of the Law" at the office of Benjamin Prat.[48] Prat's career is a model of advancement. He was born in village Massachusetts, the eighth son of a farmer and ironmonger. Originally destined to toil in field and at forge, Prat discovered his other talents quite by accident. A fall from an apple tree forced the amputation of one leg. His life thereafter was never without pain, but this misfortune, while it crippled the body, seemed to free the mind. Just as Silvester Gardiner, the sickly youth, found a crucial patron in James MacSparran, his sister's husband, Prat too was helped by a clerical brother-in-law. After five years of preparation, he entered Harvard with the class of 1738. He was a decade older than most of his fellow students.[49]

A series of scholarships allowed the impoverished Prat to earn his degree and extend his studies. He trained for the ministry but, within a few years, abandoned it for the law. He read with Robert Auchmuty, a Scots-Irish immigrant and successful provincial lawyer who was, by the time Prat knew him, Boston's vice-admiralty judge. Prat married Auchmuty's daughter and rented a pew at his church, King's Chapel. He became one of the town's most engaged and respected attorneys; the Kennebeck Proprietors were among his many clients.[50] Thus he made Silvester Gardiner's acquaintance and became the logical choice to train Gardiner's son.

Prat had many qualities to recommend him. John Adams, who began his practice in the late 1750s, wrote admiringly of his "strong, elastic Spring, or what we call Smartness, and Strength in his Mind."[51] His learning and powers of memory were the stuff of minor legend. An infirm but ambitious man was naturally prone to a narrow bookishness, and Prat's knowledge sometimes got the better of his sense. One colleague silently laughed upon seeing him "lugg a Cart load of Books into Court to prove a Point as clear as the Sun."[52]

Prat's success—and the methods and manners that attended it—put some distance between him and his origins. He belittled "the common People" for their stupidity but was quite happy to leave them unimproved. "The People ought to be ignorant," Prat once said. "And our Free Schools," he added, "are the very bane of society. They make the lowest of the People infinitely conceited."[53] He also appreciated how the established Church might coddle and ultimately order the popular superstitions. These rather high sentiments were perhaps an extravagant display by which Prat meant to screen his scrambling ascent, but he came by his cynicism honestly. Poor health agitated a mordant wit. When asked what was the chief end of man, Prat shocked the callow Adams by replying, "to provide food for other Animals." Some grim, good poetry also survives:

> Late in a microscopic worm confin'd,
> Then in a 'prison'd foetus drows'd the mind,
> Now of the ape-kind first for sense and size,
> Man eats, and drinks, and propagates, and dies . . .

Scheme after scheme the dupe successive tries,
And never gains, but hopes to gain the prize;
From the delusion still he ne'er will wake,
But dreams of bliss, and lives on the mistake.[54]

This poem came to light immediately after Prat's death, and he might have written it during his final illness. As will be discussed later, that last year also saw him placed in an imperial office, a "prize" he did not so much enjoy as suffer.

In spite of his crabbed disposition, Prat was a minor political success. He was elected moderator of the town meeting in 1757, and he was the first professional lawyer to represent Boston in the General Court for more than one term. His elections augured well for his colleagues at the bar. In 1761, James Otis, the hero of the writs-of-assistance cases, began the first of his ten terms.[55] The lawyer's preeminence in American politics had begun. Prat encouraged professional strength and solidarity. His parting admonition to the Suffolk bar was "Let brotherly love continue and forsake not the assembling yourselves together." Like many of his fellows—and despite his own Toryish sympathies—Prat opposed Thomas Hutchinson and his faction, which, among other things, engrossed legal offices without regard for professional qualifications.[56]

John Gardiner was on hand to witness Prat's electoral success, and, of course, he closely observed Prat's conduct as a lawyer. Whether by chance or influence, Gardiner adopted much of his mentor's character. His recall was impressive and his learning extraordinary, but these often did not combine to good effect. Gardiner's intelligence, like Prat's, was too easily indulged. Both men behaved rather imperiously in public, though each retained an attractive, if cutting, sense of humor. Finally, Gardiner would, as Prat before him, savor the practice of letters and the company of lettered men.

There were important differences. Gardiner was a rich man's son, and he enjoyed advantages Benjamin Prat never knew. The scope of Gardiner's ambition was larger. He was probably aware that Prat's father-in-law, Robert Auchmuty, and the governor, William Shirley, attended the Inns of Court, and that this experience opened doors for both. He could have practiced law in Massachusetts without further education, but he was not thinking along strictly provincial lines. In May of 1758, he entered the Inner Temple in London.[57]

According to one point of view, it was not the most propitious moment to be at the inns. Attendance at one of the four societies—Lincoln's

Inn, Gray's Inn, and the Inner and Middle Temples—remained the necessary step for those men who would become English barristers and argue causes before the central Westminster courts: King's Bench, Common Pleas, Chancery, and Exchequer. In the early modern period, the Inns of Court constituted the "Third University of England," and to it flocked the sons of the elite. Some stayed for only a few years, but even so short a residence taught a familiarity with the common law and with Greater London, both of which were useful to lords and squires who would govern the nation from their manors and from the houses of Parliament. Before the Civil War, students could hear senior members of the inns lecture on the law, and those students who genuinely aspired to the bar had to perform at moots. These practices, however, had ceased by the end of the seventeenth century, and the inns ceased to be institutions of learning or societies of the first rank.[58]

In his magisterial *Commentaries*, William Blackstone bemoaned the state of legal education in England and pinned much of the blame on the inns. Their governors made no attempt at instruction, leaving that task to the ingenuity and—even more doubtfully—the diligence of the members. Blackstone certainly thought little of the sort of person who populated the inns at midcentury. One gentleman observer, an old Templar, reached the same conclusions much earlier, in 1700. The children of "mechanics, ambitious of rule and government" were supplanting the young men of his type and standing.[59]

A historian of the eighteenth-century English bar echoes these assessments, describing the inns of that time as "moribund." Their decadence had a wider cause. During the eighty years before 1750, the number of cases heard in the Westminster courts declined sharply, and calls to the bar shrank appropriately. The inns became cash enterprises, renting their rooms to outsiders and fining their barristers for lectures they were no longer expected to deliver. To receive their call, students had only to register at their inns for the statutory period: at first seven years, then five after 1762, but, informally and in Gardiner's case, even fewer. And who were these students? As Blackstone suspected, they no longer represented the nation's political leadership as well as they once had. In the Tudor and early Stuart eras, nearly half of the members of the House of Commons attended an inn; in the Georgian era, less than a quarter did.[60]

On the other hand, the Georgian bar, though smaller and less blooded, was "fitter" and led by men ready to serve a society marked by commerce and nascent industry.[61] Britain's economy was becoming more and more of a bourgeois concern, and the bar followed suit. By the time of Blackstone's critique, two-thirds of the barristers were from middling families. Of course, land was still the prime source of wealth and standing, and both barristers and attorneys profited from its disputes and improvements, as well as from the business generated by banks, manufactures, and mercantile trade. Land was also the desire of all sorts of men and women, and lawyers were notable members of— and more numerous than merchants in—the modern squirearchy.[62] Political success was the inevitable companion of the social. Many an obscure young man found his way into the great offices of state after brilliant works in law. Philip Yorke, the attorney's son who became Lord Chancellor Hardwicke, is but one very good example. Accomplishments such as his inspired hundreds to try a career at the bar, where relatively few prospered, and to come to the inns, which, by John Gardiner's admission in 1758, offered little except grand hopes and an expensive opportunity to fail.[63]

Students at the inns had to seek out their education. John Rutledge, the wartime governor of South Carolina and later chief justice of the U.S. Supreme Court, recommended a catholic program of study to his younger brother, a Templar, in the late 1760s; his curriculum included learning shorthand, reading the best English historians and other authors, attending the more elegant churches to hear good preaching, and visiting the theater to take in Garrick's lessons in elocution and presence. The most serious of Rutledge's peers would apprentice with an attorney or pleader in order to learn the practicalities, and students of all stripes enjoyed visiting the courts of Westminster. There they could watch England's best barristers at work. The reasoning, the rhetoric, the styles of person and performance: these made for a better day than parsing Coke upon Littleton.[64] If the bar was not stimulating enough, the audience could always turn its attention to the bench. Its incumbents were barristers as well, and barristers worthy of emulation. Their skills and connections had raised them to the top of the legal apparatus.

Gardiner and his contemporaries were particularly lucky, for they had before them the model of William Murray, Lord Mansfield, the chief justice of the King's Bench and the most influential practicing jurist of his century. John Dunning, who, like Yorke and Murray before him, gained a peerage through the law, remembered how, as a young Templar, he and his fellows made a point of going to Westminster whenever Murray was due to speak: "Sometimes when we were leaving the court, we would hear the cry, 'Murray is up,' and forthwith we rushed back, as if to a play or other entertainment."[65] Dunning was called to the bar the same year Murray was elevated to the Lords and to the bench; the two met many times thereafter as counsel and judge. On at least one such occasion, John Gardiner was at Dunning's side, in service to the same cause. We can be sure that he happily took part in a show he, like his senior partner, had earlier watched from the gallery.[66]

Mansfield's genius was not eccentric; his successes were attuned to many of the structural changes that concerned the philosophers and political economists of North Britain. Mansfield was himself, rather notoriously, a Scot. He was born two years before the Union, the fourth son and eleventh child of a poor Scottish noble. The Murrays were Jacobites; one of William's older brothers was a courtier to the exiled Stuart. This same brother arranged for William to leave Scotland for London in 1718, but this move did not at first loosen young Murray's ties to Jacobitism. He was enrolled at the Westminster School exactly because its dean was Francis Atterbury, who would be banished a few years later for plotting against the Hanoverian king. Murray exhibited better judgment than his master: he never returned to his homeland after leaving it; his was to be an exemplary British life spent at Britain's English center.[67]

Murray was aware that his heritage was a liability, and his efforts to distance himself from it were so earnest as to be easily exaggerated. As a fledgling barrister, he in fact relied upon his Scottish connections for business, and he was not without ancestral pride. Shortly after the 1745 revolt, a critic wrote that Murray, hopeful of preferment, had from his youth "smeered over" his true character with "a little English erudition." Murray responded with spirit:

> why should it be an indelible reflection on Englishmen that a Scot, with more merit and virtue than any of his co[n]temporary pleaders, should be placed in a high station. The Union gives him an equal right with the English professors of the law . . . 'Tis peculiarly remarkable that the prejudice to the Scotch and Irish in England, is confined to the males only; the English fair being too discerning and generous to indulge a native, interested, unjust prejudice to all who are not born among themselves.[68]

Murray was by then married to an Englishwoman and serving as the king's solicitor general. He would shortly demonstrate his loyalty and professionalism by prosecuting the Scots earls who had aided the

Pretender's rebellion. Rumors of a Jacobite past would continue to dog Murray, but his career progressed magnificently.[69]

His judicial opinions are his legacy, and they obscure whatever historical baggage he might have brought to his practice. Edmund Burke's appraisal is unsurpassed:

> His ideas go to the growing melioration of the law by making its liberality keep pace with the demands of justice and the actual concerns of the world—not restricting the infinitely diversified occasions of men, and the rules of natural justice, within artificial circumscriptions, but conforming our jurisprudence to the growth of our commerce and of our empire.[70]

In other words, his ideas were forward looking in a way well known to many Scots. The Union spread their concerns through the imperial dominions. The commercial spirit became the soul of politics, replacing the old Scottish fidelities and institutions. Though no merchant, Murray was interested in the growth of empire. As a barrister, he profited from boundary disputes in the American colonies; when he was attorney general, Silvester Gardiner and his Kennebeck partners sought his opinion on their claims.[71]

Murray was sensitive to the needs of business. Anything so massive and messy as the common law could not be stiff, but much of it had coalesced into doctrines protecting and maintaining real property, the land. When Murray became Mansfield and sat at the head of the common law, he imported into its practice many of the equitable notions he had learned under Lord Hardwicke in Chancery. The entrepreneur was happier for these flexibilities. Mansfield valued coherence and predictability as well, but, like his countrymen Hume and Smith, he understood that these goods emerged from a wealth of many considerations and not just those prescribed by writ.[72] If John Gardiner did not conscientiously absorb Smith's theories of jurisprudence at Glasgow, he at least witnessed their tendencies in action at Westminster.

◆⟩§ · §⟨◆

Gardiner's greatest teacher, however, was neither Mansfield nor Smith; London itself was the master of masters. Its discipline and lessons ran the gamut: from the crushing to the indulgent and from the comprehensive to the minute. Many commentators regretted London's influence on students at the Inns of Court. Blackstone hinted at the perils: "A raw and unexperienced youth, in the most dangerous season of life, is transplanted on a sudden into the midst of allurements to pleasure, without any restraint or check." How unsurprising it was that students should abandon their all too independent studies and "addict themselves wholly to amusements, or other less innocent pursuits."[73] Charles Carroll, an American and Gardiner's exact contemporary, visited London in the early sixties and recorded the same downward spiral: "law books are thrown aside, dissipation succeeds to study, immorality to virtue, one night plunges them in ruin, misery, and disease."[74] In nearby Ram Alley, off Fleet Street, every house was bawdy; the most infamous, the *Maidenhead*, sat close to where the alley's end abutted the Temple grounds. According to "Mary Midnight," a mid-century chronicler of London's street life, Templars and other law students did more than their part to sustain the vicious trade.[75]

More reputable establishments also drew the young men of the inns. Coffeehouses and taverns crowded the neighborhood. During John Gardiner's London tenure, the writer Oliver Goldsmith often found his supper at the Globe before he found his final resting place in the Temple churchyard. Poet and Inner Templar William Cowper favored Dick's. Peele's was home to moneylenders. If students wanted a larger assembly, they could always take in a concert or show. Dunning may have thought Murray and his Westminster fellows were entertaining company, but the finest plays and performers in the English-speaking world were just ten minutes' walk from the Temple, at the Drury Lane Theatre. The streets themselves were a promiscuous exhibition. An intermittent rain of slop threatened a parade of modish and castoff finery. Shopkeepers and peddlers hawked their wares; in the street, a buyer could find most anything: rabbits and gingerbread, lavender and lace, almanacks and candles.[76]

London's offerings were abundant and, if liberally enjoyed, expensive. A student's or barrister's fees and room rents were not that taxing. John Gardiner kept rooms at the Inner Temple into the middle 1760s, and their rent required only a tenth of his allowance. The remainder was readily spent. Well after John's call to the bar in June of 1761, his father continued to grant him forty-five pounds a quarter, nearly the amount a wealthy baronet of that period allowed his son at Oxford.[77]

James Boswell had to be happy with a similar portion when he visited London in 1762. His father, one of Scotland's chief judges, did not like to indulge James's considerable whims and had at first promised less. In addition to an equivalent allowance, the younger Boswell and John Gardiner enjoyed other common experiences. Boswell attended Adam Smith's lectures at the University of Glasgow. He lived at the Inner Temple for several months during his visit to the capital; he and Gardiner might well have crossed paths. Boswell delayed his call to the bar for twenty-five years, but he appreciated the Temple's charms from the start. Samuel Johnson, his new friend and future biographical subject, resided there. The grounds had the air of a retreat but were deliciously near London's most bustling districts. Boswell described life at the Inner Temple as "the most agreeable in the world for a single man."[78] A Templar could come and go at all hours and get along fairly well without a servant. Boswell took advantage of the opportunity. He could not live extravagantly on his £200 a year, but he could hire a sedan to Drury Lane when the weather was foul. He also hired prostitutes to satisfy his "carnal inclinations." Given Boswell's gregariousness and tastes, his introduction to John Wilkes in the spring of 1763 comes as no great surprise, and, with this meeting, his experience again converged with John Gardiner's.[79]

How Gardiner came to meet Wilkes is unknown; what is certain is that the young barrister entered Wilkes's employ and, to some degree, his social orbit before that libertine's first moments of national fame. When the king's messengers arrested Wilkes in April of 1763 for his part in writing and publishing the *North Briton*, Gardiner was in the small gang of admirers that convened at Wilkes's home in Westminster. According to Gardiner's own recollection, it was he who pushed open the door over the messengers' objections. Wilkes had already been spirited away, but, for the next three hours, Gardiner and friends harassed the king's men as they ransacked the house in search of incriminating papers.[80] Gardiner and Arthur Beardmore, a solicitor and printer whose *Monitor* anticipated the tone and politics of the *North Briton*, then made their way to the Tower of London, where Wilkes was confined. They were unable to see their client; one week later, Charles Pratt, chief justice of Common Pleas, ordered his release on the grounds of parliamentary privilege.[81]

Thus began a series of legal adventures in which Gardiner was engaged as junior counsel. Many Wilkites major and minor profited by these suits, but more important to posterity was their effect on the economy of language. The inflation of "Liberty" was dramatic. In order to root out the king's abusive critics, his secretaries-of-state issued a general warrant, which allowed for blanket arrests and seizures. John

Wilkes was the primary target, but many printers and printers' apprentices were also detained. Over a dozen of these men brought actions of trespass, assault, and false imprisonment against the king's men. The case of William Huckle set the trend. Gardiner introduced Huckle's complaint to Pratt's court when it sat at the City's Guildhall in July.[82]

Huckle was a laborer in the shop of Dryden Leach, who had published an earlier number of the *North Briton*. When the messengers came looking for no. 45, Huckle and his mates were rounded up and held at a constable's house. While their confinement only lasted until the early evening and was improved by what one apprentice called "a hearty Dinner" of beefsteaks and porter, the jury awarded Huckle £300, much more than he could have earned in a year, let alone a day. Huckle's companions won similar judgments. When the losers moved for new trials, claiming excessive damages, Chief Justice Pratt vindicated the juries. He admitted that the award was disproportionate to Huckle's suffering, but that mattered little once "the Liberty of the whole Kingdom came in Question." He remarked that the general warrants constituted "a publick Invasion in General on the Liberty of the people."[83]

Pratt reiterated this decision in the case of Arthur Beardmore and his clerk, David Meredith, versus the Earl of Halifax, one of the signatories to the general warrant. John Gardiner was principal counsel for the plaintiffs, and his efforts met with considerable success: the jury delivered a £1,500 judgment. Beardmore expressed his gratitude by presenting Gardiner with a handsome silver waiter, a trophy the barrister and his descendants brandished proudly.[84] As before, Pratt had to defend the large award, and while doing so he defended Gardiner's right "to harrangue the Jury upon Topicks of aggravation," meaning those topics that elevated the matter above a simple loss of time into the headier realm of political history. If one took these aggravations seriously, the issue was no longer "the case of Mr. Beardmore only, but it is a Struggle between the Power of the Crown and the Liberty of the People." Gardiner had clearly delivered exactly what Pratt wanted to hear, a brand of ideological abstraction that was to become more and more popular and effective in the succeeding decades. Of course, this abstraction was incomplete. The grand political concept still required a face, and the cheer of the hour was "Wilkes and Liberty."[85]

Wilkes's first contest with the government ended to his advantage, but the victory enlarged his troubles as well as his reputation. John

Gardiner helped him control the damage. Wilkes was particularly anxious to recover his papers; he guessed that officials held a copy of the *Essay on Woman*, an indecent parody of Pope's *Essay on Man*, which Wilkes had planned to circulate among his louche friends. In an attempt to outflank his adversaries, Wilkes had Gardiner arrange for a newspaper advertisement that announced the government's forthcoming publication of obscenity. This cheekiness did not help Wilkes's cause in early 1764, when he was tried before Lord Mansfield for publishing the essay himself.[86] Similarly ineffective were his cronies' efforts to sway the jury with pamphlets such as "The Trial of John Peter Zenger." Mansfield was a loyal government man and, unlike Pratt, not easily moved by broad appeals to freedom. Wilkes's lawyers, including Gardiner, could do little to prevent a guilty verdict. The accused, having seen the writing on the wall, fled to France well before the trial. Thus began four years of outlawry, during which time Gardiner and his most illustrious client had little or no contact.[87]

Wilkes had, however, deeply impressed his young counsellor; Gardiner's public persona would ever after bear a Wilkite stamp. Like Boswell, Gardiner relished his introduction into a circle of wits. He was friendly with Charles Churchill, Wilkes's fellow profligate and mischiefmaker. Churchill was an accomplished and bestselling poet; his most famous work was *The Rosciad*, a satire on the theater. Gardiner liked to think of himself as a man of letters, and he often quoted Churchill in his later speeches and writings.[88] These quotations are the plainest evidences of the influence that London and the Wilkite project exercised throughout the rest of Gardiner's life. Less obvious, but of significance to a study of eighteenth-century ambition, was the exemplary nature of Wilkes's career. He was an original, to be sure, but he was also a model of political versatility.

David Hume had suggested that the future would belong to men from the "middle station of life"; John Wilkes was one of their champions. His supporters came from all ranks, but most numerous among them were the merchants and tradesmen of Greater London. Under the banner of "Wilkes and Liberty," the boldest elements in the middling sort hoped to reform the political system so that it might respect their interests and economic clout. These reforms were not realized until the next century, but Wilkites successfully pioneered a style of politics that reflected their style of life. One historian calls their undertaking the "commercialisation of politics" and Wilkes the "first political entrepreneur." He was a highly marketable hero, and, where his cause was active, printers sold more paper, brewers more ale, and artisans more paraphernalia bearing his face and slogans.[89] Scottish writers such as Hume described how Europe entered an age of commerce and how the law and other governing structures of society tended, at their best, to meet the needs of that age. The Wilkites, though relentless Scotophobes, incarnated this process as faithfully as the North Britons explained it.

While Scottish liberalism adopted the dry confidence of the account book, the Wilkite faith was celebrated as at a black mass: wildly and festooned with contraries. Hume thought the uproar was barbaric; Wilkes and his followers invoked a mythic vocabulary in the service of a campaign that deep historical change could win on much more reliable terms. On the other hand, scientists rarely make policy, and historians rarely fight the country's battles. Wilkites carried forward the civilizing process—the Scots' master narrative—but their understanding of the problem was old-fashioned, dependent on a primitive, static history and the violent pieties that guarded it.[90] In a letter to Wilkes, John Gardiner called himself and his confederates the friends of "old England." They pursued reforms so that they might protect an antique constitution. They feared Scottish encroachments, but even as their ritual use of "45" summoned, for purposes of derision, the ghost of Stuart tyranny, it also recalled Prince Charlie's rebelliousness and bonhomie, qualities flattering to Wilkes and Wilkites. Not too surprisingly, a number of gentlemen Tories made common cause with these "radicals." Both groups were full of true blue patriots and vigilant foes of the court party.[91] Their enterprise presaged new priorities but relied upon old symbols and songs. It was a totemic politics, and its chief idol was John Wilkes himself.

He was well suited to the role. Wilkes was a child of the middling sort: his father was a prosperous distiller; both parents were Dissenters. As befit his religion, young John attended the University of Leyden. His best friends there and for several years thereafter were Scots. In 1754, he toured Scotland and met David Hume. Wilkes had a talent for meeting people, and he had to apply it if he were to succeed in politics. Any man who aspired thus, and particularly one of his background, needed influential patrons. Wilkes gained the notice of Earl Temple and, through him, two future prime ministers: Temple's brother, George Grenville, and his brother-in-law, William Pitt. Wilkes's first attempt at a parliamentary seat was an instructive failure. He disputed the return, alleging bribery. Three years later, he contested another seat and spent £7,000 to win it. When he wasn't busy practicing high libertinism, Wilkes was seeking preferment and office. He lobbied hard to be the first British governor of Quebec, but his rise was stopped by the ascendancy of Bute, George III's Scottish favorite. Wilkes soon went into opposition.[92]

He did not lose his elasticity as he entered this radical phase. As has been seen, people came to his cause as he began it: with a variety of motives and predilections. If he did not share all of the ideas of his followers—and he was apparently doubtful of the more progressive ones—then he was better able to represent a broader range of sentiment. After the *North Briton* controversy, a correspondent joked that he knew not whether to find Wilkes "in the Tower, the Bastile, the Elysian Shades, Quebec, or at the Treasury Board."[93] The man was difficult to pin down because, at every turn, he adeptly seized new opportunities and cultivated new sources of power. In the 1760s, his interest lay with the mob. In the 1770s, Wilkes pressed his advantage in the City and became Lord Mayor of London. A sinecure eased his financial woes and his return to respectable society. During the Gordon Riots of 1780, he took up arms to defend the Bank of England against the ruffians who once rallied to his name.[94] Although John Gardiner did not witness the rogue's progress in full, he was a quick study and assumed from the beginning of his own career a similar facility. The lesson of John Wilkes, the last of Gardiner's education, would prove useful in the coming imperial crisis.

The Revolution of Opportunities

John Wilkes was an engrossing politician. He staked his personal ambitions to those of the middling classes, and he put his stamp on ideological ventures old and new. Wilkes focused popular concerns but designed to rise above them. Similarly, many eighteenth-century British-Americans couched their own ambitions in a liberal vocabulary that balanced social progress and private advantage. This philosophy was grounded in experience. For example, the profession of law taught a strategic versatility: lawyers had to connect particular arguments to general rules and commanding schemes of thought, and they were well placed to profit by the relations of parish, province, and empire.

Where long-established structures of government and jurisprudence had achieved an impressive and sometimes perplexing density, lawyers were the masters of detail. Where procedures were less settled, as in the American provinces, lawyers could bring to bear their knowledge of distant authorities, while drawing on an often powerful base of local contacts. And when the highest authorities were questioned, as in the Wilkite episodes and during the Revolutionary crisis, many lawyers were skillful managers of disruption for the same reasons that others were the best defenders of the status quo: because they used a language that was at once traditional and presumptively universal, because they were professionally engaged with different sorts of people, and because they were gifted, or at least experienced, in matters of public representation.

John Gardiner's career demonstrates how a lawyer—and especially one who worked in many far corners of the British Atlantic world—might play a sharp game, trading one opportunity for another as chance demanded. But his adventures also delineated the limits of an unmoored opportunism. As this cocky provincial moved from London to Wales and then to the West Indies, he accumulated a certain (though never very large) amount of real and political capital, but it was not bankable until he committed himself to one place and one position. It is fitting that the end of his active phase as a practicing lawyer would see him return to his native Boston, an apparent champion of America's lately victorious cause to free itself from the control of the very empire his professional hopes had embraced.

The twilight of his career—which, as we shall see, was rather purple in its excitements—had much to remind one of what Gardiner was before the Revolution, for he could not entirely escape the imperially cosmopolitan frame of reference that shaped his youth and early middle age. He did not want to escape it, except in matters of politics and social advancement. He did, however, make a choice that irrevocably bent his destiny to an American design. As this chapter shows, John Gardiner, for his own reasons as well as for those forced upon him, had fashioned himself as a kind of superprovincial, a citizen of the Anglophone world ruled from London. Then the scope of his career narrowed, and the constitutional face of Atlanticism fell away. It had always been largely a state of mind, and so it remained: memories and attitudes recorded in the common law, in literary culture, in the continuing entanglements of commerce, and in the liberal ideology that the ambitious professionals and provincials of the old empire had propagated by word and deed. This was what Gardiner brought home with him, and what he and other Yankees would bring to bear on the problems of nation and commonwealth.

◀§ · §▶

In the 1760s, Gardiner's whole career lay ahead of him. Wilkes and his confederates were not the young lawyer's only clients. Like most fledgling barristers, Gardiner relied on contacts from home to bring in the business. He was his father's agent in several small mercantile transactions, and Benjamin Prat helped him to recover at least one Londoner's money from a debtor in Boston. Gardiner's first big case also came from Massachusetts. His client was Richard Derby, the Salem shipping magnate. He was some catch for a twenty-three-year-old still a few months shy of his call to the bar. Derby first broached the matter with one of his business correspondents, but it soon passed into Gardiner's inexperienced hands.[1]

Derby's problem arose during the Seven Years' War. Wars are disorderly occasions during which reputations rise and fall quite suddenly, and this war was particularly unsettling. It was a contest for empire that saw the French driven from Canada and the West. British subjects as different as John Wilkes and George Washington coveted these lands and the new offices attached to them, and the Crown bureaucracy disappointed the hopes of these and smaller men at some cost. The war was good and bad for Richard Derby, but in neither case did it lash him more tightly to Britain's imperial destiny.

He was never the most loyal of subjects; a businessman of his kind could not afford to be. He continued to peddle French sugar through the war, and, in the matter that fell to John Gardiner, he was caught in the act. One of his ships, the *Ranger*, took on the contraband in Monte Christi, a port in Hispaniola, which Spain kept open to British trade. Derby thought the secondhand nature of the transaction relieved his liability; the British authorities thought otherwise. Privateers captured the *Ranger* and directed it to the Bahamas, where the vice-admiralty judge and governor condemned it as a prize of war. The governor was William Shirley, once Silvester Gardiner's fellow vestry-man at King's Chapel and his occasional accomplice in the Kennebeck claims. As the governor of Massachusetts and the dispenser of government contracts, Shirley as much as anyone had benefited from the North American wars. Military incompetence and rumors of malfeasance had relegated him to his last, tropical post. He remained an active servant of the Crown. By seizing ships like Derby's, he served both its interests and, as a party to the spoils, his own.[2]

John Gardiner took up Derby's cause early in 1761. He promised his client that he would embarrass Shirley and "bring that old greyheaded Villain to condign Punishment." The young barrister was given to bold promises. He wrote to Derby of his connections at Whitehall and Westminster. He had friends in the Commons, dined with a lord of trade, and filed petitions at more than one important office. Gardiner was anxious to impress Derby and forthrightly stated his hope that Derby's friends would engage him as their English advocate.[3] He would have to capitalize on his provincial roots if he were to succeed at the bar, or so Gardiner supposed at that early stage of his career, when he had just begun to ride circuit in the outlying counties. Gardiner would make new contacts in these other, older provinces, but Derby's business was good work for any lawyer.

While lawyer and client were American, the costs of Derby's case were decidedly metropolitan. Gardiner was careful to point this out: he practiced in London, at the central courts of kingdom and empire, and he charged appropriately. He even sent Derby an account of charges incurred by another American who appealed to the London courts, so, in Gardiner's words, "you may not be hereafter surpriz'd at the Expence."[4] Gardiner added that it was his custom—probably instituted for this occasion—to take a 2.5 percent commission on the amount appealed. Other agents asked for twice that; according to Gardiner, his client was getting a good deal.

Derby was less likely to agree with each passing year. He was at first as eager as his barrister. He encouraged Gardiner to move against Shirley and his second, Judge James Bradford. They were a "Piraticall Combination" that harried American shipping and grew rich on bribes and seizures. Derby advised counsel to seek damages in the amount his cargo would have fetched at its destination, a sum nearly four times its cost to him.[5] Gardiner considered several modes of action, but he was hamstrung by Shirley's absence. The Commons might punish a corrupt governor, but Gardiner chose the more regular course of complaining to the Board of Trade. This prosecution, though it lends the affair color, was of less moment than the *Ranger*'s appeal before the Privy Council. Here Gardiner was hopeful, for the lords of appeal had recently overturned the condemnations of two other American ships with similar trading histories. Gardiner happily reported this news to Derby, along with portents of Shirley's recall and Benjamin Prat's appointment in his place.[6]

By the end of 1763, however, Prat was dead, and the council had confirmed the Bahamian judgment. Derby decided to cut his losses and ordered Gardiner to cease his action against Shirley. In 1765, Gardiner sent his client the bill for his services; in it, he charged a commission against the value of the forfeited ship and goods. Derby and his London financiers were not about to pay. They backed away from the high figure at which Derby himself had rated his loss; then they demanded a refund of much of what they had advanced their lawyer in the early years of the case. They found Gardiner hard to pinch.[7]

So did the principals and agents of Connecticut's Susquehannah Company. This group was organized in 1753 to settle some five million acres of Pennsylvania wilderness.[8] In 1764, the company's representative in London was planning his return to New England and tapped Gardiner as his replacement. By this oblique approach the lawyer entered his family's business, land speculation. Silvester Gardiner had left the fields and pastures of Narragansett for a life shaped by cities and professional attainments, yet reshaping the land became his life's great object. His son, John, followed a similar course, leaving America to pursue a professional and metropolitan career (elder brother William became the gentleman farmer). Then, in London, Yankee land interests came a-calling, but Gardiner did not serve them with his father's unceasing application. He did little, if anything, to advance the company's claim. What was worse, he seems to have absconded with the supporting documentation that more conscientious agents would need if they were to succeed where he had failed. The company despaired of ever retrieving the fees already paid Gardiner for services never rendered. His corporate record was not, however, a complete blank. The ledgers show that he sold several parcels of Susquehannah land to curious, or gullible, Welshmen.[9]

◄◊§ · §◊►

John Gardiner first traveled to Wales in the spring of 1762. Not all barristers rode so far afield to find work, but most did not earn their keep in London. They derived much of their income from practicing on circuit. Twice each year, normally during the Lent and Trinity vacations (late February to March and July to early August), the Westminster courts went on the road. Judges, lawyers, and their retinues split into bands and traveled a traditional route that connected several neighboring counties. The court sessions, or assizes, lasted less than a week in each shire, but they were eventful days.[10]

In his charge to judges about to commence their circuits, Francis Bacon reminded them of the considerable tools they carried: "you do carry the two glasses or mirrors of the State. For it is your duty in these your visitations to represent to the people the graces and care of the king; and again, upon your return, to present to the king the distastes and griefs of the people."[11] In 1617, when Bacon sat in the Star Chamber and spoke these words, the assizes were near the height of their influence. Their judges were the Crown's roving political managers. They conferred with the local gentry and kept the justices of the peace and other magistrates in line. Upon riding into town, the judges read their mandate, which usually stretched beyond rote formula to summarize Whitehall's current priorities. Thus the judges were also heralds, even evangelists. The assize sermon was the ecclesiastical escort to the judges' charge—and often just as pointed. If the sermon was to the judges' liking, it could expect a large printing. Religious and political turmoil would fatally interrupt the Stuart dynasty, and following the interregnum, King and Council handed many of the judges' administrative responsibilities to the lords lieutenants. The assizes, however, continued to be a potent medium of state power.[12]

That power was expressed judicially and symbolically. The assizes were courts, first and foremost. They brought the king's justice into the country. The local bench punished many crimes, but most felons had to wait for Lent or late summer, when the assize judges came and delivered the jails. The judges also heard civil causes, matters pled before the central courts and sent by writ of *nisi prius* into the counties for jury trial. Such cases offered various opportunities to the parties involved. To barristers, the civil proceedings meant fees and perhaps a minor fame. As these proceedings often concerned local disputes, they offered jurors—important men of town and county—another chance to play at politics and to shape, intentionally or no, the law that sought their decision.[13] Of course, power flowed both ways, and more readily from the top of the polity. The hearings at Westminster and the trials on circuit translated the disputes of the shire into the pleadings and principles of the common law. No person or institution controlled that law, and it might potentially work to the benefit or harm of any subject, but, in almost every instance, the law's performance—the expression of a national tradition—ratified the unity and order of the kingdom.

The assizes were celebrations of hierarchy and, as such, spectacular and pompous events. A popular history of Haverfordwest, the Welsh borough where John Gardiner practiced law and sired his children, records the excitement of the first day in the "size week." Town and country were astir. The ceremonial guard donned their livery and took up their javelins. As the official cavalcade approached, trumpeters went forth in greeting. Closer to town, a curious throng gathered in anticipation. At last, the judges arrived, and "their lordships entered the Sheriff's carriage as he stood bare-headed to receive them."[14]

While this scene was the same on all the circuits, justice wore a slightly different guise when it called on Wales. The assizes there, though they resembled their English cousins, had their own name and history. They were the Great Sessions, and, quite importantly, their authority proceeded from the acts of union that bound Wales to the English nation. The Sessions were the consequence and reminder of one of the original acts of English statecraft, without which Bacon's invocation of the "State" would have meant much less. Indeed, were it not for Henry VIII's domestic troubles and the apostasy that followed, England might very well have directed its future by a different compass, with little bearing on North America. But troubles there were, and Henry chose an independent destiny for himself and for his country. England became Rome's enemy and, in the coming age of discovery, a competitor of Catholic Europe.

Like all revolutions, the Henrician had its key words and documents. Particularly significant was the preamble to the Act in Restraint of Appeals (1533). Here is the crucial portion:

> This realm of England is an Empire . . . governed by one Supreme Head and King having the dignity and royal estate of the imperial Crown of the same, unto whom a body politic, compact of all sorts and degrees of people divided in terms and by names of Spirituality and Temporalty, be bounden and owe to bear next to God a natural and humble obedience.[15]

Earlier English kings had claimed an imperial title, but Henry's "Empire" was different: it was not a plurality of kingdoms but an uncontested sovereignty or *imperium* to which were uniformly attached all subjects and subject territories in the nation. Henry and his minister, Thomas Cromwell, had conceived—or, we might say most accurately, rationalized—nothing less than the modern state. In order to realize their conception, the two men had to exclude the Crown's ecclesiastical rivals. The Act of Supremacy (1534) and the later confiscation of church property worked to that purpose. Additionally, Henry had to regularize his government in every place he claimed sovereignty. Wales was particularly wanting of correction.[16]

The Welsh could fairly say that they had fostered the Tudor monarchy. Henry VII was born in Pembroke, well away from the Wars of the Roses that would ultimately end in his coronation. The road to Bosworth and victory began at Milford Haven, on the Welsh coast, where Henry's army landed after sailing from France. His son, if not grateful to Wales, was certainly attentive. His designs on that land extended his father's ambitions. When young Henry ascended to the throne, he did not rule Wales as he ruled Kent or Cornwall. It was a patchwork of jurisdictions, many of them obnoxious to his absolutist scheme. The old principality governed the far west and north, and the lords marcher held much of the rest. The marches were essentially petty kingdoms; their Norman rulers assumed the privileges of the Welsh chieftains they had conquered. The Normans and their descendants maintained their own armies, courts, and administrative systems. While these lords, along with the princes of Wales, recognized the English king to be their feudal overlord, he could not easily interfere in the lordships' affairs. As the saying went, "The Lord King's writ does not run in Wales."[17]

Henry VIII changed all that after his break with Rome. Two acts of union, in 1536 and 1543, incorporated Wales into the realm, subordinating it fully to what the first act called the "imperialle Crown." Henry's government abolished the feudal boundaries and franchises and organized Wales into shires. Politically, Wales became a bunch of English counties. A few discrepant entities remained, but their purpose was not to retard integration but to further it. The Great Sessions were such an institution. Nominally and, to some small degree, functionally, the Sessions were modeled after a system active in the northern part of the principality since 1284. The Sessions enjoyed an original jurisdiction in Wales. Welsh actions at law began at the Sessions and not in Westminster, though these suits could and did find their way to England by appeal or special writ.[18] In the main, however, the Great Sessions behaved just like the English assizes: they kept the same schedules and traveled circuits with the same ceremony.

Moreover, when John Gardiner practiced before the Sessions of southwest Wales (a circuit connecting Carmarthenshire, Pembrokeshire, and Cardiganshire), its judges exercised the political functions that their English counterparts had largely abandoned at least fifty years before. The Welsh judges had seen their privileges expand. Since the beginning of the eighteenth century, they alone nominated the sheriffs in the counties they traveled, a task they had earlier shared with the President and Council of Wales. The judges kept a hand in other local matters, especially those that affected their comfort and dignity. In 1761, they fined the burgesses of Haverfordwest £400 for not renovating their town hall. Sir John Philipps, a member of parliament (MP) and sixth baronet of Picton Castle, quickly gave half that sum to alleviate the cost of repairs.[19]

Philipps's relationship with the judges was not adversarial; to the contrary, knight and judge represented the same trend. The Great Sessions married their Welsh name to an English style of administration, a style outmoded in its home country by the middle of the eighteenth century but still appropriate to annexed Wales. And the gentlemen of Philipps's class were the chief beneficiaries of the Tudor settlement. In a process very like that described by the Scottish historians, the Tudor modernization of Welsh law and government humbled the great lords and allied the monarch's interest with that of the gentry. While these men usually boasted a longer Welsh pedigree than the disenfranchised nobles, they inevitably adopted English manners as they accepted and dispensed official favor.[20]

Again, the Welsh judges reflected a similar pattern of influence, though from a different angle. The judges who presided over the Welsh circuits were not, as in England, the same justices who presided over the high courts of Westminster. Indeed, the Welsh judges of the eighteenth century were often undistinguished barristers, but they were well connected MPs and by that token worthy of the king's patronage. Only a small fraction of the Welsh judges were in fact Welsh.[21] They were political appointees who strengthened the Crown's stake in Parliament and its authority in Britain's ancient western province.

While the judges of the Great Sessions were not the kingdom's best, they were able to address matters unheard of at the English assizes. The old Sessions of the principality were also courts of equity, and, after the union, the new courts retained that jurisdiction. The caseload in equity was quite small when compared to that in law, and the two practices were distinct, except at one or two points of commonality. For example, the same counsel served in both courts. There being no master in chancery to decide if the exceptions of a case warranted a hearing in equity, this task often fell—"whimsically," thought one critic—to the greenest lawyer available. A later chapter will discuss John Gardiner's law reforms; worth noting now is this experience, in the earliest years of his legal career, of moving back and forth between law and equity. He was already an admirer of Lord Mansfield, who went some way toward reconciling the two sides of jurisprudence. Gardiner was also aware of the chicaneries by which the law courts reached equitable solutions. Breaking entail by common recovery was one such method; Adam Smith belittled it in his lectures as an anachronism. At the Great Sessions, the needs of equity occasionally demanded these fictitious actions at law. While an assize equity was idiosyncratic to Wales, its rules and style followed that of the High Court of Chancery.[22] This is not so surprising, given that the barristers on the Welsh circuit were London trained.

John

Judicial practices in Wales conformed to the metropolitan standard, and institutions at the center pressed for even more control. The King's Bench had always been the court of appeal for most actions commenced at the Great Sessions. By the early part of the eighteenth century, it was able to remove Welsh proceedings to England by writ of *certiorari*. Gardiner worked the Welsh circuits in the final years of their already suspect independence. In 1769, the court of King's Bench established its right to a concurrent jurisdiction in Wales. The Great Sessions were rendered obsolete, and Parliament dissolved them fifty years later.[23]

Developments in jurisprudence cemented Wales to the English, and then British, political conglomerate. Much of the process was cultural as well as legal, for the conduct of the courts was closely associated to the conduct of society. Language was one key issue. By statute, the Sessions were in English and English only. This was less of a problem in Pembrokeshire, long an outpost of Englishry, but elsewhere a multitude came to court and left for the pillory or gibbet without understanding much of what was said at their trials.[24] Naturally, few of the judges and counselors understood Welsh. The assizes employed lawyers, like Gardiner, who were unfamiliar with the people they represented, though time and ambition mitigated this deficiency. Remember Bacon's mirrors: the courts carried forth the image of the state and bore upon returning the image of the country. Barristers on circuit were experts in the higher law, but they were beholden to local clients, local material, and local juries, all of which brought the law to life.

◦§ · ?◦

The assizes were highly charged events. Commerce and entertainment were accessories to justice and worked to the same purpose, a closer compact among the king's subjects. Eighteenth-century attorneys were often bankers as well. The assizes promised them legal fees and the chance to gather in a makeshift exchange where credit and capital found a ready outlet. Theatrical players typically rode a circuit pegged to the courts. Before the judges met with sheriff and gentry to discuss the county's affairs, the players sought out these local worthies to secure their favor. The audience could expect a quality performance; as in other provincial companies, actors in Welsh troupes wanted and won jobs at Drury Lane and Covent Garden.[25]

Nevertheless, the strolling player's life was barely respectable. He had to take extra measures if society were to accept him. Some actors joined the Freemasons, whose organization enjoyed a wide currency in middling and genteel Britain. Others practiced a useful trade, teaching townspeople to dance or pulling their rotten teeth. The example of John Potter is instructive. This Irishman first came to Haverfordwest with a band of players. He stayed in town, ran a printing press, and married a native. Potter expanded his business to include the sale of patent medicines and London journals, and he eventually established one of the largest circulating libraries in Wales.[26] His career demonstrates the quiet, binding power of itinerants and of itinerant fora such as the theater and the assizes.

Actor and lawyer kept busy catering to the needs of the gentry, the landowning county families that supplied the local pulpits and magistracy. The squires, their seconds, and very often their wives and children flocked to the court towns for assize week. One historian describes the assemblage as a "county parliament," and, as in London, a parliamentary sitting was more than a political event. In Haverfordwest, the winter capital of the Pembrokeshire elite, the Sessions capped the social season. In addition to the usual run of plays and card parties, the week saw balls hosted by the sheriff, the grand jury foreman, and the county MP.[27] For the man who made his living on circuit, the assizes were lucrative as well as festive times. The richest and most contentious people from the nearby towns and surrounding countryside congregated in one spot.

These were exactly the people John Gardiner needed to cultivate when he came to Haverfordwest in the early 1760s. What took him to Wales in the first place is uncertain. Perhaps he thought he could make a bigger splash in a remote locale. Perhaps the other circuits were already full of barristers.[28] Perhaps he was in flight from his creditors and unhappy clients. In any case, his success in Wales was by no means assured. He had to have friends in high places, patrons who could push business his way. He at least had the ear of George Rice, the MP and lord lieutenant of Carmarthenshire. Rice sat on the Board of Trade, and it was in this capacity that he offered Gardiner his assistance in Richard Derby's appeal. The Welsh squire was from an influential Whig family; for many years, he actively supported the Duke of Newcastle's political causes. Rice was not, however, overscrupulous in his loyalties. He shrewdly aligned himself with the Earl of Bute, who rewarded him with his seat at the Board of Trade and the £1,000 a year that went with it.[29]

Gardiner also came to know another of Bute's Welsh friends: Sir John Philipps, the Pembrokeshire baronet and a leader of the country interest in Parliament. At the time of their acquaintance, Gardiner was a raging Wilkite and vehemently opposed to the Scottish favorite. Philipps's politics had earned him abuse in the *North Briton*, and he took the matter up with the young lawyer over dinner at Picton Castle in August of 1763. It was an intriguing meal, as Gardiner reported in a letter to Wilkes. When the time came for a *digestif*, Sir John ordered the servants to bring clean glasses. By mistake, Gardiner received one emblazoned with the white rose and "emphatical *Fiat*," the signs of the Stuart Pretender. The young lawyer left the table well fed and in good humor. He told Wilkes that his host was "certainly in private Life an amiable man, but in Politicks profoundly contemptable."[30]

Over the next several years, Gardiner consorted with Welshmen— and at least one Welshwoman—who assumed Jacobite airs. As he no doubt learned, these people were not impossibly backward. Their half-secret fraternity was politically and culturally effective within its provincial sphere, and their romantic imposture screened a variety of political attitudes and allegiances. In the early eighteenth century, Jacobites in northern Wales formed the Cycle of the White Rose. Its most famous member, and indeed the most famous Jacobite in the principality, was Sir Watkin Williams Wynn. He was at his most disaffected in 1722, the year of the Atterbury plot. Wynn aided one of the suspects and reportedly burned the king's likeness. He was more cautious afterward. In the '45, he had kind words for the rebel prince but did not assist him materially. Wynn was a champion among Tory squires: doggedly opposed to the Robinocracy, obeyed without pause in three counties, and roundly admired elsewhere. He was also one of the last of his kind. After 1749, when Wynn died in a hunting accident, no country gentleman could command the same respect.[31]

Sir John Philipps was one of many considerable Tories who tried to fill Wynn's shoes, and, though Philipps cut a smaller figure at Westminster, he was, like "Great Sir Watkin," a power at home. His wealth and standing were strengths, and so was his membership in the Society of Sea-Serjeants. This society formed in 1726 and throughout its life enrolled the same sort of person: men of good family and Tory inclinations from the southwest of Wales. The Sea-Serjeants were reputedly Jacobite, and, as John Gardiner noticed at Picton, these rumors had the ring of truth. On the other hand, the society's Jacobitism probably never left the dinner table. Western Wales sent no men to the

Stuart's aid in 1715 or 1745. Toast making was one thing, treason quite another. The Serjeants were practical men and keen to control the affairs of their region. Under Philipps's leadership, the Society packed the common councils of several towns and manipulated the elections to county and parliamentary office. Haverfordwest was particularly subject to its influence.[32]

The Sea-Serjeants also dominated the social life of their shires. They convened annually in a Welsh seaport, and their families and friends—in other words, a large portion of the local gentry—joined them for a week of balls, cockfights, feasts, and races. Perhaps the only comparable events on the calendar were the assizes, and they drew the same quality of people. Tellingly, the Serjeants' sociable aspect became more prominent as the Pretender's cause faded. A few years after the '45, they began electing a "Lady Patroness" to preside over their festivals. The meetings ceased altogether in 1762, at a time when, through Bute's agency, Philipps and other Tories were again being heard at court after decades of proscription.[33]

Some Tories stayed in the political dark and wedded their complaints to the emerging radicalism. As noted earlier, Wilkite emblemata borrowed heavily from the Tory stock, and the sons and grandsons of Welsh Jacobites joined Gardiner in Wilkes's camp. The libertine's grasping and seemingly congenital versatility gratified, rather too impishly, an impulse felt by many. His celebrity had a genuine ideological content, but this content was flexible and traveled well. Different admirers conjured the Wilkite magic to meet their particular needs. Some true believers magnified his radicalism; others were charmed by the energy of his persona and cause. That energy might have served, in the first instance, the ambition of the man himself, but it also emboldened middle-class electors, bumptious English patriots, the contrary sons of the Welsh gentry, and a broad cross-section of British-Americans. His iconography was current far from its point of production and farther still from any place the very metropolitan Mr. Wilkes would have cared to spend his days. Even the most conservative Sea-Serjeants played at a similar game of cultural appropriation; their hero was also a rebel, happily distant: the dissolute bonnie prince.[34]

Gardiner could not have avoided the Sea-Serjeants if he had tried, and indeed he came as close as a man could to marrying one. "I have done a thing lately which you perhaps will think very foolish," he wrote to Wilkes, who loved women but not matrimony.[35] A week earlier, in

September of 1763, Gardiner had married Margaret Harries, a former lady patroness of the society. She was a famous beauty from an honorable family. Her uncle, a Serjeant and Philipps client, had served as Cardigan's member of parliament.[36] Somehow a young, landless outsider like John Gardiner was able to enter her genteel circle. Two of her sisters married Serjeants, and at least one other Serjeant assiduously courted her. Gardiner knew better when he wrote to Wilkes of his foolishness: the barrister had made a shrewd match that undoubtedly opened doors for him.

Harries's heritage was a capsule history of—to use the Henrician term—"imperialle" progress. The Harrieses claimed descent from Wyzo, a lord of the Flemings whom the first King Henry hired to protect and extend the Norman conquests in Wales. Haverfordwest was the Fleming stronghold and bore the marks of their presence into the late nineteenth century. Even before they arrived, Viking marauders had wrested much of future Pembrokeshire away from the Cymric Celts. The invasions of Norsemen, their Norman cousins, and Fleming mercenaries put Welshry to flight and cleared the ground for "little England beyond Wales," as the southern hundreds of Pembrokeshire came to be known. Although Margaret Harries came of age in Haverfordwest, her family's seat was in the Dewsland hundred, in the county's Welsh-speaking north. Tradition held that Bonnie Prince Charlie took refuge in Dewsland with a Tory family, and Margaret's cousin married one of its daughters—perhaps the very imp who, according to legend, blew a hunting horn and sent the wary prince scurrying for cover.[37]

But Margaret's pedigree could not buy her husband success. She was unlucky in her finances. Her father mistakenly neglected her in his will, and her brother, an established squire, did nothing to help her. Her most enthusiastic champion was also the most unwanted. Before Harries met Gardiner, she unwittingly fascinated an aged baronet who had already buried three wives. This silly old knight often rode out after dusk to observe her darkened window; he even pushed lovesongs through her family's keyhole. Worse yet, his executors discovered upon his death that he had willed all his property to Miss Harries. She recognized the injustice and cooperated with her admirer's son and daughters in their attempts to regain their patrimony. The issue was unresolved at the time of Harries's marriage, and her husband became a party to the case. The baronet's children sued the Gardiners in the High Court of Chancery.[38] It was a completely amicable arrangement, but John could not be blamed if a few bitter thoughts hid behind his smile. Like every lawyer, he dreamt of making a fortune at Westminster, and he returned there to lose one.

◅§ · ℈▻

Gardiner did not move his bride to London; instead, he began to spend more time in her native Pembrokeshire, a commitment that deepened with the birth of their first child, John Sylvester John, in 1765. By the beginning of 1768, he rarely ventured from Wales. His debts, rumored to be considerable, discouraged residence in London.[39] He did not, however, go native; he could not afford to. He could not support a family on his barrister's fees. Such a failure was common enough, and so was his response: seeking an office that would provide a respectable income and position. From the colonies he had come, and to them he might return, armed with the king's commission. In the end, his search for a more secure place within the imperial system acquainted him with the empire's limits. Like many Americans, he found that he could better achieve his ambitions independently.

Gardiner's mentor, Benjamin Prat, was especially well versed in the frustrations of imperial office. He was an ally of Thomas Pownall, Shirley's successor as governor of Massachusetts, and Pownall, upon returning to England, recommended him for the chief justiceship of New York. This prospect may have dissuaded Prat from arguing the writs-of-assistance cases; both the government and the merchants tried to engage his services. He was understandably reluctant to leave behind a lucrative practice in his home province and move to a strange town for a position with uncertain privileges. On the other hand, he had within his grasp the highest legal office he could have ever hoped to gain. The Hutchinsons and Olivers were monopolizing similar offices in Massachusetts; New York was his last best chance. He had connections within the province. His brother-in-law, Samuel Auchmuty, was already the rector of New York's Trinity Church. Prat accepted the appointment and took up his new work in late 1761, but his wife and children did not join him. Prat was wary, and for very good reasons.[40]

No one was more aware of New York's problems than its lieutenant governor, Cadwallader Colden, with whom Prat corresponded in the summer before his arrival. Colden was a dedicated and accomplished civil servant. Born in Ireland to Scottish parents, he returned to Scotland to study medicine at the University of Edinburgh. While in government service, he published several important scientific and historical works, including a treatise on yellow fever and a history of the Iroquois nations. By necessity, he was also a student of politics, and his observations are as anxious as they are intelligent. As the guardian of the Crown's interest, Colden was sensible of the designs and tendencies that threatened to reduce it. Most worrisome of all were the province's lawyers. They typically came from, or were otherwise connected to, New York's proprietary families, which owned large parcels of land in the Hudson River valley. The judicial system was extraordinarily subject to private influence. Colden thought the situation unprogressive: "The People of this Province are truely in the state in which the People of England were, when their Properties were determined in the County Courts."[41] Kinship and dependence were weightier than the principles of law.

A further crudeness compounded New York's dilemma. Its major proprietors were not equivalent to the English gentry. They were, according to Colden, "in our own Memory . . . arisen from the Lowest Rank of the People."[42] In this society, lawyers could aspire to a unique leadership. They were the province's mandarins, its educated and most active political class. As the rare men of letters, they made the press their own. As practicing lawyers, they insinuated themselves into the affairs of many people, both great and small. They made a popular politics work for them, and the king's government suffered. Colden did not lack for enemies in New York, but by the early 1760s, he reserved his harshest criticisms for the "triumvirate" of William Livingston, William Smith Jr., and John Morin Scott. These men had agitated the province against the colonial government in the fifties, most effectively in their short-lived literary periodical, the *Independent Reflector*. With the passing of Governor James DeLancey in 1761, they hoped to take charge of the assembly as leaders of what Colden called a "new set of Men." The three were lawyers and, what was worse to Colden's mind, Presbyterians. They had attended Yale and "imbibed the Independent principles" of Connecticut.[43]

Benjamin Prat was to be the antidote to the lawyers' craft. Colden found him to be the intellectual match for his adversaries, and one who was able to restrain their "licentiousness." Because Prat was a "Stranger," he was a better instrument of the king's justice and the governor's authority.[44] He had no local interests that might compromise his integrity. Prat understood the role he was expected to play. He knew that New York's judiciary was an adjunct of its proprietary class, and he could calculate the cost of this arrangement to the empire. As he wrote to the Lords of Trade:

> All the Colonies are vested with Legislative Powers, by which the Systems of their Laws are gradually varying from the Common Law, & so diminishing, in that Respect, their connection with the Mother Country: And if the Judgments of the Supreme Executive Courts, are only vague and desultory Decisions of Ignorant Judges; it must augment the mischief; & this cannot be guarded against, without some such establishment for the King's Judge, as to render the Office worth a Lawyer's acceptance.[45]

The last sentence is key: Prat was not a rich amateur; he was, by his own estimation, a professional who respected the law and could halt its colonial drift. He did not deny either his mediocre estate or the high income he earned in Massachusetts; they were both proofs of his merit.[46]

His tenure and salary in New York were controversial, and the dispute pointed to the larger problems of empire and of the lawyers' place within it. Under young King George and his ministers, Whitehall tried to strengthen its control of the colonies. Crown appointees, such as New York's superior judges, were to hold their offices at pleasure rather than during good behavior. Prat accepted his office on these terms, though with the hope that the authorities would in time revert to the older, more agreeable convention. His honor was at stake, as were the rights Englishmen had enjoyed since the Glorious Revolution. Prat guessed that the New York Assembly would despise the change and him for his part in it, and he was right: the legislators refused to vote him his salary. Nevertheless, the new chief justice was in no mood to surrender, especially after he discovered that the assembly at its most cordial paid judges half of what he had made in practice. He was expected to rely on a private fortune he did not have. Colden and Prat had to propose an obnoxious alternative: the chief justice would be paid out of the colony's quitrents.[47]

To New York, Wales offers a useful, if slightly unfair, contrast. On the Welsh circuit, barristers mixed with the provincial landowning class. They were not of that class, as in New York—and this is an important distinction—but successful lawyers were the gentry's advisors and advocates. Yet while tending to local needs, barristers and assize judges also advanced the imperial design. Most were not Welsh, and they were oriented, legally and culturally, to the metropolis. Because the judges on the Great Sessions did not rotate their bailiwicks, they fraternized with the same people season after season, but their appointments and salaries were the government's responsibility. Of course, there were no circuits under sail. Judges and barristers could not shuttle back and forth between America and Westminster. When the governments of the 1760s tried to rein in the colonies, they did more harm than good.

Colonial lawyers faced difficult choices. Their profession enabled them to "mix with every Company," but could they exploit their provincial connections without leaving the empire—the laws, the offices, the cosmopolitan spirit—that framed their ambition?[48] Lawyers who made different choices may not have been very different men. Benjamin Prat may not have been born into wealth, as William Livingston was, but what Prat wanted was simple and commonly sought. He wrote to Cadwallader Colden: "The Center of all my Wishes in Life, has always been to be in Circumstances that would permit me to Devote a great Part of my Time, to Speculation, Literary Ingagements, Correspondence with Friends of that Taste, and to the Doing [of] Some thing for public Emolument."[49] Unfortunately, time was one thing Prat did not have; good health was another. He died in January of 1763 and was buried under Trinity Church. John Adams was deeply affected by the news; the following month, he dreamt of Prat sitting all alone, on a rock surrounded by sea, beneath a gathering storm.[50]

The departed justice did leave a literary remnant. A poem, "Written in Sickness," appeared in *St. James's Magazine* the May after his death. This journal had Wilkite ties; John Gardiner was undoubtedly a reader and probably submitted his friend's poem.[51] He and Prat had kept in touch. When the New York Assembly withdrew its support, Prat asked his former student, along with Thomas Pownall, to petition Whitehall on his behalf. Gardiner valued the Pownall connection. To Richard Derby, he bragged of his friendship with John Pownall, Thomas's brother and the longtime secretary of the Board of Trade. The Pownalls were practiced at upsetting William Shirley, but neither of them proved to be of any help in Derby's case. Gardiner was also disappointed by Prat's death; he had hoped that his mentor would replace Shirley as governor of the Bahamas. In any event, Gardiner did not lay aside his own desire for office. Later in the decade, he lobbied for Prat's last job, the chief justiceship of New York, and for the job that launched William Shirley's official career in Massachusetts, the advocate general's position in Boston's vice-admiralty court.[52]

Gardiner was still hopeful of preferment when he left for the Caribbean island of St. Christopher, commonly known as St. Kitts. The lawyer had contacts within London's large cadre of West Indian merchants and absentee planters. Barlow Trecothick, a future Lord Mayor and the owner of the front pew in King's Chapel, maintained a considerable trading interest in the Leewards. Florentius Vassall owned plantations in Jamaica and, under Silvester Gardiner's supervision, a share in the Kennebeck Company. A Vassall relation had recommended St. Kitts to the younger Gardiner, and Florentius himself gave John ten guineas to ease the costs of emigration.[53]

Gardiner's was not a singular itinerarium. Consider the example of Anthony Stokes, who came to the Inner Temple's bar in 1760. Like his junior fellow, Stokes practiced on the Oxford and South Wales circuits. Unlike Gardiner, he was Welsh born, but he construed his attachments broadly: he once remarked that the word "English" properly modified things Welsh and Scottish. Stokes's Welsh heritage was in any case of little use to him on circuit. He abandoned Britain for the West Indies less than two years after commencing practice. There he succeeded in making a name for himself. He landed on Antigua in 1763; in 1766, he was named to its provincial council. He never sat, having moved to St. Kitts the same year. Thus he was on hand when John Gardiner arrived. Their tenures did not long overlap, although those few shared months were enough to see them at odds in court. Stokes left the Caribbean in July 1769 to become the chief justice of Georgia. He had traveled some distance to find an office, and he entered into it at a particularly troubled time. Revolutionary elements harassed and, in 1776, expelled him. He returned with the British army in 1779, but defeat forced a permanent leavetaking.[54]

The same conflict that pushed Stokes back to London brought to Antigua an American lawyer, Samuel Quincy, who attested to the islands' remarkable effect on a stalled career. Quincy, a Bostonian, knew both Gardiners; he even trained with John in Benjamin Prat's law office. At the time of the Boston Massacre, he had a hand in the prosecution of the implicated British officers, but he had no stomach for rebellion. He chose an English exile instead. As the war dragged on, he decided to try his luck in the Leewards, knowing full well of their questionable security. "[A]s a citizen of the world," he wrote, "I am but a Passenger & must follow the fortunes of the day."[55] He certainly pursued a most fortunate course by coming to Antigua. Despite the fact that he had not practiced law in five years, Quincy had no trouble finding clients. He was pleased with his earnings and noted that they would have far outstripped his Boston receipts, if not for the wartime suspensions of business. He reported to his relatives in Massachusetts: "It is a common saying here that it rains sugar & rum, and exactly in that ratio is the proportion of Lawyer's Fees."[56]

Antigua's neighbor in the Leeward chain, St. Kitts, was even more bountiful. It was the most fertile of Britain's sugar islands, and its fertility exaggerated the already grotesque character of life in a tropical colony. Fortunes were quickly made, quickly lost, and recklessly paraded. The St. Kitts plantations were very profitable—they could return 15 to 20 percent—but, as sugar production was so capital intensive, many planters were heavily indebted to London merchant houses. Most of the capital was invested in slaves. Over twenty-three thousand of them lived on St. Kitts in John Gardiner's day; he and his fellow whites numbered less than three thousand. The labor system depended on brutality and fear, and fear was as much its fruit as money or molasses. The threat of insurrection hung over the Leewards. The governor wrote of one scare in the year before Gardiner's arrival. The blacks, he conceded, were cunning. They had planned to rise on St. Patrick's Day, when most whites were deep in their cups. The governor added that the ringleaders "were not insensible to the power of Beauty, but had cast lots for the ladies who they intended to carry off the Island to Porto Rico."[57]

Had this plot succeeded, the slaves would only have been repaying their masters in kind. St. Kitts harbored a lively market in mulatto girls. White mistresses commonly profited by the sale of their slaves' virginity. Overseers were especially profligate. These men, often young and unmarried, reduced many of their charges to the further slavery of the harem. One observer noticed that poor emigrants were the worst masters, and he lamented their preponderance: "when one considers how these adventurers are usually collected, how often the refuse of each man's connections, of every trade, and every profession, are thronged in upon them, much sentiment, morality, or religion cannot well be expected to be found within the circle of their influence."[58] Checks on their behavior were few. The island's productivity allowed for an even higher rate of absenteeism than was normal for the West Indies. In the second half of the eighteenth century, first professionals and then estate managers—glorified drivers, really—began to join the remaining grandees in the governing circle.[59]

Lawyers were very much a part of this adventure. Stokes we have already noticed. Two others, who knew John Gardiner from their shared probation at the Temple, made his acquaintance again on St. Kitts. One, Anthony Bryan, was connected to the island's richest creoles. The other, John Stanley, had strong ties to Nevis but few certain prospects. His father had mortgaged and lost the family's estates.[60] The law promised his son a chance to recoup, especially on St. Kitts, where barristers enjoyed special privileges. In Britain, they increasingly relied on attorneys to direct clients their way, but, due to an assembly statute of 1764, lawyers who came to the island could themselves act as attorneys and solicitors. By so doing, they engrossed the community's legal business. During the sixty years prior to 1764, only four attorneys could practice at the island's court of King's Bench and Common Pleas, but those four's qualifications were left to the judges' discretion. To be an attorney in that period was to be in an enviable position. Not so in the mid-sixties, when three attorneys and solicitors petitioned the Board of Trade. Their complaint was simple: the assembly's innovation had destroyed their livelihood; the island was awash with refugees from the London courts and assize circuits.[61]

These barristers were much better educated than the attorneys they supplanted, but they had come to St. Kitts precisely because they had not succeeded in the more traditional arenas of their profession. The island rewarded a superficial excellence, as Anthony Stokes observed:

> Most of the questions that arise in the Colonies are founded in litigation, and not in intricacy; and, as the gentlemen of the bar in general go out there at an early period in life, before they are arrived at any considerable share of knowledge, they have it not in their power to gain much experience in the Colonies, and most of the Judges not being bred to the profession of the law, the Advocate, who has the greatest fluency, may sometimes be considered as the ablest lawyer.[62]

Despite their inexperience, West Indian barristers pursued the work that was most lucrative. In the Leewards, that work was in Chancery. As in Wales, the rules of practice conformed to the English rule. John Gardiner's bound record includes many of the standard forms.[63]

The proceedings were typical of equity: parties seeking injunctions to suspend judgments at law or halt contested transfers of property. Legacies were often at issue, and Gardiner filed bills on behalf of widows, infants, and other exceptional plaintiffs. One of his clients was a free mulatto named Thomas Tyrell Kelly, who probably objected to the unfair execution of his white father's will. And Gardiner must have enjoyed his successful representation of Margaret Gardner. Like his wife of the same name, this Margaret was a child whose father had died without adequately providing for her. Gardiner prevented the estate's sale until the girl's claims were satisfied. Of course, these were not charity cases, and Gardiner was not a choosy advocate.[64]

He did well enough to buy a few properties in the town of Basseterre and in the parish of Trinity Palmetto Point. This last holding was small and carried a mortgage, but it raised Gardiner, just barely, into the planting classes. When a hurricane blew through St. Kitts in 1772, a great many plantations were damaged, including Gardiner's. The storm's chronicler noted that the barrister's fruit trees and gardens had taken a beating, but there was no mention of leveled sugar. Gardiner probably lacked the resources to raise much, if any, cane. He owned slaves, however; they no doubt lived in some of the outbuildings destroyed by the blow. Perhaps they took refuge in the great house's rum cellar, cowering in the dark with the Gardiner family: such arrangements were typical during the emergency; Kittitians of both sexes and all ages and races had no recourse but to take up with one another, in the close but secure commons of the island's basements and cisterns.[65]

Such allowances were rare. In John Gardiner's first year on the island, he filed a brief on behalf of the Reverend Jonathan Flemming, whose slaves had murdered another black, a canebreaker. The dead slave's owner sued and won a judgment against Flemming, who then appealed in Chancery. Gardiner's brief was extraordinary for that court, but its emphatic and personal tone had become his trademark. He wrote, "Are we to be Answerable for the Villainies of our Negroes? God forbid. Should we become liable for such Villainies, what mischiefs and ruin must ensue! Neither our Lives nor our Fortunes would be one Moment secure!"[66] This was perhaps a dicey interpretation of tort law, but it shows how easily Gardiner could adopt the Caribbean's racial regime. He did not, however, lose his taste for improvement or reform: after several years on St. Kitts, he invited Moravian missionaries to catechize his slaves.[67]

In addition to his holdings in blood and land, Gardiner earned a reputation for gouging. When William Mathew Burt, governor of the Leewards in the late 1770s, wrote to Whitehall about excesses in Chancery, Gardiner provided the most damaging exhibit. In one matter, which ended in a judgment of £120, he presented the loser with a bill for £1,800. The unfortunate party had to flee the British dominions when Gardiner refused a £1,000 settlement.[68] John Pinney, the Nevis grandee, was another sufferer. Gardiner threatened to manage a suit against Pinney's British correspondents—who had engaged the lawyer on occasions past, to his great reward—and demanded a petty consideration. Pinney paid, but not happily: "The rapacity of this man is scarce to be equalled; he publickly declares, that he wishes to be released from his engagement with you, for he says, he can make more Money to be concerned against you."[69] Imagine Pinney's anger had he known of Gardiner's future exploits as a law reformer opposed to unreasonable fees.

John Gardiner was a sharp and notably aggressive lawyer, but his efforts were hardly out of place. St. Kitts was a thoroughly litigious society. Even governors unconcerned by the schedule of costs maintained their firm jurisdictional control of Chancery proceedings. The inhabitants could not be trusted to run such a court. They could barely be trusted with their own political councils. The population was very small, and, as one governor put it, "connections of every kind are so intimate that scarcely any Matter of Litigation can be started, which does not occupy the Heart as well as the Judgment of almost every Individual."[70] Eighteenth-century politics were especially sensitive to the repercussions of private disputes.

◄§ · §►

Gardiner stumbled onto the island's political scene at an especially factious moment. At formal issue was the franchise of councillors: could these men vote in assembly elections? The question was more than a constitutional nicety. The electorate was tiny and often evenly divided at the polls. One man's vote could decide more than one election, for men voted in the several parishes where they held property.[71] The issue began simmering in the autumn of 1768. In less than two years, Hillsborough, the secretary of state, was complaining to Governor Woodley that the affair had spread into the London press. Week after week, "inflammatory Publications" attacked the government for its handling of the crisis, of which Hillsborough still knew very little.[72] He was aware that the controversy had taken a serious turn in October of 1769. At its first sitting, a new assembly resolved, once again, that councillors could not vote in its elections. Three members were unseated by this decision, and seven more bolted from the room once the purge began. An eighth member tried to leave but was forcibly detained to preserve a quorum. The rump then ordered the arrest of the contrary seven. John Gardiner was their lawyer.[73]

This quarrel raised questions of a high political order, but the fundamental problem was money. A contemporary described the argument, with only a few reservations, as "credit and property against debt and poverty." The characterization was self-serving, for this observer's loyalties were with the purged members. Nevertheless, his report is accurate: the rogue assembly lowered the interest rate by two points. Gardiner construed the debate in much the same way. In the midst of it, he pressed an islander for repayment on behalf of London merchants. Pursuant to a parliamentary statute governing the recovery of colonial debts, these creditors secured an affidavit from the Lord Mayor of London. Thus armed, Gardiner compelled the debtor's arrest on St. Kitts.[74]

At this point, John Stanley intervened. Stanley was Gardiner's "quondam Friend and very old Acquaintance," a Templar and a Wilkite, and the two men had worked together as arriviste barristers to squeeze the island dry. Yet they drifted into different political camps. Stanley led the debtor faction and masterminded its electoral victories. By controlling the register's office, Stanley was able to manufacture phantom or otherwise dubious freeholds and pack the assembly with his formerly disenfranchised supporters. This was the new majority that turned on its betters, including Gardiner's clients. The opposition was criminalized, and Stanley and company intimidated their rivals in the legislature, in court, and at the polls. The rebel's profane style became part of the equipment by which a strongman bullied his opponents. Stanley made a point of defiling the parish churches in which elections were held. During one poll, he demanded that a bowl of punch be brought to the communion table, for, as he put it, "I'll be damned if I ever drink any other liquor here."[75]

Though no angel himself, Gardiner had taken the side of credit, against the man he now called the "Supreme Dictator" of the island's upstart assembly. Stanley did what he could to stymie Gardiner's collections and prosecutions. In the case just mentioned, he alerted a friend on the island bench to the debtor's troubles; this judge discharged the prisoner on the basis of a local law that required plaintiffs to swear their affidavits before local magistrates. As Gardiner wrote to John Pownall at the Board of Trade, this judgment did not bode well for British commercial interests: "no Debt due from any one here can be safe."[76] Gardiner was not always the loser in such actions. During one court session, he successfully represented two creditors of Edward Gillard, Stanley's ally on the "Grand Committee of Privileges and Elections." The judgments were large, amounting to nearly £6,000 current money.[77]

Gardiner also mounted a more direct challenge to Stanley's purge. He brought a writ of *habeas corpora* demanding the release of his seven clients, but the island's chief justice did not honor it, citing legislative privilege. The speaker of the assembly upbraided the prisoners, informing them that they were "guilty of the highest offences that can possibly be committed; offences which tend to annihilate their very Constitution." He added that the assembly's authority exceeded that of "any and every Court of Law." The assembly reprimanded Gardiner for his *habeas*. By claiming that it unlawfully detained his clients, he had excited the house's anger:

> Legal and Illegal are Terms, in the Sense you use them, with which this House is unacquainted. The Courts of Common Law are guided by the Rules of Common Law, but the proceedings of Parliament are quite by another Rule. The Matters of Parliament are to be discussed and determined by the Custom and usage of Parliament and not by the Law in the inferior Courts.[78]

The assemblymen closed with a warning. They suspended any further action against Gardiner, on account of his poor health at the time, but he was told to recollect their justice with "Terror." The lawyer was not easily intimidated. He was afterward heard vilifying the legislature and declaring in public company that he "wou'd damn every act that shou'd be passed this Session."[79]

His clients spent sixteen days in Basseterre's damp, infested jail. One of the seven, Aretas Akers, reported that the mosquitoes and fleas were so abundant that the prisoners were "almost eat up." Fortunately, there were mitigating comforts. The prisoners were the cream of island society, and they did not suffer unattended. Each day as many as ten carriages arrived at the gaoler's door laden with friends, family, and gifts. A rowdier bunch of admirers also gathered and threatened to free the prisoners by force. At Gardiner's urging, the deputy provost marshal relented and the seven returned to their estates. At least one of them did not long enjoy his homecoming. Anthony Bryan, Gardiner's and Stanley's contemporary at the Inner Temple, fell ill while under guard and never recovered. His death added a dreadful note to the controversy and precluded its easy resolution.[80]

At the end of March 1770, Gardiner's clients sued their gaoler and the assembly's sergeant-at-arms for trespass, assault, and false imprisonment. The assembly ordered the chief justice to discontinue the suits with costs, and Gardiner once again stood before the house to answer for "his insolent and menacing Behaviour." Finding him defiant, the legislators ordered his arrest a few days later. When taken into custody, Gardiner asked for his pistols, in case he met an assemblyman willing to contest the issue personally. The sergeant granted this request, but his charge passed into jail without incident. Governor Woodley, in his capacity as chancellor, refused to free the barrister, who then filed a *habeas* writ in the island's court of King's Bench and Common Pleas. John Stanley argued the assembly's side. He claimed that the king ruled St. Kitts by right of conquest and thus independently of his government in Britain. The king had granted the island's inhabitants a charter that vouchsafed to them certain liberties and privileges. It established an assembly with original and unimpeachable legislative powers—in other words, a new House of Commons. This assembly was "above the Courts and Judges of the Common Law"; no person or institution could countermand its warrants, including that for Gardiner's arrest.[81]

Gardiner responded to Stanley's "unconstitutional Doctrines" with a long and strident speech, which he later published. He pointed out that St. Kitts had no charter. Before 1711, when Queen Anne approved an assembly act regulating its conduct and election, the island's legislature met according to the royal instructions, which the monarch could revoke at pleasure. Even if a charter existed, under no construction of law could the king grant an arbitrary power to imprison. He did not enjoy that power himself. The judgments of the law were inescapable, and so were its protections. As Gardiner put it:

> The common Law of England is in Force within the Island . . . Should Business, or any other lawful Occasion, oblige me to quit Great Britain, and settle here, merely because I cross the Atlantic, and reside here, do I forfeit the Rights of a British Subject? Am I not still intitled to the same Liberties, the same Privileges, which, as a British subject, I enjoyed at home?[82]

"Home" was not Boston or his Palmetto Point estate; it was Great Britain. Gardiner drew readily on his metropolitan experiences. He imagined how Lord Mansfield would smirk upon hearing that the island's assembly had declared its unimpeachable jurisdictional superiority.[83]

Gardiner saw the debate as a matter of law but also as a matter of perspective. He had had a proper view of Britain, and he could arrange its parts into their rightful places. For example, he explained that the "City of London is certainly of as much Consequence to the British Empire as this Island can be."[84] The city's common council and the island's assembly passed bylaws for discrete areas within a greater whole, but one area, the city, was a thousand times more populous than the other. Even so, London's council never assumed that it could jail the contemptuous without fear of contradiction. Gardiner acknowledged that a sitting House of Commons could do exactly that, but he violently rejected any analogy between the Commons and "the little, trifling, twopenny, pretended-corporate Charter Assembly of Saint Christopher's." The Commons were more than superior; they were supreme:

> they derive not their Existence, they claim not their Privileges, *ex gratia*, from the King or his Ministers: They derive the same from as high a Source as the Kings of Great Britain hold the Crown, from the Constitution itself . . . The House of Commons, with the other Branches of the supreme Legislature, can annihilate the Legislature of the Island in an Instant, and can regulate the whole British Empire.[85]

A more forthright statement of the Whig imperial order would be hard to find. Many of Gardiner's fellow Americans would have found it obnoxious in the extreme.[86]

Gardiner, on the other hand, did not shrink from metropolitan attachments. They worked to the advantage of persons who understood the system of authorities and were ready to use it. He would protest the assembly's outrages and apply for redress with the imperial powers. Appeals were pending in English courts of law. If all of these applications failed, Gardiner promised to leave St. Kitts. Even an absolute monarchy would be preferable to the assembly's little tyranny. The barrister concluded, "it is more noble, far more honourable, to fall by a lion, than submit to be thus gnawed to Death by Rats."[87] His enemies were unmoved. When Gardiner's speech appeared in print two months later, its author was still under lock and key. In a preface, signed and dated from Basseterre's prison, Gardiner reiterated his opinion of the assembly and its usurpations. He hoped that the public would appreciate his speech, and he anticipated the decisions of the courts and Privy Council in Great Britain.[88]

The island's political troubles resonated through its society. The crisis inevitably affected the small white population; even more alarming was its feared effect on the blacks. Just ten days after John Gardiner addressed the Court of King's Bench, Governor Woodley reported to Hillsborough that the "Principle negroes" from Palmetto Point—Gardiner's neighborhood—had been behaving rather strangely. Every Saturday night, they convened a kind of mock government, constituted after the English fashion with a council and assembly. Woodley happily wrote that their meetings were as yet harmless, but he guessed that this project, "to imitate their masters," might have eventually led to insurrection.[89]

The governor might also have been nervous about his support for Stanley's legislative coup. News of his conduct had reached London, and the secretary of state was displeased. In fact, Woodley's tenure was drawing to a close; he left the Leewards in July. St. Christopher's political disputes began to fade under his lieutenant, and the new governor, Sir Ralph Payne, arrived in January of 1772 in no mood to brook further unrest. He was a solid man with powerful connections. Mansfield supposedly wrote Payne's maiden speech to parliament, a speech denouncing John Wilkes.[90]

To no one's surprise, the authorities in London did not credit the assembly's claims. In the summer of 1771, the Board of Trade affirmed that members of the governor's council on St. Kitts could vote in assembly elections. Then the Privy Council considered John Gardiner's causes. He had asked the king to set aside the irregular discontinuance of his clients' lawsuits (and of his own: after his arrest Gardiner sued the speaker of the assembly, who promptly ordered a judge to dismiss the complaint). The kingdom's chief law officers recommended an affirmative response, finding that "the House of Assembly seems to have corrupted its own Constitution by affecting a power which they have not, analogous, and coequal to that of the House of Commons." They also advised the king to instruct his governor in the Leewards "to keep his Assembly within the legal Bounds of a provincial Council." The St. Kitts suits dragged on through the mid-1770s and finally ended in judgments for the loyal six and their lawyer. Aretas Akers decided to press for the last shilling, if only to force his bounding rivals to admit their poverty.[91]

Gardiner had won large awards from political actions before, in his Wilkite days, and he compared those efforts with his work on St. Kitts. In his April 1770 speech, he argued that the assembly's prior exercise of a commitment power was of no consequence, for bad usage did not make good law. His example was the general warrant, which the government had used scores of times until the Wilkes case established its illegality. Gardiner reminded his listeners and readers of his own part in that affair.[92] He might also have been thinking of the electoral controversies that erupted after he left Britain, during which the House of Commons repeatedly denied Wilkes his fairly won seat. In the West Indies, Gardiner's "radical" past served rather conservative ends. He was an advocate for the conventional hierarchies of credit and empire.

❧ · ☙

Like Wilkes, Gardiner collected a political dividend from his controversial fame. He was still in Basseterre's jail when its freemen first elected him to the assembly. The other members immediately expelled him. No doubt they hoped that jail would be the death of him, as it had been for fellow barrister Anthony Bryan, but Gardiner was a tougher nut to crack. One observer credited his survival to a "vigorous constitution" and his "happy stock of spirits."[93] At the end of 1770, he was returned by two parishes, but Stanley's "Grand Committee" prevented him from sitting. He was again proscribed in January of 1772, but that month also saw Sir Ralph begin his successful generalship. The assembly fell into line, and Gardiner represented three different parishes from 1773 to 1775.[94] He did not flinch from joining a "twopenny" parliament; he knew to take his gains where he could find them. His metropolitan bias informed and even encouraged his provincial ambitions. Gardiner's nemesis, John Stanley, was similarly versatile. The eventual defeat of his faction did not stop his rise within British politics and society. He was the solicitor general for the Leewards from 1771 to 1781 and then attorney general until the end of the century. He married an heiress worth £25,000—her brother was one of the imprisoned seven—and these riches helped Stanley win a seat in Parliament.[95]

Not every British colonial could so ably coordinate his activities and orientations at "home" and abroad. This was an especially difficult task during the American Revolution. West Indians of property faced a nearly untenable dilemma. Their ties to mainland America were strong. They depended on their northern neighbors for food and fuel.

The unruly New Englanders were also good consumers of sugar. On the other hand, they were not the most faithful of customers, because French sugar was cheaper than British. The planters of Jamaica and St. Kitts needed the mercantile protections that Bostonians wanted to undermine. West Indians were vulnerable to seaborne attack and slave revolt, and these weaknesses, like their second-rate produce, bound them all the more tightly to London. Furthermore, most whites on St. Kitts were British natives, and many intended to return to Britain once they had secured their fortunes.[96]

Aretas Akers was one planter who preferred the islands to the English capital and countryside; nevertheless, he was a loyal subject whom the war severely tried. He regretted the government's heavy-handed tactics in America, and, while visiting London in 1775, he petitioned for appeasement. He did not waffle once blood was shed. He was the navy's agent for St. Kitts, and his boys aided in the defense of Brimstone Hill, the island's citadel, in early 1782. Under the command of William Shirley's son, Thomas, its garrison held out for over thirty days against a determined French assault. Many islanders were not so brave. The bulk of the Basseterre militia refused to follow Shirley into the redoubt. Inhabitants betrayed their own cannon to the French, who then turned these guns on the last stalwarts. Nevis surrendered without a fight, and its chief councillor begged the Comte de Grasse for an occupying force strong enough to protect the planters from their own slaves.[97]

Akers, too, enjoyed cordial relations with the French, though he had the good grace not to dine with their officers until after the fall of Brimstone Hill. Because he had treated French prisoners with some courtesy, he hoped his property would not suffer during the occupation. A year later, he was disappointed to hear that a Frenchman was plundering one of his estates. As peace neared, this villain transported the plantation's negroes, cattle, and copper stills to Martinique. Akers went to Paris seeking compensation and, to his joy, found favor at court. His own countrymen were less accommodating. Because he was a naval agent, many British merchants and privateers made claims upon him. Akers suffered from both sides, a common experience among West Indians. Fortunately, he had the wherewithal to survive the crisis, but his family's future was in England, which he thought a charmless place.[98]

John Gardiner did not withstand the empire's troubles; indeed, he did not try. He let the revolutionary changes carry him away, first to an office under another king, and then back to his first home, where he reclaimed his American birthright. Before the war even started, Aretas Akers discovered that his lawyer was an unreliable friend. By late 1774, he and Gardiner had not corresponded in some time, and Akers felt the snub: "Oh! tempora. I wish all my heart for his own sake as well as his amicable wife's, that he would act as well as he speaks, but in neglecting me he neglects himself also."[99] John Pinney, another of Gardiner's clients, would have welcomed such disregard. Gardiner demonstrated his loyalty to the French conquerors by informing on Pinney, who as receiver of the *droits* of admiralty was holding over £800 due the British Crown. Well before the French invasion, Gardiner had consorted with men like Dr. Benjamin Clifton, who was indicted for pro-American activities. Now he could profit by his principles: Gardiner became King Louis XVI's attorney general on St. Kitts and Nevis.[100]

Gardiner had, after long and circuitous efforts, made it onto the civil list. He would later claim that he joined Louis's service out of patriotic motives. He saw himself as a dispenser of liberty; the last item in his Chancery notebook is a copy of a certificate, signed by the French governor, which proved "the Freedom of a Negro Woman." Gardiner did not, however, manumit his own slaves when the negotiations at Paris prompted thoughts of departure. These slaves numbered eight in 1783, and he signed them over to a trustee, along with the rest of his personal estate: the family china, linen, furniture, carriages, and "Liquors of every sort." The houses and land at Palmetto Point also went into trust, the proceeds of which Gardiner earmarked for the amortization of the mortgage, for the payment of debts, and for the future support of his wife, Margaret. The properties in Basseterre he sold outright. Finally, he extracted a couple favors from the French military command. These officers had protected him from the island's poor creoles—who were not quietly enduring the war's hardships—and now their letters of introduction would smooth his return to the mainland.[101]

◄§ · §►

It was at this point that John Gardiner's life once again intersected with his father's. In January of 1783, Silvester was a Tory exile living in Dorset, but he had never despaired of recovering his place in America. Through Boston contacts, his son discovered that there might not be much to reclaim. The elder Gardiner's property in Massachusetts, including his massive estates downeast, faced dissipation on the auction

John

block. In a letter to his father, John reported this fact and—strange co-incidence—his own plans to come home. He suggested that Silvester send any correspondence by way of Boston but to include, "not one word of Politicks for God's sake—as I know not yet the disposition of the People there. I am," he continued, "a staunch, thorough revolution Whig you know and abhor all Kingcraft and all Priest Craft." These scruples had not prevented him from taking "a Place under his most Christian majesty," but King Louis's patronage was fungible. A letter from the French government earned John an audience with George Washington upon arriving in America. The war had been kind to him, and he meant to extend this good fortune. He even declared in his January letter that he was "so selfish as ardently to hope there will be no Peace before the next winter."[102]

After a pleasant stay in Philadelphia, where he was "much ca-ress[e]d," John returned to New England and began making the best of a messy situation. He inquired after the state of his father's houses and lands and even took legal action to protect them. At the same time, he relished the novelty of his position and wanted to keep Dr. Gardiner away from Boston, where he might cast too long a shadow. John strongly recommended that Silvester remain in England until the family's affairs were more settled. This advice was seconded by John Hancock, the elder Gardiner's business partner and now the governor of the commonwealth.[103]

Despite his good references, some Bostonians were unsure of John Gardiner's status. When he applied for admission to the bar, some of its members wondered if he was really a citizen and recommended natural-ization. Gardiner bridled at taking this step, because it would imply that he was once an "Exotick." At his urging, the General Court passed a special act that confirmed his citizenship and that of his Welshborn wife and children. The language of the act suggests that its authors were un-aware of Gardiner's turns as parliamentary suprematist and imperial officeseeker. He was, rather, "at all times opposed . . . to the System of Tyranny fabricated by the Administration of Great Britain."[104]

In another petition, Gardiner asked the legislature to restore his pa-trimony, which Silvester, by his political sympathies, had nearly for-feited. Rumor had it that John went even farther in private conversa-tion. According to one observer, he "cursed" father, king, and church "in order to ingratiate himself with the ruling party."[105] Silvester got wind of these remarks and disavowed any connection with his son. This is not so surprising, for John had never been a model child. Of more interest is the reaction of Silvester's chief agent in Boston, his son-in-law Oliver Whipple. He defended the younger Gardiner from what he regarded to be undue rancor. To Whipple's mind, John was at least a man of principle, even if those principles were mistaken and his methods obnoxious. And more importantly, his entry onto the scene had been a quick success. Notwithstanding the doubts of a few colleagues, John Gardiner was a lawyer of increasing influence, and his reputation boded well for the recovery of the family property.[106]

That property included two adjacent pews along the center aisle of King's Chapel. Before evacuating, Silvester Gardiner entrusted their upkeep to one John Haskins. As the final peace approached, Haskins inquired whether he might oversee their sale or continue as proxy. Silvester chose the latter course; he did not intend to abandon his place. When his son arrived in Boston, he found Haskins and family seated according to Dr. Gardiner's plans, and at first John acquiesced to this arrangement. He assured his father, "there are a great number of Places of rel[i]gious worship in this place and thank God I am no bigot. All sects of protestant Christians are to me alike, tho' I prefer certain services in the Church of England."[107] These preferences apparently got the better of the younger Gardiner, for within a year he owned one of the family pews and was attending closely to the chapel's business.

These events were a source of great discomfort to Silvester, as were all of the changes at the church he helped to build. Now settled in Newport, he demanded an account of the chapel's conduct. He could not understand how the wardens could sell his pews, given his record of service and the fact that Haskins had faithfully paid the rent. For their part, the wardens referred their old compatriot to his son, "as we rely on his judgment as a lawyer to warrant our proceedings."[108] Of course, to Silvester's mind, his son was part of the problem. A sinister design was at work in the chapel, and the seizure of pews abetted its accomplishment. As the elder wrote, "it was with a View of carrying into execution the plan of a set of men who live by the Vice and follies of their neighbours . . . they are now labouring to corrupt the faith in the ever blessed Trinity."[109] He was writing of lawyers, a group of men with whom Silvester Gardiner was intimately familiar. He had underwritten his son's expensive stay at the Inns of Court. As a tireless advocate for the Kennebeck claims, he was something of a lawyer himself. Even now, he threatened to resolve the chapel's problems by legal action. All this was evidence of Silvester's own follies, perhaps, but one must admit that his interests were more than material. He was genuinely alarmed by the new theological posture adopted by the men who had taken charge of his church.

A celebratory history of King's Chapel describes the typical supporters of its Unitarian apostasy as "young entrepreneurs" with an "energetic" and "optimistic" approach to Boston and its culture as well as to their own careers. This was the same set that, seven years later, campaigned against the ban on theatrical entertainments. A strident enemy of their efforts would echo Silvester's complaint when he accused "puppies" in the legal order of spreading corruption under the guise of liberality.[110] In early 1785, a lay committee met to discuss revisions in the chapel's prayer book. Among the members in favor of the changes were two men who would take noticeable roles in the theater debate: Perez Morton, who co-wrote the town meeting remonstrance that called for the ban's repeal, and John Gardiner, the wayward son.[111]

The chapel reforms of the mid-1780s were to some extent a consequence of the Revolution, but they also crystallized broader intellectual trends that had little to do with colonial politics. After Henry Caner and a number of parishioners fled in 1776, the congregation worshipped without a pastor until 1783, when James Freeman took the job after six months as a probationary reader. Freeman was a Harvard graduate and had preached in Congregational pulpits. His doubts about the Trinity precipitated the changes in the chapel's liturgy and organization, but he was hardly alone in his beliefs. When he was invited to read in 1782, the wardens left the use of the Athanasian creed to his discretion. For a time in the 1780s, Trinity Church, which officially held to orthodox Protestant Episcopacy, dropped the same creed from its services. Freeman's church, however, was the first in America to formalize its Unitarian stance.[112]

The chapel published its prayer book in 1785. Its compilers acknowledged their debt to Theophilus Lindsey and Samuel Clarke, the English liturgical reformers. They also took their cue from the "late happy revolution," which made certain alterations "expedient." These changes involved not a positive reconstruction of theology but a divestment from those awkward claims and positions that cramped the church's appeal. The preface reads: "The Liturgy, contained in this volume, is such, that no Christian, it is supposed, can take offence at, or find his conscience wounded in repeating. The Trinitarian, the Unitarian, the Calvinist, the Arminian will read nothing in it which can give him reasonable umbrage."[113] Aware of the diversity of human experience, the compilers were careful not to presuppose or limit God's mind. Theirs was an iron tolerance, however, for the liturgy was to encompass all possible and "reasonable" diversities. No dissent was credible.

The chapel's iconoclasm extended from its prayer book into church government. James Freeman was still unqualified to administer the sacraments. He courted Bishop Samuel Seabury and other church officials, but, owing to Freeman's heterodox opinions, an Episcopal ordination seemed unlikely. The members of the chapel decided to take matters into their own hands and ordain him themselves. Three lawyers planned the ceremony: its form was that of a contract. The first party identifies itself as "we the Wardens, Vestry, Proprietors and Congregation." Its power to ordain did not arise from any Biblical or ecclesiastical source but rather from the third article of the state's declaration of rights. Freeman's obligations and privileges are delineated. All the precise redundancies are observed: and so, on the eighteenth of November 1787, "said Freeman" joined the established clergy of "said Boston."[114]

The innovators guessed that their manner of proceeding would "perhaps be thought new and unprecedented," and they enclosed a long vindication in the church record. Therein they attempted to confirm the authority of the congregation to ordain its minister while retaining the chapel's links to the Episcopal Church. One strategy was vaguely historical and invoked the opinion of William Blackstone: "lawful authority" had resided in the King and Parliament and not in the bishops. With the American Revolution, that authority had devolved upon the people:

> For what is *lawful authority?* It is that right which every individual has to conduct in conformity to the laws of the land, and which every corporate society has, to make rules and orders for their own regulation, not repugnant to the general laws of the Legislature of the State under which they are formed.[115]

This "right" did not participate in a higher sovereignty or mission. Quite the contrary, it emptied society of any restraints or duties beyond the barest reverence to law. There is no firm talk of what was good or what was fair. Their accomplishment was entrusted to the various individuals and interests that operated freely within the wide expanse of allowable endeavors. As the document happily admitted, this was the philosophy of the corporation.

Such a novel ceremony was bound to excite controversy. In the same paper that reported the proceedings, a "Spectator" added more pointed comments. After Freeman, the "mock priest," withstood an ordaining tap from the senior warden, "the infidel hand [was] raised in triumph . . . All distinction was levelled with the dust, and that sacred building which was formerly consecrated to order and propriety, [was] disgraced by the projects of an irreligious junto, and ambitious sectiary."[116] The vitriol is typical of the period, but its emphases are still informative. The "Spectator" assumed that church practices and structures had to mimic the natural proportions of society. To overthrow this relation was impious and insincere. Beneath the hypocrisy lurked ambition.

In the next edition of the *Centinel*, John Gardiner rose to the defense of the chapel, and his style was similarly caustic. He affirmed the right, extended by the "God of nature" and guaranteed by the civil constitution, of any group to elect its own officers. By exercising this right, the congregants had "undermined the pompous fabrick of hierarchical usurpation" and "pricked the puffed bladder of uninterrupted succession." Rather than inhale "sacerdotal effluvia," Gardiner and his fellows at the chapel practiced an "unadulterated Christianity."[117] Here was a familiar rhetoric: eliminate the clutter that retarded human capacities and a better society would emerge. Why tolerate the props of a pretended order if they choked the free range of merit and reason? Gardiner certainly did not, as he made clear by his attacks on the American episcopacy.

John Gardiner and Samuel Seabury, the first American bishop, were second cousins, a fact not mentioned in the biographical notices. One might call their kinship a bizarre accident of history, had Gardiner not been so adept at turning on his family. Seabury had corresponded with Gardiner's father and informed him of his successful application to the Scottish bishops after the English declined to ordain an American.[118] We do not know Silvester's reaction, but we can guess that it was friendlier than his son's. In March of 1786, during the bishop's visit to Boston, John abused his cousin in the town's newspapers. Seabury was the "sole Vendor of the pretended, late imported Spirit, from Scotland." His church and his ministry represented "bigotry" and "selfish priestcraft." This scorching line of critique—not voiced by Gardiner alone— tolerated no superiors above the people but their laws and their God.[119]

The episode also reminds us of the difficulty many Americans faced as they disclaimed their colonial status. Their colonial past, furthermore, could not be shed and was often not shed willingly. Samuel Seabury had abandoned all hope of a political link with Great Britain, but he clung to an apostolic connection routed through the old imperial circuits. Other Episcopalians—William Smith comes immediately to mind—sought to reknit the Anglican communion according to American patterns. John Gardiner and his mates at King's Chapel followed this logic so far as to leave the communion entirely, though even Gardiner remained an admirer of Anglican vocabulary and style. And while these issues were particularly fraught for churchmen, they were attached to a problem of identity that was not confined to religious experience. When Gardiner impugned Seabury for his contraband Scottishness, he was attacking a now antiquated British allegiance, but in a manner that betrayed his own familiarity with and instinctive reliance on the English (and here Wilkite) lexicon of radical complaint. But the past had American inputs as well, and we are reminded of this fact by unlikely referees. Silvester Gardiner was a Tory exile, but no one was more invested in America or more anxious to see the country's development continue untroubled by political disagreement. Improving America's land was, after all, the fundamental task of both the once and future empires.

So Silvester had had enough of ideological nicety. His will, signed a month after his son's paper assassination of cousin Seabury, held its own daggers. John received one guinea. Codicils added a house in Boston and a large farm in Pownalborough to this legacy, but John, as the second son, had stood to inherit the bulk of the estate upon the death of his childless older brother.[120] However, no great bitterness haunts his correspondence or speeches. He discovered other ways to prominence. He adapted quickly to local environments, even as he maintained a link to extralocal sources of authority. In Wales and St. Kitts, he relied on his common law training and on the institutions of empire. In the infant United States, he cast himself as a model of ideological rectitude.

◆§ · §◆

Even before his very public abuse of cousin Seabury, John Gardiner had managed to cut quite a figure in Boston politics and society. Two years after settling in his native town, its citizens asked him to deliver the annual Fourth of July oration. This was a man who left America before the writs-of-assistance cases and did not return until independence was certain. His speech, delivered at the church he had so recently helped to transform, did not ignore the Revolution, but its review of martial valor was brisk and came late in the text. Gardiner's aim was higher and wider. His true subject was the progress of freedom, commerce, science, and letters. War alone could not effect such a great change. Instead, citing Blackstone and Hume, Gardiner pointed to a "revolution in manners" that had its roots in the Middle Ages and accelerated with the Reformation and the introduction of the printing press. The "middling rank" came into its own as the Catholic Church diminished in influence and the nobility alienated their estates in a vain attempt to rival the merchants. America promised to fulfill these trends; Americans would be as polite as they were free.[121]

While Gardiner spoke in universal terms, his understanding of historical process implied a kind of distinction: the civilized person rode these changes to their furthest extent and became the agent of progress. This person let no backward loyalties hinder his rise, for "where nothing existed to depress or contract its elastick force, the human mind expanded freely, reached the sublimest heights of elevation."[122] Gardiner was describing the same "new set" he would later celebrate in his theater speech. He was also describing himself, an "elastick" man who stayed on top of the forces that moved his society. This buoyancy could not be taken for granted. For all his talk of general improvement, Gardiner knew that progress came at a high cost. England, for example, profited by the Norman conquest: "at the battle of Hastings, gleams of scientifick light began to beam through the Gothick cloud . . . the vanquished nation were put into a situation of receiving the rudiments of science and of cultivation, and of emerging from their former barbarous and rude state of manners."[123] In the long appendix to his speech, Gardiner admitted that William, who perversely enjoyed the name of Bastard, pushed England forward with cruelty and violence. David Hume had handled this subject before and with less embarrassment.[124] Good ends from bad could come. The key for men like Gardiner was to stand at the right end, to be the refined products of turmoil rather than its victims.

Gardiner's liberality had its lacunae, especially in 1785, when republican pieties bristled at signs of a postwar complacency. The orating Gardiner did not smile on material refinements. He condemned America's new taste for luxuries and its reckless importation of British manufactures. Quite against the grain of his character and experience, he recommended the passage of sumptuary laws. He had not lost his cosmopolitan perspective, that natural consequence of his imperial career, but he did adjust the frame of reference. He asked his listeners to look upon their vast country and find a "world within ourselves": "Every article of commerce and almost every article of luxury, now imported from abroad, may be produced in one part or another of this our great, our wide extended Empire."[125] America had broken with Britain, but the young nation would not abandon the ambitions it had inherited from the old. Gardiner's concern for public virtue bespoke a deeper confidence. If the country delivered on its promise, it could keep its virtues and its riches too.

This confidence, along with the bare facts of political expediency, should discourage any historical interpretation that fastidiously combs the liberal from the republican. The new American empire could accommodate both attitudes at once, and in the same persons. On the other hand, liberal and republican tendencies did not rest in systemic balance. The two phenomena were not equivalent. Republicanism was—and would remain—a powerful critical idiom, but it did not describe the way most people truly lived in the eighteenth century. Liberalism was an index of hopes—and hopes less nostalgic than those harbored by republican discourse—but it also transcribed the behavior of a commercial economy. The next chapters will gauge how broadly the liberal mode was adopted in the politics and culture of early national Massachusetts.

John Gardiner was, by his own account, a liberal man, but he remains hard to situate historically. At the close of Samuel Seabury's visit to Boston in 1786, a satirist reviewed the cousins' quarrel in the *Independent Chronicle*. In an imaginary dialogue, the bishop disparaged his adversary for being a lawyer, to which Gardiner responded: "Our profession it is true, have much to do with knaves and fools, and it is perhaps the habit of finding them out in the course of my practice, that has enabled me so easily to detect you. The *consistency* of my character will always induce me to expose you as much as I can."[126] Those italics invite a question: in what ways, if any, was John Gardiner consistent? During the Revolutionary period, he seemed ready to say and do what opportunity beckoned. On the other hand, he was never one to moderate his principles. The question arises again in the dissection of his legal reforms.

Lawyers and Leadership

Lawyers operate best in the interstices between contending persons and powers. John Gardiner certainly thrived on conflict. While on St. Kitts, his income in Chancery derived less from the size of a case than from its difficulty: a solicitor's fees increased with the length of a dispute and the complexity of the actions it required. Professional endeavors were unavoidably political. The coincidence was immediate on a tiny Caribbean island, but lawyers were always amplifying local arguments. They incorporated discrete issues—their clients' problems—into a vast body of historical and constitutional discourse. Similarly, they mediated between the various authorities that ruled the British Empire. As a barrister on the Welsh circuit and as a party to the St. Kitts Assembly row, Gardiner had a hand in imperial administration.

His peers in Massachusetts played the same role, though perhaps not so abandonedly. In the mid-eighteenth century, provincial lawyers courted official favor at every level, from the county to the Crown. During the imperial crisis, half of the province's barristers were of Loyalist sympathies, and a third left rebellious New England to prove it. Their Patriot colleagues—some with similar regrets—left the empire, but they did not lose their transactional advantages thereby.[1] In the future, however, they would have to speak of them openly. The Revolution quickened its advocates' rise in the social and political structures, and rivals took notice. Lawyers, it was said, were trying to build a new establishment, one more insidious, even, than its Hutchinsonian predecessor. In defending their claims to authority, lawyers naturalized what the empire had taught. Their broad experience of the world and their talent for finding opportunity in unease were, they argued, the best qualifications for leadership in a free society. Gardiner, as law reformer, was only holding his colleagues to their liberal rhetoric.

While Gardiner understood that progress came at a price, he often buried his tolerance for these social costs in the historical excursions that crisscross his speeches. "Senex," writing in Boston's *Herald of Freedom* in 1788, was more forward. Noticing that the "world is a series of revolutions, an assemblage of varieties," the essayist admitted that "the mind is generally wafted to the point to which the capricious winds of fortune direct, and rises and falls according to the weight of external circumstances." This, however, was no cause for concern:

> the man who opens his mind to things human and divine; who traces their nature, operations and relations, discovers that the effort of all the parts of the system tends to the preservation and good of the whole. He believes a partial distribution of evil necessary to preserve a system which consists of evils and remedies, poisons and antidotes. If the adverse winds of misfortune irresistably hurry him from some favourite post, where every prosperous gale seemed to conspire with his wishes, he considers this sudden alteration as the course of nature, in pursuing the course of general happiness.[2]

Here was Gardiner's "elastick" man. He understood the forces that moved him, and he shared in the larger successes that accrued from their interplay.

Confidence could not wander far from commerce; each pushed and pulled at the other. Liberalism was the vernacular of their conversations. In the same paper that published "Senex," another writer celebrated America's potential. "Experience is teaching us wisdom with rapidity," he wrote, and "trade and commerce are regulating themselves, infinitely better than all the short-sighted schemes of moonshine politicians could ever do."[3] Nevertheless, politics would not be without its own wisdom if conducted according to a similar economy. When operating freely, the world produced its own best managers. These were the late 1780s, and supporters of the freshly minted constitutional settlement adopted the same rhetoric.

Jonathan Jackson was one of many writers who imagined a proper national government. Jackson was a prominent Essex County merchant, and his *Thoughts upon the Political Situation of the United States*, while national in scope, considered the particular needs and opportunities of his native Massachusetts.[4] Jackson's outline of government—

like the federal design he backed—was fitted to an active, commercial society. He admitted that people were not born politicians; a traditional aristocracy had no place in America. But the country did have its "wise men," who, by devoting their talents to long service, had learned "the art of managing well." The trick was to collect them in one place, so that the nation might profit by their experience. Such leaders would not only be competent but also blessed with "extensive open views." Having risen to a special position, they had gained the broad perspective necessary to govern the rude bulk from which they were "refined."[5] Like the authors of the *Federalist*, Jackson believed that this refinement proceeded best within a large republic. Again like James Madison and Alexander Hamilton, he received these ideas through David Hume. Jackson acknowledged the debt and quoted Hume at some length.[6] The sensibility is by now familiar: progress does not falter, but it is often perversely, even crassly, accomplished.

Jonathan Jackson did not for a moment believe that "wise men" entered government out of goodwill. He conceded that "[t]o expect men in publick, any more than in private life, will act without interested motives, is to expect what is never to be found in human nature, nor ought to be looked for."[7] Public office had to excite the ambitions of men who, after all, were likely to succeed in other employments. Jackson regretted the "wretched parsimony" of government. "Superiour workmen," he said, "are entitled to superiour pay."[8]

Jackson recognized the dangers of his scheme. High wages were enticing, but power was a real stimulant. The able and famous might conspire against the government. With a nod to John Adams's *Defence of the Constitutions*, Jackson argued that the best way to "disarm" the able was to grant them constituted authority. Rather than deny them their interests, well-made governments aligned these interests with the nation's. The best system isolated the ambitious and put them to use. Dangers were better managed than disowned.[9] This practice made for an "energetick" government, much as it improved the economy. Of first importance was the strategic allocation of resources, for, as Jackson noted, "the division of labour is the great modern expedient of bringing all works of human industry to their utmost perfection."[10]

While of obvious utility to Constitutional advocates, this economic understanding of leadership was active in other debates. In late 1790, a correspondent to Boston's *Independent Chronicle* wondered why lawyers were so numerous in government when they did not truly represent the community. A better accounting would see more farmers and artisans in the state legislature.[11] Another writer rose to the lawyers' defense and delivered a cold rebuttal to their critics. The proportion of lawyers in government was deservedly high because they represented by far the largest interest in any population, "the litigious and bad part." Government and its laws assumed a degree of wickedness. Lawyers were best acquainted with the flaws and passions of human nature and so made the best governors. Their experience was the broadest of any men in the state. They did not attach themselves to any one enterprise; instead, lawyers "harmonised" the various endeavors of the commonwealth. Their interest lay with "the promotion of the whole."[12]

Notwithstanding the generous leaven of sophistry, these arguments were certainly of the same bent as those recommending the federal experiment. Lawyers as leaders transcended the segments of their society but in their independence oversaw its integrity. They knew how society worked from its base to its top and could comprehend its general happiness. And finally, these advantages brought success. Lawyers were men of property with a considerable stake in government.[13]

Although adept at winning office, lawyers as a group were never popular. The 1780s were particularly unfriendly to the Massachusetts bar. Inland debtors became increasingly desperate, eventually taking up arms under Daniel Shays. Lawyers, of course, were credit's hangmen. And in that rebellious year, 1786, there was the additional challenge of Benjamin Austin Jr., who, as "Honestus," proposed the abolition of the legal "order."[14] Austin favored laws reflecting the "genuine principles of Republicanism." The lawyers, he thought, preferred distortion. Like "Romish priests," they guarded their craft as a "wonderful mistery." The epithets are telling: lawyers stood accused of backwardness as well as sharp practice. To Austin's mind, they hid behind "Old English Authorities" that embarrassed American justice.[15]

Even worse, lawyers made sport of the merchant's distress. For all his republican bywords, Austin's first concern was commerce rather than virtue. Lawyers interfered where they were not wanted; they oversaw commercial relations they did not understand. Austin suggested that merchant referees might better arbitrate disputes. Courts were inefficient and usually multiplied problems they were meant to solve. In later years, Austin would win dubious acclaim as a "jacobin," but he was an unconvincing radical. He meant not to overthrow the system but to insure its clean operation. Lawyers were antiques and hindrances. For the agrarians and their battles "Honestus" had little sympathy. In early 1787, he condemned the Shaysite outrages.[16]

Austin's newspaper rivals recognized that his position was half baked. One suggested that he clarify matters with a day's journey to the west and into the insurgents' camp. Another hinted brightly that Austin's complaints had little to do with reform. He manufactured ropes, the demand for which would rise with lawyers on the scaffold.[17] The issue was interest, not principle. It was a subject on which lawyers wrote knowingly and well. As they defended their profession from Austin's attacks, they revealed how close they were to the spirit of the times, quickly disproving his most grievous charge against them.

"Mentor," for example, was happy that "Honestus" had denounced the mob but wondered if Austin were fully aware of modern realities: "Rogues there always will be in all trades and professions. But shall we therefore, abolish the arts and sciences, and return to savage life?"[18] Other writers assured Austin that merchants and lawyers were not at odds. They were both looking for an "equal chance" in a game of guile and risk. "The same contagious spirit of enterprize actuates the lawyer," wrote one defender, "he is willing to hazard the loss of time and trouble, and is accordingly admitted to participate [in] the gain."[19] Here we see the liberal sensibility in calm exposition, with none of the anxiety witnessed in Austin's attempt to play at once the republican and the friend of commerce.

But then, that era was free and easy with labels, and a writer calling himself a "Free Republican" offered the most elegant example of the liberalism peddled by Austin's interlocutors. The same writer provoked "Honestus" by daring to state that lawyers were a "necessary order" in America. In an earlier essay, he elaborated a general scheme of society. Because "variety pervades the system," because of differences in ability and disposition, "equality seems inconsistent with the plan and economy of things."[20] The more able citizens enter the professions or the countinghouse, where they live from others' labor:

Some at least of that class, who are supported from the labours of their fellow men, seem at first blush to be useless, the mere drones of the hive; but it is to be remembered that we are not to quarrel with the destination of things, but must take mankind as we find them. They ever had, and probably ever will have, their follies, their vanities, and their vices, which they will gratify, and their diseases, which must be cured. This general spirit of gratification gives riches to the merchant, the maladies of mankind to the employment of the physician, and the necessity that their follies and vices should be checked, to the business of the lawyer and divine.[21]

The philosophical tradition of private gains and public benefits was at work in Massachusetts. Within a few years, the U. S. Constitution's authors would appropriate it to lasting effect, but this rendering of the social economy continued to shape other debates. Not least among the critical issues was the role of the legal profession.

The "Honestus" controversy inspired John Gardiner's first public declarations on that subject. A rumor circulated that he was the ghost responsible for Benjamin Austin's tirades. Gardiner answered by disavowing any attempt to abolish lawyers as a class. He reminded Bostonians that he was "bred to the bar"; to dissolve it was to "cut his own throat." He did admit to concerns about certain laws, such as estates-tail, and certain establishments, such as the bar association. Gardiner asked his readers for patience and hinted that a reform bill of his devising would appear in due time.[22]

Like much of his life, John Gardiner's legal career presents quite a tangle. Upon returning to Boston in 1783, he took his rightful place among the town's senior lawyers. He was a barrister, after all, and had argued cases before the most important courts in England. He did not shrink from the privileges of membership; in fact, he persuaded his colleagues to revive the custom of wearing black gowns.[23] He also attended the meetings of the Suffolk bar, but it was there that he began to sour on his job. When, in 1785, he presented his son to the meeting as a probationer, Gardiner's peers refused the suit. While the young man's classical training was impeccable, he had never been to college. This incident fed rumors of a collaboration with "Honestus" the following year.[24] Shortly thereafter, John Gardiner withdrew from regular practice.

He almost left the scene altogether. As noted earlier, Silvester Gardiner's will threw a spare guinea in John's face but reserved more considerable properties in the codicils. Among these bequeaths was a farm in Pownalborough, hard by the Kennebec River. The barrister moved there after his father's death in 1786. He did not forsake the law, but his attention was often elsewhere. He took in a student, James Bridge, who found that Gardiner's pedagogy confined itself to the first volume of Blackstone and family games of backgammon. Sensing a lack of rigor, Bridge joined his friend John Quincy Adams in Newburyport, where they studied under the heavier hand of Theophilus Parsons, the future chief justice of the Massachusetts Supreme Judicial Court.[25]

From Maine, Gardiner corresponded with friends in Boston, where he owned a house by Silvester's legacy. He wrote to Samuel Adams about the state of his gardens and begged some seeds from the old patriot's wife. He arranged, through Adams, to donate a number of books to the Harvard College library. Included were several legal compendia, a book of heraldry, and a copy of Handel's *Messiah.* These donations, the casual remains of his English career, eventually won for Gardiner an honorary Harvard degree.[26]

While Gardiner complained of his ignorance of events in the wider world, he focused on his immediate surroundings. He was a respected man in Pownalborough, and that comes as no surprise, given his name and experience. As a justice of the peace, he married some of his neighbors and ordered others to the whipping post. He also occasionally served as moderator of the town meeting. At one such meeting, in May of 1789, Gardiner saw fit to expand his aims. He traded against his local position for the sake of a promising venture in state politics. The people of Pownalborough voted to accept his gift of three hundred acres, which was reserved for the support of schools and ministers. At the same time, the town voted to send John Gardiner to Boston as its representative to the General Court. Sadness at home might also have encouraged a change of scene. Maine did not agree with Margaret Gardiner. Her health faltered, and she returned to the West Indies in the hope of restoring it. She died on St. Kitts in 1789.[27]

Gardiner was ready to reenter the larger public life of the commonwealth—with a vengeance. He would take this opportunity to effect his "intended Reformation" of the law. He told Sam Adams, "I consider myself pledged to my country to carry this matter through or perish in the attempt."[28] The hyperbole is characteristic, though in this case not entirely misplaced: four years' time would see Gardiner dead and many of his reforms unborn.

◆§ · §◆

His initial efforts were vigorous, as were the sallies of the opposition. In January of 1790, Gardiner moved that the full House of Representatives resolve itself into a Committee of the Whole to consider the state of legal practice in Massachusetts. More speeches and proposals quickly followed.[29] Rather than examine his measures in detail, most writers diminished the man. They also had not forgotten his family's rebuff by the Suffolk bar. Five years before, its members dismissed Gardiner's "unskilled offspring . . . a son whose knowledge of the law was as deficient as his Sire's talent at defamation is prolix." Now, the father offered to improve law and lawyers both; surely "a spirit of the blackest revenge" animated his plan.[30]

Other detractors suggested even baser motives. Gardiner was determined to make a name for himself. Beneath the lofty rhetoric, he was really chasing fame and fortune "through the lowest, and most dirty paths of ambition." One wit compared him to a child who tried to jump a moving coach: "Now this I think's the very case / With our Reformer, all so high! / He hopes to gain the envied place / And duns the 'Order' with his cry." The poet further speculated that Gardiner had designs on a federal seat. To make "a ladder of the Lawyers, thereby to mount into publick office," was a proven stratagem.[31]

In other words, many people questioned if John Gardiner was sincere. Gardiner himself acknowledged a rumor that the lawyers had bribed him to undermine his own scheme. A correspondent to the *Centinel* had a similar idea: Gardiner was the stooge of another, lesser "Order," a cadre of quacks and pettifoggers opposed to the legal establishment. Meeting in secret, they appointed "a rosy-gilled brother to do their drudgery." Gardiner would obfuscate the issues with rambling discourses on English law, but his employers' real object was an undeserved share of the legal business in Massachusetts.[32]

For all their bluster, Gardiner's critics sensed the direction of his reforms. The law could become too established. Its practitioners might, in welcoming the security of old methods, reduce the law's currency. In his first reforming speech, Gardiner argued that impressions and ideas attached themselves to the human constitution and hardened into prejudice. These fixations even marred the habits of "liberal and expanded" minds. While both an "eminent modern" and Gardiner's favorite legal author, William Blackstone was nevertheless a man whose prejudices had sometimes gotten the better of him. He defended Latin proceedings and the "barbarous" black-letter script. These were mysteries to (and here Gardiner bought slander with smugness) "all but the Priests—I beg pardon, I mean the Professors of the Law." If men like Blackstone were so inclined, what of the "little men of the Profession"? In Massachusetts, they stuck to their "contracted systems" and resisted the course of reform. Prejudice obscured reason and hobbled fair practice.[33]

Gardiner had found another priesthood to blast. His ridicule of high-church Episcopalians had been merciless. Their superstitions and hierarchies retarded progress toward an unadulterated Christianity. Many attorneys were just as culpable. Their traditions offended the clarity and facility of the law. Moreover, their private meetings set a bad precedent for even the regular ministers of God. Gardiner noted that clergymen had begun to gather in associations like those of lawyers. "One monster," he wrote, "has produced another."[34]

In the long title to his reform act, John Gardiner proposed to render the law as he and others had made the King's Chapel liturgy: "easy, safe, and intelligible." The act itself was rather crowded, running to twenty-one chapters. Of course, one of them outlawed the bar association, or, as the bill's author liked to call it, the "Bar-call."[35] His animus was personal but not inconsistent with the general tendencies of his thought. Bar meetings represented a larger problem. The law worked best when it worked openly. Under the cover of secrecy, lawyers twisted the law to partial uses.

Gardiner needed to put faces on these crimes, and he started with a favorite scapegoat, "that tall, thin, half-starved, parricidious traitor, Tom Hutchinson," under whose watch the bar association had developed. (And so it had, though many lawyers, like Benjamin Prat, viewed Hutchinson as a threat. As Prat's student and friend, Gardiner understood these vexed relations.) The Suffolk meeting grew into the "unlawful combination and conspiracy" of the 1780s. It was a "self-created Legislature." Within a decade of Gardiner's efforts, many a good Federalist lawyer would hang the same tag on the Democratic-Republican societies beginning to dot the political landscape. But then, a politician in early national Massachusetts was often implicated in what he despised. As an example of the bar's sinister reach, John Gardiner cited a passage from the Suffolk association's record in which the members appointed three of their number to consider how delinquent sheriffs might better execute their offices. Gardiner thought this measure a "usurpation" of civil power. As a former member of the committee at issue, he was, perhaps, in a position to know.[36]

His strictures on the legal profession appeared in concert with other reforms. The bill he offered in January of 1790 was really a jumble of ideas. The first chapter harkened back to the Puritans and to the Mosaic laws they never enforced. Gardiner was not so reticent, proposing that perjury in capital cases be punishable by death. Other chapters seemed to orient the law along a popular bearing. Insolvent debtors would no longer suffer imprisonment. The poor would be allowed to act as their own attorneys. While Gardiner's bill encouraged others in the practice of law, it chastened lawyers already in practice. There was the matter of the "bar-call" and a section on excessive charges. Gardiner also proposed an end to special pleading.[37]

Under the common law, special pleading framed legal actions according to a narrow set of questions. This limited juries to deciding only matters of fact, whereas cases decided on the general issue saw juries enjoying wider discretion. This is a crucial topic in American legal history. By one account, the prerevolutionary adherence to common law forms resulted in the local resolution of legal issues. This argument relies on an inside joke gone bad: lawyers and judges were so distracted by the system of writs that they left substantive law to the juries. Special pleading was the peculiar exception to the rule. It was an old common law creature that ceded little to juries. It was, however, rarely seen in colonial America. While there was an increase in special pleas just after the Revolution, that era was more remarkable for its reform of all common-law pleading. At the same time, lawyers were coming into their own, professionally and politically.[38]

Indeed, lawyers became more powerful as the common law shed its arcana. They rose upon a looser foundation. Judges, now uniformly lawyers, wielded the common law as a policy tool and not as a traditional standard. The law itself had changed. No longer the index of stability and landed authority, it had grown responsive to a commercial society wherein property changed hands quickly. Lord Mansfield, Gardiner's model jurist, presided over and encouraged these accommodations, which had begun long before his tenure. So even as "Honestus" vainly hoped for merchant arbitrators, lawyers secured their place as the managers of transaction.[39]

Returning to John Gardiner's reforms, the chapters on special pleading and other popular causes begin to look more like loss leaders. Of greater salience are and were those sections that accommodated law to commerce. His temperate view of bankrupts anticipated Federalist legislation that decriminalized financial failure in order to monetize it and return failed merchants to a fluid marketplace. Chapter 10 broadened the negotiability of bonds, and, in the next chapter, Gardiner suggested that judgments on money contracts and securities might themselves bear interest.[40] The law had become something more than a model of a just society; it was becoming a financial instrument. In making this case, John Gardiner was as much the lawyer's companion as his reformer.

The thirteenth chapter of Gardiner's bill proposed an end to the further creation of estates-tail and suggested a method by which legatees might easily dock entails then in existence. Under the doctrine of entail, a property holder could restrict his heirs from dividing their estates.

The law was akin to primogeniture in its social intent. Real property was to pass undiminished through the same families, generation after generation.[41] Gardiner's own experience as an heir had been difficult. When the matter came up for debate in 1791, he argued that such difficulties had become the common lot in the law of inheritance. But this he would seek to change; his proposed act repeated the promises of the previous year. Whatever the language of conveyance, all land was to be owned by fee-simple. Tenants-in-tail could escape the conditions of their tenure by registering a new deed with a justice of the peace and the appropriate clerk. This last procedure improved on the "common recovery," which had been the only remedy for centuries. Gardiner discussed its origins at some length; the *Centinel* dubbed the speech "A learned Law Lecture."[42]

To anyone who had heard or read his Fourth of July oration, the history had a familiar plot. When German barbarians invaded Roman Europe, they brought with them a system of feudal obligations. The "rude" Saxons extended this system to Britain by all manner of "Gothick cruelty." The poor Celts fled to Wales or Brittany, where, according to Gardiner, their descendants still displayed "many excellent good qualities," including the imprudent hospitality that delivered their homeland into German hands. (He too had imposed on his Welsh hosts.) The Saxons got their comeuppance at Hastings, as one invader punished another. The Norman conqueror refined Saxon feudalism by replacing gavelkind, or partible inheritance, with primogeniture. A further innovation was the conditional estate, whereby tenants producing male issue by their lords' daughters won a more secure title to the land. In the thirteenth century, the barons enforced these conditions on future generations, thus inventing estates-tail.[43]

During the Wars of the Roses, English judges, with Edward IV's blessing, found a way to break entails. They turned to a device contrived by "designing selfish Priests." The Church and its monasteries, having spread the gospel of "no Pence, no Peter," wanted to accept alienated land as payment for absolving its owner's sins. By a "common recovery," the monastery (or buyer) would bring a false claim against the penitent's (or seller's) estate. As a matter of process, the seller warranted his lands to a third party, who, to complete the sham, would default by his absence from court. Appropriated by the secular authorities, "common recovery" became the standard means by which lands held by fee-tail were converted to fee-simple. "Priest-craft," said Gardiner, "became a piece of law-craft."[44] The first settlers of New

England had none of this skulduggery, but, under James II and his co-lonial Dominion, "avaricious, pettifogging Lawyers" imposed the doc-trine of entail on their neighbors. The practice of "common recovery" continued even as Gardiner spoke. He related how all parties seeking this remedy in Suffolk County hired the same mulatto to vouch for es-tates and then flee the court. Such behavior, said Gardiner, was an af-front to reason and good sense. His method of redress would set the commonwealth aright.[45]

His account of entails tells much about his ideas in general. On the one hand, the law and its practitioners were encumbered with the traditions of an unenlightened past. To follow these forms in Amer-ica was ridiculous, as ridiculous and unhelpful as a pope on Boston Common. However, Gardiner was also recounting a story of prog-ress. He had told the same story in his oration of 1785, with all its Gothic trappings and unexpected twists. The alienation of large es-tates was a key factor in the "revolution of manners." David Hume explained how the Saxon nobility were men of small credit. They could not risk their lands in expensive ventures, and there were no "middle ranks of men" to profit from these risks.[46] As Gardiner found in Blackstone, this situation improved under the Tudors. The popish clergy were put to rout, and many nobles sold their estates in order to keep up with their middling rivals. To Gardiner's mind, the end of this inexorable process was in sight. The merchants and profession-als were the winners, and their elevation would be complete once they cast off illiberal notions best left to priests and aristocrats, the creatures of the past.[47]

This vision of progress was tolerant of conflicts. The "middle ranks" were the beneficiaries of a long, greedy history, and vice did not disappear with the Saxons. Lawyers tended conflict and kept it from exploding unproductively. The "Free Republican" knew this, and so did John Gardiner:

> Were all mankind, as their beneficent Creator made them, in a state of
> perfect innocence and virtue . . . there would be little, if any occasion, for
> this Order of men in society; but while mankind are as we know they
> are, this Order . . . will be found absolutely necessary in all free govern-
> ments, where they ought to be kept on an exact line of level with the
> other liberal professions in the State, neither degrading them below, nor
> permitting them arrogantly to exalt themselves above, the great body
> of their fellow citizens.[48]

John

Gardiner understood the lawyer to be a part of the system. Many thoughtful lawyers agreed. What set the reformer apart, however slightly, was his readiness to apply the same ideas in a critique that others used for vindication. Society bettered itself in the gross, and this general improvement relied on a complex mesh of interests and endeavors. When lawyers assumed too many privileges, they clogged an apparatus they were meant to grease. He could make that argument—and perhaps wanted to make it—because he was an almost marginal figure. He studied and worked abroad, returned to Boston rather late, and soon left again for Maine. Most lawyers had more to protect and little reason to change. Small wonder Gardiner's reforms did not move very far in the legislature.[49]

Despite his wayward career, John Gardiner was still "bred to the bar." Even in the midst of his row with the legal establishment, he made common cause with it as a legislator. Along with Theophilus Parsons, he supported a bill raising the salaries of judges on the Supreme Judicial Court. His argument was realistic and quite similar to Jonathan Jackson's view of public employments. Jackson condemned the government for its "wretched parsimony"; Gardiner bemoaned the judges' "pitiful salaries." These could not reliably attract lawyers of ability. "Who will leave the profits of a lucrative profession which enables him to live in splendour," Gardiner asked, "and at the same time lay by large sums in the Bank, for the future use of himself and [his] family, merely to starve honourably on the Bench?"[50] Talent craved a more tangible reward than honor. Governments would do well to follow the same economy.

Lawyers inspired a model of social policy. Many of Gardiner's measures would have reduced their earnings, but he warned against undue regulation:

> The Law is, or at least ought to be, a liberal profession, and its professors ought to be paid liberally, though not extortionately. If we screw them down too hard, we may force them into dishonest practices to gain a livelihood; if we attempt to starve them we shall compel them to steal and thereby let loose a band of thieves upon our fellow citizens.[51]

The good society was not a pure society. Virtue tempered vice but did not try to expel it. The various elements of success did not work independently of each other. They had to mix more or less freely, with no one piece mastering the rest.

Some people, of course, were more at ease in the compound. On the same day that he recommended liberal pay for lawyers, Gardiner explained to the House of Representatives that mistakes will happen. If a man took his broken watch to a blacksmith, that was his error, and so it was with the law. The best practitioners would thrive. One legislator had heard enough of thieves and blacksmiths and asked for a retraction. Gardiner was having none of it, and he decided to teach this unwanted monitor a lesson. He offered a law maxim in Latin and then translated it for his opponent's benefit. The maxim was, "there is no superiority, no power, among equals," to which Gardiner added, "I hope, therefore, Mr. Speaker, that the gentleman will never again presume to interrupt his equal."[52] The newspaper records much laughter in the room, for Gardiner's point was well taken. An open system was friendly to merit, and, as any smart lawyer would have understood, merit depended on a knowledge of the terms that defined that system. By this criterion, John Gardiner was an expert at his craft and a worthy representative of his guild.[53]

◆§ · §◆

In the late months of 1790, even as the remnants of his law reform bill crawled through the committee process, Gardiner denounced another group of men for its malignant claim on privilege. This group was the Society of the Cincinnati, and Gardiner was not the only critic of its hereditary design. The occasion of his particular remonstrance was friend William Tudor's "Gratulatory Address" to the Massachusetts Cincinnati. Writing in the *Chronicle*, Gardiner found Tudor's speech to be a "new species of New England, anti-republican manufacture." The society was a "novel, self-created, aristocratic, military order of pretended nobility."[54] Neither Gardiner's response nor its vehemence came as much of a surprise.

Less expected, perhaps, was his attack on a genuine noble. After the French National Assembly abolished the aristocracy, one Boston paper published the dissent of the Duc de Broglio. Gardiner again took up his pen and asked, "What is there in these supercilious Nobles, that is not equally common to all the human species, that they should claim such superiour rights and privileges?" This was a question most Americans could have comfortably posed. Fewer would have rejoiced with Gardiner if "this very lordly Duke is confined to a mad house for life, has his head shaved and well blistered, kept constantly upon a light, cool regimen, [and] occasionally put into a straight waistcoat."⁵⁵ Here was liberal punishment, indeed.

Such energetic censure—and from such a source—was sure to draw some reply. "A Card," writing in the *Centinel*, thought Gardiner had better not mention straightjackets, considering his "late quixotick exploits." The same writer, after Gardiner's "rhapsodical, bombastical, pompous Phillipick" against the Cincinnati, reminded the reformer that he still owed the one hundred guineas he had pledged to the society in 1783.⁵⁶ Having spread himself between so many causes, several of them contradictory, Gardiner made a large target. He happily veered toward the most dangerous issues. During his Cincinnati address, William Tudor referred to the bloody sacrifice of America's sons during the Revolution, and Gardiner scolded him for abusing the "Litany of your Church." Tudor's church was King's Chapel; with its litany Gardiner had himself made free. Because Tudor was "too orthodox a Christian, wantonly to sport with things sacred," Gardiner blamed his entire speech on a "strange effervesence of the brain."⁵⁷ In Gardiner's hands, a phrase like that was all edge and no handle.

There was, however, a method to John Gardiner's madness. He consistently attacked privilege when it grew too imposing. Lawyers had become obnoxious; so had the Society of the Cincinnati. Another potential threat was the federal government. In his speech to the Cincinnati, Tudor called the United States "a Consolidated, and not a Confederated Republic." Gardiner thought this opinion affronted the commonwealth's sovereignty. The particular laws of Massachusetts would, under this dreadful scheme of consolidation, "be totally absorbed, entirely swallowed up, in the General." The state would lose its capacity to protect and punish.⁵⁸ Both state and nation would be better served by a truly federal apportionment of powers.

This issue came to a head in late January of 1791. The town of York elected David Sewall to the state House of Representatives, even though President Washington had appointed him to the federal bench in the District of Maine. The General Court had faced this problem in the previous year. Christopher Gore found it impossible to keep his job as U.S. Attorney and his place in the legislature; he left the latter under pressure from his colleagues.⁵⁹ In June, Gardiner spoke before the house on the propriety of seating federal officers. The *Gazette* published this speech when it became clear Sewall intended to honor his election. Gardiner claimed to have heard "a voice from Heaven," which pronounced that "No man can serve two masters." He argued that the interest of federal officers lay without the government of Massachusetts. Though they be men of the best intentions, they represented a "foreign" influence.[60] He would repeat these arguments as the whole house considered Sewall's eligibility.

The debate issued from the diffidence of the Massachusetts Constitution. Its writers had not thought that a resident and citizen of the state would hold office in a contending or even higher jurisdiction. The national government was then embryonic, and subsequent statute law had not yet caught up to the new contingencies. The state constitution did prohibit justices of the Supreme Judicial Court from sitting in the legislature. Sewall reasoned that his position was an inferior one in the federal system. He was the equivalent of a state judge of common pleas, one of whom already sat in the House. Moreover, the constitution did not strictly disqualify him; any further ban would be arbitrary. In response, one legislator said that this construction would allow an old woman into the senate. "Would not the Hon. Senate," this member continued, "exercise a discretionary power, and reject the female Senator with disdain?"[61]

John Gardiner concluded the debate in convincing fashion. He explained that as a federal judge, Sewall could interpret laws he might make as a state representative. This possibility offended that part of the Massachusetts Constitution that forbade the confusion of the judicial and legislative functions. Judge Sewall held more potential authority than all of the justices of the Supreme Judicial Court put together. In the face of that reality, thought Gardiner, the General Court "ought to expound the Constitution liberally" and deny the aspirant a seat. Sewall, for his part, was tired of being dismissed as an "alien." He tried to engage Gardiner in an argument over legal technicalities. The member from Pownalborough rejoined that "he could quote Law-Maxims as well as the learned Judge—and if he chose it could go on until the morrow's morning." Instead, Gardiner offered several Latin wisdoms from Coke that substantially disagreed about the nature of the common law. He then put a question to Sewall, "that had no Latin in it; that was plain English which everybody might understand: 'How could he consistent with the Constitution and Bill of Rights of this Commonwealth, take his seat in that House?'"[62] The speaker immediately put the matter to a vote, and Gardiner carried the day, one hundred and eleven to four. He did not always play the contrarian. How could he, when, despite his eccentricity, he personified the trends of his age? Liberal motives animated the gestures of a patriotic tribune.

The episode in the House of Representatives also illustrated how essentially personal these controversies were. The parties said more about each other than about the substance of their debates. As we have seen, Gardiner and the lawyers were closer on the issues than they may have cared to admit, but each side rushed to portray the other as antique and unprogressive. Gardiner found the priestly charade of the "common recovery" occasionally performed in Suffolk County, but nearly everybody in the early national period thought entail was an anachronism. The practice was uncommon before the Revolution and certainly on its way out when Gardiner delivered his "learned lecture." He also falsely charged Massachusetts lawyers with confounding the common and statutory laws.[63]

Gardiner's interlocutors played a similar game. The reformer, they said, wanted to erase the laws of the state and replace them with his "incoherent" ramblings. Even worse, he would have deeds and writs recorded on expensive parchment. He sought a revival of "English fees and English practice." Theophilus Parsons seconded this view: Gardiner may have known the laws of England, but he was ignorant of American laws and courts. His attempts to impose the one on the other were selfish and obnoxious. Parsons added that laws relied on the good "character" of their administration. Gardiner's reforms addressed a corrupt magistracy, which existed in his own mind and nowhere else.[64]

Despite their low regard for human nature and their attention to general goods, the writers of that day stressed the importance of individual character. Certain persons circulated to the top of the social economy; they focused a system of great complexity. Origins mattered less than the fact of their success, but, for that reason, their position was speculative. The persons who presumed to speak for others had little to support them but good fortune and the confidence of their peers and constituents. Not everyone could make it work. John Gardiner knew the quality of leadership in modern times was elastic and unstable. Counterfeits were bound to appear, such as the scribbler to whom Gardiner dedicated Swift's couplet on "horse turds": "[Which] say to the apple plump and prim, / See how we brother pippins swim."[65] One could not trust everything that floated.

Gardiner's critics expressed the same doubts. They maligned his "character" and his "credit." In the *Independent Chronicle*, "Junius" saw Gardiner representing license rather than liberality. His influence was as unsteady as his passions, and "the public will see the buble burst."[66] Another writer put like sentiments to verse:

Learn hence ye statesmen, who to fame
   On midnight fogs ascend,
Ne'er tempt your fate, while Sol's bright flame
   Through ether shall extend:
Lest while far borne aloft ye sail,
   Like Satan high and proud,
Your wax shall melt, your wings shall fail;
   And where's the nitrous cloud?[67]

Setbacks are rarely that dramatic. Before Gardiner sank, a drowning man, to the bottom of the Atlantic, his life would take a few more turns. His attempts at legal reform sparked an abusive row in the press. In the next round, the contest moved back into the courtroom.

◄§ · §►

On February 2, 1790, less than a month after John Gardiner proposed his reforms of the law and its practice, an article attacking his character appeared in the *Herald of Freedom*. As we have seen, he was no stranger to such criticism. This piece, however, was especially aggressive. The critic struck at predictable points: Gardiner's "turbulent temper knows no rest—troubles and tempests have attended him, wherever he has resided." He decried prejudice, but no man was more in its thrall. Gardiner acted from a "prejudice against quietness and peace—Prejudice against sobriety and temperance—Prejudice against every one, who appears to differ from him, in opinion who opposes his injudicious schemes, or who stands in the way of his importance."[68] Gardiner's sobriety had been questioned before: remember his appearance as a "rosy-gilled brother." This author carried the attack much further. Gardiner was a rummy and, even worse, an impious rummy: "Even on the Lord's Day, his God receives no part of his adoration, but the *spirit of New-England*, rises so high as to remove the centre of Gravity."[69]

These were light touches compared to the article's treatment of Gardiner the family man. One might expect any critic to have revisited the troubled relationship of father and son. The *Herald*'s correspondent thought John's abuse of the dead Silvester "would strike even a Savage, with horror and amazement," but Gardiner did not reserve his venom for the older generation. According to the paper, he openly belittled his own daughter, Ann, "whose innocent and modest appearance, one would think, were sufficient to disarm a Russian." However, what moved Gardiner to action was this short phrase: "A Wife, murdered by his cruelty."[70]

The author of this piece never came forward. Gardiner immediately confronted the *Herald*'s publisher, Edmund Freeman, and hauled him before a judge. Gardiner reminded the court of his past services on behalf of a free press. He had been at the heart of the great English controversies of the 1760s. He had defended the *North-Briton*'s printers. He had remained, in America, a foe to tyranny. And apparently, he was still very much a lawyer. Gardiner brought his copy of Hawkins's *Pleas of the Crown* and cited its passages on libel. Defamation was criminal when it tended to breach the public peace, when it was so malicious as to incite acts of revenge by the injured parties. State justice offered a safer form of redress. A libel on an officer of the state was doubly upsetting and particularly subject to prosecution. Along with these definitions, Gardiner introduced a distinction between liberty and licentiousness that would figure prominently in the case.[71]

The counsel for the defense, Harrison Gray Otis, speedily found fault with the accuser. Even at this preliminary hearing, John Gardiner was on trial. Of course, he had broached the matter of his personal experience with libels; Otis simply offered tit for tat. Gardiner's complaint was "extremely confused and desultory." He might have resorted to an old Massachusetts statute against lies and libels, but he had chosen to commence the sort of common law process—full of "prolixity" and "inconveniences"—that normally drew his reforming ire. Gardiner, Otis suggested, had let a private issue get the better of his principles.[72]

Otis did not mount a full defense because, on this occasion, the clever lawyer was an even better prophet. Gardiner could not get out of his own way. The hearing of early February 1790 ended in his favor. Freeman had to make bail and stand to answer the charges of libel before the Supreme Judicial Court that same month. Gardiner was determined to prosecute the case himself, and, after receiving sureties in the amount of one hundred pounds, the court granted him that privilege. To the delight of his enemies, Gardiner mishandled the job and forfeited his bond. He was persistent, however, and secured an indictment in August. On February 22, 1791, one year after publication, Edmund Freeman again stood before the commonwealth's highest bench.[73]

By that day, Gardiner's reforms did not excite as much interest. Some fugitive pieces from the original bill, such as the measure docking estates-tail, were still making their way through the legislature toward a rare enactment. The Freeman trial recovered some of the old buzz, but the curiosity it inspired did not proceed from questions of policy. Indeed, curiosity had become its own excuse. The editor of the *Independent Chronicle* remarked on the "novelty" of the episode and presented a sketch to his readers "with pleasure."[74] While the freedom of the press was at issue, it was never really at stake. All the principals agreed on the character of that freedom. The trial grabbed notice inconsiderate of ramifications.

Despite its shallow impact, the case was novel: the first criminal prosecution for libel in the state's history.[75] John Gardiner knew this. So did the attorney general and the presiding justices. Harrison Gray Otis made the most of it. In his opening remarks to the jury, Otis noted that the trial was unprecedented. During the period of arbitrary government and factional animosity that saw the colony break with Great Britain, there were no such prosecutions. "How strange and extraordinary," said Otis, that "the first instance, is brought forward by a gentleman, who has professed himself an advocate for the liberty of the press, and the rights of mankind."[76]

The prosecutor, attorney general James Sullivan, always seemed a step behind the opposition, but he had to play a straighter part. He also had to argue on behalf of John Gardiner, a difficult ally and a magnet of ill will. Gardiner wanted to handle the prosecution again or, at the least, to aid in it. Understandably, Sullivan balked at this idea. He thought it unwise to digress from regular procedure, especially in a landmark case. Sullivan was particularly upset at the prospect of sharing the prosecution with Gardiner; he preferred to relinquish the matter entirely. The justices opted for a saner proceeding, and Sullivan carried out his duty without what he described as the reformer's "interference."[77]

The attorney general began with a summary of the pertinent body of law. He explained that a libel's crime was provocation, the incitement to violence. For this reason, the truth or falsity of libelous words mattered little; indeed, truth was often the stronger agitant. While Sullivan voiced some personal reservations about the applicability of this doctrine in the United States, he did not dwell on the matter because he sensed the defense would not either: truth was not Freeman's excuse. At the close of the case, two of the justices expressed like opinions. While they hinted that truth might eventually bring acquittals, they refrained from speculating at length. By then the justices knew what Sullivan had earlier guessed. Harrison Gray Otis never directly challenged the familiar common-law emphasis on provocation, and he did not attempt to establish the truth of his client's article.[78]

James Sullivan needed to reconcile standard libel law with the liberty of the press. Of course, English jurisprudence had already attended to the same need, and Sullivan could resort to his Blackstone, from which he read a large passage into the record. While Blackstone admitted the importance of a free press, he defined that freedom as the absence of "previous restraints upon publications." Once published, malicious language deserved censure. As Blackstone wrote, and Sullivan repeated, "Every freeman has an undoubted right to lay what sentiments he pleases before the public: to forbid this, is to destroy the freedom of the press; but if he publishes what is improper, mischievous or illegal, he must take the consequence of his own temerity."[79] From this understanding of the law arose the distinction between liberty and licentiousness that Gardiner had cited at the preliminary hearing. Sullivan relied on the same distinction in the full trial of 1791, although he allowed "that it is very difficult to draw the line."[80]

This lack of assurance was typical of the prosecutor. He was too willing to dissipate the force of his arguments. We have witnessed his attempt to dissociate himself from the common law's disregard for truth. Sullivan also worried aloud that past libel laws had been too partial to authority. He went out of his way to describe how the Star Chamber abused libel prosecutions.[81] In his closing statement to the jury, Otis remarked on the embarrassments of his adversary. Sullivan was uncomfortable with the English precedents, which, Otis noted, often reflected the design of an "arrogant Nobility." Seven years later, as a chief sponsor of the Sedition Act, Otis would affirm Blackstone's distinction from the floor of the U.S. House. In the Freeman case, however, he argued that the distasteful body of English law vindicated the "extensive latitude" with which he conducted the defense.[82]

Otis really had no choice but to be inventive; the facts of the case clearly pointed to his client's guilt. However, his strategy was not radical. He did not object to the fundamental direction of libel law: words and pictures, once published, were punishable. Rather, Otis tried to convince the jury that latitude was the common practice of public argument. The competitive environment of business and politics tolerated roughness. The standard for criminal prosecutions did not evaporate, but it had stretched.

Like any enterprise, the press was most productive when it had the opportunity to make mistakes. Otis wondered "whether greater mischief would not be introduced by an unreasonable restriction upon the press, than could possibly arise from casual licentiousness." While he "did not however mean to advocate licentiousness . . . Still some exceptions must be allowed—or we renounce all the advantages derivable from a knowledge of the failings and misfortunes of others."[83] Lawyers had already argued the same position for their own sake. The legal profession depended on human shortcomings for its utility and profits. Who else but a lawyer could apologize so winningly, so perversely, for a free press? "Moralists may preach," said Otis, "but their examples will be Libels."[84]

Although not as lucrative as the law, the press was very much a business, and that business was to attract readers. According to Otis, this basic interest accounted for the occasional scurrility. Freeman was a young printer who naturally wanted to close the gap between himself and his more senior rivals. Surely, thought Otis, this situation encouraged his client to publish questionable material. Freeman may have erred against discretion, but his errors arose from the pressure of economic contest. His intent was not malicious and, therefore, not criminal under accepted law.[85] Because all printers trafficked in a great deal of information, a certain faulty or vexatious amount was allowable as a hazard of the trade. Besides, printers did not generate the information themselves. Otis explained: "Mr. Gardiner, at this time was pouring forth torrents of eloquence in the House of Representatives; Freeman, with avidity was collecting the little streams into his paper, and these it seems were sometimes rather muddy."[86]

While the newspapers tried to channel the swollen flows of information and polemic, authors failed to control their own words. Gardiner was a good example. The *Herald* article closed in this way: "the Gentleman himself has told us that a reverence for the memory of the Dead ought not to tie the tongue, nor ought the pen of the historian, and certainly a reverence for the character of the living, who have rendered themselves infamous by their conduct ought not to have this effect."[87] Sullivan directed the jury's attention to this passage in order to prove what everyone already knew: that John Gardiner was this "infamous" gentleman. The prosecutor brought Gardiner to the stand and asked him if he had ever spoken on respect for the dead and its tendency to confine debate. Gardiner freely admitted that he had challenged the maxim *nil de mortuis, nisi bonum* in his first reforming speech against the lawyers. The episode had appeared in the papers; the last paragraph from the *Herald* applied to him and no one else.[88]

Otis found the case less simple. Gardiner's vision of his own speech varied slightly from the crucial excerpt in Freeman's newspaper. The story had passed through many hands, and the connection to its original source was tenuous. One could not easily assign responsibility to words once they entered the ether of publicity, a habitat in which Gardiner frequently sojourned. Otis submitted that "by reading, sentiments become our own—and at length we know not whence they were acquired. It is language only, which in some measure alters the property—and a gentleman of Mr. Gardiner's extensive erudition, had, no doubt, frequently engrafted on his speeches, beauties which he ought not to arrogate to himself."[89] Otis was asking the jury to tolerate in the *Herald* the same liberality of expression that John Gardiner practiced with untamed vigor.

The defense strategy aimed to undercut any presumption of malice by establishing that Gardiner invited abuse. The invitation was literal. Gardiner had informed Freeman that all of his speeches were promised to Benjamin Russell, the editor of the *Centinel*, as long as Russell also printed "everything that the Black Birds [meaning lawyers] wrote against him, however black and smutty."[90] Otis maintained that this promise, once known, bucked its private terms and implied a general license to publish anything and everything about the reformer. Gardiner relied on a messy, freewheeling exchange to raise his name and his efforts in the public's considerations. He courted exposure of the worst kind. His agreement with Russell only seconded his provocative behavior. Harrison Gray Otis undoubtedly spoke for many of his fellows as he recounted Gardiner's savage insults to the profession. "Like the ruffian who strikes first," Gardiner had "no right to complain, although the blow be returned with disproportionate severity."[91] As James Sullivan listened, some part of him must have smiled. While he was Gardiner's advocate on that day, one year earlier, when the reform controversy raged and the case against Freeman began, Sullivan had attacked Gardiner in the *Chronicle*. Writing under a pseudonym, the attorney general pilloried the renegade as a "licentious and indecent man."[92]

Such a man, Otis told the jury, could not legitimately call for restraint. Near the end of his closing statement, Otis wondered if he would risk a lawsuit by inserting, "in a public news-paper, that Mr. Gardiner upon his first arrival in this country, wore the Barrister's wig and gown, and was attentive to all the etiquette and formality of the profession, but has now relinquished the whole."[93] Gardiner had thoroughly abandoned form. In the hope of gaining some advantage with general opinion, he railed against professional privilege. He furthered his designs by vicious speech on the House floor, an abuse of legislative privilege. Finally, Gardiner's "smutty" publishing arrangements forfeited his claims on the protections of law.

In the end, *Massachusetts v. Freeman* turned on a technicality, the delight of lawyers. Gardiner countered the defense argument of implied license by bringing evidence that he had excluded accusations of treason and murder from his agreement with Russell. This was a tender issue. The article told of a wife "murdered" by a husband's cruelty. It was this line that originally angered Gardiner and incited his legal action. The indictment took these words seriously: the libel was thought to accuse Gardiner of actual murder, of killing with malice aforethought. This interpretation was Otis's opportunity. He explained to the jurors that if they found the meaning of the article to be other than that represented by the indictment, they were bound to acquit. At the same time that Otis was excusing his client from charges of malice, he found himself needing to do the same for John Gardiner, the "ruffian." Otis assured the court that there had been no real murder. When Margaret Gardiner died, she was on St. Kitts and her husband was in New England. If anything, the pain of separation had been too much, and she died of a broken heart. It was a shameless argument, necessitated by a shameless use of precedent. Despite his stated misgivings about English libel laws, Otis relied on one of Lord Mansfield's decisions from the King's Bench, a ruling that demanded an accurate match of indictment and innuendo.[94]

Edmund Freeman's trial lasted one day. In the afternoon, the three justices of the Supreme Judicial Court gave their instructions to the jury. Two of them, Francis Dana and Increase Sumner, agreed that the Mansfield decision was especially important. However, the jury charges were generally favorable to Gardiner and the state. The defense argument of implied license swayed Sumner alone. All of the judges thought the facts of the case were clear. The libel intended to defame Gardiner, and Freeman was its publisher. The jurors, after "considerable deliberation," reached their verdict. The foreman, Paul Revere, read it the next morning: Freeman was "not guilty."[95]

Immediately, a rumor circulated that Gardiner would retry the matter as a civil suit in Pownalborough, his hometown.[96] The contrast with his father's methods is striking. If Silvester did not win his point in Massachusetts, he sought a higher court across the sea. His son, though quick to recall his Westminster days, had to repair to a smaller and safer forum. Harrison Gray Otis taught the barrister a lesson. John Gardiner had overextended himself. He had bridled at the liberality that lifted his own ambitions. In the short life left to him, he seemed to pick his spots with more care. The next debate found Gardiner and most other lawyers in agreement on the value of licentiousness.

The Independent Province

The Commonwealth of Massachusetts saw a number of institutional controversies in the 1780s and 1790s. The imperial collapse was responsible for much of the tension. Boston, having disowned its metropolis, now was compelled to emulate it. Some townspeople opposed the changes as affronts to local custom and virtue. Others, more cosmopolitan in spirit, welcomed the signs of a continuing refinement. Citizens wrangled over new financial, governmental, and cultural establishments, and about whom these establishments would benefit. Although the outcomes of these controversies varied, the issues and personalities involved usually did not. John Gardiner had a part in nearly all of these debates, and, in this, he was not alone.

More consequential than the common participants were the common rhetorics. Among these, liberalism was the most significant—because it was so readily used, and because it was flexible. To say that rhetoric is broader than policy is to state a commonplace, but liberal rhetoric was more than just the standard political idiom. It also informed an ideology of political and social advantage. A liberal understanding of political economy explained how a fortunately positioned few might benefit from the efforts of the many. It also assumed a multiplicity of positions and opportunities that precluded one set of actors from consistently realizing its ambitions. No one could expect fortune's blessing; everyone had to ground their hopes in particular endeavors.

When Gardiner and the other advocates for a more forward-looking Massachusetts set about developing metropolitan institutions, they did so in a historically fraught atmosphere. The Revolution dominated the collective memory, and projectors had to contend with those who decried their projects as faithless to New England's and America's patriotic traditions. The progressives did what they could to ease their opponents' fears, though some younger men chafed against the fusty virtuemongering of the Revolutionary era. Whatever their temperament or inclination, the reformers and boosters of the postwar period employed a fairly explicit vocabulary. Prosperity and excellence were to be found all the more easily in those communities that understood the partial nature of these and all such gifts. Enterprises, both cultural and commercial, should be allowed to pursue their objects without the interference that the standards of community or some vestigial covenanting spirit had hitherto demanded. The liberals, in most cases, had a strong sense of order—many if not most of them were Federalists— but they believed that society had its own ordering instinct, which tended to bring laudable results when tempered by the economies, refinements, and laws of Anglophone civilization.

The liberalism of the late eighteenth century was more or less openly espoused because it spoke to common urges. The best outcomes might be exclusive property, but the speculative pursuit of one's desires could not and should not be a closed game. Thus we find, in Massachusetts especially, a rage for incorporation. Enterprises multiplied as one group after another plied the commonwealth's legislature for the chance to leverage shared risks into private gains—and advance the public good along the way. The corporate surge meant more people than ever before were involved in the concerns of large businesses; it also brought more lawyers into positions of commercial and financial leadership.[1]

Lawyers were accustomed to being leaders in argument. Their political engagement in the age of resistance and revolution had trained them to serve a general clientele as well as particular clients. Now, and to a much greater degree than previously, lawyers (and many other Americans with ready money) became personally interested in projects that aimed to pay dividends as they improved the nation's capital. This growing pool of investors was becoming practiced in a life of risk and return, and the language and liberal perspective of commercial adventure colored the politics of the time because these investors were the political class.

Lawyers and doctors were the most articulate members of that class, and it is important to remember that they were instructed in their liberalism by past experience as well as the economics of the early national present. Their progressive yet quite hardheaded rhetoric made use of the ideas generated from within Britain's empire—ideas that had special resonance for England's provinces—but it also intellectualized (and so made explicit) habits and orientations adopted during the long imperial moment. The British Empire, like modernity, taught those who would listen that richness and danger were linked: one could not exist without the other. This was, moreover, the wisdom of professionals. They thrived on others' wants and failings, and their practice and influence grew as, in the case of America, the colonies became more and more exposed to the economic and cultural possibilities brokered by the British Empire of the eighteenth century. We should not be surprised that at least two of the postwar innovations championed by many Boston lawyers and their comrades in the "corporation party"—namely, theatrical entertainment and municipal reform—had provincial antecedents closely associated with the extension of metropolitan power.

But all of the efforts and innovations of that time were controversial, not least because the contest of interests was transparent. Some men proposed the independence of Maine because their claims to authority were insupportable in the commonwealth at large. Other citizens formed banks in which they might enjoy a controlling interest. These enterprises were points of leverage, stakes in the general arithmetic of prosperity. Liberals could and did operate on both sides of the equation. They pursued close ends even as they wrote on behalf of an open society, free from settled advantage. Everyone found their proper level eventually, or so it was assumed. This chapter ends with John Gardiner finding his, but it is more concerned with how he and several of his acquaintances—important men in Massachusetts—generalized their ambitions in philosophical terms. We begin with the theater, an issue upon which all liberals agreed and one that saw them muster a full range of arguments.

⟢ · ⟣

In late March of 1793, the General Court substantially repealed the ban on dramatic entertainments in the Commonwealth of Massachusetts. The legislature permitted the construction of a theater in Boston, and this theater opened on Federal Street the next year.[2] The intense period of debate that preceded the legislature's action lasted less than two years, but the quarrel over the theater's role in society was ancient and enduring. One might easily turn to the Greek and Roman sources, but, in the context of New England, one would do just as well to recall the Puritans' animosity toward the stage-play and any other sort of mummery. The prohibitory act dated from 1750, and it quite likely appeared out of a late necessity. Notwithstanding the casual scenes performed in private company or by students, professionally mounted productions were extremely rare in the mainland colonies before the middle of the eighteenth century. That century saw the stage flourish in England, where John Gardiner became a devotee.[3]

The theater's success in Europe had inspired its critics there, the most famous of which was Jean-Jacques Rousseau. His dissent was prompted by Jean d'Alembert's article on Geneva for *l'Encyclopedie*, which asked Rousseau's native city to forsake its prejudices against the dramatic arts. In 1758, Rousseau published his rebuke. He retreated from the universal claims and commitments of the other philosophes. He frowned on the attempt to establish reason as the "common measure" of humanity. He offered "that one ought not to seek among us for what is good for men in general, but only what is good for them in this time or that country."[4] Writing as a "Citizen of Geneva"—while listing in the title page d'Alembert's affiliation with the learned societies of Paris, Prussia, London, Sweden, and Bologna—Rousseau readily defended the narrow pieties of his home.

He did so, of course, by broad and reasoned argument. The theater, Rousseau suggested, was only permissible in an already corrupt society. He reviewed the various advantages a theater might bring: commerce with foreigners, a fluid currency, artistic stimulation, a distraction for rich and poor, an improved taste, and a means "for covering the ugliness of vice with the polish of forms." Bostonians would cite all of these advantages in supporting the dramatic cause; for Rousseau, these effects prevented "bad morals from degenerating into brigandage."[5] In Geneva and in any town where virtue remained, the theater was a malign influence.

Plays could not alter public opinion, for the playwright depended on the public for success. Drama was therefore an exercise in flattery. Even if it presented moral lessons, it was a decadent spectacle that alienated an appreciation of the good from what was more important, the practice of the good. Rousseau explained, "In the quarrels at which we are purely spectators, we immediately take the side of justice, and there is no act of viciousness which does not give us a lively sentiment of indignation so long as we receive no profit from it. But when our interest is involved, our sentiments are as soon corrupted."[6] Other friends of the theater defended it less for teaching morality than for purging immoral passions. Rousseau doubted that this was a "well-administered remedy." He asked, "Is it possible that in order to become temperate and prudent we must begin by being intemperate and mad?"[7]

John Witherspoon, the Scottish divine, expressed similar misgivings in his *Serious Enquiry into the Nature and Effects of the Stage* (1757). He found stage-plays to be "medicine of a very questionable nature." The theater's sinful effects constituted an "infection," and they were not to be encouraged. Even if God tolerated sin, the Christian could not afford to be so generous. The mixture of good and evil in this world did not license persons to pursue good ends by risky means. Witherspoon explicitly rejected Mandeville's view of a healthy society.[8]

Rousseau and Witherspoon make useful reading because they explored themes crucial to the Boston theater controversy as an intellectual event. But neither man's work was really present at that debate. One friend of the theater referred briefly and disgustedly to Rousseau's strictures on knowledge. One opponent identified with the Genevan philosopher but did not describe his argument at any length. While the antitheatrical cause depended on the language of republican virtue, Bostonians did not turn to Rousseau for their script.[9]

John Witherspoon's essay was available to the debaters, but there is no evidence that they made any use of it.[10] Witherspoon was an important figure in America for other reasons. A decade after he published the *Serious Enquiry* in Glasgow, Witherspoon emigrated to the colonies to become president of the College of New Jersey. Through his good offices, many young Americans made their first serious acquaintance with Scottish philosophy. One of the youngest and brightest, James Madison, would pass from Princeton through the critical period to Philadelphia, where there appeared a Constitution that owed as much to him as to any other author. Madison's views on government were no less indebted to Scottish thinkers, and Hume—Mandeville's reluctant heir—was first among them. Despite these uneasy associations, President Witherspoon was undoubtedly proud of his star pupil. Along with Madison, he embraced the cause of the United States; he was the only clergyman to sign the Declaration of Independence.[11]

The Revolution affected the theater's opportunities in America more than did any treatise. In October of 1774, the delegates to the First Continental Congress resolved the following: "We will in our several stations, discourage every species of extravagance and dissipation, especially all horse-racing, and all kinds of gaming, cock-fighting, exhibition of shews, plays, and other expensive diversions."[12] As the revolutionary element in the colonies assumed its best poker face, the most prominent acting troupe west of Bermuda, the American Company of Comedians, decided to close up shop. Its principals withdrew to friendlier climes: David Douglass left for Jamaica, never to return; Lewis Hallam and John Henry went to London, where they found work at Drury Lane and other theaters.

Of course, drama did not disappear entirely. The British occupiers brought unwelcome relief. In besieged Boston, they effected a shocking conversion: Old South Church became a riding school, and Faneuil Hall—once the den of Patriots—became a playhouse. General John Burgoyne was playwright-in-residence. His *Maid of the Oaks* took to the London stage the same year he arrived in Boston, where he mounted its American debut. To another play at Faneuil Hall, Burgoyne added a prologue that lampooned the "Boston prudes" and their Puritan antecedents. Eventually, the cannon of Dorchester Heights halted these exhibitions, and theater fled Massachusetts on the same ships that carried Silvester Gardiner and his fellow Tories.[13]

Yet neither the departure of the British nor America's final victory over them could stop the broader cultural debate. If anything, that debate became more heated. At issue was the character of the new republic. Would its citizens maintain their martial rigor? Would they continue to avoid luxury as a threat to their virtue and liberty? Or did they imagine another destiny? An ambitious people might tolerate the occasional extravagance. Refinement would become the index of progress. In Boston, these matters seemed especially relevant in January of 1785, when the Sans Souci controversy erupted in the local papers.

The Sans Souci Club was—and was also known as—a "tea assembly." There a young man or woman could sip tea or, for a small outlay, punch in the company of other Bostonians very much like himself or herself (and no doubt much innocent pleasure arose from putting hims and hers in such close quarters). Dancing never went out of style. Less innocent perhaps were the card games allowed at the assembly hall, but house rules kept the stakes small. Nevertheless, these "free and easy" affairs did not amuse Samuel Adams. He thought the assembly "totally repugnant to virtue." It threw aside "every necessary restraint—those being esteemed the politest, who are the most careless;—and the most genteel and accomplished, who can, like the figures at a masquerade, mix in each scene, however devoid of delicacy."[14] To Adams's mind and in the minds of other stalwarts who joined their warnings to his, the commonwealth had entered a prodigal phase.

The friends of the assembly were quick to respond. Harrison Gray Otis was the club's organizer and chief advocate. Writing as "Sans Souci," he objected to Adams's malice and severe tone, learned in "some sequestered corner" where he "broods over the virtues of the ancient republics."[15] Another clubman thought his opponents naive:

> If you wish to separate commerce from luxury you erect an impossibility; let us break the bands of society, refuse all connection with the arts and sciences which live under the patronage of commerce and retire to the woods; let us learn of the savages' simplicity of life, to forget humanity, and cut each other's throats without remorse, and even with satisfaction, for the inestimable reward of a garland of parsley, or a wreath of pine.[16]

This argument and the scorn that colored it would linger in Boston as one controversy followed another. Supporters of the tea assembly— and of the theater—valued growth before caution. Progress might have been a mixed blessing, but it promised the most to those who could appreciate what was best.

Like many evacuees, dramatic entertainment returned to America soon after the war. Late in 1785, Hallam and Henry revived the American Company. It was not a promising venture. Other troupes began to compete for the public's attention, and many state legislatures and municipal governments enacted measures against such performances. In Massachusetts, for example, the General Court renewed the ban of 1750. Other events, however, suggested that the immediate postwar reaction against the theater was the reflex of an expiring historical impulse. In 1787, Hallam and Henry produced *The Contrast* in New York, and the play was a notable success. Its author was an American: Royall Tyler, Harvard class of 1776. Two years later, the Pennsylvania Assembly repealed its antitheater laws.[17] A new trend had begun, and the Bay State was just behind the curve.

While the ban on theater remained in place through the 1780s, visiting players presented odd scenes and bits of monologue. A correspondent to the *Herald* praised these entertainments and regretted that a real theater could not yet be built in Boston. Other townspeople were not so welcoming. The theater inculcated "liberal doctrines of gratifying every caprice without hesitation or remorse." Actors were the worst kind of pickpockets, for they preyed on the poorest citizens. Moreover, their "sham theatres" were congenial to the smallpox.[18]

In June of 1790, Hallam and Henry asked the General Court to rescind the ban. They assured the legislature that their company would confine its performances to Boston. A committee appointed by legislators would oversee dramatic content. These concessions played to the town's insular tendencies, but Hallam and Henry directed the main thrust of their arguments elsewhere. A theater would encourage foreigners and Americans from other states to visit Massachusetts. "And an influx of strangers," the petition explained, "must be beneficial, in a pecuniary view at least, to any country: Not to advert to the advantages that must spring from the citizens of all parts of the Confederacy becoming more generally acquainted with each other." A theater would establish a national standard of taste and improve national manners. That improvement might best be measured in the language, for tasteful performances would gradually destroy "those provincialisms which are so disgusting to strangers, and so obnoxious to correctness."[19] In addition to raising and uniting American habits, a theater would more closely bind the various ranks of American society. Money would flow readily from the rich to the poor.

This impressive petition did not convince the legislators. The commonwealth was slow to change its ways. Hallam and Henry's arguments were not exactly new to Bostonians, and soon enough they would be familiar. The theater controversy began in earnest a little over a year after the petition's failure. This time, the push came not from outsiders but from the traditional center of Boston politics. In October of 1791, the town-meeting asked the legislature to repeal the prohibition against theatrical entertainments. An overwhelming majority of attending townsmen made this demand; one report put its number at three-quarters of the whole.[20] When the House of Representatives opened its January session, legislators friendly to the theater's cause initiated the process of repeal. William Tudor moved that the house name a committee to study the matter. After some hesitation, this motion passed at the urging of other representatives, including John Gardiner, Tudor's friend and sometime antagonist. Gardiner served on the committee, but, despite his best efforts, a majority of its members recommended inaction. While the house accepted the committee's negative, the public debate intensified.[21]

In the newspapers, the theater's enemies articulated an austere moral and economic critique. Private amusements desolated public virtue; the stage was a showplace of the obscene and the decadent. Critics did not have to invent or anticipate these perils; in 1792, mendicant actors infested the town, thinly disguised as moral lecturers and acrobats. Referring to the latter, "A Ploughjogger" wrote that "the Tight Rope applied to the legs, is not so effectual to refine the morals of the people, as the old fashion way of applying it to the neck."[22] Almost as bad as the players were their patrons—or at least those patrons who should have known better. "Alfred" scolded well-educated supporters of the theater for "not only giving a specimen of the depravity of their own tastes, but also vitiating the taste of their fellow townsmen." Another critic, passing himself off as "a plain countryman," wondered if the "Aristocrats" were agitating for repeal in order to derange the people's "republican principles." These principles were, after all, a matter of priorities. The average tradesman or laborer, it was argued, could not frequent the theater and still hope to support his family.[23]

Republican critics appealed to their traditional allies, the tradesmen, precisely because that alliance was no longer secure. Repeal was a popular cause; the town-meeting had proven that. One "Citizen" thought that the theater's enemies were unfairly severe. They wound "the machine of Society" too tightly and denied to mechanics all the best things in life. The writer remembered that Thomas Hutchinson had been just as stingy. "A Mechanick and Voter" accused those who opposed the town-meeting's decision of acting out of "aristocratick, monopolizing principles." He asked, "Are we not able to take care of ourselves and our purses?" As the drama faction assented to this question, it was able to define its interest as liberty's interest. While critics spluttered that the "solemn ideas of natural and unalienable rights" had nothing whatsoever to do with the "frolics" of playgoers, advocates succeeded in making that very connection.[24] In this way, the Bostonians who spoke for the theater could convincingly speak for the people as well.

The character of public opinion was the crucial issue in a debate that arose within the larger controversy. The personality of this debate is as interesting as its substance. James Sullivan, whom we have met before as Gardiner's unlikely advocate and as the attorney general of Massachusetts, wrote as "A Friend to Peace." In 1792, an outlaw theater was doing a good business on Boston's Board Alley, and Sullivan was alarmed by the brazen defiance of legal authority. He stressed that the "will of the people is the only proper support of a free government. And the first dictate in a republic is the submission of the minority to the voice of the majority."[25] Laws expressed the popular will, and if persons objected to a law, they could seek two constitutional remedies: they could elect likeminded legislators and hope for a new majority, or one of their number could offer himself up as a test case before the courts and hope for a favorable verdict. To Sullivan's mind, the theater's friends had pursued neither course. Instead, their insolent challenge to the law was a kind of violence against the commonwealth.[26]

His opponent, "Menander," was John Quincy Adams. Adams was introduced to Shakespeare by his mother, the redoubtable Abigail, and had seen plays in Europe while traveling with his father, then a Revolutionary diplomat. After the war, young Adams went to Harvard and, soon after his matriculation, was to be found reciting passages of *Macbeth* before the assembled college in Holden Chapel. This performance complemented two others from the same period. Adams's maiden speech before Phi Beta Kappa affirmed the idea that "civil discord is advantageous to society." Although Adams was no friend of disorder (or Daniel Shays, whose rebellion was on everyone's mind), he did think that much good could come from what was in itself inadvisable or even immoral. When, at another college exhibition, he was asked to defend the legal profession, he did so by pointing out that all professionals— lawyers, of course, but doctors and clergymen too—were sustained by human vice. Five years on, Adams rose to the theater's defense.[27]

He thought that an offensive law had to be "openly violated"; only then would the authorities confront the pressing issues. The citizen who violated the law did not invite prosecution so much as test the government's will. The typical theater-man was not so full of "Hibernian blood" as to deliver himself up to the sheriff.[28] As for the "will of the people," Adams construed that concept much more broadly than Sullivan had. He was not deferential to the General Court. When claiming their rights, the people might appeal directly to the state constitution, which was superior to legislative statute. Adams declared that "every individual in the community has the same right with the legislature to put his own honest construction upon every clause." Of course, individuals had to obey the law, but legislators also had to take care, lest they "suffer the continuance of any Statute, which the spirit of the people will not allow the execution." Reformers were always quick to grant radical powers to public opinion as long as they could freely invoke it. The Federalists pursued this strategy in recreating the United States.[29] The friends of drama labored in the same tradition.

They represented what they thought to be the largest and most vigorous part of the community: the Bostonians who wanted to have fun, who were not ashamed of wanting it, and who counted a good time among their liberties. The advocates made bold claims: "The great body of the people WILL this species of amusement: Their WILL finally must triumph over opposition." The ban of 1750 suggested "a distrust of the people to pursue their own happiness."[30] During the theater controversy, happiness—always the bottom line in politics—came to the fore as a critical issue.

The opponents of the theater saw in its friends an excessive mirth. Natural rights were a serious business, and the playhouse gang was too young, too gay, and too high-toned to do them justice. One critic looked at the theater's supporters and asked, "Are any of them known by their dissipation, their nightly revels, their debauched manner of life?"[31] The question assumed an answer and made a point. Although supporters cried freedom, their goal was to advance their own vicious lifestyle. The same critic also noticed that young lawyers— "puppies," he called them—were especially prominent in "the Play House party." He reminded his readers that the legal "Order" could talk broadly of rights but was apt to interpret them in an exclusive and perplexing fashion.[32]

The theater's friends, in turn, made much of their opponents' narrowness. We have already seen how the antitheatrical faction appeared to be miserly with other people's money. According to "Rights of Man" and other writers, it was also a party of killjoys. The Bostonians who defended the ban were "restless Croakers"; they had "no relish for amusements." This ill humor, unpleasant as it was, evinced a more damning offense: the theater's enemies were backward. "Candidus" wrote, "In vain then may the gloomy Bigot vent his spleen . . . The progress of light and reason is rapid, ignorance and superstition are fast wasting away, and the time I trust is near at hand, when the Americans will cherish all those refinements, which tend to meliorate the condition of humanity."[33] These were not original sentiments. Hallam and Henry linked the theater to the improvement of manners in their petition to the General Court. They stated their case carefully. When the Massachusetts House reopened the debate at the beginning of 1792, its members enjoyed a boisterous version of the same argument, courtesy of John Gardiner.

Gardiner's speech on the theater came two years after his reforming speeches on the law and its practitioners. That was an uncomfortable memory for some of his peers, and his advocacy might have hindered as much as helped the theater's cause.[34] However, his position was no longer eccentric; most lawyers and most Bostonians shared it. His speech, delivered in January, was published that summer in expanded form. In the preface, he warned that "furious bigots" would strive against repeal; fortunately, "a few of the more learned, liberal, and enlightened, may applaud that effort which attempts to dispel the dark fogs of an absurd, blind, superstition, and to permit the cheering beams of the enlightening Sun of Manly Reason to shine in upon us."[35] In each of his endeavors, this vision of progress was constant. It was also the least controversial of his expressions. While aggressive to be sure, this celebration of liberality was large enough to subsume a world of disputes.

Gardiner spoke as a man of big ideas and as a man of experience. He reminded listeners and readers of his theatergoing abroad, in London, Bath, and other British cities. He also brought to the debate a tolerant sensibility formed during his English career. Tolerance—one should add—of a sort; Gardiner had no patience for the Society for the Reformation of Manners, which tried to purge all moral squalor from London's streets. He charged that this "self-created" society had fallen into disrepute for harboring sodomites. A hatred for the "helpless sex" drove its reforms. The society caused general warrants to be issued for the arrest of all lewd women. To a Wilkite, this was obnoxious policy on at least two counts. He fondly related how one jailed innocent sued before Lord Mansfield and "recovered handsome damages against the brutal Reformer."[36]

Indeed, Gardiner argued that one could make too much of innocence. In London, he had seen no reason to persecute whores, the "Sisterhood of the Strand." Prostitution had always lingered about the stage, and that association would continue after Gardiner's side carried the argument. The builders of Boston's Federal Street Theatre made the customary allowances for a courtesans' row, and they provided a discreet exit to those patrons busy with assignations.[37] Gardiner and other likeminded advocates held that blanket reforms meant to quash all untoward behavior were misguided and, in the end, dangerous to the freedoms that inevitably civilized a society.

Many of the same writers accepted the need for some regulation. Bostonians were not so liberal as to dispense with every safeguard. Some genuinely believed that the theater, if properly controlled, might become a moral showplace. Undoubtedly others wrote of controls in order to placate the fearful.³⁸ John Gardiner suggested that the town-meeting choose five censors from all walks of life, mechanics and merchants, lawyers and ministers. He reminded the clergy "that they are directed not to be righteous over much—not to act the part of Brutish Churls, to condemn every species of decent, gay, good humour . . . nor to renounce all the innocent recreations of a polished society, in which their profession constitutes them gentlemen."³⁹ This was odd regulation indeed. The judges were the judged. If they were so unenlightened as to restrict the theater, then they had no place in the audience or among the leaders of an improving commonwealth.⁴⁰

Another advocate for drama, William Haliburton, was even more attentive to the social consequences of improvement. Under the name of "A Bostonian," he wrote the *Effects of the Stage on the Manners of a People* in the same year that Gardiner delivered and then published his theater speech. There were other similarities. Haliburton was born in Boston in the late 1730s; he and Gardiner might have met as pupils at the Latin School. Haliburton was a lawyer, but the bulk of his professional life had been spent out of the thirteen colonies. In 1761, he moved to Nova Scotia, where he lived until his death in 1817. He returned to Massachusetts now and then to visit family. On one such visit, he submitted his treatise on the stage.⁴¹

Like Gardiner, Haliburton carried the marks of Scotland's influence. He was half Scottish, and he corresponded with the most famous Scott of all, Sir Walter. Haliburton's writings betray his familiarity with the work of Adam Smith, Gardiner's instructor in ethics and jurisprudence. Early in the *Effects of the Stage*, Haliburton discussed the moral sense, the "medling Observer in his bosom station'd." The functional society depended on this sense, not because it was infallible, but because it was common: "Whence, all the species from the highest to the lowest, are subjected to the observation and censure of each individual; and each, when inclined to sit in judgment on his peers, remembers that he in his turn shall be judged by others."⁴² These ideas found their most enduring expression in the *Theory of Moral Sentiments*, wherein Smith argued that "[e]very faculty in one man is the measure by which he judges of the like faculty in another," and therefore:

The man within the breast, the abstract and ideal spectator of our sentiments and conduct, requires often to be awakened and put in mind of his
duty, by the presence of the real spectator: and it is always from that
spectator, from whom we can expect the least sympathy and indulgence,
that we are likely to learn the most complete lesson of self-command.[43]

Social stability was not the individual conscience writ large; instead, it
was the product of anxious considerations and exchanges. As Haliburton told his daughter, "So may your virtues, like the action and reaction
of profitable Commerce, serve to increace the sum of your own Felicity,
while it enlargeth that of Others."[44]

A theater in Boston would, according to its champions, promote a
happy society. One of its necessary conditions was the division of labor.
In *Effects of the Stage*, Haliburton explained that "[t]o perfect the social
union, strength, wealth, talents, genius and capacity (the gifts of heaven)
are bestowed on different persons and in different proportions."[45] He was
more explicit in private. Human beings often complained of inequalities,
but these were "useful beauties in the Divine System." In fact, "[n]oth-
ing could produce greater evil in society than uniformity of sentiment,
taste, and opinion." Equals would covet the same land, the same horse,
and the same woman; they "would become as useless, and as indifferent
to each other, as cattle who graze the verdant meads!" Inequality, on the
other hand, connected the "human race in one golden chain of love."[46]

A likeminded Bostonian, writing that same year in the *Columbian
Centinel*, warned against jealousy of the rich. He asked the townspeople
to reflect on what one of their number had accomplished by building a
large mansion among them. This fortunate man employed many poor.
Yes, he took pleasure in his home, but, the writer reasoned, "his very
happiness becomes mine by sympathy, and I am further indebted to him
for the pleasure excited in me, every time I behold his fine house."[47] And
a playhouse would be no different. Its maintenance would require all
manner of industries and attract the interest of all manner of people.
Haliburton compiled a long and detailed list of necessary employments,
and Gardiner wrote of the "emolumentary advantages" to Boston's artisans. These workers would then become the theater's patrons as well
as its builders. While trying to convince Sam Adams of the stage's utility, Elbridge Gerry argued that the universal popularity of theater
smoothed over the fractures opened by social envy.[48]

But patronage was discriminating. The stage was to inspire the
taste and talents of Bostonians who were already blessed with some

measure of privilege. Taste, as Haliburton pointed out, depended on leisure. Only men and women of means could properly cultivate "the polite arts." A theater confirmed that a society had reached a certain level of sophistication or—more to the point—that it could support different levels of opportunity and accomplishment. The theater also trained the privileged to use their leisure properly. One advocate explained that the human mind was naturally indolent; some external stimuli were necessary to excite its ambition and push "to maturity its various fruits." The bar, for example, was full of capable men who could devote to the dramatic muse "many hours which might otherwise glide away with little advantage to themselves or to society."[49] The best commonwealth made the most of its most able citizens.

Liberality and distinction went hand in hand. The friends of the theater were not afraid to let society develop as it would. They were confident of progress and hoped to be in its van. Economic growth would be good for nearly everybody and especially kind to those people with the smarts and the savvy to exploit new opportunities. The ban on theatrical entertainments stifled growth and, with it, excellence. Men and women, said theater's advocates, should spend their money and their time as they wished. If they chose wrongly, someone would benefit from their mistake. That was how the economy worked if all of its resources were brought into play. Freedom was messy but conducive to what Haliburton called "the general fitness of things."[50]

Health was no longer a function of purity. In the midst of the theater controversy, the merchant Nathaniel Cutting returned to Boston after a few years abroad. Between visits to the outlaw playhouse, Cutting toured a sailcloth factory normally worked by "blooming girls." On that day, however, the girls were at the inoculating hospital. They undoubtedly returned as productive as ever and all the more reliable for their stay.[51] Boston was winning the war against smallpox, but an epidemic was alarming still. The General Court fled to Concord during the same year it reconsidered the theater ban. Disease and the theater were often proximate in political conversations. The *Independent Chronicle* spliced a report on the Federal Street Theatre with news of yellow fever in Philadelphia.[52] The comparisons were unfriendly in the main, but the exceptions are telling. Unlike Witherspoon and Rousseau, William Haliburton thought drama was the perfect remedy for social ills. "As in pharmacy," he wrote, "the most efficacious medicines are those which are capable of doing most mischief; so the stage and music, having the greatest effect on mankind, are capable of doing the most hurt, and the most good." Another advocate of repeal seconded this prescription; a theater would make an excellent "substitute" for the whorehouse and gambling den. These writers knew that any promising enterprise held an element of danger.[53]

The theater interest understood Boston's potential in terms of this tolerant political economy. Boston was more than a town; it was, or at least should have been, a metropolis. Such a city exerted considerable cultural influence, but it did so at some cost. Haliburton asked the people of Massachusetts, and especially those living in the state's "sylvan bowers," to reflect on the merchants and mechanics "labouring on from day to day, in the dirt and smoke of Boston, stunned with the din of trades, and the rattling of cars, breathing naught but infected air, to procure you, from every quarter, the necessaries, the comforts, and delights of life."[54] These were ominous words to spend on a seaport of eighteen thousand inhabitants. London or a future New York might better have fit the bill, but then, the supporters of theater liked to think ahead and to think big. A proper metropolis had problems to match its achievements. A theater helped to manage these stresses, but it also represented the sum of skill and indulgence and ambition that was the modern city. The stage, though occasionally licentious, ratified a city's greatness, and a great city, for all its ugliness, improved the country. If Boston became the metropolis it promised to be, it would raise the value of land in the outlying districts, and its manners—"be they what they may"—would set the tone for the commonwealth and, perhaps, for the republic.[55]

In the early 1790s, however, these speculations were as yet idle. There was no theater in Boston, and the town lagged behind its rivals. One advocate for drama wondered, "Is the Legislature of Massachusetts less enlightened than that of Pennsylvania, or will it be less liberal?"[56] Pennsylvania's assembly had legalized the stage, and Philadelphia was reaping the benefits. The *Centinel* noted George Washington's presence at that city's new playhouse. Boston, on the other hand, did not attract the right company. Unlike Philadelphia and New York, the capital of Massachusetts was a dull place. Surely a theater, wrote one booster, would "afford amusement to strangers, who universally complain, that their residence in this town is a blank in their lives."[57] If the town conformed to the cosmopolitan expectations of merchants who circulated through it, the region's professionals and entrepreneurs who shared their liberal sentiments were confident of large material and cultural gains. Boston would become a center of wealth and culture, and those persons who advanced the town's designs would see their own fortunes and influence grow.

Not much could be expected, however, of fledgling enterprises like the Board Alley Theatre. Defying the ban, five local investors opened this establishment in August of 1792. At least one visitor, Nathaniel Cutting, was not impressed. He thought the theater a "rough boarded hovel," and at one performance, he found that an actress "assassinated both the language and sense" when delivering her monologue.[58] Bostonians were not really fooled, but they were also not disappointed. The merchant Samuel Breck remembered many a good laugh had at the theater. He also remembered it as a muddy, almost indecent place. Young men were prominent in the audience, and women were usually absent. On one occasion, a stage hunter almost killed a black servant impersonating a bear. The wadding from the huntsman's musket apparently penetrated the poor fellow's hindquarters, despite the protection of a "shaggy costume." Before the extent of his injuries was known, "he lay kicking amid a thunder of applause, and we all agreed that he died very well and very naturally." Breck commented that such "gaucheries occurred often . . . among a people in an incipient stage of playhouse amusement."[59]

This theater almost came to an appropriately rowdy end. In December, Governor Hancock asked his attorney general, James Sullivan, to move against the outlaws. After the second act of Sheridan's *School for Scandal*—the play within the play that so mystified the Yankee Jonathan in Royall Tyler's *Contrast*—a sheriff mounted the stage and arrested the theater's manager. A brief riot ensued. At a hearing held the next day at Faneuil Hall, Harrison Gray Otis and William Tudor, counsel for the defense, proved that the arrest warrant violated the state constitution. Sullivan was heckled for his error, though rumor had it that he sabotaged his own case out of sympathy for the liberals. Hancock raised a mob against the Board Alley, but even had these roughs succeeded in demolishing the crude playhouse, they could not have stopped the theatrical cause.[60] Later that month, the town-meeting again remonstrated for repeal, and, of all the men there, only one dissented. In the spring, the General Court cleared the way for the more elegant structure designed by Charles Bulfinch, the chief architect of the federal style.[61]

Throughout the theater controversy, the prohibitionists sensed the issue slipping away from them. The popularity of the stage was obvious and galling. The progressives who led the repeal campaign were, in their opponents' minds, exactly those Bostonians who most wanted to distinguish themselves from the common townspeople. How odd it was, complained one critic, that members of "the Corporation and Play House party" would court a class of citizens which, on other occasions, they had dismissed as rabble.[62] This writer, still smarting from the December town-meeting's near unanimous call for repeal, was probably comforted by thoughts of past debates, when the rhetoric of the pretentious elite had fallen on deaf ears. As his partisan epithets suggest, one such debate concerned the incorporation of Boston.

The capital of Massachusetts was not, after all, a city. Until 1822, it was a town. All of the men who attended town-meeting were its formal governors. While the town elected selectmen and constables and hogreeves, these functionaries did not lead a representative democracy. They performed basic maintenance, but every important matter of government passed through Faneuil Hall, where the town met as a body. Not everyone bothered to come to meeting, of course, and critics of the town system made much of that fact. These reformers wanted Boston to assume the privileges of a city. Once the legislature passed an act of incorporation, a mayor and a council—the titles varied— would exercise decisive powers, and an effective police force would enforce city ordinances. These plans appeared as early as 1708, and they incited a number of political rows after the Revolution.[63]

Many of the disputants would take part in the theater controversy as well. At a town-meeting in May of 1784, the reformers proposed the corporate reorganization of Boston. Their chief spokesman was Joseph Barrell. In the late 1780s, he mounted the *Columbia*'s pioneering voyage to Canton via the Pacific Northwest, a source of marketable otter pelts. As Barrell expanded opportunities abroad, he did not ignore a chance to liberate his home port. He was one of the proprietors of the Board Alley Theatre.[64] In 1784, however, his proposals ran into the brick-hard morality of Samuel Adams. This old naysayer held incorporation, the theater, and the Sans Souci Club in equally low regard. He responded to Barrell by remarking that some Americans had "a hankering for the leeks and onions of Great Britain." Among the men who took exception to Adams's curious turn of phrase was William Tudor, a supporter of the city plan who would defend the theater in the courts and in the House of Representatives.[65]

Each party to the argument strained to describe the other's destructive interests. Sam Adams began in a conservative and sentimental fashion. The town government had time and glory on its side. Adams wondered why anyone would tinker with good fortune. Why fix what was not broken? He had an answer, of course. Aristocrats were not so known by their intransigence as by their selfish innovations. "A love of novelty, and a desire for changes, had been," Adams warned, "an avenue through which aristocracy had entered."[66] Another jeremiah contended that while "the buzy and impetuous" geniuses of incorporation built their utopia, Boston would fall under the control of the few. Worse still, these few would probably be lawyers. "A Mechanick" pictured them as the agents of "the *better sort*," a mushroom gentry who despised the town system as a brake to their ambitions. After incorporation, the people would decline into vassalage, and their new masters could have the theater they always wanted.[67]

"Publicola" saw a "detested Hutchinsonian plan" at work. He wrote, "Could we draw aside the curtain, and peep behind the scene, should we not find those at whose instigation the diabolical scheme for incorporating the town was brought . . . to be some of the identical recreants who bowed the knee to the calf of Britain, who in their hearts are inveterate enemies of republicanism?"[68] The first accusation was dubious; the second, perhaps, was nearer the truth. More interesting than either was the city faction's view of interestedness, of its dangers and its expediencies.

In many instances, these reformers repaid their critics in kind. They explained that Hutchinson and "the aristocrat" were hobgoblins who hid their conjurors' desire for fame. Incorporation's foes would cluck over these and other bogeys, but what they really feared was any change in a system by which a small number of demagogues exerted an undue influence on the town. Joseph Barrell estimated, rather outrageously, that a Bostonian who came to every town-meeting lost a tenth of his working life. No responsible tradesman or merchant could afford to do that, and as a result the meetings were often sparsely attended. The management of all was left to a leisured clique.[69]

The city plan would professionalize the uneven nature of government. What was once conspiracy would become the model of efficiency. If a few leaders inevitably exercised the power of the many, then Boston's wisest course was to adopt a system that ensured fair representation and enabled the representatives to govern effectively. This argument was similar to that made almost half a century before, when Boston's leading merchants tried (and failed) to establish a central market at Peter Faneuil's hall. The town was outgrowing its old ways, and there was no time for half-measures. "Anti-Aristocratick" was sure that any attempt "to restore our rotton, worn-out constitution, is like sewing patches of new cloth, upon an old thread bare garment." Boston needed to purge itself in order to make room for new methods and perhaps new men. One advocate described incorporation as a "radical cure." The city that emerged would be more energetic, and its government, unlike the town's, would be full of "competent persons."[70]

As in other debates, the two sides competed for the artisan's vote, and this contest had a clear winner when the city plan was broached in the mid-1780s. Incorporation did not offer something tangible, like a theater, and soon enough Bostonians would enjoy the theater's amusements without having relinquished their ancient prerogatives. Much of the rhetoric in the town-and-city controversy amounted to little more than shadowboxing. The city party tried to convince the mechanics that they were the victims of demagoguery, and the town party told them they were about to be.[71] Bostonians made up their own minds. In June of 1784, the town met to consider the reforms Barrell and others had proposed the previous month. One observer thought Faneuil Hall had never been so full. When reformers tried to discuss their plan, they were shouted down by calls for "the Question." The plan failed by an overwhelming margin, and the hall shook with the roar of "No innovations." The *Centinel* drily commented "that it would have been more to the honour of the town, had the same business been performed with more civility."[72]

For the reformers, Boston's dignity was precisely the point. They were anxious about the town's prospects. New York was a city, and it was growing rapidly. The other cities in America were not about to abandon their governments and become "paltry towns."[73] Boston had to keep up. An "American" argued that incorporation was a part of progress. Drawing upon William Robertson, this author described how European towns had weaned themselves from the protection of the nobility by winning city privileges. Liberty brought with it an enriching spirit of industry. The choice for Massachusetts and its principal towns was obvious, and the town loyalists were obviously backward: "they are opposing a measure to which we are indebted for the reformation from popery, for the excellence of the manufactures we import, and for the punctuality of foreigners in their dealings: A measure which must sooner or later be adopted; or we shall be poor—destitute of money, credit, or friends."[74] Here was an argument John Gardiner might have easily made, whereby local politics telescoped into a grand revolution of manners. But in 1785, he set his pen against the city cause.

◄§ · §►

Gardiner remained true to his peculiar historical vision, and some of the best history, to his taste, was personal history. Writing as "Old Whackum," he informed his readers that he had lived in the largest cities in Great Britain, including the mighty London. For all their regulations and police powers, he found nothing in their governments worth a Bostonian's envy. As any Wilkite knew, London was a disorderly place, but more alarming by far were the abuses committed in the name of order. Gardiner referred to Vaughan's *Reports* and the case of Edward Bushell, a juror whom the city magistrates imprisoned for failing to convict William Penn of certain "tumults." The details escalated from there; Gardiner could not escape the rich idiom of his British career. One of his "Whackum" pieces begins with these lines: "Let not a mob of tyrants seize the helm, / Nor titled Upstarts league to rob the realm, / Let not, whatever other ills assail, / A damned Aristocracy prevail."[75] The poet was Charles Churchill, the ribald vicar and friend of Wilkes.

Even more telling than his past attachments was the history Gardiner told but had never experienced. In his critique of the city reforms, he further extended the myth of New England. "Our manly Ancestors," he explained, flew to America from the tyrannies of church, state, and city too. Then, in the early eighteenth century, when the first attempts were made to incorporate Boston, "the free spirit of our democratic republican fore-fathers burst forth at once, and instantly crushed that whelp of the aristocratick monster."[76] Other Yankees (John Adams most prominently, in his "Dissertation on the Canon and the Feudal Law") had long since discovered the Puritan libertarian. John Gardiner, the scion of an Anglican Rhode Island family, still saw promise in this material.

In the same vein and with similar nerve, he raised the "hedious spectre" of Adams's departed nemesis, Thomas Hutchinson. This "canting hypocritick ambodexter" had hoped for Boston's incorporation. In a 1770 letter to Hillsborough, the secretary of state, Hutchinson explained that the selectmen were "the Creatures of the Populace." Only a mayor and aldermen could manage the lower classes. Commenting on this letter, Gardiner declared that "these low folks" had brought more honor to the town than its best people. The Revolution had practically begun in Boston's town-meeting.[77] Of course, Gardiner himself was not even in mainland America during those heady days. In 1770, the year of the Boston Massacre, he was petitioning the Privy Council to quell St. Christopher's upstart assembly. Fifteen years later, he was running from his father's Toryism, though not necessarily his father's property. When reading Gardiner's anti-city pieces of 1785, one must remember that the author was an alien in his hometown. He returned in 1783 and over the next three years threw himself into controversies of church and state. By the end of 1786, he was a leading citizen of Pownalborough on the Kennebec.

The advocates for incorporation renewed their efforts in 1792, and, once again, "Old Whackum" stalked the *Centinel*'s pages. This time, however, he did not seem to notice the reformers. Gardiner was busy with Abraham Bishop, a Connecticut native who had traveled Europe disguised as a mendicant friar. Returning to New England, Bishop lectured from his *Visions of Clio*, a meditation on science and religion. He also disapproved of the theater, prompting Gardiner's lyrical mockery.[78] Gardiner associated Bishop with the major varieties of nonsense: the prudish, the superstitious, and the provincial. This last association is clear from one footnote, wherein Gardiner lampooned the "Country Yankees of Connecticut, as well as of Massachusetts."

Most disturbing to him was their abuse of language. Noah Webster, whom Gardiner described as Bishop's cousin and the "scourge of all grammar," had the gall to recommend spelling "neighbour" as it sounded: *nabor.* (Here Gardiner anticipated the Anglophilic hauteur that characterized his son's circle of Federalist literati.) Turning away from this New England model of erudition, Gardiner relied instead on the wisdom of Jonathan Swift, who, upon noticing the several London dialects, warned against confounding orthography with speech.[79] Whatever his opinion of city government, "Old Whackum" believed that Americans—and New Englanders in particular—had a lot yet to learn from the wider world.

Provincialism was a politically charged issue in 1792 Boston. Its adherents and critics clashed in the theater controversy, and its rhetoric colored the debate over municipal reforms. At the beginning of the year, a committee recommended several improvements. The town would divide into nine wards and annually elect a legislative council. This council would have the power to appoint and remove most of the town's executive officers. These plans were alarming to many Bostonians. One wrote that many of the reformers were "exotics." The town could not entrust its future to newcomers who had no interest in its past.[80]

"A Town-Born Child" put no stock in these accusations. He reminded readers that most of the members of the reforming committee were natives of Boston. He remarked on how New York and Philadelphia were "totally lost to all these patriotick home born feelings" and yet grew richer each day. Boston would do well to think as broadly. After all, "a town is a mere creature of legislative authority, and this authority is again a mere creature of the sovereignty of the people's in a whole State or Commonwealth." Change made much more sense as one moved away from the particulars of each case, or the customs of each town, to the general requirements of a productive society. The enemies of reform seemed to think in the opposite direction. "Town-Born" wondered how they could tolerate the national government, in which the states united as one, if a city was already too "aristocratical" for their comfort.[81]

This reformer's Federalist bias may be clear, but his example should not encourage a partisan reading of the town and theater controversies. In the early 1790s, political affiliations were much more various than was the case ten or even five years later, when national parties started to consolidate loose factional interests into more disciplined— and, from the historian's point of view, more easily remembered— blocs.[82] In Boston, men who later found themselves in very different camps could agree that the town needed a playhouse and a less antiquated form of government. They shared a liberal disposition toward progress and enterprise. As we have seen, this was still a controversial attitude, and its wide currency among men of clashing political stripes is just as important as the issues that occasionally separated them.

Consider two men who spoke on behalf of the city plan of 1792. One is not surprised at the advocacy of Harrison Gray Otis. He was, in his biographer's words, the "urbane Federalist." The casual student of American history remembers him as one of the principals at the Hartford Convention. He survived that scandal and lived long enough to be a mayor of the belatedly incorporated Boston and one of the city's grand old men. Born to a family of famous Tories and even more famous rebels, Otis multiplied his fortunes in the practice of law and in real estate. He was one of the developers of Beacon Hill.[83] Readers of this essay are already familiar with the young Otis, the presiding genius of the Sans Souci and the defender of Edmund Freeman and the Board Alley Theatre.

One of his partners in the municipal scheme of 1792 was Dr. Charles Jarvis. He was a prominent supporter of John Hancock and Sam Adams. After Jefferson won the presidency, Jarvis's reward for long service was an appointment to the Federal Marine Hospital in Charlestown. The good doctor was not, however, as tightly wound as Adams, his political patron. One Sunday evening, when an acquaintance asked him if he were on his way to church, the fighting cock hidden in his coat crowed evidence of a different pastime. He was one of the proprietors of the Board Alley, and it was his unfortunate servant who played the "Bruin" too well and so nearly became Boston's first martyr for the stage. By the standards of the day, neither Jarvis nor Otis was narrowly provincial, and, what is more certain, neither man encouraged that reputation. On the other hand, they were not "exotics," to use the language of the city debate. They were locals, and they were popular. During the 1790s, both men won over a majority of Boston's voters. Jarvis represented the town in the General Court; Otis did so in the U.S. House of Representatives.[84]

Despite their popularity, they could not save their municipal reforms from defeat. At a meeting in late January of 1792, the town declined to act on the committee's recommendations. The tally was 517 for and 701 against the plan. John Quincy Adams remembered the meeting this way: "seven hundred men, who looked as if they had been collected from all the jails on the continent, with Ben. Austin like another Jack Cade at their head, outvoted by their numbers all the combined weight and influence of wealth and abilities and of integrity, of the whole town."[85] Benjamin Austin Jr.'s role was an accustomed one. He had been a confirmed troublemaker since his "Honestus" days, if not before. Nevertheless, one cannot take Adams's account at face value. At least one wealthy and influential citizen stood on the negative side of the question. His name was Perez Morton.

Like Otis and "Honestus," Morton is a character we have met before. He helped to bring a unitarian liturgy and lay ordination to King's Chapel. His approach then was quite opposite to the one he took at the town-meetings of early 1792. As one of the lawyers who drafted the chapel's apologia, he used the language of incorporation to break with the past.[86] Morton was a flexible and enterprising fellow—as flexible, even, as John Gardiner, his chapel comrade. He was born in Plymouth but grew up in Boston, where his father owned the White Horse Tavern. After attending the Latin School and Harvard, Morton studied the law in time to test his training in the Revolution. He prosecuted some Tories and defended others, though he was himself the thorough Patriot, serving on the town's Committee of Correspondence and Safety. Toward the end of the war, he married Sarah Wentworth Apthorp and thus joined one of Boston's most prominent Tory families. His wife's grandfather was Charles Apthorp, a warden of King's Chapel and a Kennebeck Proprietor.[87]

Morton was active in many notable controversies, and his positions were usually not what one would expect of an old town conservative. He and his wife frequented the Sans Souci Club. He remonstrated against the ban on stage-plays, and he was a stockholder in the Federal Street Theatre. A critic very likely had Morton in mind when he wrote of the "debauched manner of life" and "domestic quarrels" of the theater's advocates. While Sarah was an acclaimed poetess, Perez contributed to literature in a different fashion. He seduced his wife's sister, Fanny Apthorp, and the scandal of her subsequent ruin and death inspired William Hill Brown to write *The Power of Sympathy*, regarded by many scholars as the first American novel. Morton's career continued without a check. He was, like Charles Jarvis, a consistent supporter of John Hancock and Samuel Adams. In time he became one of the state's leading Democratic-Republicans, but he was one of the few members of that party to live in a house designed by Charles Bulfinch.[88]

Morton's lifestyle, extravagant though it was, could not deliver the attorney general's office, which he in fact occupied for twenty-two consecutive years in the nineteenth century. Perez Morton was a successful politician because he cultivated particular loyalties and constituencies. This son of a tavernkeeper quickly learned that broadmindedness needed a spine of tenacity. His first lessons in organizational grit came at the Green Dragon, which the Freemasons of St. Andrew's Lodge purchased in 1765. Morton joined St. Andrew's, and he began his public life by eulogizing its grand master, Dr. Joseph Warren, the hero of Bunker Hill. In the 1790s, the Green Dragon was the home of the Massachusetts Constitutional (or Democratic-Republican) Society. Morton was one of its chieftains, though enemies portrayed him as a man embarrassed by the low company his politics forced him to keep.[89] Whatever his private feelings, he knew that there was strength in such company, and that was why, during the town fight of 1792, he took his place with "Jack Cade" and the seven hundred.

Morton's example is instructive to the student of liberalism in early national Massachusetts. The liberal argued that the happiness of a society would increase if its constituent elements—"the parts of the system"—were free to act as their natures demanded and their abilities allowed. This idea could turn in many directions. To the merchant, it promised a lively business. To the optimist, it affirmed the promise of human potential, while the pessimist consoled himself with the knowledge that imperfections served a higher purpose. To the ambitious and capable, liberalism confirmed that persons found their proper stations. In all cases, it was a vocabulary that connected private considerations to the commonweal.

Liberalism was not, however, an end in itself. It described a process, which depended on the pursuit of various ends that were often contradictory. At King's Chapel, Perez Morton preached free association in order to advance the interests of the new proprietors. John Gardiner and most of his professional opponents were of the liberal persuasion; their disagreements arose because Gardiner had little to lose. The theater campaign was a rousing success because, in material terms, there was no real conflict. No one had an abiding interest in the ban, and principled objections could not carry the debate. In short, if one is to understand the social function of liberalism, one must examine the investments fundamental to and extended by it.

◆⟨ · ⟩◆

The 1790s were years of intense financial speculation. Money continued to pour into the woodscapes of Maine and New York. Petitions poured into the state legislatures, requesting acts of incorporation that would enable factories, bridges, academies, and banks to organize the underdeveloped resources of the new nation. Banks were doubly important because financial capital was itself a resource as well as the instrument by which other forms of capital—environmental, industrial, even literary—might be employed. The federal government, under Hamilton's leadership, was a partner in speculation, assuming state debts and strengthening the position of creditors.[90]

Boston was caught up in the rage. In 1790, when John Quincy Adams considered his prospects as a fledgling attorney, he noticed that the town's most successful lawyers were dealing in public securities. Christopher Gore and Harrison Gray Otis, for example, "played at that hazardous game . . . and have been enabled by the temporary possession of property belonging to foreigners, to become masters of sums to an equal amount before they have been called upon for payment."[91] The theater's advocates were right: "strangers" *were* good for business. In 1792, during the debate over municipal reforms, one observer asked

Bostonians not to heed the opinions of "a few overgrown six per cent. gentry, those drones in the hive of society." That same year, the *Centinel* carried this dispatch from Boston's municipal rival, New York: "We are all Banking Mad, here. Speculation absorbs every principle, and one would suppose from the immense sums subscribed, that this city was the tunnel of the mines of Peru, and the rivulets of Indostan. Much it puzzles me to guess the issue."[92] However baffling, similar projects were afloat by Massachusetts Bay. One of them was the Tontine Association.

On the thirteenth of January, 1792, a few days before he introduced the question of the theatrical ban's repeal, William Tudor presented to his fellow legislators at the General Court an incorporation request from the Boston Tontine Association. He was supported in both actions by John Gardiner, who spoke on behalf of the Tontine Bill shortly after delivering his more famous dramatic lecture. European governments in need of revenue had in the past resorted to tontines, and the Boston scheme followed the same conventions. Subscribers purchased shares that declined in price with the rising age of the buyer or beneficiary. In 1850, the survivors would divide the fund between them, but this final disposition of the tontine's capital mattered less than what was done with it in the interval. During its lifetime, the tontine would act as a bank, loaning money to individuals and corporations. The interest on these loans would return to the members in yearly dividends.[93]

The promoters of the Boston Tontine Association made broad appeals for support. They argued that their bank would better serve the general public. The high price of a share in other banks had prevented the "mediocrity" from investing. As a result, these shares were "circumscribed within the narrow limits of a few individuals . . . whose fortunes have enabled them to monopolize every advantage."[94] Membership in the tontine came cheaply, and investors might come from all walks of life. This "diffusiveness," as one booster put it, promised to cement the commonwealth, because no one group would turn against another if everyone were united in a profitable venture. Even farmers would be included, for the tontine's organizers would place a sizable portion of their funds in land mortgages.[95]

The tontine presented itself as the everyman's bank. Benjamin Austin Jr. was one of its agents. Many of its trustees, however, were of a different sort. Stephen Higginson was a rich merchant from Essex County and close to Jonathan Jackson, the federal theorist. Abiel Smith was such a success in trade that he retired in 1787, almost thirty years

John

before his death. He stayed active in town affairs, where he remonstrated against the theater ban, and in his church, King's Chapel, where he was a proprietor and vestryman. (Only John Hancock kept a better carriage.) While touts described the tontine as the most "republican" of banks, another trustee, David Greene, was a former Tory. He had fled Boston in 1775 for London and then Antigua. William Phillips Jr. was no Loyalist, but he was the son of the largest stockholder in the Massachusetts Bank. In the newspapers, the tontine's supporters hinted at this bank's exclusive practices.[96] Its early history explains a great deal about other financial institutions and about the character of opportunity in early national New England.

The General Court incorporated the Massachusetts Bank in 1784. It was the first of its kind in the newly independent state. Sitting alongside the senior William Phillips on its first board of directors were some of the state's most prominent men. There was James Bowdoin, the Kennebeck Proprietor who would soon replace fellow mogul and political nemesis John Hancock as governor. And there was George Cabot, the former privateer and future U.S. senator and Federalist icon. Within a couple of years of the bank's founding, Bowdoin, Cabot, and a number of other investors sold their shares in the corporation. Phillips and his conservative allies engineered this consolidation of the bank's assets. They came to understand that many of their original partners had purchased stock in order to borrow against it on easy terms. Creditors were too ready to accumulate debt, and the bank's integrity was vulnerable. Because Phillips owned 40 percent of the shares—by far the largest stake—his interest lay in dividends, not debt.[97] The proprietors who favored a looser policy were simply not as established as he was in that particular institution. They needed easy money for enterprises in which they enjoyed or hoped to enjoy a similar advantage. When the Massachusetts Bank trimmed its sails, these entrepreneurs looked to other expedients.

Some of the disappointed paused to complain, though with a definite purpose. The tontine's promoters offered one alternative, and James Sullivan, the old bank's loudest critic, was never without an angle of his own. His *Path to Riches: An Inquiry into the Origin and Use of Money; and into the Principles of Stocks and Banks* appeared in 1792. It was a liberal document. Sullivan wrote that the individual's "desire of dominion over external things, and a thirst for that superiority which arises from wealth" happily tended "to the advancement of the public interest." He also accepted that persons shared the ability to succeed less evenly than they partook of ambition. That was God's wisdom. Human legislators could not be so prejudicial, and the rules of society were not to favor one group over others.[98] Sullivan distinguished merit from privilege; in his view, the proprietors of the Massachusetts Bank profited from the latter. Incorporating a bank that welcomed everybody's business would remedy the injustice. He admitted that such an inflationary measure would lead to more failures, but, he added, "we are to take mankind as we find them. To contend against all the follies and weakness of the people would be but a poor way to govern them."[99] Sullivan was prepared to let the chips fall where they would, for he was confident of his own rising fortunes.

Whether open or closed, the economy of the early republic was kind to him. He was as involved as anyone in the corporate system that bound private desires to the public interest. He was a member of the West Boston Bridge Company, the Boston Aqueduct Corporation, and the Massachusetts Mutual Insurance Company. Sullivan was the president of the Middlesex Canal Company from its incorporation in 1793 until his death in 1808. He was a fixture in politics and—when his politics were successful—in government. His career peaked in 1807, when he became governor of the commonwealth. During this lifetime of achievement, no one day told more of Sullivan's methods than the fourth of July, 1782, when the General Court asked him, along with William Phillips, George Cabot, and Stephen Higginson, to consider how to raise the state's revenues. And on the same day, he and Perez Morton secured a letter of marque for their privateer sloop. Its name was the *Fair Trader*.[100] A piratical ambition and a liberal—though consciously clever—disposition were married to an active interest in the public welfare.

Sullivan's rhetoric was, in many ways, that of the tontine's supporters, but he objected to the scheme, as did the Massachusetts Senate in a tight vote. (Prior to the senate's action, the house passed the Tontine Bill—and it was bribery that won the day.) An observer commented that the organizers might succeed if they abandoned the death lottery and stuck to straight banking. By the middle of 1792, they did essentially that, dissolving the tontine and depositing its funds in the newly incorporated Union Bank. Tontine-men directed this institution as well. On the original board sat Higginson, David Greene, and William Tudor. The bank set up shop at the corner of State and Exchange in the old Apthorp mansion, then owned by Morton. Like its rival, the Massachusetts Bank, the Union Bank was unable to satisfy the demand for credit. Eight more banks sprang up in the next ten years. John Gardiner could not join the debate over these incorporations, but he voted for the Union Bank as well as for the tontine. He was not, however, a major player in either project.[101] He had investments of his own, but they were rather more civic than financial. The independence of Maine became his special concern.

❧ · ☙

The eastern counties had long been the scene of enterprise and whimsy, and they would retain their unsettled character for some time, as the United States and Britain haggled over the northern border (while British money was invested indiscriminately on either side of it) and as common farmers donned Indian costume and terrorized the landlord class that had survived revolution and independence. The early 1790s were especially wild times, excited as they were by commercial ferment. As one observer put it:

> this is a day of Speculation. Strange ideas have got possession of Peoples Minds and they don't feel themselves at ease unless they are trying projects. The Bubble by chance may burst and fall very heavily upon the pates of some people . . . some are Land Mad, some Tontine mad, some scrip Mad, some Bridge Mad, some Canal Mad and some seperation Mad.[102]

Land madness was particularly virulent in Maine. The district's vast wilderness was an abundant and debased coin. Investors traded and accumulated millions of acres, often to no great end. Profits issued from the very process of trade or from small, productive concessions cut from the unrefined whole. In Silvester Gardiner's heyday, the most active Kennebeck Proprietors saw a better return from mill and shipping rights than from the land itself. After the Revolution, Massachusetts also learned to sift real gains from imagined riches. The state government sold large chunks of Maine in order to reduce its debt burden.[103]

One of the most aggressive buyers of eastern lands was William Bingham. By the time of his major purchases, Bingham was one of the nation's richest men. He made his fortune in the West Indies, where he served as trade representative and privateer for the warring colonies. He returned to his native Philadelphia and became a director of the Bank of North America. His household, under the management of his remarkable wife, Anne Willing Bingham, was the most important salon in early America and a kind of "Republican Court." William Bingham took his turn in the Pennsylvania Assembly and the U.S. Senate, but he made his mark outside politics, by the extravagance of his lifestyle and speculations. He owned a good bit of western Pennsylvania, and he founded Binghamton in New York State. In 1792, he began to acquire sections of Maine, which, at their greatest extent, amounted to two million acres. The following year, in the hope of boosting emigration, he published a pamphlet describing Maine's natural advantages. John Gardiner was a contributor.[104]

Maine never really delivered on its initial promise. Bingham's huge investment brought with it huge and ongoing obligations. The terms of the sale required him to develop and settle his lands. Rich and powerful though he was, Bingham could not carry on alone. He sought the aid of the Barings, a British family that gave its name to the influential merchant bank. Even this partnership, cemented by the marriage of Alexander Baring and a Bingham daughter, was insufficient to hold the grand scheme together. Bingham died in 1804, and the Maine partners who remained could not meet the settling duties. Disintegration meant opportunity for some; Harrison Gray Otis was one of the men who tried to prevent the forfeiture of the Bingham lands in return for a share in the speculation.[105]

Settlers and money were moving westward to more productive land in New York and Ohio, and the settlers who stayed in Maine could be a troublesome lot. In the late eighteenth and early nineteenth centuries, large proprietors worked to secure title and income at the expense of squatters and smallholders who had labored most to improve the wilderness. The clash of interests was occasionally violent. Savvy men like Robert Hallowell Gardiner, the primary heir to Silvester's Kennebeck estates, learned to moderate their claims and compensate their lessers for the appreciation in land values. The General Court codified this wisdom in a betterment act of 1808. John Gardiner—whose disinheritance was nephew Robert Hallowell's bounty—had hinted at this solution in his proposed reforms of 1790.[106]

After returning to Massachusetts from his long absence abroad, Gardiner depended on the family's eastern holdings as the refuge of his ambitions. When his professional career sputtered in Boston, he moved to Pownalborough and settled into the role of town father. His neighbors rewarded his service and generosity with a seat in the legislature. Even as his law reforms died on the vine, Gardiner looked to new labors and larger fame. Toward the end of 1790, after an inconclusive first ballot in the federal elections, he decided to challenge Maine's incumbent representative to the U.S. House, George Thatcher.[107]

Thatcher acquired the eastern clients of James Sullivan when that worthy lawyer pursued fortune and office to Boston. He was an admirer of the scientist and unitarian Joseph Priestley, and a friend warned Thatcher than many constituents found him "a little heterodoxical." Gardiner was not the type to be bothered by such beliefs; his campaign, though negative, followed a different script. Writing under the guise of "Lincolnshire," he advertised Thatcher's advocacy of an exorbitant pension for Baron Friedrich Wilhelm von Steuben, the Prussian military advisor to the Continental Army. In the *Centinel*, one "Agumenticus" rose to Thatcher's defense and disputed Gardiner's facts. Gardiner responded by calling "Agumenticus," among other things, a "tomahawking Mohawk" and an "impudent liar." After another member of Congress testified to Thatcher's opposition to the Steuben grant, Gardiner "chearfully" acknowledged his mistake.[108]

The argument mattered little by then. In the poll of late February 1791, Gardiner finished last among the four listed candidates. His tally was twenty-one votes; George Thatcher finished first with 1,137. The *Chronicle*, on the very page that reported this result, announced the verdict in the Edmund Freeman libel trial. It was not a good day for the old barrister, though he would again, as before, demonstrate an admirable resilience. Just below the disastrous totals came word that certain representatives to the General Court were reviving plans to separate Maine from Massachusetts. John Gardiner was at their head.[109]

"An Address to the Numerous and Respectable Inhabitants of the Great and Extensive District of Maine" appeared the next month. Gardiner authored the piece and chaired the group of Maine legislators who signed it. The address outlined the reasons for separation; the most compelling were distance from the capital, the district's size and promise, and unfair taxes. The list was straightforward and the document bland—exactly what one would expect from a committee. Gardiner's personality does not scream from the newsprint as it so often did in other efforts. He is most present in the grandiose opening: "The time draweth nigh, when ye must be, as the God of Nature intended ye should be, a Free Sovereign and Independent State."[110]

In a polemical essay supporting independence, William Symmes, alias "Alcibiades," extended this train of thought. Considering the language, we should not be surprised that at least one critic thought "Alcibiades" and Gardiner were the same man. Symmes explained why "force of habit and former usage" could no longer tie Maine to Massachusetts:

> This force is sufficient to govern lazy and unenterprizing minds. This band is strong enough to connect bodies that are at rest. But that it cannot resist the liberal spirit of reform that periodically pervades enlightened countries, America herself has been and France now is a glorious proof. All absurd subjections, all inconvenient usages, give way before the penetrating philosophy of the present day . . . Let us improve the critical season, or own that it is already past.[111]

Maine's statehood would be one more push for progress. The district's connection to the elder commonwealth—like entails and the Trinity and the ban on theater—was inconvenient to reason and enterprise. Men and women of large understanding could see a better, richer future.

In an important and familiar sense, then, the separationists were big thinkers, but the size of their ambition also underlined the limits of opportunity. There was resentment in the separationist essays, resentment by the somewhat fortunate for the already successful. In the same article as above, "Alcibiades" contrasted Maine and Massachusetts and complained, "we make but a small figure at her side." He wondered, "why should we be submissively dancing attendance on her when we could just as well do our own business in a quarter of the time?"[112] To separate was to "economize" and pursue advantage in a contracted, less competitive situation. This strategy was characteristic of the separation movement. Gardiner, Symmes, and their fellow advocates were not out to remake society so much as to make a place within it. They could not be the leaders of Massachusetts, whom they otherwise resembled, so they designed to lead a new state.[113]

Among the "seperation Mad" was Daniel Davis. Though rejected by Harvard, this Cape Cod native still managed to join the bar and establish a practice in Maine. He married Louisa Freeman, whose brother would become the controversial minister of King's Chapel. During the courtship, James Freeman assured his sister that, while Davis was not formerly a "courtier," he had become a gentleman with a promising career ahead of him. Freeman added that he wrote "with an ease and elegance which would have done honour to Addison himself." Davis agreed and to Louisa's brother boasted, "in point of smartness, I am a very considerable young man."[114] Still, he was not as considerable as he would have liked. In the late 1780s, his enemies questioned whether he owned enough property to be elected to the General Court. Davis found a way to succeed. He represented Portland in the Massachusetts House, and he later sought preferment within the federal government. In a Fourth of July oration, delivered at Portland in 1796, Davis warned against Virginian infidelity and "the black froth of democracy." During the presidency of John Adams, he was appointed U.S. Attorney for the District of Maine.[115]

Before his entry into national politics, Davis published on behalf of Maine statehood. He was particularly concerned with the manufacture of elites, and given his life's course, this concern should not surprise. In a 1791 address, he argued that the new state would attract learned men "who happen to be a little tinctured with ambition." The original vacancy of state offices would "open a field for their ambitious and aspiring geniuses."[116] These new elites would, in turn, elevate the whole of society. They would spend their salaries locally, encouraging trade and circulating money throughout Maine. By mixing and conversing with the people, they would raise the level of information available to all citizens and inculcate in all the habits of respect. Davis's good society was the more generally prosperous because it valued distinctive accomplishments.[117]

William Symmes was aware of such bargains, and he, too, hoped that the people of Maine were willing to make them. The separation movement saw its share of venality, but interest was at play in any project. The public had to trust in final outcomes. In the first "Alcibiades" letter, Symmes wrote:

> Some men are ever restless and uneasy, fond of change, and never satisfied—Some are ambitious, and fond of empty rank—Others avaricious, and always dreaming of the loaves and fishes. But even such men as these may seek their own ends by means that may benefit the public; and their advice may be good, although they mean only to serve themselves.[118]

One can never know for sure how Symmes arrived at this formula. Part of the answer must lie in what is a primary concern of this narrative: the potency and accessibility of liberal notions in the late eighteenth century. These notions could arrive in odd containers. Symmes was a Freemason, and he recited on one occasion this choice bit of Masonic wisdom: "All discord (is) harmony not understood, / All partial evil universal good." Humanity may have been "eccentric and irregular," but Symmes was sure it tended to grand achievements.[119] He tried to peg Maine's independence to this happy process. He encouraged the doubtful to look beyond interests and personalities, for these were but grist for the mill. John Gardiner, however, was a hard man to ignore, and opponents of statehood concentrated on its most eccentric advocate.

Gardiner's prominence in the separation movement confirmed its speculative nature. "Under the patronage and direction of the Sachem [the barrister's most common nickname]," one observer wondered, "what height of perfection will they not reach?"[120] A writer in the *Centinel*, "a White Bird," was no friend of separation, but he was happy to find Gardiner localizing his efforts. He joked that Gardiner's law reforms might have met with more favor in the General Court had they applied to Maine alone.[121] A more devastating treatment appeared in the *Herald of Freedom*, surely Gardiner's least favorite paper. The author envisioned a district convention whereat "the eloquent Sachem" bid for the governorship of the new state. He made a rather pompous demagogue. Upon election, he planned "to cloathe myself in scarlet and fine linen, and my barrister's gown and three tailed wig, and wear besides my silver waiter [the plate presented to Gardiner by his grateful Wilkite clients]."[122] This pseudo-Gardiner's style was not suited to the rugged terrain downeast, but he aspired nonetheless to fashion a free Maine in his own image. While he admitted that his constituents "know no more of Latin than the logs [they] saw," he promised that they "shall be taught to chop Logic as easily as to chop fire wood." Maine's "Loggers" would become "Literati." The satirist's point is clear: the district was too immature to deserve independence, and Gardiner was too decadent to lead a rustic challenge to the established order. His schemes floated above realities and evaporated, almost without a trace.[123]

❧ · ☙

The story of "almost" is the last to tell of John Gardiner. Most of his reforms came to naught, and those that succeeded—like the theater ban's repeal—did not need his help. On a number of occasions, he caused quite a stir in the commonwealth, but he did not change its political and social structures. That was never his aim, though he would have welcomed higher office. What Gardiner left behind was the tale of his exploits. He may not have been a governor or great proprietor, but he was undoubtedly a character.

The best contemporary sketch appeared early in 1786, about the time of his Pownalborough remove and well before his very public legislative career. The author, known as "P," did not mention Gardiner's name; instead, he called him "Silenus," the drunken god. This incarnation blazed an unsteady path through Britain and St. Kitts and across his father's memory. In Boston, his methods were outlandish, for they were "exactly calculated to the meridian of London," the city of Wilkes, "an abandoned Debauchee," and George III, that "despicable Monarch." Gardiner was an outrageous man: "his conduct in every situation, appears to have been almost precisely the reverse of what it ought to have been."[124] He was not without talents or opportunities, but he seemed determined to squander them. While disposed to "convivial hilarity," Gardiner celebrated the austere manners of wartime. Despite his considerable knowledge of the law, he could not retain a client. He offended men of congenial tastes and sentiments. In sum, he was a traitor to his best interests.

A few years later, coincident with his legal reforms, Gardiner increasingly became the object of satire. As we have seen, the attacks could be vicious, and Gardiner sued in only one instance out of many. Some of the satires were in verse; a strong example is "Jack the Giant-Killer's Third Phillipick." The poet was a discerning judge of the "Killer's" prospects. In Gardiner's mouth, he put these words:

> Ye lonely wilds of Kennebeck!
> Thy deepest, darkest shades I seek,
> To prowl alone: Well pleas'd to hear
> More kindred Calls of Wolf and Bear
> There, how it glooms the tardy hours,
> To view my empty book of powers.[125]

Here was a chronicle of failures—and it was accurate enough—meant to set the reformer back, but it and other satires also granted the notoriety he was supposedly chasing.

As misadventure mounted upon controversy, Gardiner made a name for himself—many names, in fact. A squib in the *Centinel* listed seven, and that was not a complete catalog. Most of them were the pseudonyms he attached to his various polemics. He was an old hand at caricature, and, if he called himself the "Eastern Sachem," he was probably not surprised to find others calling him the "Wild Man of the Woods."[126] Gardiner even rated comparisons with widely known comic figures. One writer placed him in the company of Laurence Sterne's Yorick and Corporal Trim. A fellow legislator compared him to Don

Quixote. Another observer was reminded of New England's own Stephen Burroughs, whose criminal audacity excited the public imagination during the years of Gardiner's greatest fame. Later in the 1790s, Burroughs published his memoirs, and the book sold well in several editions.[127] Unfortunately, John Gardiner never produced an autobiography or in any other way profited materially from his eccentricities, but he did have the satisfaction of becoming, for a brief period, an established rogue in the print culture of Massachusetts.

His reputation extended beyond the comedy of his failed reforms. The papers recorded his jokes from the Massachusetts House floor, regardless of context. The *Chronicle* ran a piece called "Food for the Humorist!" in which Gardiner offered the first course in wit. The *Centinel* printed an "Advertisement of the Eastern Sachem, to the Western Beauties." It read in part: "Wanted, a Wife.—She must be handsome, because I am not an Adonis . . . She must be always rational, because I am often mad;—and if I like her, she may be rich, because I am poor."[128] The author was obviously no friend to Gardiner, but he did not hint at any particular dispute. The notice merited publication because of who the "Sachem" was by the middle of 1792. His celebrity had outgrown its political origins.

Of course, for all his activity, John Gardiner was reluctant to enter into the compromises and commitments that brought success in any enterprise, and in politics especially. He preferred to step into character. One of his correspondents, upon learning of his designs on Thatcher's seat, wrote with honesty:

> I extremely regret that your Country cant have the benefit of your great abilities and extensive knowledge owing to your obstinate persisting in what every man but yourself knows to be erroneous. Can it be thought your friend Churchil ever imagined you would carry his sentiments the length you have done? I abhor and detest that "hackneyed Strumpet," as much as you can . . . but my friend, shall we be so blind to our own interest as to carry our resentment so far as to defeat our good intentions of usefulness?[129]

The reference is to "Night," a poem Charles Churchill wrote in 1761, the same year Gardiner passed the English bar. The success of *The Rosciad*, a satire upon the theater, had allowed Churchill to indulge his dissolute proclivities. "Night" was a defense of his conduct. The pertinent section goes as follows:

Whilst frank Good-Humour consecrates the treat,
And [Woman] makes society complete,
Thus Will we live, tho' in our teeth are hurl'd
Those Hackney Strumpets, Prudence and the World.[130]

Gardiner quoted this poem himself at times, and he liked to salt his essays and speeches with other bits of Churchill.[131] From his correspondent's perspective, he pursued matters to absurdity. Gardiner had ambitions; we have seen him stretch to achieve them. What he lacked, however, was a firm grip. He was too devoted to his contrariness, to the perverse sensibility of "Night."

Even in his death, John Gardiner was faithful to type. During the controversy raised by his law reforms, a critic dedicated to him this nasty verse: "Better, far better, had it been for thee / Had mill-stones drown'd thee in the depth of sea." In October of 1793, Gardiner was on the packet *Londoner* when it foundered in a gale off Cape Ann. His body was never recovered, but a passing ship found his trunk bobbing on the surface. It contained a bundle of his papers, including the revised copy of his theater speech, which he had intended to deposit at the Harvard College Library.[132]

Gardiner was a bridge-figure in the history of late-eighteenth-century Anglo-American politics and society. Indeed, he halted at mid-span. The lawyer who was somehow too English for comfort proposed reforms that were, with a few exceptions, attuned to an American future. His theater speech expresses the hope that even the rustiest patriots might make merry and be the better for it. His example guides us through the tangles of early national speculation, though he was himself no entrepreneur. And he demonstrates (like the counterfeit Burroughs) how a man's ambitions, a man's life, could be liquidated and traded like merchant scrip. Gardiner's paper might have been denominated in the bawdy argot of the British past (just as many American accounts were kept in sterling long after independence), but it was endorsed by national and provincial usage.

Reverend John Sylvester John Gardiner (1756–1830),
Gilbert Stuart (1755–1828), ca. 1815, oil on panel.

Letters and Distinction

Also found amid the flotsam was *The Widowed Mourner*, Gardiner's most sustained poetic effort. Its 160-odd lines commemorated the life of Margaret Gardiner, who died in 1789. John published the poem in late 1791, several months after the libel trial provoked by suggestions of spousal cruelty. The *Mourner* is an affecting and awkward tribute, as these verses attest:

> Affliction's keenest pangs, alas! I've borne!
> A kind, endearing, tender wife I mourn!
> My soul's deep-cherish'd love, my Friend sincere!
> To my poor bleeding heart, than life, more dear![1]

Obvious too is the author's emphatic personality; these four lines apparently deserved five exclamation points. The reader never forgets that the poet is also the title character. The barrister's style is inescapable. Besides the aggressive punctuation, there are quotations from Virgil, Pope, Milton, and the book of Titus. Even more characteristic are the footnotes, which are as long as the poem itself.[2]

Gardiner may have indulged himself and his love, but the *Mourner* was more than an act of fancy. It sublimated his disappointments. Silvester Gardiner had turned his back on John, and John, when remembering his wife, was very attentive to her disinheritance. Margaret's father, George Harries, had neglected to amend his will upon her birth. Mr. Harries died when his daughter was an infant, leaving her nothing, though he had not intended the exclusion. According to Gardiner's poem, the saintly Margaret never sought the remedies available in a court of equity, even though she bowed to equity in the case of her dotty admirer. Luckily, some minor legacies mitigated her loss, a saving grace that husband John understood well.[3] Silvester did not deny his son the family home in Boston. It was the small, manageable tragedy that appealed to John Gardiner's poetic sensibilities.

The *Mourner* was keen to the charms of lost causes. In these causes and their remembrance, Margaret Harries and her demi-Jacobite family were practiced hands. In the late 1750s she was a patroness of the Sea-Serjeants and presided at one of their last meetings. Gardiner would not come to Wales for several years yet, but, as a widower poet, he described the pageantry and his wife's role in it with intimate rapture. "Recal that fav'rite period," he wrote, "when she shone, / Of all the Cambrian nymphs, fair Queen alone!" There was her silken robe and, pinned upon it, her badge of office, a silver dolphin brooch. Small wonder that she set "all Llewhellin's youthful sons on fire!"[4]

Thirty years on, John Gardiner joined in the celebration retrospectively. Strange doings, this, at least at first consideration: he was an outsider in Wales, and he despised the Stuarts. Late in life, perhaps, he was beginning to put his contentious career in perspective. The Sea-Serjeants offered a comforting example. Their political wrangles melted into the picturesque haze of the Welsh seaside. Gardiner wrote of "soft zephyrs" and "gentle breezes," and the reader can almost see them slowly polishing the edges off the Jacobite's complaint.[5] Similarly, Gardiner as elegiac poet refrained from dividing history into rights and wrongs. Instead, he attended much more closely to cultural detail.

The Widowed Mourner was a consciously belletristic project. In one footnote, Gardiner took issue with his "literary friends" who objected to his use of the phrase "chaste desires." Turning to Johnson's *Dictionary* and to Milton, the poet assured his expert readers that an active marital fidelity was also pure. In the advertisement for his work, Gardiner declared that the poem was really meant for a narrow audience, a "circle of ladies" with which he was acquainted.[6] If this was not a new association, it at least signaled a new stance for the brash reformer. For John Gardiner's eldest son, however, belles-lettres was a serious avocation. John Sylvester John Gardiner's life and writings did not escape the sting of popular politics, and at times he savored it. But he devoted his career to elaborating the different tendencies one sees at play in the *Mourner:* a precision in language, the appreciation of antique beauties, and the culture of memory.

New England's Federal-era literati do not enjoy a brilliant reputation, nor should they: the derivative, even defensive, character of their work won few admirers in succeeding generations, and contemporary interest, if one can find it, is academic or antiquarian. Nevertheless, young Gardiner's shortcomings, and those of his peers, must not blind us to what was modern and ambitious in the Federalist literary project. Gardiner and company did not pine for the disowned king and mother country, but neither were they pleased by the bald nationalism of many American writers. To them it was an infant's baldness, evidence of a sloppy and griping immaturity. Worse still, the crudeness was willful: the Anglophone tradition in letters was a rich one, and Americans could respect it while honoring their own political choices.

Federalist literati were pessimistic, but they did not deny what history had wrought. They were aware of the social bases of that history and of the culture they hoped to protect. Good literature was the product of refinement, but a society's intellectual and aesthetic health also depended on the versatile excellence found in men of learning and experience, the professionals who were the natural leaders of a nation, the United States, that was at once great *and* middling. One reason for J. S. J. Gardiner's pessimism was his fear that the learned classes were narrowing their sights and skills. Hemmed in by philistine greed, the increasing technicality of their professions, and the disturbance of Atlantic comity, Americans who should have known better instead made common cause with the vulgar. Mandarins like Gardiner and his most gifted colleague, Joseph Dennie, believed in talent, and their understanding of its role was shaped by the same expectations of liberal political economy that emerged from the late imperial era to shape the Federal constitutional order.

◄§ · §►

J. S. J. Gardiner was born in 1765 in Haverfordwest, Wales, his mother's hometown. At a very young age, he went to Boston, where he spent several years in his grandfather's care. During America's war for independence, John sent his son to England for an education. J.S.J.'s schoolmaster was Dr. Samuel Parr, and Parr's rigorous manner and classical technique made a definite impression on Gardiner. As a critic, J.S.J. reflected Parr's prejudices; as a teacher, he replicated Parr's methods. Their personalities were also congenial, or perhaps Parr's was simply influential. Certainly in this most memorable description of Parr, one can see the man Gardiner would become:

Though by nature temperate and even frugal, he nevertheless delights in luxury, in rich food, rare vintages, soft beds and purple coverlets. And, though of humane and kindly disposition, he is much given to argument and contention . . . He is accustomed to assert that all foreigners should be swept away like so many noxious insects, and that once every five years the first minister of state should be put to death . . . to sum up, he is a man skilled in ringing bells, poleaxing cattle, petting kittens, [and] out-Heroding Herod.[7]

Moreover, Parr was exactly the sort of teacher one would expect John Gardiner to hire. He is remembered as the "Whig Dr. Johnson." He was a supporter of John Wilkes and of the American cause. He almost lost his house to the same "Church and King" mob that razed the unitarian Joseph Priestley's. In 1800, when J. S. J. Gardiner was settling into the severe politics of his maturity, he remembered Parr as an excellent scholar hamstrung by ideological folly. As if mimicking what many people thought of his father, Gardiner came to believe that Parr enjoyed talent and prudence in inverse proportion. But in 1783, when J.S.J. returned with his father to Boston, the teenager was still adhering to the models of parent and teacher. John reported to the exiled Silvester that his grandson "bids fair to be a good Whig. Algernon Sidney upon Government is his daily Catechism."[8]

J. S. J. Gardiner was very much his father's boy, though they led quite different lives. Throughout his peripatetic career, John Gardiner committed to nothing except his sense of self-importance and the demands of his idiosyncratic conscience. He had ambitions, but they were wayward (if occasionally well served by his elastic nature). His son, once he had decided upon a profession, stuck to the same post for nearly forty years. J.S.J.'s life did not lack for variety and achievement, and the men of his generation certainly did not lack opportunities. There was opportunity in the corporations whose charters raced past John in the General Court. There was opportunity in the new western territories and in trade with the Far East. Yet, as the American economy grew larger and more sophisticated, its offerings were more discrete, and it developed a texture marked by many narrow bands of expertise.

J. S. J. Gardiner was a perceptive young man, and he knew that, for all of his advantages, not every field would be open to him. Upon arriving in Boston, he informed his grandfather that, despite his inclinations to the law, he had "little Hopes of succeeding in this Part of the World as the Bar is her[e] already overburthened."[9] Aided by his father, J.S.J.

pressed ahead, but, as we have seen, he was stymied by the increasingly rigid standards of the Suffolk bar association. He had a superb classical education but no college degree and therefore, according to the bar's disingenuous judgment, no knowledge of the mathematics, ethics, and metaphysics so necessary to the practice of law in Massachusetts.[10] John Gardiner, of course, never forgave the slight.

J. S. J. went about finding another career, and, within a couple of years, the able catechumen in Whiggery took up the very prayer book his father disavowed. Early in 1787, J.S.J. began reading the service at the church his grandfather built in Pownalborough. Later that year, he entered the Episcopal diaconate at New York City and traveled south to begin his parish duties in Beaufort, South Carolina, not far from Charleston. In 1791, he returned to New York, where Bishop Provoost completed his ordination. The proprietors of Trinity Church, Boston, elected him their assistant rector. Upon the death of the Reverend Samuel Parker in 1805, Gardiner ascended to the rectorship and held it for the rest of his life. His father did not seem too upset that J.S.J. had followed in cousin Seabury's footsteps. When John wanted to hear "Jack" preach, he went to Trinity and read aloud from his renegade liturgy.[11] As far as we know, the young priest did not mind the intrusion, though of course he only had to endure it for a year and a half before his father died at sea. In time, J.S.J. Gardiner lost patience with the heterodox, first in politics and literature and then in religion as well.

Within a few years of Gardiner's installment at Trinity, the United States entered a period memorable for its acrimonious political culture. In the controversies of the late 1780s and early 1790s, the aggressive and successful relied on a liberal rhetoric. Letting the people do as they would was popular and promised to serve the interests of the few. The last years of the eighteenth century witnessed a rhetorical contraction. One can see its effect on George Cabot, who, when discussing the Whiskey Rebellion with Theophilus Parsons, was finding it harder to invoke "the general will."[12] Cabot and many other political leaders in New England sensed that the will of the people, broadly construed, no longer worked to their advantage. Politics, while still a very personal game, was increasingly the business of organizations. Federalists organized themselves into a party as they were losing their hold on national power. By inclination and out of institutional necessity, they shortened their gestures and appeals. New England, and Massachusetts in particular, was safe territory for the Federalists, and their politics took on the sharp accents of the region.[13]

Gardiner's published sermons and speeches were surely more controversial than the unpublished majority; nevertheless, they are a telling source. By Jefferson's first term, the sermons assumed a definite color. Gardiner assured the Massachusetts Humane Society that Christianity did not preclude "those partial attachments, which our regard for relations, friends, and country inspires." Jesus was a patriot, and there was no reason for good Christians to be anything less. Moreover, the "rigid rules of Christian charity" demanded that they expose and counter "the designs of wicked men."[14] In other sermons, Gardiner was not shy about naming the face of evil. Before the Massachusetts Convention of the Protestant Episcopal Church, he complained that the "pestilence" of French thought raged through the country; even New England, the "Palladium of correct morals and sound religion," was susceptible.[15]

Despite Gardiner's reservations about New England's future, a strong regional bias is evident in his work. "Extravagant theories" found most of their adherents in other states, and in Virginia especially. New Englanders were a happy race, superior to other Americans in intelligence, spirit, enterprise, and sobriety. "The purity of our blood," Gardiner explained, "is but little polluted by the intermixture of foreigners," and, fortunately, the "motley rabble, that infest other parts of the Union, would find no asylum here, where idleness would starve, and profligacy be punished."[16] But for all its forbidding virtue, Gardiner's New England could not shut out the problems of the wider world.

By April of 1812, only the good sense of the eastern states kept the nation from "the worst of all calamities," a war with Great Britain. In a fast-day sermon delivered from his pulpit at Trinity Church, Gardiner blamed the administration for leading Americans into the crisis. It had squandered their commercial advantages through the "philosophistical mummery" of embargo and non-intercourse. It had offended the parent country, the land from which America derived its freedoms and religion, and courted instead a warmongering tyrant. Notwithstanding this ruinous course, Gardiner held out some hope that Massachusetts could dissuade its fellows from a final and evil decision.[17]

Events soon disappointed him. In a little over three months' time, after the declaration of war, Gardiner again stood and spoke in Trinity Church on a day of public fast. His text was from Psalm 120, the seventh verse: "I am for peace." His tone, however, was bitter, his message discordant. The war was the "baneful" effect of Jefferson's government (Gardiner considered Madison to be a mere puppet).[18] The country was taking a lesson in southern patriotism, which Gardiner excoriated with a paraphrase of that most contrary—and to Gardiner's mind, conscientious—southerner, John Randolph:

> The southern patriots . . . expend all their sympathies on the Little Turtle and the savage tribes, whom they are anxious to furnish with blankets, to enable them to make a more successful attack upon us, and with scalping knives and tomahawks to murder our women and children. With regard to those, who speak the same language, and are governed nearly by the same laws as ourselves, their rancour is implacable, unrelenting as the grave. But with regard to France they are true spaniels and fawn upon the hand that scourges them.[19]

The French Revolution was "the first cause" of the 1812 emergency. Gardiner allowed that newly independent Americans had justly sympathized with their allies' struggle, but as that struggle degenerated into an anarchic bloodbath, affection for France became an infatuation among the unsound and the "semi-barbaric." This partisan madness aggravated a widespread antipathy for Britain, which had existed (and not without cause, he noted) since the Revolutionary War. The original rulers of the United States—Washington, Adams, and Hamilton—could have governed these dangerous sentiments; unfortunately, their moment had passed. Gardiner looked southward to the capital and saw a crowd of disreputable placemen.[20]

He advised the citizens of the eastern states to cleave to their interests, even to the point of disobedience. They were to protest the war vigorously. They were to resist the likely presence of French troops. Finally, Gardiner spoke of secession:

> the conclusion is inevitable, that there is an essential difference of interests between the southern and eastern states of the union . . . you must either, in the language of the day, *cut the connexion*, or so far alter the national constitution, as to ensure yourselves a due share in the government. The union has long since been virtually dissolved, and it is full time that this portion of the *disunited* state should take care of itself.[21]

Admitting that these were grave matters, Gardiner entrusted them to a convention of the northern and eastern states. Two years later, the meeting at Hartford made a prophet of the priest, though the wisdom of that body lay precisely in the moderation he belittled that summer of 1812.[22]

J. S. J. Gardiner was an old hand at harsh judgments. He surveyed the American scene, and where he did not see naiveté, he more often than not saw corruption, the good gone bad. The nation's leaders betrayed its heritage by their policies and its dignity by their incompetence. Their mistakes were painfully obvious. In religion, the danger was rather more insidious. Gardiner grew up in a latitudinarian age. He was the son of a unitarian, and he worked closely with others. But in the early nineteenth century, theological loyalties were stiffening. In 1811, Gardiner delivered *A Preservative against Unitarianism*. He brought to the subject the same acidity that would mark his fast-day sermons. "The Unitarians," he said, "are forever harping upon candour and liberality, which they display by ineffable contempt for all sects but their own. The candour of an Unitarian resembles the humanity of a revolutionary Frenchman. It is entirely confined to words."[23] Unitarians also demonstrated a Jacobinical recklessness in their attempts to "find out the Almighty to perfection." In fact, God was a dark mystery no one understood and few could approach.

By worshipping a knowable God, Unitarians upset tradition and authority. In a sermon before the state Protestant Episcopal convention of 1813, Gardiner put his case frankly:

> notwithstanding the babble about freedom of inquiry, and liberality of sentiment, and what not, there is not, nor ever can be, one christian in a thousand, who has inclination, or leisure, or capacity to settle abstruse points of divinity by inquiring himself, but must necessarily take his faith from others; and, if so, from whom will he take it, but from men of the most extensive learning and brilliant talents?[24]

These men, "the guides of publick sentiment and of publick taste," were almost invariably believers in the Trinity. In the *Preservative*, Gardiner declared that all of the giants of science and literature were Trinitarians. His examples included Milton, Edmund Burke, and Dr. Johnson.[25]

The Book of Common Prayer was another bulwark of the faith. It was a digest of Christian knowledge and style and was superior in every way to extemporaneous worship. "Unpremeditated prayer," Gardiner opined, "is extremely apt to degenerate into enthusiastick absurdities, or disgusting familiarities. At the one, true taste revolts, and at the other, true piety." Here it becomes clear, if it has not already, that language was implicated in Gardiner's vision of the world. While bemoaning France's travails in one of his earliest published sermons, he snarled that the "revolutionists have made as free with the purity of language as of morals."[26] And one need not rely on the evidence from Gardiner's life in the church to study his concern for words. Before he was rector at Trinity, he was one of the most important literary figures in early national Boston.

◄§ · ░►

Gardiner first published in 1786; he entitled the satirical poem *An Epistle to Zenas*. Like most satires of the eighteenth century, it was political, but its politics were idiosyncratic. The poem was not about party or even faction; its subject was personality. Gardiner entered into his majority and his career in letters by extending a family tradition of discontent. "Zenas" was one pen name of James Sullivan. Silvester Gardiner had nearly hired him to recover his debts and confiscated estates, but Sullivan angered the family by sponsoring a Massachusetts House bill that was unfriendly to Tory absentees. He helped John Gardiner return to Boston, but the two men would prove to be—as in the Freeman libel case—poor allies at best.[27] At worst, their relationship was a circuit of slander. Sullivan's attack on Gardiner in an April number of the *Continental Journal* was what inspired Gardiner's son to take up the pen on his father's behalf.

Sullivan called his piece "Pompus—A Character." He remarked that a young and industrious America had little experience with persons such as "Pompus," whose singularity was better nourished in Europe. Indeed, after an impudent but precocious boyhood, "Pompus" left for Scotland, "where the soil is naturally productive of genius without virtue." In this manner, Sullivan traced Gardiner's path from the Inner Temple through Wales and the West Indies to Boston, which mistakenly welcomed its prodigal son. Sullivan did not mince words in describing the barrister: "He is prophane in religion—A bigot in free-thinking—Scurrilous in politeness—Deceitful in friendship—Mean in politicks—And a pedant in Science." At one point, Sullivan went too far, calling Gardiner's daughter, Anne, a "Miss Fortune, who was never courted by any body." His retraction appeared the next week.[28]

For Anne's brother, J.S.J., Sullivan reserved a rare kindness: he thought him a promising fellow; his only fear was that the father's "noisy indelicacy" might wound the son's tender mind. *An Epistle to Zenas* undoubtedly confirmed this misgiving, but Sullivan should not have been surprised. His "Pompus" piece responded to John Gardiner's recent lashings of the Suffolk bar, and Gardiner had turned against his peers because they had snubbed his son. J.S.J. was a party to their argument—really the sole injured party in the entire affair. Thus one finds these passages of gleeful violence in his *Epistle:*

> List, Zenas, list! the faithful tale attend,
> Thou noxious viper, thou perfidious friend . . .
> Close to thy trembling bed behold me stand,
> The scourge of Satyr threat'ning in my hand.[29]

Sullivan's chief sins were the sins of a lawyer: greed, duplicity, and obscurantism. The poet did not ridicule Sullivan's family as Sullivan had his, though the lawyer's woodsy upbringing was an irresistible target. J.S.J., kept from the bar by a lack of credentials, jumped at the chance to expose a worse deficiency in one of the legal worthies: "The dews of education ne'er refined / Thy Mohawk manners, and thy rustic mind."[30] By contrast, Gardiner brandished his refinement. *An Epistle to Zenas* was as much a learned exercise as a political satire. In this exercise, the son followed his father's lead.

The *Epistle* could have passed as John Gardiner's work, and it was, in a way. One report has it that the elder Gardiner found his son's poem and published it of his own accord. John was likely the author of the poem's preface and notes, which delight in the many allusions to famous works. When "Jack" aped Virgil or Shakespeare or Pope, John was waiting in the margins to provide the original and secure father, son, and the ghosts of Western literature in one band of cleverness. The elder Gardiner must have been especially pleased to see his son borrow "the thund'ring force of Churchill's Song."[31] J.S.J. was a good child to his father, and he began his literary career in that role. He gamely fought the family's battles, and his early poetry was firmly rooted in his father's past. He would never lose the Gardiner spirit; with time, he would bring it to new debates.

J. S. J. Gardiner did not publish another satire until the end of 1794, more than a year after his father's death. *Remarks on the Jacobiniad* originally appeared as a serial in the *Federal Orrery*, then Boston's newest paper. Its editor was the twenty-one-year-old Thomas Paine, known to history as Robert Treat Paine. (He took the name of his dead elder brother. Rumors had it that he was happy to distance himself from the other Tom Paine, the famous deist and firebrand.)[32] That he would publish Gardiner at all demands some explanation. There was no love lost between the Gardiners and Thomas's father, the most senior Robert Treat Paine. As a young lawyer, he had worked for the Kennebeck Company; like another company hire, John Adams, he became an important politician and a signer of the Declaration of Independence. As the attorney general of Massachusetts in the 1780s, he had overseen the attempted confiscation of Silvester Gardiner's estates. In the *Epistle to Zenas,* Silvester's grandson intended the following words to be a grand insult to the next attorney general, James Sullivan: "of law the blemish, man the stain, / Inferior scarcely to that monster ———— [Paine]."[33] Gardiner further vilified Paine in a verse appendix to the *Epistle* entitled "Cerberus." In early 1795, after the *Jacobiniad* commenced its run in young Paine's *Orrery,* a critic wondered how the son of "Cerberus" could bear to deal with its author. Paine deflected this query, calling it the weak retort of a wounded jacobin. "Cerberus" was a youthful work instigated by "paternal resentment." Paine would come to know these sentiments firsthand as his literary career and lifestyle estranged him from his father's love.[34]

For the youngest Robert Treat Paine was America's first dissolute poet. That he is not remembered as such—or even remembered at all—speaks to the quality of his verse, but, in his day, he was one of New England's most honored. The notices began in 1794, when his prologue was chosen for the opening of the Federal Street Theatre. His intimate knowledge of the stage and of some of its players contributed to his family troubles. Yet when he launched the *Federal Orrery,* he was very much a rising star. A precursor to the Federalist newspapers of the Jefferson years, the *Orrery* devoted many of its pages to belles-lettres. It did not ignore politics, of course, and its political pieces were often of a bilious temper. Gardiner, for example, meant to provoke, and some offended readers of his satire responded energetically. One of them thrashed Paine in the street, and a mob assaulted his boarding house.[35]

Gardiner avoided the melee; the *Remarks on the Jacobiniad* were his brickbats. Like his father, the priest was a ready hand with personal invective. The style of older controversies lingered in the *Jacobiniad,* as did one of their main players: Benjamin Austin Jr., better known as "Honestus." This chronic pest had led the charge against the lawyers in the 1780s. John Gardiner was thought, then and now, to have been Austin's sponsor, but he denied the association. By 1792, the barrister and "Honestus" were on opposite sides of the theater question.[36] The barrister's son widened the breach with his *Remarks.* Austin was a leader of the Massachusetts Constitutional (or Democratic-Republican) Society, of which Gardiner's piece was a mock history. The satire was merciless, and its treatment of "Honestus" was characteristic. When he rose to speak, Gardiner found him obscenely postured: "His lean, left hand he stretched, as if to smite, / And, manful, groped his breeches, with his right."[37] Even more embarrassing was Austin's delivery, or lack of it. In the *Jacobiniad*, he could hardly manage a word.

The real "Honestus" was effusive. He addressed a number of open letters to Gardiner in the *Chronicle*; these discussed the poet's depravity at some length.[38] There were other critics, but all seemed to follow the same line. Gardiner was a coxcomb and a disgrace to the pulpit. He preferred to "bellow out applauses at the Theatre, and to show his dexterity and spirit at a card table, than to study and write sermons." (Gardiner supposedly justified his theatergoing with the wisdom of Ecclesiastes: "There was a time for every thing under the Sun.") His opponents found his behavior quite out of place. One of them recommended that he return to the goat-ridden hills of his native Wales or, more cruelly, that he move to Africa, "where monkies and baboons so greatly abound, and which you so much resemble."[39]

These criticisms—of Gardiner's profligacy, hypocrisy, and general inappropriateness—had a familiar ring: much the same had been said of his father. Indeed, many writers thought the priest's heritage was revealing. What else but knavery could one expect from the Sachem's "very spawn"? A critic remembered how an adolescent J.S.J., laden with law books, had dutifully waited upon the barrister in the mid-1780s. Ten years later, the son was still following in the father's footsteps and gave every sign of becoming "a finished blackguard." True, the younger Gardiner practiced superstition and priestcraft, two of the elder's favorite bogeys, but such inconsistencies were easily overlooked.[40] As before, and perhaps as ever, character and connections drew more notice than policy.

Even in the short span of time that separated John's outrages from the publication of the *Jacobiniad*, the political climate did change in significant ways. Political discussion continued to delight in personalities, but the clash of these personalities was increasingly pegged to issues of national and international scope. The title of J. S. J. Gardiner's poem was telling. In 1790, New Englanders were almost unanimous in approbating the French Revolution; their disagreements were mainly parochial. With the execution of Louis XVI, the Reign of Terror, and the entanglement of American shipping in the European war, events abroad catalyzed the formation of distinct parties in the United States.[41]

The Democratic-Republicans were the first to organize, and the friends of the government, looking to bloody France, called them "jacobins" for doing so. Washington himself denounced the "self-created societies" in late 1794. Gardiner's *Jacobiniad* appeared in this speech's wake. The poem was full of Boston men and Boston problems, but the poet could link them all to faraway matters: the Whiskey Rebellion, Genet's embassy, and the bathtub assassination of Marat.[42]

Each of these events ended to Gardiner's liking, but he was not particularly interested in discussing the resolution of crises. He did not even dwell on the federal government's victories and virtues. Instead, he was obsessed with the crudities of the opposition. Austin's awkwardness was indicative; with few exceptions, the heroes of the *Jacobiniad* were rubes. Gardiner passed along to his readers a "copy" of the compact that members of the Constitutional Society repeated upon their induction. It closed in this way: "as grate sekrecy, is much wanted in this bisness, wee binde ourselfes, not to lett any thing, sed or dun in our socity, git abraud, lest wee oversett our apple-cart, and so stick our foot in it."[43]

And this was an extraordinary effort. Gardiner described how a committee of seven was appointed to answer his satire; it consisted, he added smugly, of every literate member. This committee then considered a poetical model for its reply. One fellow mentioned Pope (whose *Dunciad* was obviously on Gardiner's mind), but the others, having never heard of him, thought his admirer was a papist and drove him from the room. Finally, wrote Gardiner, "the poor jacobins, embittered with despair and disappointment, swore eternal enmity to all literature, and passed a resolution, that, in future, no member of that society should suffer any one of his children to learn, either to read or write!"[44] There is an overweening quality to this satire, which hints at the anxieties of the author and the vulnerability of his politics. Within a few years, "despair and disappointment" would be the Federalists' lot, and, for some of them, literature offered a rare consolation.

In the meantime, Gardiner's opponents were not impressed with his learning. Without acknowledging its excellence, they saw its display as a sign of effeminacy. One of them predicted and clearly hoped that a citizen would ignore the priest's "petticoats," the "protection which you enjoy with every female," and administer the rough justice Gardiner deserved. Another contributor to the *Chronicle* remarked upon the literary pilferings of the "right reverend plagiarist." By exposing these, he wanted to incite "a little tete-a-tete among his [Gardiner's] female circles in the gay world."[45]

J. S. J. Gardiner did not intend to leave the world of letters; there he was proficient and comfortable. In the *Jacobiniad*, he paraded his familiarity with literature, often to the detriment of his political agenda. He appended to the second part of the *Jacobiniad* a parody called "Benjamin's Feast," which took as its material a democratic jubilee, presided over by the usual suspects: Austin, Perez Morton, et alia. In a footnote, Gardiner admitted that if the reader were "unacquainted with Dryden's 'Ode on Alexander's Feast,' he will probably pronounce the foregoing a very dull performance."[46] One might apply similar reservations to the whole of his *Remarks*. Its first number commences not with a summary of the present dangers, but with a discourse on the epic. His opponents' clumsy alexandrines interested him more than their conspiracies.

Of course, those bad verses were really his, not theirs. The *Remarks on the Jacobiniad* were a mix of poetry and prose. Gardiner transparently offered up the former as the work of an anonymous scribe, although the "jacobins," as speakers, provided many of their own lines. The authorial presence was strongest in the prose gloss. For example, after the goddess "Faction" sang her henchmen's praises, the author commented:

> A rigid critic would object to these lines, as the two former appear ironical, and two last, serious . . . But it should be remembered, that the person, here speaking, is no less than a divinity, who, consequently, has an absolute command over every figure of speech, without confining herself to those established rules of composition.[47]

Gardiner's choice of role is telling. He was not a political actor, and he was only rarely a poetic celebrant of those politicians who acted on his behalf. Gardiner was not, in fact, a prolific poet at all. Given his talents, the *Jacobiniad* was a most appropriate construct: he wrote awful poetry and assailed it ruthlessly. He had defined himself as the "rigid critic" with a sense of humor. The troubles ahead would encourage him in that role.

◗§ · §◖

By the end of 1800, New Englanders had to come to terms with the Republican victory. Writing in December of that year, a correspondent to the *Massachusetts Mercury* listed the grim possibilities: "anarchy, convulsions, a contraction of national credit . . . want of confidence at home, contempt abroad, a foreign war and a civil war." He hoped that the leaders of the new government would preserve the principles of the old and become "federalists in fact." They could then demand the loyalty of even the most disgruntled citizen. In any case, New England's influence in national affairs was sure to wane.[48]

The *Mercury* adjusted itself to the new dispensation. With its first issue of 1801, it assumed another name and a defensive posture. In an address to the public, the editors of *The Mercury and New-England Palladium* (and this second name was the more prominent on the masthead and in the historical record) offered the wisdom of the wounded. A century of progress had drawn to its close, a century so eventful and promising as to encourage a belief that progress would continue without check. Happily, in the paper's view, many people had now left the world of dreams and concluded instead "that modern liberty and equality, the emancipation and regeneration of the world, the perfectibility of reason and all the farrago of political creed mongers, are founded in the vanity, pride and wickedness of the human heart."[49] Recent political events provided numerous examples of corruption and suggested that more was to come. The people of New England were the most likely to brave and perhaps stem the evil. Their forefathers, "who first settled this country, brought with them the true principles of liberty . . . their literary, civil and religious establishments have been, from that time to this, its only solid support."[50] The *Palladium* devoted itself to the maintenance of New England habits. The country's future depended not on its advancement but on its memory—indeed, on the memory of one part of the whole. The Federalist mind, once so expansive, was falling back on provincial impulses.

Naturally, New Englanders thought these impulses reflected universal goods and truths. They were lessons to be taught, though not everyone could take to them. The *Palladium* understood, for example, that if it did not speak for the nation politically, it could at least "diffuse a correct taste in literature." The new paper attended much more closely to letters than did the older *Mercury*. Essays were commonly found on the first page of eighteenth-century journals, but essays primarily concerned with questions of literary merit were rarer. Not so in the *Palladium:* in its first month there began a series of "Observations on the Corruptions of Literature." The paper did not confine its criticism or its praise to New England writers. It excoriated Wieland and

Godwin, and it wished good luck to the *Port Folio*, Joseph Dennie's journal in Philadelphia.[51]

Dennie once was, in Nathaniel Hawthorne's words, "esteemed the finest writer in America." His *Lay Preacher* essays were popular at home and earned praise from abroad. He created and edited the *Port Folio*, the most important literary magazine of the early republic. For the last eleven years of Dennie's life, the practice of letters was his sole vocation. How he arrived at that point is at least as interesting as what he produced once there, in part because he was a more productive writer before he settled unequivocally upon a literary calling.[52] Moreover, Dennie had to confront directly the problem of how his society dealt with talent. His opinion was not fairly and not liberally. His experience, however, provides a more nuanced answer. Joseph Dennie wanted to believe that the talented—always an articulate elite, though possessing other skills—could sit astride society and partake of all its advantages. They deserved riches and respect because their excellence was general. They were at once the best wits, the best advocates, and the best companions. Yet Dennie also knew that the economic and political systems of his day matched particular rewards to very particular efforts.

Joseph Dennie was born in Boston in 1768. His mother's family was active in publishing, his father's in the West India trade. At the age of sixteen, Dennie became a clerk in the countinghouse of James Swan.[53] One can only speculate about how this master influenced his charge, but Swan was a daring and erratic schemer—just the man to fire a young imagination. A Scottish emigrant, Swan cast his lot with the American cause. He was a Tea Party Mohawk and was wounded at Bunker Hill. He bought into the first stock issue of the Massachusetts Bank, from which he borrowed rather recklessly. Swan read his countryman Smith. He knew wealth might have an unseemly foundation. Debt and vice were profitable if managed correctly. He purchased state notes and converted them into eastern landholdings. He consulted with William Bingham on Maine's development, and an island south of Bar Harbor still bears his name. In a tract entitled *National Arithmetick* (1786), Swan recommended that the commonwealth increase its revenues by licensing stage-plays and other entertainments. Like the theater advocate John Gardiner, Swan saw a chance to improve himself in the Revolutionary crisis and aftermath. He purchased the confiscated estate of a Tory who had fled with Gardiner's father in 1776. He parlayed his connections with the Marquis de Lafayette and other prominent Frenchmen into a lucrative agency, which continued to pay off even as his original patrons lost power or worse in the terrors of the early 1790s.[54]

Swan spent the last twenty years of his life in a French jail because he refused to acknowledge a debt he had the means to pay. His American wife sent enough money to keep him in relative comfort, but he remained in captivity until the July Revolution of 1830 emptied the prisons. His death followed almost immediately upon his freedom; he had just enough time to see his old friend Lafayette. Thus, like Gardiner again, Swan was a shifty operator who, in the end, proved to be bizarrely stubborn. These kindred spirits were surely familiar: they served together in the King's Chapel vestry.[55]

Swan's apprentice knew good company when he saw it, and he was determined to see as much of it as he could. In 1785, Dennie proudly reported to his parents that he would accompany Harrison Gray Otis to Harvard commencement. Otis was soon embroiled in the Sans Souci controversy, and Dennie exhibited the same "free and easy" temper at college. He matriculated at Harvard in 1787, as a sophomore. Josiah Quincy, the future Harvard president and Boston mayor, was in the same class, and he would write of Dennie: "he might unquestionably have taken the highest rank . . . but he was negligent in his studies, and not faithful to the genius with which nature had endowed him."[56] The campus was used to the misconduct of gifted students. Royall Tyler, class of 1776 and Dennie's literary collaborator, had been sent down to Maine after he and Christopher Gore—later Governor and Senator Gore—caught the president's wig with a hook and line. Tyler studied law in Cambridge after his graduation and fathered a child with a college maid.[57]

Harvard's finest were no better in the late 1780s, and they may have been even worse. The college prescribed a strict dress code, including a prohibition on silk, in order to keep its swells in line. The students did not receive these regulations well. One professor noted their misdeeds in a "Journal of Disorders": biscuits, teacups, even knives thrown at tutors; dogs thrown down a well; members of Dennie's class tossing pennies in chapel; Dennie himself, found drunk.[58] It is not a distinguished record. In his senior year, Dennie went too far. Cribbing from a speech by the elder Pitt, he publicly abused the college authorities, who in turn rusticated the offender to Groton. This was an upsetting blow, but not crushing. The faculty restored Dennie to his place before commencement. In the meantime, he enjoyed his sojourn among Groton's "liberal and spunkey" lads, and his removal to the west allowed him to visit a favorite girl in Concord.[59]

Dennie's college antics deserve our attention because they informed his literary projects. His work, like most of that produced in his day, was about the appreciation of virtues; Dennie just made a point of admiring a broader range of abilities. His models were not careful or solemn. They were as inspired at play as they were on the job. During Dennie's exile, one of his schoolmates, John Callender, entertained him with a fantastic travelogue in which Callender joined Charles Fox and the Earl of Sandwich on a tour of Italy. Their "party of pleasures" culminated in a skirmish with stiletto-wielding Roman constables.[60] Fox was a compelling figure with a curious history. He was the great-great-grandson of Charles II, and his initial political inclinations were Tory. (He was, for example, a savage critic of John Wilkes.) Eventually, Fox was disappointed in his hopes for advancement in George III's government, and he settled into the role by which his fame persists, that of the Whig reformer.

Fox's personality was always notable. By the 1790s, his reputation as a carouser and a rake was long established. His youthful exploits on the Continent were the subject of a book that might well have been the source for Callender's story. In one of his first published essays, Dennie eulogized Fox, "who, like a man of spunk, at brothels and at Brooke's, wenches, gambles, and drinks all night, and like a man of genius, harangues in the house all day."[61] The young American roué looked up to the great Brit, whose excesses matched his ambitions. Fox's life was an example of energy, of talent unbound.

Dennie also knew that Fox was a dangerous hero. Few of his literary admirers could direct their energies "into a regular channel," and Dennie was thinking of himself when he wrote this. As a collegian, he imagined the sort of writing that would use his somewhat unreliable gifts to their best advantage and appeal to readers of a similar character. Such a work would be diverse in its interests in order to "gratify that thirst of variety inherent in man." It would make for pleasant reading, so pleasant, in fact, that its moral and social benefits would seem incidental: "though the essay may be read with a view to waste time, it will probably contribute to its improvement." In short, the ideal literary effort would "fix volatility."[62] Dennie struggled with this, his own mandate, throughout his life and works. Volatile persons were charming, and often, the most capable, but, to be productive, they had to accept the harness of social needs and norms.

Joseph Dennie stared this problem in the face as he prepared to graduate. The time had come for him to choose a profession. With Roger Vose, his best friend at Harvard, he discussed all three: law, medicine, and divinity. Dennie dismissed the last because it did not pay and involved "a starchedness of thinking and behavior totally repugnant to our liberal views." In the not too distant future, Dennie would reconsider this position, but, in the spring of 1790, neither the pulpit nor the bar held a candle to medical practice. It was potentially lucrative and demanded fewer literary exertions. Vose saw the error in his friend's logic. He reminded Dennie that his talents were precisely literary. He might make a good minister, if he were to conduct himself with more gravity, but the law was the obvious choice. Dennie's powers of memory and elocution promised a first-rate legal career. He had a chance to prove "that Massachusetts can produce a Madison."[63]

That winter, Dennie apprenticed himself to a lawyer in Charlestown, New Hampshire. The Madisons and Marshalls need not have feared for their places. Joseph Dennie was never an eminent lawyer, and, if we believe his friends, he did not take his job seriously. Jeremiah Mason, who would become a leader of the New Hampshire bar and a U.S. senator, described Dennie as a "most aerial, refined, and highly sublimated spirit." Dennie's legal knowledge amounted to some "queer phrases" from Plowden's *Commentaries,* which he repeated for others' amusement. Royall Tyler recalled Dennie's maiden speech before the court, when his fine language left the judge dumbfounded. According to Tyler, Dennie resolved upon this occasion that he would never again try "to batter down a mud wall with roses."[64]

However, if Dennie badmouthed the law, he did not abandon it entirely for many years. Mason's and Tyler's recollections had the privilege of hindsight; they appeared after Dennie was an established literary figure. Throughout the 1790s, he was a reluctant practitioner who cherished letters above the law, but he did not think that one endeavor excluded the other. His approach was typical: most early national writers were lawyers, many were unhappy ones, but several wrote their best work before they left the profession for good. Washington Irving and William Cullen Bryant were of this group, and so was their predecessor, Joseph Dennie.[65]

He began publishing his first series of periodical essays while still a clerk. The original number of the *Farrago* appeared in the *Morning Ray* (of Windsor, Vermont) in February of 1792. He promised to carry out his design with "the restlessness of indolence" and "the volatility of a humming bird." He claimed to be a privileged member of society, free to wander and observe.[66] This was a standard pose of the English essayist: witness Johnson's *Rambler* or the *Spectator* of Addison and Steele.

Dennie probably found some relief in the persona as he pored over legal treatises in his village office. There was a strong biographical element in the second and third numbers, which described the kind of law students who had talent and taste but no focus: "Their judgment, pronouncing sentence against themselves, acknowledges the utility of fixation of thought, and marks, with mathematical precision, the point, on which attention should rest; but their wayward imagination is eternally making curves."[67] The exemplary character in these two essays is "Meander," who prefers Shakespeare and Sterne to Blackstone. Dennie was obviously satirizing tendencies of his own, but one cannot help but wonder if there was a bit of John Gardiner in Dennie's creation. The essays appeared only a few weeks after Gardiner delivered his speech on the theater, and he was already known as a failed law reformer. "Meander" was full of ambitions and visionary projects, but these never seemed to materialize. He was more assiduous about drink and revel, and, like Gardiner, he apologized for his conduct with a nod to Churchill's "Night."[68] He represented the sensibility that found vices attractive, but he was too eccentric—too consciously literary—to distinguish the useful perversities from the merely decadent.

During one failed attempt at study, Dennie's "Meander" escaped into Hume's history of England and, in particular, the story of Henry I. This brilliant king "blended in one bright assemblage, ambition, prudence, eloquence, and enterprize." The irresolute student wondered why he lacked the prudence to complete his hopes. Dennie did not claim, as Gardiner had, to have turned his back on that "Strumpet." On the other hand, he joined the Sachem and many other contemporaries in an ambivalent respect for Hume. Dennie disapproved of the philosopher's skepticism, but he was drawn to the historian's understanding of social causes.[69] Hume knew that felicity might issue from strange and unexpected quarters. He also practiced what he preached. In the *Farrago*, Dennie noted how Hume restored his intellectual powers with a "cheerful Rubber" of whist: "From a fashionable amusement he derived that benefit, which the worshippers of Euclid would confine to their God. In fine, a mere mathematician . . . is less learned, less eloquent, and less courtly than the Beauclercs, whose superficial talents he contemns."[70] The "Beauclerc," or polite scholar, was the best sort of person. Without squelching his considerable ability, he enjoyed society in all its richness and sophistication.

At Harvard, Dennie had aggressively sought out amusement, and the young lawyer and his friends were just as determined. That stretch of the Connecticut River Valley from Windsor, Vermont, to Greenfield, Massachusetts, was home to a loose circle of legal and literary hotshots. Its activities revolved around the courts and taverns and eventually found its center in Walpole, New Hampshire. Besides Dennie, the circle included Royall Tyler, Jeremiah Mason, William Coleman, who would later edit the Hamiltonian *New York Evening Post,* and Thomas Green Fessenden, already a popular author while at Dartmouth and, in the next decade, the author of "Democracy Unveiled." By all accounts, they were a merry company, but they were no less accomplished for their indulgences: Dennie wrote essays while playing cards at Walpole's tavern. When the printer's devil ventured inside and begged for copy, the author asked a friend to assume his hand so that he might "give the devil his due."[71]

Beginning in the colonial period, young lawyers from the Boston area often had to seek their fortunes in the outlands. Dennie admitted to his parents that the pattern still held. While senior members of the bar like Theophilus Parsons and James Sullivan monopolized Boston's business, he thought he would remain in his "northern corner." He argued that learning and merit drew more notice where they were a rarer commodity. The environment was less competitive, and it was less elaborate.[72] Dennie and his fellow wits could lead in several fields: in law, in letters, and even in divinity.

In the winter of 1793–94, Joseph Dennie became a lay reader at a local Episcopal church. He recited the liturgy and a few sermons with enough elegance and conviction that a Portsmouth congregation invited him to be its pastor. If Samuel Seabury would ordain him, the congregation wrote, he could count on a substantial benefice. Dennie was never seriously interested in the offer; he preferred to combine the wages of an occasional ministry with his legal practice. He was not an irreligious person, but neither was he shy about liking money. Moreover, he liked the very idea of proving his worth in different enterprises. In a letter home and in the *Farrago,* he pointed to the example of Alcibiades, the Athenian master of war and revel, who could deliver a homily on Sunday and plead a cause on Monday. Dennie aspired to a similar "versatility."[73]

An opportunity to broaden his horizons emerged early in 1795. With the support of many prominent subscribers, including J. S. J. Gardiner, Christopher Gore, and Sarah Wentworth Morton, Dennie oversaw the publication of the *Tablet*. This Boston magazine was a novelty: it was devoted wholly to belles-lettres; it did not print news or advertisements. Dennie's *Farrago* essays were a mainstay. His collaborative miscellany with Royall Tyler, "From the Shop of Messrs. Colon and Spondee," moved to the *Tablet* from the *Federal Orrery*. The magazine published short biographies of Adam Smith, Edmund Burke, and Charles Fox. It furnished its readers with Gardiner's original criticism of Churchill.[74]

Dennie had returned to, as he put it, the "metropolis" to advance a brazenly literary project, but he did not want to give anything up for literature. The *Tablet*, he told his mother, was the means to greater ends, wealth and general eminence. Dennie believed that his literary fame in New England's largest town would promote his legal practice in the country. He thought the magazine would bring in a steady income, and he hoped that it might win him political favor and emoluments. By October, Dennie bragged of being "more afloat" than he had ever been, but he could not be so sanguine about his magazine. It had not survived the summer, and its founder blamed the "tasteless" Bostonians for the failure.[75]

What followed was the most productive stage of Dennie's career. He moved to Walpole, where he continued to practice law even as he began the more rewarding task of editing the *Farmer's Weekly Museum*. This newspaper contained all of the various elements absent from the *Tablet*, plus the lively political and belletristic compositions at which Dennie and his friends were adept. The *Museum* was probably the most widely read village paper in American publishing history. It was the staple of literate Federalists throughout the country.[76] Its politics were correct, its prose clever. Dennie himself set the tone with his major series of essays, the *Lay Preacher*.

◄§ · §►

In the main, Dennie's "Preacher" was easygoing. He projected stability and contentment. He was sure that Christianity was a "cheerful system" secure enough to tolerate fun in moderation. He regretted that "the moping and the austere" had laid claim to true religion. Mopers were all too common in the "Preacher's" world, and he was determined to

J. S. J.

convert them to a life of peace. He met them while "on devious rambles through lonely pasture or gloomy wood." He saw them in the corner, nursing their spleen. The "Preacher" was no prig. He called on the sick at heart to mimic the publican and seek jovial companions.[77]

At the same time, the "Preacher" recognized that one had to find the proper balance between pleasure and industry, and he argued that this balance prevailed in the village and adjoining countryside. For centuries, men and women had chased their ambitions to the cities, where they found "in every street a ladder lofty enough to reach the extent of many a project." The "Preacher" continued:

> Allowing that there are some genuine delights in the thronged town, yet they tread too fast on each other and weary by constant succession . . . The pleasures of the country, pure, simple, not dazzling, not boistrous, will gently stir the stream of life . . . To saunter along the banks of the brook and allure the trout from his recess, to crop the fantastic flowers of May or the strawberries of June . . . are cheap and real pleasures, make no man a criminal, and leave no sting behind.[78]

To deserve these simple refreshments, one but had to obey the simple but oft ignored injunction to rise and work. At his most straightforward, the "Lay Preacher" was a dogged enemy of sloth.

Not surprisingly, some of his sermons praised the farmer as the stalwart of American virtue and social happiness. "What order of knighthood," asked Dennie, "can be more noble than yeomen"? In passages such as this, he sounded a republican note, but it was the republicanism of steady habits rather than of revolutionary strivings. In America, each citizen could be "the artificer of his own fortune," and the result was not confusion but independence. Industrious farmers relied on their own resources and led quiet lives.[79]

The "Lay Preacher's" politics tried to assume similarly stable airs. The federal administration, like the Episcopal faith, was an easy yoke to bear. Neither asked for wrenching sacrifices; both enforced a pleasing artificial order that might pass for natural if left to its business. The "Preacher" advised: "Be your devotions and your government equally undisturbed; attendance at church at least preserves your neatness and sociability. Obedience to government causes you to sit in peace under the fig tree."[80] Dennie first published these essays when the political opposition had begun to organize. He looked south and east to his native Boston, and he saw "irregular sectaries" convening at the Green Dragon. He bid Austin and Morton and their fellow democrats to set their complaints aside and join "the venerable and established Church of government." Such loyalty was unfashionable, perhaps, but fashion had to give way to comfort and utility. The "Lay Preacher" explained that he eschewed canonical dress; instead, he wore "a good, warm, well-made, easy garment, made to fit any one, called Federalism."[81]

In fact, Joseph Dennie was a dandy who stood out on Walpole's village lanes, and his politics were likewise an exercise in distinction. No amount of homespun sentiment could blunt the fine edges. In an essay from December 1795, he defended "energetic government" against the democrats:

> I have learned that civil liberty consists in doing whatever does not militate with laws, restraining individual excesses to promote the public weal. Observation has further suggested that there are a few, and how few! upon whom the Parent of wisdom has largely bestowed that ethereal spirit, that bold and sublime genius which He has chosen to withhold from the majority of mankind. Yet farther, it is obvious that in the race for riches, all run, and still but few reach the goal and bear the prize. It follows, therefore, that he of ample mind or ample purse will direct the councils and command the service of him who is weak or poor, and that equality is a visionary whim.[82]

Here again is the consonance of the liberal and the elitist, a consonance noticed earlier in the legal reform controversies and in Federalist political theory. The words in themselves involved no contradiction; they jar because their sentiments are naked and because they issued from an expositor of rustic mildness and self-sufficiency.

Dennie mixed his messages in other ways. Even as he called others to duty, he hinted at his own contrariness. He castigated idlers, but he also hoped his readers "will not inquire how long I court the morning pillow." His political economy taught that the line from motives to benefits was rarely straight, and he laced his sermons with a like irony. "Gather grapes from my thorns" was his advice. His anxieties were not always so obvious or so humorously couched. During lonely tramps through the northern woods, "far from the clink of Industry's anvil, far from the jocund chorus of Music's songs," did not the "Preacher" meet his own shadow in the "moping hypochondriac"?[83] This troubled soul was bent on squandering his talents, and Dennie often worried that he walked the same path.

He discussed proper employments in a number of essays. Of particular interest is an early selection in which Dennie ridiculed wine-soaked parsons, quack doctors, and country attorneys. They all claimed the privileges of craft but were nothing more than "sharpers." He then reflected on his own plight. He noted that his friends reproached him for devoting himself to such an unpromising enterprise, but he preferred "literary speculations" to any other kind. He was happy to preach simple truths and smoke "the tranquil cigar." These professions of happiness were, even then, not completely genuine. The quiet pastimes of the country, the tickled trout and ripe strawberry, did not calm Dennie's ambitions. He knew himself to be a "Mandevillean" (his word) who craved the riches of a busy hive and the sting of dangerous pleasures.[84] After four years in Walpole, his thoughts turned to opportunities available in Philadelphia, America's metropolis.

Dennie's occupational concerns informed his disenchantment with New England. His hometown had not supported the *Tablet*, and he had begun to regret his heritage altogether. Rather impolitely, he reported those misgivings to his parents. How unfortunate it was for him to have been raised among Yankees and Indians. The Puritans emigrated to shirk the obligations of debt and tithe; their cheap descendants were unfriendly to "men of liberality and letters." Dennie wished that the colonies had not revolted or, better yet, that he had been born in England. There, he believed, talent received its due. He imagined himself in the king's service, basking in the "genial sunshine of a Court." These musings were probably facetious as to substance, but the sourness is unmistakable. Dennie was ready to abandon New England. He had little to carry away but his growing reputation. The publisher of the *Museum* went bankrupt in 1799, and Dennie shared in the loss.[85]

The "Lay Preacher" essays of this period record his move and the adjustments it entailed. In one of the last numbers he prepared for the *Museum*, he remarked that his had been the observations of a hermit "who remembers what man was, rather than those of a man of business, or courtier, who holds an actual intercourse with society." The moment had come for him to cast off his rural habits. A quick wit was needed to manage the city's perplexities. Dennie never went to Britain, but he did what was to his mind the next best thing: he became a fixture in what he called "the London of America."[86]

This was outrageous flattery, but Philadelphia's late-eighteenth-century importance is too easily forgotten. At no other time in the nation's history was its political center also its largest city. The cultures of state, commerce, and literary production intermingled. Dennie, who had revisited the theme of versatility in his final essays for the *Museum*, was enthused by the possibilities, and he had good cause. Three potentially lucrative offers lured him to Philadelphia. William Cobbett, the genius of *Porcupine's Gazette* and the scourge of democrats, was going to publish a "Lay Preacher" anthology. John Ward Fenno hired Dennie to edit the *Gazette of the United States*, the country's leading Federalist newspaper. And Timothy Pickering, U.S. Secretary of State, took Dennie on as his private secretary.[87] The fugitive Yankee had established his prospects on a broad footing.

His old friend, Thomas Boylston Adams, found less cause for optimism. When he heard that Dennie might soon join him in Philadelphia, he looked forward to taking up the pen himself but had few illusions about the journal's prospects. Adams thought that the city's professionals would not encourage literature. They were narrow philistines: "I dread these mere Lawyers & Doctors & Divines, they are of no use or amusement but to their respective fraternities, and yet they are eminent men—full of professional knowledge & formidable on their own ground—soaring high in their appropriate elements & only fit to dwell therein."[88] Adams, of course, was a lawyer, and, like many lawyers, he did not love his job. Nevertheless, he saw that he was more likely to succeed if he concentrated his efforts on the law. He also guessed that Dennie would suffer for his literary sensibilities.

Dennie himself began to despair of success shortly after arriving in Philadelphia. In Fenno's *Gazette*, he worried about becoming one of Mandeville's unfortunates, a person doomed to an unrewarding and subordinate place in society. He complained that talented and energetic people did not infallibly receive their just desserts. Too often, the "rude stream" of life pushed fools to the "unruffled surface," where they enjoyed unmerited honors.[89] The promises that brought Dennie to the city were not guarantees. A libel judgment chased Cobbett back to England, and Dennie refused an invitation to join him there. Pickering left the government and returned to Essex County, where he nursed dreams of secession. His secretary remained at the State Department but acknowledged that a Jefferson victory in the election would force his withdrawal from public endeavors. The following March, Jefferson was inaugurated in Washington, D.C., a new capital conjured out of a southern swamp, far away from any cosmopolitan allurements.[90]

Dennie found consolation in the *Port Folio*. The initial volume appeared in January 1801, one day after the first issue of the *New-England*

Palladium. Its prospectus had earlier circulated to "men of affluence, men of liberality, and men of letters." This piece predated Jefferson's election, and Dennie promised therein to expose "Jacobinical misrepresentations" regarding Adams's government. Even so, Dennie was no electioneer, nor did he pretend to be. He forswore any attempt to please a wide audience; the *Port Folio* was meant for "the liberal Few." Perhaps the editor recognized that his politics were in decline, or perhaps he increasingly found political controversy distasteful, despite his flair for such work; in any event, he very deliberately made literature his priority. He bemoaned partisan bickering and "the universal eagerness for political texts," for these distracted readers from "the gentle voice of the Muse."[91]

In the first "Lay Preacher" to grace the *Port Folio,* he seemed to welcome his fate. He conceded that he had come to the city in order to seek preferment. With his hopes disappointed, he was subject to "the mandate of necessity." Nevertheless, Joseph Dennie was cheerful. Necessity was satisfied by the cultivation of his literary talents. He earned enough money to enlarge his library, and he was free to wander through the city's broad streets, an observant member of the throng.[92]

But the flaneur's pretensions can mislead. Dennie never stepped beyond the professional background that had produced him, and he knew—*pace* T. B. Adams—that practicing lawyers were numerous among the "liberal Few" who read and supported his magazine. The *Port Folio* flattered men of the bar: they were the nation's "Natural Aristocracy" as well as "the best patrons which literature can hope to find" in a country bereft of other supportive institutions, such as an established Church. Dennie could be wistful about what was lost when America gained its independence, and—to the dismay of even the Episcopalian and arch-Federalist J. S. J. Gardiner—he enjoyed playing the part of the latter-day "Cavalier."[93]

Yet when offered the chance, he did not pursue his career abroad. His talents were suited to Grub Street, but he preferred the company of his peers in the legal and other professions to the high and low of London society. He was, after all, an American and a provincial, though one especially anxious to maintain a still enriching relationship between his country and Great Britain. However much he might have hoped to see bishops and barons on the *Port Folio*'s subscription list, he understood that its core audience was to be found in the better law offices of Boston and Philadelphia. As Dennie pointed out, and Tocqueville argued thirty years later, such men were America's social and political elite; they bowed to no king, no lord, no altar. Their perspective and capacities were, nonetheless, improved by contact with the larger Anglophone community of law and letters. The *Port Folio* eased these contacts, not only as a literary organ but as a publisher of contemporary legal decisions issuing from the King's Bench and other English courts.[94]

Except for episodes of poor health, Dennie never left his editorial post at the *Port Folio*. He died in January of 1812. His estate did not equal his debts, and his mother had to provide for their payment in her will. His legacy in letters, though small, was kinder to its heirs. Early in his career, he wrote that the "scholar, like the merchant, should exult at petty gains, and, from their accumulation, form his capital."[95] In this way we might also appreciate Joseph Dennie. Other writers extended what he had begun. One of them was Washington Irving, who called on him in 1807. At that time, Dennie was the master of the light satirical essay. Irving was a fan and an imitator. He became the success Dennie never was: an author widely read and well patronized both in Britain and in the United States.[96]

◄§ · §►

In the mid-1790s, when Dennie published the *Tablet*, J. S. J. Gardiner contributed to its short run with several articles of Churchill criticism. In 1799, he canvassed support for a secret literary magazine to be published under his direction.[97] Nothing came of the scheme, but with the emergence of the *Palladium* and the *Port Folio*, he did not lack a forum. In March of 1801, he commenced a long essay series called "The Restorator" in the Boston paper, and Dennie quickly picked it up for his periodical.

In its first number, Gardiner situated himself within the tradition of English essay writing. Behind him stood the hallmark examples of Addison and Steele's *Spectator* and Johnson's *Rambler*. He declined to comment on his present competition, partly out of professional courtesy and partly—he seemed to hint—out of charity.[98] He also explained the title of his series. For some time, a Boston hotelier named Julien had advertised his establishment as the "Restorator." (Anglophones would eventually accept the French word *restaurant*.) He set an enlightened table, its offerings endorsed by Continental science. On the advice of Tissot, he provided turtle soup for the consumptive. For the flu-sufferer, Julien stocked oysters and barley soup. The town also relied on him for "truly republican entertainment." In 1795, when the friends of France gathered to celebrate that country's military successes, Citizen Julien was their caterer. Gardiner mentioned none of these activities. He simply welcomed readers to the new "Restorator" and promised that there "every intellectual epicure may be gratified with his favorite dish."[99]

This was false advertising. Gardiner's tastes were extremely particular. He held most contemporary authors in contempt, especially those whose reputations depended on the latest philosophical fad. Both their work and their sympathies deserved opprobrium. One could not expect to find the "flowers of poetry" on the "dung hills of democracy." Because critics praised the "Sans-culotte school" of literature, readers had to tolerate "the asinine strains of Coleridge, and the dull malignity of Southey."[100] Americans would do best to look to older models: Pope, Dryden, and Milton. According to Gardiner, these English poets could not be surpassed, though the quality of English poetry had been deteriorating since the reign of Queen Anne.

Gardiner's critical aesthetic depended on decline, and to this aesthetic his politics were adjunct. They complemented rather than drove his criticism. He scolded his friend Dennie for his seeming love of all things English, as it supported the view that Federalists were consistent partisans for Great Britain. Gardiner was a patent Anglophile, but he did not hesitate to decry what he saw as absurdity, no matter the source. Throughout the English-speaking world, the literati at best imitated their predecessors; at worst, they abused the language by their innovations. "Every new word," he warned, "tends to corrupt."[101]

Turning to the narrower subject of American letters, the "Restorator" again saw much to scorn. Americans deformed their writings with "vulgarisms and provincial peculiarities."[102] Noah Webster was the most outrageous offender, for he took it upon himself to indulge provincial American practices while tinkering with the language for reason's sake. He thus combined the bad with the horrible, the vulgar with the strange. Webster became Gardiner's favorite whipping boy, and Gardiner's friends joined the attack in later publications. The fifteenth "Restorator," nodding to Burke, described Webster's English as appropriate for the "swinish multitude." The nineteenth joked about Webster's half-measures. Rather than adopt a "Babylonish dialect," would it not be better to revert to aboriginal speech? Gardiner hoped that some citizens might be allowed to study English as a dead tongue. The language, as he knew it, did not require improvement; instead, "literary men" were obliged "to guard against impurities and chastise, with the critical lash, all useless innovations."[103] So much for epicurean generosity. In Gardiner's mind, the finest literary judgments were often severe.

This standard was rarely met, and America's critics were as disappointing to Gardiner as its writers. "There is no art," he wrote, "in which our superiority over the Europeans, is more evident, than in the art of puffing . . . every new production is a masterpiece, and every new author a first rate genius."[104] This loose way with praise indicated a lack of discernment, and it amounted to a betrayal of the public's trust. As arbiters of taste, critics were responsible for leading their audience down the straight and true path. Gardiner explained this responsibility in the second "Restorator": "The majority of readers are incapable of appreciating the literary merit of any work, and generally suspend their judgment till they are acquainted with the opinions of profest literati."[105] Here was the same view he held in religious matters: authority rested in an articulate elite.

One of the early problems of American culture was that the nation could not reliably foster a mandarinate. Gardiner looked to the colleges and their "slender" endowments: "few of their professorships hold out any great temptations to avarice or ambition." Men of talent might linger around their schools for a brief period, but they inevitably moved on to business or the professions. The students who remained as tutors were made of lesser stuff. They were, in Gardiner's words, "a succession of tyros, who, in many instances, attempt to teach what they themselves have but imperfectly learnt." On the other hand, Gardiner was proud that knowledge was widespread in America and "that society, in the aggregate, is, in no part of the civilized world, on so good a footing, as in New-England." He even invoked the region's "free and enlightened yeomanry." These conditions boded well for the future.[106] The question was how to concentrate the country's intellectual resources, how to achieve sophistication. This was a social question, and if it were to be answered, American writers had to rely on, and even revel in, their social experience.

◆§ · ❦◆

In Boston, the most important literary venture between the Revolution and the War of 1812 was the publication of the *Monthly Anthology*. Its run began inauspiciously in 1803, under the direction of David Phineas Adams, two years out of Harvard. Within a year, the magazine passed into abler hands. William Emerson, minister of Boston's First Church and Ralph Waldo's father, became editor, and J. S. J. Gardiner began contributing. Emerson and Gardiner were among the founding members of the Anthology Society, which oversaw the journal's operations. This group also included two future professors of the Harvard Medical School, a few Congregational pastors with Unitarian sympathies, and, of course, a small bunch of reluctant lawyers. William Tudor, Jr., the son of John Gardiner's friend and fellow liberal, would extend the society's labors as the first editor of the *North American Review*. William Smith Shaw was Abigail Adams's nephew, and he served as private secretary to Abigail's husband in the late, troubled years of his presidency. While John Quincy Adams contributed to the *Anthology* here and there, cousin Shaw threw himself into the magazine and the Athenaeum, which sprung from it. Another active member was Arthur Maynard Walter, a great-great-grandson of Increase Mather and the son of a Tory rector who preceded Gardiner in Trinity's pulpit. Walter avoided the law with a tour of Europe before joining the society, which briefly enjoyed his company until his death in 1807.[107]

Walter's close friend, Joseph Stevens Buckminster, just outlived the magazine, but dying at the age of twenty-eight gilded an already lustrous career. Buckminster was famous for his scholarship and elegance. With the aid of James Freeman at King's Chapel, he broke with Calvinism; his sermons at the Brattle Street Church delighted Boston's fashionable. His Phi Beta Kappa oration, "On the Dangers and Duties of Men of Letters," exemplifies the Anthologist mind. Buckminster regretted the French Revolution and its consequences for literature. "The foul spirit of innovation and sophistry," he said, "has been seen wandering in the very groves of the Lyceum, and is not yet completely exorcised."[108] America was particularly vulnerable to these upsets, because its literary character lacked maturity and form. Education in the United States was superficial and did not instill the discipline required for genuine scholarship. The nation entertained notions of equality that sapped its taste and ambition. A young American scholar could too easily squander his talents: "he prematurely takes a part in all the dissensions of the day. His leisure is wasted on the profligate productions of demagogues, and his curiosity bent on the minutiae of local politicks."[109] By these mean exertions, he turned "his literary credit to the quickest account." The priorities of the past were overthrown as American men of letters published more than they studied.

Yet even if literature participated in society's ills, Buckminster assured his audience that it also provided the anodyne. The life of letters ran against the grain of common American pursuits. This was a dangerous opposition, for while the orator was sure his country was fast becoming "an empire unparalleled in extent," he was less sure that it would honor literary endeavor. Letters would, however, continue to offer pure satisfactions to their habitués. Buckminster wrote, "that literature, whether it be her pride, or her misfortune, will disdain to divide the empire of your heart. She scorns to enter into partnership with the love of money . . . Hardly will she submit to be encumbered with the common worldly anxieties, much less to follow in the train of lust and corruption."[110]

Buckminster was no fool. He knew that his listeners followed the main chance down divergent paths. Literature represented a unity; it resisted these otherwise necessary divisions. "For," he noted, "however different our professions, opposite our connections, wide our opinions, or uncertain our destinies in life, in this we agree, that letters have been our study, perhaps our delight."[111] Letters offered a constant in the midst of change, and it was the duty of the lettered to respect this enduring quality and see that others did the same.

This was the task to which the members of the Anthology Society assigned themselves. Buckminster's oration of 1809 was a summary of the arguments he and his fellows had been making for the last four years. J. S. J. Gardiner had been tracing the same line for much longer, first in the *Remarks on the Jacobiniad* and then in his "Restorator" essays. When the society convened in 1805, he was the only member to have reached the age of forty. Most of his colleagues were in their twenties; some had just left Harvard. Gardiner had been instructing young Bostonians in the classics since 1794, and a few Anthologists cut their teeth on Homer and Virgil under his supervision. As the group's premier classicist, he was also its critical conscience.[112] No one was readier than he to articulate the conservative standard of what was, and continued to be, good literature.

Gardiner's fellows elected him president of the Anthology Society at its first meeting. He remained at the post for five years—the greater part of the magazine's life. Because the group arrived at its decisions jointly, the position carried with it more honor than power, but this distinction meant something to the members, who styled themselves "a society of gentlemen."[113] They had sense enough to know that their journal would never turn a profit, and despite their consistent Federalism, they did not deign to canvass votes or comment regularly on current events. They eschewed these functions. By emphasizing the literary nature of their fellowship, the Anthologists underlined their claim to expertise.

The Anthology Society was a club, and Gardiner was its best host. It held its first meeting—and many subsequent—at his home, where he tried to set a "sumptuous" table. A good meal was important to the members, and the society's minutes describe many pleasant nights when supper was the only business they could manage. In other modes of conviviality, Gardiner again took the lead. Meetings lasted longer when he attended; the president often "outsmoked midnight" as well as his younger partners. Notwithstanding his acquaintance with the "vulgar hour," Gardiner took his literary responsibilities seriously. He was one of the most faithful contributors to the *Anthology* in its early years.[114] His work sounded a crisp, unrelenting tone.

He was especially keen to expose the deficiencies of American literature, which he blamed in part on the narrowing course of professional development. While professionalization had once served the concentration of political and social talent, now it seemed to militate against it:

> Our literary discipline is well calculated for common purposes, and our professional men are little inferiour to those of other countries in the knowledge of their profession. But here our claims to praise must end. Our lawyers are mere lawyers, our physicians are mere physicians, our divines are mere divines. Every thing smells of the shop, and you will, in a few minutes conversation, infallibly detect a man's profession. We seldom meet here with an accomplished character, a young man of fine genius and very general knowledge, the scholar and the gentleman, united.[115]

Of course, a narrow education was increasingly the norm. Gardiner repeated his complaint from the "Restorator": because schoolmasters and tutors earned little more than a day laborer, these employments did not attract talent. While disdainful of common endeavors, Gardiner and the other Anthologists were aware that letters appeared on the same balance sheet with any undertaking that consumed social capital.[116] They knew the price of sophistication, but they also tried to obscure the connections between the shop and the salon.

The contributors demonstrated their worth by passing judgment on those who dared to publish. None of the members pretended to be a literary great, but at least they knew quality when they saw it. Such discretion was rare in the United States, and Gardiner, for one, was determined to use a sharper calculus than other readers. He dismissed the "enlightened criticks" who thought American literature rivaled that of Europe. Comparisons of this kind proceeded from "the grossest ignorance, or the most insufferable vanity"; as a reviewer, Gardiner almost gleefully went about correcting the one and pricking the other. Responding to a correspondent who thought unkind his treatment of David Humphreys, the Connecticut wit, the rector wrote, "Colonel Humphreys, Sir, we can assure you, is not vain of his literary talents, and so far from placing himself in the first rank of English poets, would modestly retreat to the sixth, though the world in justice would willingly assign him a station in the fourth."[117] He reacted to a piece by Eliphalet Pearson, Harvard's professor of Hebrew, in this way: "We have, on the whole, been tolerably satisfied with this lecture of the learned professor, since it is not below the mediocrity we expected."[118]

Gardiner did not muffle his criticism to save his politics. His forthrightness, already evident in the "Restorator," became more aggressive in the *Anthology*. He was disgusted to see the *Port Folio* rank Thomas Green Fessenden's "Democracy Unveiled"—a libelous satire of the Jefferson administration—with the poems of Churchill. When he reviewed a collection of essays in which several Connecticut Federalists lampooned the democratic newspapers, Gardiner could find nothing to compliment except the volume's paper and type. He added, "We are not yet arrived at a sufficient height of civilization to write satire like gentlemen."[119] One wonders if he regretted his own earlier forays in that genre. The critic's role was now more congenial to his understanding of American letters.

He had certainly lost all patience with Robert Treat Paine, the publisher of his *Jacobiniad*. Paine had contributed to a volume of sketches and verses honoring the Spanish resistance to Napoleon. Gardiner applauded the book's sentiments: "as New Englandmen and Bostonians, we are members of a state and town, which are not to be overawed by the menaces of a foreign despot, nor philosophized out of their rights and liberties by the audacious experiments of his Virginian viceroys."[120] He was just as definite about Bostonians' efforts to express these sentiments in rhyme. Some of the songs he almost liked, calling them "good specimens of perishable mediocrity." Paine's, however, were horrible. "Such is the production," Gardiner remarked, "which ignorance has praised, and folly admired, a lamentable proof of the slight progress which polite literature has made in this country."[121] No critic has since stepped forward to gainsay this opinion.

More troubling are Gardiner's aesthetics, which were brittle and prim. They seemed to expect disagreement. In a short essay on Pope, one of his favorite authors, Gardiner railed at the poet's detractors:

> They prefer the wilderness to the garden, though the latter may possess all the beauties of nature, without her deformities. But true taste admires nature only in her charms, not in the gross. Neither poet nor painter would describe a quagmire, nor expose to view those parts of the person, which decency clothes.[122]

This is a wonderful example of the neoclassical mind bridling at the Romantic sensibility. The Romantics would soon be in the ascendant, and they were not at all shy about preferring the wilderness or even indecency to safer material. To Gardiner, beauty depended on proportion. This was the accepted view of aesthetic philosophy. The problem lay in the sublime. Gardiner did not want to relinquish this category, but neither could he impute to it the characteristics described by Edmund Burke. Long before the American and French Revolutions, Burke wrote the influential *Philosophical Enquiry into the Origin of our Ideas of the Sublime and Beautiful*. He explained that, while the beautiful and stately object comforted the senses, the sublime worked upon our fears. The sublime involved the terrible, the awesome, and the obscure. Although Gardiner admired Burke and his politics, he would not bow to the great conservative in this matter. To find the sublime in obscurity was to welcome an absurd and enthusiastic drift in the arts.[123]

These aesthetic concerns were at issue in a minor controversy between Gardiner and his colleague Buckminster. Their argument was incited not by any contemporary lyrics but by the work of a poet who had been dead for over thirty years. In the July 1808 issue of the *Anthology*, Buckminster praised Thomas Gray's difficult odes. Gray's fame still relies on his simplest poem, "Elegy in a Country Churchyard," but he was a literary adventurer who studied many languages—Icelandic among them—and indulged in formal experiments. Buckminster admitted that Gray attracted extreme opinions: "If he is not excellent he is supremely ridiculous; if he has not the living spirit of verse, he is only besotted and bewildered with the fumes of a vulgar and stupifying draught." The young critic also allowed for the poet's obscurity, but he made the best of it, on Burke's authority.

"The most thrilling touches of sublimity," Buckminster wrote, "are consistent with great indistinctness of images." The critic who dwelt upon the "blemishes" in Gray was like the tourist "who could sit coolly by the cataract of Niagara, speculating upon the chips and straws that were carried over the fall."[124] This person could not appreciate the sublime.

In a couple of subsequent numbers, Gardiner belittled what Buckminster had praised. As was so often the case, J.S.J. seconded the decision of Dr. Johnson, who was also a Gray doubter. Gardiner turned to his Virgil and his Milton and saw sublime lines that were "perfectly intelligible." Obscure poems were incorrect and appealed to the reader's fallibilities. Gray was the "Whitfield of poetry"; like the legendary New Light, he encouraged irrationality and deviations from form.[125] To a traditional rector, these methods were especially obnoxious.

Nevertheless, if Gardiner's stiffness is evident in the Gray controversy, so is his impishness. He probably inspired Buckminster's defense when he parodied the poet several months before. Gardiner did not then introduce the aesthetic implications of Gray's work; instead, he objected to a stylist whose gimmicks might be easily imitated. As proof, Gardiner submitted two odes. Both are inside jokes. An "Ode on Summer" included a paean to Gardiner's seasonal retreat: "While sickening crowds in cities pant, / And suppliant sue for air, / To thy wild, wave-wash'd rocks, Nahant, / Behold thy bard repair." The "Ode to Winter" hinted at another withdrawal, also pleasant and available only to a few: "Doubtless I brave thy boisterous breath, / Whene'er the lettered circle meet, / Nor dread to tempt at daylight's death, / The dangers of the slippery street."[126] The Gray controversy ended in the same jesting spirit. At a meeting of the society in October, Gardiner read another piece on Gray but tore it up, "with much good humour," according to the secretary, before his peers voted to publish it. It was "all stuff," Gardiner said, and he wrote it for no other reason than to satisfy Buckminster on one point.[127]

The chief historian of the *Anthology* understands the Gray dispute as an omen of Gardiner's break with the society, then two years distant. There may be some truth to this, for Gardiner would come to publicly despise the Unitarianism favored by Buckminster, but the correlation is otherwise weak.[128] Whereas the religious debate was willfully divisive, an argument about poetic virtues and vices affirmed the society's vision of itself. It wanted to be New England's belletristic forum, where "gentlemen" could speak freely of things about which most men and women knew little or nothing.

J. S. J. Gardiner believed in the "lettered circle," and he did much to shape it. He supported the institutions of literature. He was an active contributor to the journal. He was an exemplar of clubbability. He had an important hand in the one institution that survived the society and still survives today. When the society began, its members established a periodical library for their use. Gardiner was the first donor, offering many volumes of the *Gentleman's Magazine*. Shortly thereafter, several members looked into making permanent arrangements. At Gardiner's house, they wrote a "Proposal for the Establishing of a Reading-Room in Boston." This project resulted in the Boston Athenaeum. Gardiner discussed the need for such a place in one of his early *Anthology* pieces. The town lacked "a publick library"; all it had was "a contemptible book-case" that housed "a repository of literature well adapted to the improvement of boarding-school misses, chamber-maids, and apprentices." Obviously, Gardiner did not think much of sentimental and manners literature; moreover, he held to a rather narrow understanding of what was "publick." The Athenaeum was privately subscribed, and it became the library of Boston's elites.[129]

The Anthology Society reveled in its vigilance, but it also claimed the privilege of arbitrary grace. No member combined the severe and the hospitable so convincingly as President Gardiner. Despite his distaste for impure or provincial language, he was an admirer of Robert Burns: "We labour with pleasure through a barbarous glossary, that we may fully relish his beauties."[130] Gardiner even invited a bit of darksome fancy into the magazine. The following is an excerpt from a piece he read before the society:

> To attempt to describe my feelings, or to particularise each howling horrour around me, were vain. It is not the thousand rivers of water, that tumble from above . . . nor the piled-up precipice of slippery crags . . . nor the furious whirlwind, driving like shot the spray against you, threatening at each gust to throw you into the merciless jaws of death below . . . not all these, that bring each its particular terrour; but the whole of them together, striking the mind at once, appal the senses, and the weakened judgment gives way to the idea, that the rock above, which of itself supports the mighty whole, has loosened . . . amidst this seeming crush of worlds.[131]

Frederic Tudor, the Anthologist's brother, recorded these fevered observations after a visit to Niagara. Tudor's future was in commerce rather than letters, and in frozen, not falling, water: he made a fortune selling Yankee ice to the tropics.[132] But who would not pay to have heard J. S. J. Gardiner—foe to obscurity and enthusiasm—recite Tudor's words, no doubt after several rounds of claret? One wonders if Buckminster had forgotten this performance when he suggested that Gray's critics were blind to the cataract's sublimity. Though a stern judge, Gardiner was not afraid of the occasional indiscretion. He kept his eyes open for the rare or rising talent.

Indeed, Gardiner spotted William Cullen Bryant when that major American poet was a child. Bryant's first publication was a clever splash of Federalist vitriol. His pleased father brought it to Boston, where in 1808 it appeared under the title "The Embargo, or Sketches of the Times; a Satire." The author was identified only as "A Youth of Thirteen." Reviewing the poem in the *Anthology*, Gardiner called the boy's command of the language extraordinary, and he predicted that the poet would bring honor to American literature. The critic pretended to scold Bryant for aiming "the satirick shaft against the breast of our most excellent President," but Gardiner could not resist quoting lines such as these: "Go scan, philosophist, thy [Sally's] charms, / And sink supinely in her sable arms; / But quit to abler hands, the helm of state, / Nor image ruin on thy country's fate!"[133] Here was Gardiner and literary Federalism at their splenetic worst, but mingled with the vulgarity and illwill was the recognition of something finer. The *Anthology* may have sponsored and repeated many ungenerous sentiments, but it also cultivated a rare sense of achievement. In 1817, William Tudor published Bryant's "Thanatopsis" in the *North American Review*. It was not a poem Gardiner could have written. Perhaps he would never have thought to attempt such a work. It vindicated his judgment nonetheless.

J. S. J. Gardiner was a conservative, but he was also a preparatory figure in the history of New England letters. In addition to his criticism and clubmanship, another medium of his influence was the classical instruction he offered to Boston youth. He opened his school in 1794 to meet the financial demands of marriage and family. He closed the school ten years later, upon becoming rector of Trinity, but he continued to see pupils. His pedagogy followed that of his old teacher, Dr. Parr; his methods were exacting and systematic. They apparently brought good results. Josiah Quincy, among other things the president of Harvard University, credited Gardiner with reviving classical study and raising the standards of admission to New England's colleges. Two of his students, William Hickling Prescott and George Ticknor, became Harvard professors. Ticknor was the most prominent scholar of his generation. Among Yankees, he was a pioneer of the European grand tour. He was the father of the Boston Public Library. At Harvard, he was the first occupant of the chair in Belles-Lettres. Appropriately, one of Gardiner's last acts as an Anthologist was to nominate Ticknor to the club.[134]

◗ξ · ϟ◖

The keenest student of the Anthology Society describes as absurd its members' attempts "to consolidate" and direct the republic of letters. As the body of human knowledge grew into a monster of special fields, "men of letters" could no longer assimilate the full range of cultural expression. Literature, in other words, was at this time becoming a constituent, rather than a presumptively unifying, enterprise. After the eighteenth century, European and American literati were more likely to resist society than to pretend to represent it.[135] However, there was considerable pretense in this alienation as well. To the extent that the modern writer was alienated at all, his image was at odds with his opportunities. The republic of letters may have dissolved, but, in its place, there emerged a previously unimagined market for literary production. By the twentieth century, writers might have stood contrary to the material success of their society, but they were clearly its beneficiaries. They were the fortunate cousins of the canary in the mineshaft: their song, despite its stridency and content, bespoke a prosperous environment.

J. S. J. Gardiner complained that American letters smelled of the shop, and he and his colleagues—professionals, almost to a man—formed their gentlemanly salon in order to shut out the stench. The common villain of many Anthology pieces was the diffusion of knowledge in America. One essayist pointed to "clowns, who ought to be brightening their plowshares, instead of dog-earing their spelling book." As a result of such wasted efforts, everyone rated himself an expert on government, and "political methodists" infested the land, preaching "the new light of reason." In a similar though more considered piece, J.S.J.'s cousin, Robert Hallowell Gardiner, wrote that the multiplicity of colleges in New England tended to scatter the "rays" of knowledge: "Collected into one focus, they might . . . give light and warmth to an age, but now, dispersed, are lost on too wide a surface."[136] Gardiner was not thinking of authors in particular, but William Tudor was when he faulted the superficial character of American education. Too many authors thought they had a claim on the public's attention. Tudor explained that these "worthless weeds" stifled "the valuable plants, that are slower in their growth."[137]

The Anthologists were one-eyed liberals. They understood the concentration of talent to be a process that operated at all levels of society, but they looked to finished products instead of raw democratic materials. The relationship between the two was hidden in these and other essays, but it was always assumed. Tudor's metaphors are competitive. R. H. Gardiner was proud of the country's growth and was confident that merit from whatever source would find its reward. "Private and publick liberality," he wrote, "might make ample provision for exciting into action those latent sparks of genius, which now lie concealed in the humble walks of life."[138] What the Anthologists might not have anticipated is how amply those Americans equipped with ease and shallow learning would provide for their authors. That time had not yet come, and the Anthologists found their support elsewhere.

We might accuse J. S. J. Gardiner of leaning too hard on the past or even of being its creature. He was, after all, John Sylvester John, named for his grandfather once and his father twice over. In Gilbert Stuart's two portraits of the youngest Gardiner, we see, above the priest's collar, a ruddy, pleasant countenance in which Silvester's heft and John's humor are favorably combined.[139] (Stuart—like Benjamin West, John Singleton Copley, and John Trumbull—was the product of a stubbornly transatlantic milieu. He was also, like Silvester Gardiner, a child of Rhode Island and a parishioner of the Reverend James MacSparran.) Silvester's last bride had Maine connections; Catharine Goldthwaite's father commanded Fort Pownall until America's independence. And J.S.J. found his wife downeast, in the rather well-appointed ruins of empire. In 1794, he married Mary Howard; her father, Colonel William Howard, was one of the Kennebec's richest men. His extended family occupied the decommissioned Fort Western, on the site of present-day Augusta.[140]

In an amusing letter, written nearly three decades after their wedding, Mary Howard Gardiner sketched her husband's foibles and perhaps revealed a few of her own. Her correspondent was their son, William Howard Gardiner, whom she implored to look after their house in

Brookline (near Boston) while they were away in Maine. J.S.J., it seems, had left everything in the care of their servants. Mrs. Gardiner, less trusting, asked her son to collect the spare keys and double-lock the cellar, where several hundred dollars worth of wine sat in what must have been, given Gardiner appetites, an uneasy repose. She admitted to William that she was "wonderstruck at the entire want of common prudence in your Father." Having that virtue in spades, her final recommendation was that William burn her letter once he digested its contents.[141]

Imprudence was a trait that cropped up here and there in the Gardiner family, especially in the male line. John Gardiner, with Wilkite perversity, wore his imprudence as a badge of honor, and we are reminded again that "Jack" was very much John's son. The noted English actor (and lush) George Frederick Cooke made a point of attending Trinity Church during his triumphant 1811 tour of Boston and other American cities, because "Parson Gardiner" was the only clergyman in town to attend his performances. Cooke slept through the sermon, but his drowsiness owed more to his morning toddy than to Gardiner's preaching.[142] A love of the theater came to Gardiner honestly. Neither he nor his father hid their affections, though both men were taken to task for them.

As much as J.S.J.'s younger colleagues at the *Anthology* admired his scholarship and his bonhomie, they were sometimes taken aback by the rector's apparent indifference to decorum. This perceived shortcoming proceeded from his taste for a particular kind of British literature and British company. When Gardiner inserted into the magazine a bawdy tale of Alexander Pope's and Colley Cibber's visit to a brothel, Arthur Maynard Walter and his fellows destroyed the original printing and sold instead an expurgated second run, without J.S.J.'s knowledge. Joseph Stevens Buckminster thanked Walter for excising such a "vile story." Furthermore, the young Anthologists did not think it wise for Gardiner to skip his Sabbath duties for a day of birdhunting with the British consul.[143]

But J. S. J. would have seen little to distinguish his activities and preferences from certain impulses of the saintly Buckminster, who was cheered by the tones of the King's Chapel organ and by the friendly advice of the Reverend East Apthorp, whom Buckminster met in England. Before the Revolution, Apthorp caused a stir with his Anglican mission to Cambridge, Massachusetts (a mission made all the more obnoxious by Apthorp's Episcopal—that is, expensive—habits), but the postbellum generation could appreciate his liberality.[144] To renew such contacts was healthy and cosmopolitan. Gardiner was less happy, of course, when Buckminster and his contemporaries exchanged good sense for puritanism—as when the young editors clucked at his improprieties—or, worse still, Unitarianism, which carried, in Gardiner's mind, the Jacobin taint.

His last published sermons, like much of his work, are shaded by disappointment. Bitterness had, however, made room for the bittersweet. In an 1823 sermon, Gardiner again took up the matter of New England's relative decline. No jeremiads were forthcoming; instead, Gardiner redefined the region's clout. Its influence survived in its enterprising natives, who were settling the rest of the country. They issued from their "Eastern hive" and carried learning and religion with them. New England would not lead the nation, but it would have a part in the nation's best achievements, in much the same way as the instincts of the imperial era motivated cultural, commercial, and municipal projects in the early Republic.[145]

In a later sermon, Gardiner recast this message for the individual who feared that he had fallen short. The aging rector explained that death did not demean a life's work; it passed that work on to abler hands. As he put it: "We are mutually connected by the ties of society, and gifted with various capacities, which we are bound to employ for the public and private advantage of our fellow citizens. We may comprehend projects, which the life of no man can execute, and leave to others their accomplishment."[146] Gardiner asked his listeners to retire with dignity and in the knowledge that they had made room for those to follow. He asked them to die as he had learned to live.

By his own life's end, J. S. J. Gardiner had traveled a strange but satisfyingly full circle. In 1830, he returned to Britain in an attempt to save his faltering constitution; he is buried in a Yorkshire churchyard.[147] Despite his contrary nature, Gardiner managed to represent the significant tensions of his era. A child of the British Empire who came of age with the United States, he was always plumbing the foundations of British-American culture, always trying to seal the cracks as they appeared in early national politics, religion, and literature. This rather comprehensive mission was beyond him, and, as a result, his sermons and essays exhibit a brittle, desperate quality. Yet it was not Gardiner's fate to despair in the end: his fundamental wisdom and good humor never left him. His trusteeship of the eighteenth century's legacies might have been imperfect, but they endured nevertheless. And Gardiner, as churchman, teacher, and belletrist, had built upon the old bricks and paved the way for more adventurous reconstructions.

Retrospect

I n the early 1820s, William Howard Gardiner went to Washington, D.C., to work in the office of Daniel Webster, the Massachusetts congressman and future senator. Until he was compromised by the slavery issue, Webster was the great Yankee hope, a lawyer and politician much admired by New England's literati for his principles and the eloquence with which he stated them. J.S.J. Gardiner was a fan: he thought Webster's Plymouth oration rivaled Edmund Burke's best; he also thought it offered a particularly fine history of America's "separation from the parent country." Ever the critic, Gardiner occasionally quibbled with Webster's choice of words, but his advice to his son was direct and material. William had moved to Washington, "that monument to national folly," but he was to keep his head about him—he was enjoined to mind the "main chance."[1] This was the same advice that Royall Tyler—in *The Contrast*, America's first play of significance—brought forth from the mouth of his New York patriarch, Van Rough. He dispensed this wisdom to everyone within earshot but most pointedly to Colonel Manly, the heroic, and very stiff, representative of Yankee and Revolutionary virtue.[2]

New England would lead the nation again, perhaps not politically, but certainly in industrial technique and in the techniques of social and cultural organization that industrial success afforded. J.S.J. Gardiner was closer to these developments than he might have guessed. Imagine him as a young man in 1784, accompanying his father to the (once and future) King's Chapel to reclaim the family's pew. The Revolution was over, but all of its fruits were not yet fallen. Capitalizing on the absence of Tory proprietors—J.S.J.'s grandfather among them—John Gardiner would abet a tiny revolution within the chapel's walls and in its book of prayer. Its rector, Henry Caner, was gone too, his home by the chapel burying ground confiscated and eventually sold to John Lowell, a lawyer who had prospered in the war. He sat near the head of the Suffolk bar, which would, in a year's time, deny the privileges of membership to young J.S.J. Here, though, Lowell interests us less than his son, Francis Cabot, who grew up within sight of the chapel and of the old linen manufactory, also on Tremont Street, to which Silvester Gardiner was an active subscriber.[3]

Francis Cabot Lowell accomplished what an earlier generation of Boston merchants could not. He came to Harvard in Joseph Dennie's final year. Like Dennie, Lowell was both a very bright student and one rusticated for misconduct, but he showed a talent for application that the belletrist lacked. He accumulated a small fortune in shipping and, in doing so, worked himself to the point of collapse. In 1810, he sailed with his family for Glasgow, beginning a long and much needed vacation. Overseas, Lowell found more than his health. The country between the Clyde and the Thames had changed since John Gardiner's day. The industrial revolution was shifting into high gear. The Lowells toured a landscape dotted with mills, and, in Lancashire, Francis memorized the mechanical designs that the British government guarded so jealously. Just as colonial merchants had profited by the imperial trading system and then profited even more by transgressing it, Lowell's Federalist affinity for Great Britain paid a venal dividend.[4]

Thus began the important success story of the Yankee mill owners. These businessmen noticed that if there was little to prevent one from reaching the top of America's social order, there was almost nothing to hold one there. Lowell and his associates believed in talent and hard work, but they were also family men who wanted a secure future for their children. Maritime commerce did not offer that security, but the merchants reasoned that manufactures might. They admired Smithian political economy and the Scottish improvements that had turned worn-out estates into going industrial concerns. The Lowells, the Appletons, and other increasingly connected mill families folded their manufacturing riches into a variety of commercial and philanthropic organizations: banks, insurance companies, hospitals, libraries, and— never to be forgotten—Harvard College. Status came to depend on these institutional affiliations, which were resistant to the vagaries of the market.[5]

Even so, the social and the political did not conform with any exactness. The associated mill owners were active and influential in politics at various levels, but at no level were their wishes consistently respected.

Moving back into the eighteenth century, when the social structure was less firm, the political picture is muddier yet. Statistical studies of provincial Boston have failed to establish a significant correlation between officeholding and socioeconomic position. (Silvester Gardiner, for example, never held town office.) In the critical period, the state's otherwise dominant commercial interests were unable to control the lower house of the General Court.[6]

The authority of Boston elites is thus a perplexing issue, as are their origins. An old but enduring interpretation looks to the Revolution and its aftermath. The town's imperial officeholders and many of its merchants and professionals saw their influence wane with Britain's, and a large fraction of them left Boston altogether. Creditable persons from the outlying counties filled the vacuum. Henry Cabot Lodge, for whom this was family history, called these newcomers "the country aristocracy," but most of them made their first fortunes in maritime trade or in the practice of law. Nevertheless, Lodge's account has much to recommend it. It encompasses the undeniable importance of Essex County connections in Federal Boston's political and economic life. The Lowells, natives of Newburyport, offer a classic example.[7]

There are, however, serious objections to this argument. There is little evidence of a social transformation. Patriot merchants were just as rich, if not richer, than their Tory counterparts. Men such as John Hancock and James Bowdoin were successes before and after the war. Moreover, a story of radical change supposes an almost hermetic community of Loyalists, but Tories had less obnoxious heirs and partners. The loyal Grays may have departed, but their relatives, the Otises, did not. Even John Gardiner looked after his father's affairs. Finally, outsiders with high hopes were always coming to Boston. William Phillips of Andover, the primate of the Massachusetts Bank, was the one brother of three who did not go to Harvard. The two who did went on to found academies much associated, in later centuries, with Yankee privilege, but these founders never settled in Boston. William did, over twenty-five years before independence, and he was already a merchant grandee when he served on the town's revolutionary committees. His son held title to one of Silvester Gardiner's confiscated estates, but was this junior Phillips more of an interloper than Gardiner himself, a Rhode Islander who worked his way into Boston's provincial elite?[8]

In many ways, Silvester Gardiner's acquisitiveness was like that of William Phillips or Harrison Gray Otis, but Gardiner's acquisitive projects, his professional acumen, even his style of religious worship, were developments of empire as well as of personality. Indeed, the British Empire was an experience, and it had intellectual and psychological effects. One of them, as we have seen, was the Scottish Enlightenment. The Union of 1707 encouraged Scotland's literate classes to devalue political heroism and to locate the causes of happiness in a larger economy of action, in commercial enterprise and in the cosmopolitan attachments that naturally followed upon it. If Gardiner found that his private interests cohered with the interests of civilization and empire, then the Scots refined the language to express that relationship.[9]

Silvester's son, John Gardiner, learned this language and lived it too, though in a different manner than his father had. Toward the end of his career, liberalism enjoyed a wide currency, of which Boston's theater and law-reform controversies are proof. The temptation is to recount the intellectual history—Bostonians repeating Hume—without demonstrating that a particular kind of social history preceded the ideas. Much of this history depends on its imperial setting and on the provincials whose aspirations and achievements were the mortar of the Atlantic world. John Gardiner may, like the proverbial Scot, have traveled far in search of fortune, but his major adaptive tool was very English: a knowledge of the common law. It was a tool familiar to other Americans, many of whom never left their native provinces. By such instruments were empires made and unmade, and lawyers profited by the prosecution of either case.[10]

Of course, the common law and its practice were not inherently "liberal," but to take advantage of unsettled situations and new opportunities was exactly that, according to the progressive sensibility articulated by David Hume and his countrymen. The Scots were the historians and exponents of a modern aptitude. They argued that the learned middle classes were closely attuned to the changes that had transformed Europe. Merchants and professionals could manage a heavy traffic of goods and information. They were independent, but their experience of the world taught them to dignify the connectedness of society. This connectedness was less rigidly construed than that imagined by premoderns, but it still enabled a comprehensive social vision. Articulating this vision confirmed one's liberality and merit.

Liberalism was, therefore, a political rhetoric as well as a way of looking at the world. It could and did serve narrow ends, but it was a cheaply held and widely used position. Liberals vilified the customs and institutions that blocked their social or political ascent; when defending their advantages, they referred to a "system" that favored the intelligent and the capable. "Head-work," wrote the theater advocate William Haliburton, "is now in more repute than hand-work." His fellow lawyers agreed, arguing that they made the best political representatives—better than farmers or mechanics—because they knew society in its fullness: its good parts, its bad, and the constitutional measures that kept all parts in a productive balance.[11]

Here was a definition of leadership appropriate to America's northeastern seaboard, where commerce and the professions were preeminent, yet it was little more than a speculative claim. Although politically attractive in some of its forms, liberal rhetoric did not afford an original purchase on power. Wealth and personal connections were still power's primary factors, and in late-eighteenth-century America, no person or faction possessed a decisive competence. This dynamic situation encouraged liberalism, but it frustrated the most liberally conceived ambitions to establish authority.

Consider the Federalists. Their notions of good government anticipated a filtration of talent. The best men would inevitably take their places at the head of the nation. Jefferson's success did not overthrow these notions; he too believed in a "natural aristocracy."[12] But a vibrant partisan politics convinced its participants that popular opinion could not be taken for granted. After 1800, the Federalists were still a force, especially in Connecticut and Massachusetts, but the turn in events disappointed the many New Englanders who assumed that the rich, good, and able among them would continue to win society's highest marks of approval. J. S. J. Gardiner did not wholly forsake his father's cosmopolitanism, but he no longer expected it to precipitate from an engagement with society in general. This quality had, in his mind, become the adornment of genteel learning.

The Gardiners encourage us to reconsider the Atlantic world in terms provided by its professional class. In the various controversies of colony and commonwealth—and in the liberalism that colors these controversies—we see the marks of an imperial orientation and the symptoms of its distress. Ambitious and accomplished Bostonians, like John Gardiner and the lawyers he nettled, were keenly aware of their vulnerabilities. This awareness descended, in part, from the memory of provincial aspiration and insecurity, and it rose to the demands of a republican polity. Citizens made political claims on the strength of their intellectual merits, but intelligence and authority, then as now, correlated unpredictably. J. S. J. Gardiner, Joseph Dennie, and other Federalist literati came to regard their felt intellectual advantage as its own reward, having distanced themselves from a body politic whose sanctions, they thought, were so frequently mistaken.[13] They questioned what is still a commonplace: that America is a meritocratic society. There may be some truth to such a notion, but the historian prefers to learn how notions, true or untrue, generate their force. The Gardiners do not tell the history of merit in America, but they do tell us where to begin: in the first British empire and in the rich company of provincials who were, almost, at home in it.

NOTES

A.O.   American Loyalist Claims, Public Record Office
BL Add. Mss.   British Library, Additional Manuscripts
BPL   Boston Public Library
C.O.   Colonial Office, Public Record Office
DFP   Derby Family Papers
GWA   Gardiner-Whipple-Allen Papers
MeHS   Maine Historical Society
MHS   Massachusetts Historical Society
MHS Procs.   *Proceedings of the Massachusetts Historical Society*
NEHGS   New England Historic-Genealogical Society
NYHS Colls.   *Collections of the New-York Historical Society*
RHG   Robert Hallowell Gardiner Papers
Trans. Hon. Soc. Cymm. *Transactions of the Honourable Society of Cymmrodorion*

Prospect (pages 1–12)

1. Jules David Prown, *John Singleton Copley,* 2 vols. (Cambridge, Mass.: Harvard University Press, 1966), vol. 1, plate 193.
2. Ibid., plate 318.
3. Barbara Neville Parker, *John Singleton Copley* (Boston: Museum of Fine Arts, 1938), 77.
4. John M. Murrin, "The Legal Transformation: The Bench and Bar of Eighteenth-Century Massachusetts," in *Colonial America: Essays in Politics and Social Development,* ed. Stanley N. Katz (Boston: Little, Brown, 1971), 415–449; Colin Kidd, "North Britishness and the Nature of Eighteenth-Century British Patriotisms," *Historical Journal* 39 (June 1996), 361–382; John Clive and Bernard Bailyn, "England's Cultural Provinces: Scotland and America," *William and Mary Quarterly* 11 (April 1954), 200–213; David Hancock, *Citizens of the World: London Merchants and the Integration of the British Atlantic Community, 1735–1785* (New York: Cambridge University Press, 1995).
5. J. G. A. Pocock, "Empire, State and Confederation: The War of American Independence as a Crisis in Multiple Monarchy," in *A Union for Empire: Political Thought and the British Union of 1707,* ed. John Robertson (New York:

Cambridge University Press, 1995), 318–348; Paul Langford, "British Correspondence in the Colonial Press, 1763–1775: A Study in Anglo-American Misunderstanding before the American Revolution," in *The Press & the American Revolution*, ed. Bernard Bailyn and John Hench (Worcester: American Antiquarian Society, 1980), 273–313.

6. See, for example, Bernard Bailyn, *Ideological Origins of the American Revolution* (Cambridge, Mass.: Harvard University Press, 1992), 22–54.

7. T. H. Breen, "Ideology and Nationalism on the Eve of the American Revolution: Revisions Once More in Need of Revising," *Journal of American History* 84 (June 1997), 13–39.

8. For studies of the middling and the modern set in eighteenth-century Britain, see Paul Langford, *A Polite and Commercial People: England, 1727–1783* (New York: Oxford University Press, 1989), and Linda Colley, "Whose Nation? Class and National Consciousness in Britain, 1750–1830," *Past & Present* 113 (November 1986), 97–117. On reaction and flexibility in the second British Empire, see C. A. Bayly, *Imperial Meridian: The British Empire and the World, 1780–1830* (London: Longman, 1989); P. J. Marshall, "Empire and Authority in the later Eighteenth Century," *Journal of Imperial and Commonwealth History* 15 (January 1987), 105–122; Eliga H. Gould, "American Independence and Britain's Counter-Revolution," *Past & Present* 154 (February 1997), 107–141. Gould expands on the points made in this last piece in "A Virtual Nation: Greater Britain and the Imperial Legacy of the American Revolution," *American Historical Review* 104 (April 1999), 476–489.

9. The Atlanticist David Armitage has remarked on the reluctance of American colonial historians to embrace the "early modernity" of their subject; the book before you will show no such restraint. See Armitage, "Greater Britain: A Useful Category of Historical Analysis?" *American Historical Review* 104 (April 1999), 427–445, and especially 435–436. On familial rivalry in Boston, see Bernard Bailyn, *The Ordeal of Thomas Hutchinson* (Cambridge, Mass.: Harvard University Press, 1974). A helpful article on this topic is Stanley Elkins and Eric McKitrick's "The Founding Fathers: Young Men of the Revolution," *Political Science Quarterly* 76 (June 1961), 181–216.

10. Ned Landsman, "The legacy of British Union for the North American colonies: provincial elites and the problem of Imperial Union," in *A Union for Empire*, 297–317.

11. James Kirby Martin, *Men in Rebellion: Higher Governmental Leaders and the Coming of the American Revolution* (New Brunswick: Rutgers University Press, 1973), 24–33.

12. See pp. 55–57 below, and Landsman, "The legacy of British Union," 297–317.

13. David Hume, "Of the Middle Station of Life," in *Essays Moral, Political, and Literary*, ed. Eugene F. Miller (Indianapolis: Liberty Fund, 1987), 545–551.

14. See, for example, Robert F. Dalzell Jr., *Enterprising Elite: The Boston Associates and the World They Made* (Cambridge, Mass.: Harvard University Press, 1987).

15. For a useful review of scholarly debates on the "market revolution," see Gordon Wood, "The Enemy is Us: Democratic Capitalism in the Early Republic," *Journal of the Early Republic* 16 (Summer 1996), 293–308.

16. See Lewis Simpson's introduction to *The Federalist Literary Mind: Selections from the Monthly Anthology and Boston Review* (Baton Rouge: Louisiana State University Press, 1962).

17. John Gardiner, *The Speech of John Gardiner, Esquire. Delivered in the House of Representatives. On Thursday, the 26th of January, 1792* (Boston, 1792), ix.

18. [Jonathan Jackson,] *Thoughts upon the Political Situation of the United States of America, in which that of Massachusetts, is more particularly considered* (Worcester, 1788). On the Scots, see below, pp. 50–57. On liberalism and the Federalist imagination, see Douglass Adair, "'That Politics May Be Reduced to a Science': David Hume, James Madison, and the Tenth *Federalist*," *Huntington Library Quarterly* 20 (August 1957), 343–360.

Interest and Empire (pages 15–41)

1. Caroline E. Robinson, *The Gardiners of Narragansett* (Providence, 1919), 1–3, 11, 32; Robert Hallowell Gardiner, *Early Recollections of Robert Hallowell Gardiner, 1782–1864* (Hallowell, Maine, 1936), 14–15; *Dictionary of American Biography*, ed. Allen Johnson and Dumas Malone, 20 vols. (New York, 1928–36), vol. 7, 139–140; Wilkins Updike, *History of the Episcopal Church, in Narragansett, Rhode Island* (New York, 1947), 62. All of these sources are helpful but are also unreliable in various degrees.

2. Dudley W. R. Bahlman, *The Moral Revolution of 1688* (New Haven: Yale University Press, 1957); Eamon Duffy, "*Correspondence Fraternelle:* The SPCK, the SPG, and the Churches of Switzerland in the War of the Spanish Succession," in *Reform and Reformation: England and the Continent, c. 1500–c. 1750*, ed. Derek Baker (Oxford: Basil Blackwell, 1979), 251–280.

3. These ecumenical and American connections are traced in W. K. Lowther Clarke, *Eighteenth-Century Piety* (London: Macmillan, 1944), esp. 32–42, and in Richard R. Johnson, *Adjustment to Empire: The New England Colonies, 1675–1715* (Brunswick, N.J.: Rutgers University Press, 1981).

4. Landsman, "The legacy of British Union," 297–317. On the religious consequences of Union, see David Hempton, *Religion and Political Culture in Britain and Ireland: From the Glorious Revolution to the Decline of Empire* (New York: Cambridge University Press, 1996).

5. James MacSparran, "America Dissected" (1753), reprinted in Updike, *History of the Episcopal Church*, 488; Esther B. Carpenter, *South County Studies of Some Eighteenth-Century Persons, Places & Conditions* (Boston, 1924), 103–111.

6. MacSparran, "America Dissected," 521, 530.

7. Ibid., 506, 527; Edwin S. Gaustad, *George Berkeley in America* (New Haven, 1979). See also William Davis Miller, "The Narragansett Planters," *Proceedings of the American Antiquarian Society* 43 (1933), 49–115.

8. Margaret Ellen Newell, *From Dependency to Independence: Economic Revolution in Colonial New England* (Ithaca: Cornell University Press, 1998), 169.

9. Francis R. Packard, "William Cheselden, Some of His Contemporaries, and Their American Pupils," *Annals of Medical History*, 2nd series, vol. 9 (November 1937), 533, 537; Gardiner, *Early Recollections*, 15; Silvester Gardiner to James Bowdoin, 10 April 1782, Gardiner-Whipple-Allen Papers, Massachusetts Historical Society (hereafter abbreviated as GWA).

10. Packard, "William Cheselden," 533–535.

11. *Dictionary of American Biography*, vol. 7, 140; Packard, "William Cheselden," 537; Henry R. Viets, *A Brief History of Medicine in Massachusetts* (Boston and New York, 1930), 67, 77. In the GWA, there is a deed confirming 1734 as the year of Gardiner's "permanent" return. On the third of July, he bought a sizable house in Boston for £1,070. On John Gibbins, see Clifford K. Shipton, *Sibley's Harvard Graduates*, vols. 4–17 (Boston: Harvard University Press, 1933–75), vol. 5, 315–317.

12. "Philanthropos," *Boston Weekly News-Letter*, 29 December–5 January 1737/8, p. 2; Viets, *Brief History of Medicine*, 66–67. Viets forthrightly denominates these efforts as an Anglicization of medicine (*Brief History*, 68); of course, "Britonization" would be the more appropriate term. Also see I. K. Steele, "A London Trader and the Atlantic Empire: Joseph Cruttenden, Apothecary, 1710–1717," *William and Mary Quarterly* 34 (April 1977), 285; Carl Bridenbaugh, *Cities in Revolt: Urban Life in America, 1743–1776* (New York: Capricorn Books, 1964), 199.

13. "A Medical Society . . . do establish the following Case," *Boston Weekly News-Letter*, 5–13 November 1741, p. 2, quoted in Robert Francis Seybolt, "Lithotomies Performed by Dr. Gardiner, of Boston, 1738 and 1741," *New England Journal of Medicine* 202 (16 January 1930), 109.

14. Eric H. Christianson, "The Colonial Surgeon's Rise to Prominence: Dr. Silvester Gardiner (1707–1786) and the Practice of Lithotomy in New England," *New England Historical and Genealogical Register* 136 (April 1982), 107–111. Note the mistaken birthdate.

15. William Jepson, typescript diary, Mss C 3095, New England Historic-Genealogical Society (hereafter NEHGS), Boston.

16. Jepson diary, NEHGS; "Articles of Agreement . . . Between Silvester Gardiner . . . and William Jepson," 3 May 1757, Silvester Gardiner Papers, Maine Historical Society (hereafter MeHS); *A full Answer to the Pamphlet intitled "a short Vindication of the Conduct of the Referees in the Case of Gardiner versus Flagg"* (Boston, 1768?), 22; *A true state of the copartnership of Gardiner and Jepson* (Boston, 1771).

17. The estimate is Gordon E. Kershaw's, from his book *The Kennebeck Proprietors, 1749–1775* (Somersworth, N.H.: New Hampshire Publishing Company, 1975), 46. Also see Edward Kremers and George Urdang, *History of Pharmacy: A Guide and a Survey* (Philadelphia: J. B. Lippincott, 1940), 140; Viets, *Brief History of Medicine*, 68; Packard, "William Cheselden," 537. The deed (in GWA, dated 3 July 1734) to Gardiner's house and shop on Marlborough Street identifies the new owner as an "Apothecary."

18. Kremers and Urdang, *History of Pharmacy*, 139–140; Steele, "A London Trader and the Atlantic Empire"; Silvester Gardiner to William Gardiner, 27 December 1757, power of attorney granted by Richard Speed and Thomas Windle, 14 September 1759, GWA.

19. Writ of attachment (executed on John Metcalf), 7 June 1774, GWA; "Indenture between Donald Cummings of Biddeford, Physician and Silvester Gardiner, Esquire," 7 May 1765, Donald Cummings to Silvester Gardiner, 10 June 1766, 24 July and 9 December 1767, Ivory Hovey Jr. to Silvester Gardiner, 25 May 1769, Memorandum, 9 January 1771, Silvester Gardiner Papers, MeHS; George Folsom, *History of Saco and Biddeford* (Saco, Maine, 1830), 258–259; William Samuel Johnson to Silvester Gardiner, 14 January, 27 April, and 29 May 1751, Nathaniel Rogers to William Samuel Johnson, 20 February 1769, William Samuel Johnson Papers, Connecticut Historical Society.

20. [Silvester Gardiner,] "To the Freeholders and other Inhabitants of the Town of Boston," (Boston, 1761); John B. Blake, *Public Health in the Town of Boston, 1620–1822* (Cambridge, Mass.: Harvard University Press, 1959), 88–89.

21. [Gardiner,] "To the Freeholders"; Blake, *Public Health*, 88–89, 92–93.

22. [Benjamin B. Thatcher,] *Traits of the Tea Party; being a Memoir of George R. T. Hewes* (New York, 1835), 55–57; Alfred F. Young, "George Robert Twelves Hewes (1742–1840): A Boston Shoemaker and the Memory of the American Revolution," *William and Mary Quarterly* 38 (October 1981), 561–623.

23. Elizabeth A. Fenn, *Pox Americana: The Great Smallpox Epidemic of 1775–82* (New York: Hill & Wang, 2001), 41–42.

24. John Rowe, *Letters and Diary of John Rowe*, ed. Anne Rowe Cunningham (Boston, 1903), 75.

25. [William Sullivan,] *Familiar Letters on Public Characters, and Public Events* (Boston, 1834), 12n, 13.

26. Roy Porter and G. S. Rousseau, *Gout: The Patrician Malady* (New Haven: Yale University Press, 1998), 74–75, 86–87.

27. Paul Langford, *A Polite and Commercial People*, 61–68; Albert O. Hirschman, *The Passions and the Interests: Political Arguments for Capitalism before Its Triumph* (Princeton: Princeton University Press, 1977), 59–63; Norbert Elias, *The Civilizing Process: The History of Manners*, trans. Edmund Jephcott (New York: Urizen Books, 1978), 73–80; Shawn Lisa Maurer, *Proposing Men: Dialectics of Gender and Class in the Eighteenth-Century Periodical* (Stanford: Stanford University Press, 1998), 75–79, 180–186.

28. From *Spectator* no. 69, quoted in Maurer, *Proposing Men*, 80–81.

29. [Richard Steele,] *The Guardian*, no. 1 (12 March 1713).

30. [Steele,] *Guardian*, no. 9 (21 March 1713).

31. *A Letter from Sir Richard Cox, Bart. to Thomas Prior, Esq; Shewing from Experience, A sure Method to establish the Linnen-Manufacture* (Boston, 1750), 8–11, 32–33; *Dictionary of National Biography*, ed. Sir Leslie Stephen and Sir Sidney Lee, 22 vols. (Oxford: Oxford University Press, 1967–68 [orig. 1885–1901]), vol. 4, 1339–1341.

32. Ibid., 18–22.

33. Ibid., 24–25, 31.

34. Ibid., 24, 29–30.

35. Ibid., 3–4; Eric G. Nellis, "Misreading the Signs: Industrial Imitation, Poverty, and the Social Order in Colonial Boston," *New England Quarterly* 59 (December 1986), 500–501; Gary B. Nash, "The Failure of Female Factory Labor in Colonial Boston," *Labor History* 20 (Spring 1979), 179; William R. Bagnall, *The Textile Industries of the United States* (Cambridge, Mass.: Riverside Press, 1893), 33–34; Horace E. Scudder, "Life in Boston in the Provincial Period," in *The Memorial History of Boston*, ed. Justin Winsor, 4 vols. (Boston, 1882), vol. 2, 461, 461n; Andrew Oliver et al. to David Jeffries, 10 May 1753, Silvester Gardiner Papers, MeHS.

36. Josiah Quincy, *Municipal History of the Town and City of Boston* (Boston, 1852), 13–14.

37. *The Report of the Committee to the Society for encouraging Industry (Boston, 1752); Articles of Incorporation of the Society for encouraging Industry and employing the Poor* (Boston, 1754), 1–3; Nash, "Failure of Female Factory Labor," 167–172.

38. Charles Chauncy, *The Idle-Poor secluded from the Bread of Charity by the Christian Law* (Boston, 1752), 19–20; Samuel Cooper, *A Sermon Preached in Boston, New-England, Before the Society for Encouraging Industry, and Employing the Poor* (Boston, 1753), 32.

39. Chauncy, *Idle-Poor secluded*, 6–7, 11–12, 14, 16; Chauncy, *Benevolence of the Deity* (Boston, 1784), 57–58. Chauncy's biographer guesses that *Benevolence*, like *Idle-Poor*, was a product of the 1750s. See Edward M. Griffin, *Old Brick: Charles Chauncy of Boston, 1705–1787* (Minneapolis: University of Minnesota Press, 1980), 112–113.

40. Arthur O. Lovejoy, *The Great Chain of Being: A Study of the History of an Idea* (Cambridge, Mass.: Harvard University Press, 1964), 183–185, 200–207, 244–254. On the price of labor, see *Articles of Incorporation of the Society for encouraging Industry*, 2; A. W. Coats, "Changing Attitudes to Labour in the Mid-Eighteenth Century," *Economic History Review* 11 (August 1958), 35–51.

41. John Corrigan, *The hidden balance: Religion and the social theories of Charles Chauncy and Jonathan Mayhew* (New York: Cambridge University Press, 1987), 98–101; Chauncy, *Benevolence of the Deity*, 110–112.

42. See, for example, Newell, *From Dependency to Independence*, 108–109, 163–168.

43. Chauncy, *Benevolence of the Deity*, 19; Cooper, *Sermon Preached . . . Before the Society for Encouraging Industry*, 2; Norman Fiering, *Moral Philosophy at Seventeenth-Century Harvard: A Discipline in Transition* (Chapel Hill: University of North Carolina Press, 1981), 296–297; Anthony Ashley Cooper, 3rd Earl Shaftesbury, *An Inquiry Concerning Virtue, or Merit* (Manchester: Manchester University Press, 1977), 5–14, 40–41, 54–56, 96; Bernard Mandeville, *The Fable of the Bees: or, Private Vices, Publick Benefits*, ed. F. B. Kaye, 2 vols. (Oxford: Clarendon Press, 1924), vol. 1, xlviii–xlix, lx, lxxii–lxxv, cxvii; Franklin quoted in Thomas A. Horne, *The Social Thought of Bernard Mandeville: Virtue and Commerce in Early Eighteenth-Century England* (New York: Columbia University Press, 1978), xii.

44. Joseph Butler, *Five Sermons Preached at the Rolls Chapel and A Dissertation Upon the Nature of Virtue*, ed. Stuart M. Brown Jr. (New York: Liberal Arts Press, 1950), 15–16, 23, 89. On Mandeville's critics, see Kaye's suberb introductory essay (*Fable of the Bees*, vol. 1, cxxx).

45. Bagnall, *Textile Industries*, 35–36; Nash, "Failure of Female Factory Labor," 178–179; Nellis, "Misreading the Signs," 501–502; Robert F. Dalzell Jr., *Enterprising Elite: The Boston Associates and the World They Made* (Cambridge, Mass.: Harvard University Press, 1987).

46. Kershaw, *Kennebeck Proprietors*; Alan Taylor, *Liberty Men and Great Proprietors: The Revolutionary Settlement on the Maine Frontier, 1760–1820* (Chapel Hill: University of North Carolina Press, 1990). The account that follows is heavily indebted to Kershaw.

47. Kershaw, *Kennebeck Proprietors*, 7–12, 29–30.

48. Ibid., 31, 43–45.

49. Ibid., 100, 103–104.

50. Ibid., 110, 128, 131–135.

51. "An Account of Dr. Gardiner's Holding in the Kennebeck Purchase to Feb. 22, 1768," Kennebeck Purchase Company Papers, MeHS, quoted in Kershaw, *Kennebeck Proprietors*, 135.

52. Kershaw, *Kennebeck Proprietors*, 135–140.

53. British Library [hereafter BL] Add. Mss. 15488, ff. 99–128; Queries addressed to Charles Yorke (Lord Chancellor) and Fletcher Norton, with their replies, 4 and 12 April 1765, Silvester Gardiner Papers, MeHS; Kershaw, *Kennebeck Proprietors*, 177–178.

54. Silvester Gardiner to David Jeffries, 10 June 1765, Robert Hallowell Gardiner Papers, at Oaklands, Gardiner, Maine (hereafter RHG); Kershaw, *Kennebeck Proprietors*, 178–186. Gardiner and Vassall were close partners; the doctor exercised Vassall's vote in company meetings: see Power of attorney, Florentius Vassall to Silvester Gardiner, 25 February 1761, GWA.

55. Kershaw, *Kennebeck Proprietors*, 156, 178–179; John J. Waters Jr., *The Otis Family in Provincial and Revolutionary Massachusetts* (Chapel Hill: University

of North Carolina Press, 1968), 117–119; Edmund S. Morgan and Helen M. Morgan, *The Stamp Act Crisis: Prologue to Revolution* (New York: Collier, 1963), 140–141.

56. Silvester Gardiner to David Jeffries, 10 June 1765, RHG; Kershaw, *Kennebeck Proprietors*, 180–185; Morgan and Morgan, *Stamp Act Crisis*, 167.

57. *Dr. Gardiner versus James Flagg, Merchant* (Boston, 1767), 2, 25.

58. [James Flagg?] *A Strange Account of the Rising and Breaking of a Great Bubble* ("on Sagadahock-River," 1767), 3; Kershaw, *Kennebeck Proprietors*, 52.

59. *Dr. Gardiner versus James Flagg*, 16–21; *A short Vindication of the Conduct of the Referees in the Case of Gardiner versus Flagg* (Boston, 1767), 5; *A full Answer to the Pamphlet intitled "a short Vindication"* (Boston, 1768?), 19–22, 42; "To the Public," *Supplement to the Boston Evening-Post*, 20 July 1767, 1–2; *Strange Account of the Rising and Breaking*, 8–21. See pp. 169–170, below, for an example of John Gardiner's ascribed quixoticism.

60. A map of the pews can be found on a plate between pp. 310 and 311 in the second volume of Henry Wilder Foote's *Annals of King's Chapel*, 2 vols. (Boston, 1896). In 1754, Gardiner would have been sitting in number eight, Shirley in the state pew. On this architectural bow, see Foote, *Annals*, vol. 2, 87.

61. On the organ, refer to Foote, *Annals*, vol. 2, 173. And for the stone: vol. 2, 78, 78n, 169; Joseph Allen to the building committee, 6 March 1750, King's Chapel Parish House Archives.

62. Foote, *Annals*, vol. 2, 603–604.

63. William S. Bartlet, *The Frontier Missionary: A Memoir of the Life of Jacob Bailey* (Boston, 1853), 43, 48, 63–67.

64. Henry Caner to ———, 22 December 1774, Henry Caner Letters, University of Bristol; Bartlet, *Frontier Missionary*, 84.

65. Kershaw, *Kennebeck Proprietors*, 244–245.

66. *Legal Papers of John Adams*, ed. L. Kinvin Wroth and Hiller B. Zobel, 3 vols. (Cambridge, Mass.: Harvard University Press, 1965), vol. 3, 136n.

67. For Anne Gibbins Gardiner's disposition, see Olivia E. Coolidge, *Colonial Entrepreneur: Dr. Silvester Gardiner and the Settlement of Maine's Kennebec Valley* (Gardiner, Maine: Tilbury House, 1999), 37. Appended to Coolidge's book is a genealogy of the Gardiner family, compiled by Danny D. Smith; see 254–256. For the younger Anne's portrait, see Prown, *Copley*, vol. 1, 215 and plate 39. On William Gardiner, see R. H. Gardiner, *Early Recollections*, 30.

68. Anne Gibbons Gardiner, *Mrs. Gardiner's Family Receipts from 1763*, ed. Gail Weesner (Boston: Rowan Tree Press, 1989), 55, 63–65.

69. Ibid., 15, 21, 36, 47, 67.

70. Ibid., 50; Kershaw, *Kennebeck Proprietors*, 269–270, 281n; R. H. Gardiner, *Early Recollections*, 22; Carrie Rebora et al., *John Singleton Copley in America* (New York: Metropolitan Museum of Art, 1995), 309–312, 312n.

71. Isabel Breskin, "'On the Periphery of a Greater World': John Singleton Copley's *Turquerie* Portraits," *Winterthur Portfolio* 36 (Summer–Autumn

2001), 97–123; Prown, *Copley*, vol. 1, plates 260 and 318 (but please note the re-dating of Abigail Pickman Eppes's portrait to c. 1772: Rebora et al., *John Singleton Copley in America*, 312n).

72. Foote, *Annals*, vol. 2, 345–346; Bartlet, *Frontier Missionary*, 112–114; Silvester Gardiner to ————, 9 May 1776, Peter Oliver to Gardiner, 6 September 1779, Gardiner to Sir William Pepperrell [copy], 4 July 1780, Receipts, 17 January and 11 August 1780, 18 July 1782, 12 August 1784, GWA; Gardiner to the Lords Commissioners (for American Loyalist claims), 12 December 1779, Public Record Office, A.O. 13/45.

73. Peter Oliver to Silvester Gardiner, 6 September 1779, William Vassall to Gardiner, 26 February 1781, Gardiner to James Browne [draft copy, 1779?], GWA.

74. Robert Hallowell to Oliver Whipple, 9 June 1784, GWA. Gardiner's attention to detail is also evident in "Dr. Silvester Gardiner's Memorial and Schedule," 10 November 1783, A.O. 13/45. As for Gardiner's pension, see Benjamin Thompson to Silvester Gardiner, 24 February 1780, William Pepperrell to Gardiner, 20 July 1780, Gardiner to [William?] Vassall, 28 September 1780, GWA.

75. "Dr. Silvester Gardiner's Memorial and Schedule," A.O. 13/45; Francis Parkman, *Montcalm and Wolfe*, 2 vols. (Boston, 1909), vol. 2, 261, 283–284.

76. [Silvester Gardiner,] "Some facts collected, and observations made on the Fisheries, and Government of Newfoundland," [1785,] BL Add. Mss. 15493; Power of attorney, Florentius Vassall to Silvester Gardiner, 26 July 1756, GWA; "The Memorial of Robert Earle Catherlough, Hugh Viscount Falmouth, and Florentius Vassall, Esq.," Massachusetts Archives, vol. 118, p. 181; Florentius Vassall to Gardiner, 8 May 1771, Silvester Gardiner Papers, MeHS; Mary Beth Norton, *The British-Americans: The Loyalist Exiles in England, 1774–1789* (Boston: Little, Brown, 1972), 105–106. On the revived episcopal scheme, see Henry Caner to Gardiner, 28 June 1777, Henry Caner Letters, University of Bristol.

77. [Gardiner,] "On the Fisheries, and Government of Newfoundland," 10–12, 29–30, 35–40.

78. Ibid., 2–6, 15, 44–46; C. Grant Head, *Eighteenth Century Newfoundland: A Geographer's Perspective* (Toronto: McClelland and Stewart, 1976), 85, 103.

79. Silvester Gardiner to ————, 11 October 1781, Gardiner to Oliver Whipple, 30 July 1784, Whipple to Gardiner, 4 January and 27 September 1784, GWA.

80. Charlotte Goldthwaite, *Goldthwaite Genealogy* (Hartford, 1899), 88–99, 142–143; *The Diary and Letters of Benjamin Pickman*, ed. George Francis Dow (Newport, 1928), 19.

81. John Gardiner to Silvester Gardiner, 14 July 1783, James Bowdoin to Silvester Gardiner, 10 August 1783, Silvester Gardiner to Oliver Whipple, October 1783 [copy], 10 February [copy], 17 May, and 30 July 1784, Whipple to Silvester Gardiner, 8 November [copy] and 6 December 1784, GWA; David Edward Maas, *The Return of the Massachusetts Loyalists* (New York: Garland, 1989), 402, 454.

82. *Newport Mercury*, 14 August 1786, p. 2; "Dr. Sylvester Gardiner's Last Will," 25 April 1786 [copy], Trustees of St. Ann's Church to Mrs. Abigail Whipple, 20 September 1808, GWA. Gardiner was scheming to the end; he was about to travel to the Kennebeck when death intervened. See Catharine Gardiner to Edward H. Robbins, 17 February and 25 March 1786, James M. Robbins Papers, MHS.

A Worldly Education (pages 45–69)

1. From "Verses by the Author on the prospect of Planting Arts and Learning in America" (originally composed in 1726), quoted in Edwin S. Gaustad's *George Berkeley in America* (New Haven: Yale University Press, 1979), 74–75.

2. Quoted in Gaustad, *George Berkeley*, 22–23. On Berkeley's argument with Mandeville, see 139, 148–151.

3. On Smibert generally, see Richard H. Saunders, *John Smibert, Colonial America's First Portrait Painter* (New Haven: Yale University Press, 1995), and Henry Wilder Foote, *John Smibert, Painter* (Cambridge, Mass.: Harvard University Press, 1950). On his connection to the MacSparrans, see James MacSparran, *A Letter Book and Abstract of Out Services, Written during the Years 1743–1751* (Boston, 1899), v, xxx. Oddly enough, MacSparran baptized Gilbert Stuart, another famous portraitist. His subjects included George Washington and J. S. J. Gardiner, Silvester's grandson (*Letter Book*, xxxii; Gardiner's portrait hangs in the Boston Athenaeum).

4. Saunders, *John Smibert*, 113–115, 135–241.

5. W. B. McDaniel II, "A Letter from Dr. Williams Smibert, of Boston, to his Former Fellow Student at Edinburgh, Dr. John Morgan, of Philadelphia, written February 14, 1769," *Annals of Medical History*, 3rd series, vol. 1 (March 1939), 194–196; Saunders, *John Smibert*, 124.

6. McDaniel, "Letter from Dr. Williams Smibert," 196.

7. George W. Norris, *The Early History of Medicine in Philadelphia* (Philadelphia, 1886) 205–206.

8. Older secondary sources disagree about Gardiner's age and his place in the family birth order. His entry in the university roll verifies that he was born second, after his brother William. See *The Matriculation Albums of the University of Glasgow, from 1728 to 1858*, ed. W. Innes Addison (Glasgow, 1913), 46. The baptismal records of King's Chapel (located in the Parish House Archives) confirm that he was born in December of 1737, as does "An Act to remove all possibility of Doubt touching or concerning the free Citizenship of John Gardiner, Esq.," 12 February 1784, *Acts and Resolves*, ch. 28, Massachusetts Archives. On his years at Boston Latin, see *Materials for a Catalogue of the Masters and Scholars who have belonged to the Public Latin School* (Boston, 1847), 15; "Pompus—A Character," *Continental Journal*, 27 April 1786, p. 2.

9. John Gardiner to Samuel Adams, 8 September 1786, Samuel Adams Papers, New York Public Library; *Matriculation Albums*, 46; *Dictionary of American Biography*, vol. 7, 136–137; *Sibley's Harvard Graduates*, vol. 12, 593–603 (*Sibley's* includes Gardiner because the college awarded him an honorary masters in 1791).

10. Henry Caner to John Gardiner, 9 July 1753, Henry Caner Letters, University of Bristol.

11. John Strang, *Glasgow and its Clubs* (London and Glasgow, 1857), 1, 1n, 11; T. M. Devine, "The Golden Age of Tobacco," in *Glasgow, Volume I: Beginnings to 1830*, ed. T. M. Devine and Gordon Jackson (Manchester: Manchester University Press, 1995), 140–141, 155–158.

12. Devine, "Golden Age," 161; Roger L. Emerson, "Politics and the Glasgow Professors, 1690–1800," in *The Glasgow Enlightenment*, ed. Andrew Hook and Richard B. Sher (East Lothian, U.K.: Tuckwell Press, 1995), 34; W. M. Mathew, "The Origins and Occupations of Glasgow Students, 1740–1839," *Past & Present* 33 (April 1966), 75–83. Richard Sher sounds a contrary note in his essay "Commerce, Religion and the Enlightenment in Eighteenth-Century Glasgow," in *Glasgow*, 312–359. He argues that the commercial community often regarded with unease the moderate tendencies and belletristic pretensions that the university sponsored. The following paragraphs offer one view of the divided Scottish mind and suggest that the divisions did not uniformly pit town versus gown or commerce against the academy.

13. Walter Baynham, *The Glasgow Stage* (Glasgow, 1892), 6.

14. Ibid., 7–9.

15. James C. Dibdin, *The Annals of the Edinburgh Stage* (Edinburgh, 1888), 59–60, 73–79; John Gardiner, *The Speech of John Gardiner, Esquire. Delivered in the House of Representatives. On Thursday, the 26th of January, 1792* (Boston, 1792), 92–93.

16. Walter Robert Scott, *Adam Smith as Student and Professor* (Glasgow, 1937), 163–165; Ian Simpson Ross, "Adam Smith's 'Happiest' Years as a Glasgow Professor," *Glasgow Enlightenment*, 89–90; Deidre Dawson, "Is Sympathy so Surprising?: Adam Smith and French Fictions of Sympathy," in *Sociability and Society in Eighteenth-Century Scotland*, ed. John Dwyer and Richard B. Sher (Edinburgh: Mercat Press, 1993), 147–162.

17. Mathew, "Origins and Occupations of Glasgow Students," 92–93; Ross, "Adam Smith's 'Happiest' Years," 80–85. Gardiner matriculated into James Clow's logic class, and ethics followed logic in the curriculum (*Matriculation Albums*, xii, 46).

18. Adam Smith, *The Theory of Moral Sentiments*, ed. D. D. Raphael and A. L. Macfie (Oxford: Clarendon Press, 1976), 13, 19, 23, 109–110, 153–154; Smith, *Lectures on Jurisprudence*, ed. R. L. Meek, D. D. Raphael, and P. G. Stein (Oxford: Clarendon Press, 1978), 3–4.

19. Smith, *Lectures on Jurisprudence*, 3–4, 14–16, 50, 68–70, 261; R. L. Meek speculates on the form these lectures would have assumed in the early fifties

(when Gardiner was at Glasgow) in his essay "New light on Adam Smith's Glasgow lectures on Jurisprudence," *History of Political Economy* 8 (Winter 1976), 439–477. On Smith's historical sensibility, see Duncan Forbes, "'Scientific' Whiggism: Adam Smith and John Millar," *Cambridge Journal* 7 (August 1954), 643–670.

20. Smith, *Lectures on Jurisprudence*, 340–341.
21. Hirschman, *The Passions and the Interests*, 10; Millar is quoted in Ross, "Adam Smith's 'Happiest' Years," 83.
22. Hirschman, *Passions and the Interests*, 16–54.
23. Mandeville, *Fable of the Bees*, vol. 1, xvii–xx, 7.
24. Mandeville, *Fable of the Bees*, vol. 1, 24–25, 51; Hirschman, *Passions and the Interests*, 10, 33, 48–54.
25. Mandeville, *Fable of the Bees*, vol. 1, xix, 19–20; Nathan Rosenberg, "Mandeville and Laissez-Faire," *Journal of the History of Ideas* 24 (April–June 1963), 183–196, in particular 189.
26. Gladys Bryson, *Man and Society: The Scottish Inquiry of the Eighteenth Century* (New York: Augustus M. Kelley, 1968); on 48–49, Bryson quotes Adam Ferguson, who, in his *Essay on the History of Civil Society*, remarked that "nations stumble upon establishments"; David Hume, *The History of England from the Invasion of Julius Caesar to the Abdication of James the Second, 1688*, 6 vols. (Boston, 1854, 1856), vol. 2, 514. Duncan Forbes argues that this was Hume's valediction; see Forbes, *Hume's Philosophical Politics* (Cambridge: Cambridge University Press, 1975), 309.
27. Hume, *History*, vol. 2, 509, vol. 5, 282.
28. Ronald L. Meek carefully examines this theory and its history in *Social science and the ignoble savage* (Cambridge: Cambridge University Press, 1976).
29. Smith, *Lectures on Jurisprudence*, 14 (I. 27), 50 (I. 117–118), 261 (IV. 157–158).
30. Hume, *History*, vol. 1, 160–161, 177; Forbes, *Hume's Philosophical Politics*, 91–91, 233–307.
31. Hume, *History*, vol. 2, 511–512, vol. 4, 374; Forbes, *Hume's Philosophical Politics*, 176–178, 296–297.
32. David Hume, "Of the Origin of Government," *Essays Moral, Political, and Literary*, ed. Eugene F. Miller (Indianapolis: Liberty Fund, 1987), 39; Hume, "Of the Original Contract," *Essays*, 477; Smith, *Lectures on Jurisprudence*, 207, 315–316.
33. Hume, "Of the Rise and Progress of the Arts and Sciences," *Essays*, 130–131.
34. Hume, "That Politics May Be Reduced to a Science," "Of Commerce," "Of Refinement in the Arts," *Essays*, 15–16, 260, 262–263, 280.
35. See *Federalist* no. 51, for example. The article that reopened these connections was Douglass Adair's "'That Politics May Be Reduced to a Science': David Hume, James Madison, and the Tenth *Federalist*," *Huntington Library Quarterly*, 20 (August 1957), 343–360.
36. Hume, "Of Refinement," 277–278.

37. Ibid., 270–271.

38. Hume, "Of the Middle Station of Life," *Essays*, 547–549.

39. Hume, "Of Commerce," 253–254; Nicholas Phillipson, *Hume* (London: Weidenfeld & Nicolson, 1989), 48–55; Phillipson, "The Scottish Enlightenment," in *The Enlightenment in National Context*, ed. Roy Porter and Mikulas Teich (Cambridge: Cambridge University Press, 1981), 31; Forbes, *Hume's Philosophical Politics*, 91. Adam Smith did not trust merchants and manufacturers to look after the public interest, but he admired their acuity nonetheless. See Smith, *An Inquiry into the Nature and Causes of the Wealth of Nations*, ed. R. H. Campbell and A. S. Skinner, 2 vols. (Indianapolis: Liberty Fund, 1981), vol. 1, 266–267.

40. Strang, *Glasgow and its Clubs*, 11.

41. Stewart J. Brown, "William Robertson (1721–1793) and the Scottish Enlightenment," in *William Robertson and the Expansion of Empire*, ed. Stewart J. Brown (New York: Cambridge University Press, 1997), 14–18.

42. Jacob M. Price, "The Rise of Glasgow in the Chesapeake Tobacco Trade, 1707–1775," *William and Mary Quarterly* 11 (April 1954), 179–199; Forbes, *Hume's Philosophical Politics*, 140–141.

43. Quoted in Bryson, *Man and Society*, 5.

44. Hume, *History*, vol. 1, 177; William Robertson, *The History of the Reign of Charles the Fifth . . . to which is prefixed, A View of the Progress of Society in Europe*, 3 vols. (Philadelphia, 1770), vol. 1, 23, 28.

45. Nicholas Phillipson, "The Scottish Enlightenment," in *The Enlightenment in National Context*, ed. Roy Porter and Mikulas Teich (Cambridge: Cambridge University Press, 1981), 22–31; Forbes, *Hume's Philosophical Politics*, 91.

46. Janet Adam Smith, "Some Eighteenth-Century Ideas of Scotland," in *Scotland in the Age of Improvement*, 107–124; John Clive, "The Social Background of the Scottish Renaissance," *Scotland in the Age of Improvement*, 224–244; Forbes, *Hume's Philosophical Politics*, 140–141.

47. Robertson, *History of the Reign of Charles the Fifth . . . A View of the Progress of Society in Europe*, vol. 1, 31, 59, 70; Hume, *History*, vol. 1, 459–460.

48. W. Innes Addison, *A Roll of Graduates of the University of Glasgow* (Glasgow, 1898), 211; *Massachusetts Centinel*, 30 January 1790, p. 1.

49. *Sibley's Harvard Graduates*, vol. 10, 226–239.

50. Ibid.; Annette Townsend, *The Auchmuty Family of Scotland and America* (New York: Grafton Press, 1932), 1–7; Kershaw, *Kennebeck Proprietors*, 29.

51. John Adams, *Diary and Autobiography of John Adams*, ed. L. H. Butterfield, 4 vols. (Cambridge, Mass.: Harvard University Press, 1961), vol. 1, 83–84.

52. Adams, *Diary and Autobiography*, vol. 1, 90, and vol. 2, 111; *Sibley's Harvard Graduates*, vol. 10, 228–229.

53. Adams, *Diary and Autobiography*, vol. 1, 152–153.

54. "By the late Benjamin Prat, Esquire," *St. James's Magazine* 2 (May 1763), 153–156. Although *Sibley's* misses this instance of publication, it records

others (vol. 10, 230n). And see Adams, *Diary and Autobiography*, vol. 1, 152–153, 346–347.

55. John M. Murrin, "The Legal Transformation: The Bench and Bar of Eighteenth-Century Massachusetts," in *Colonial America: Essays in Politics and Social Development*, ed. Stanley N. Katz (Boston: Little, Brown, 1971), 429–431; *Sibley's Harvard Graduates*, vol. 10, 231.

56. Bernard Bailyn, *The Ordeal of Thomas Hutchinson* (Cambridge, Mass.: Harvard University Press, 1974), 30–31, 47–54; Oxenbridge Thacher to Benjamin Prat [1762], *MHS Procs.* 20 (1882), 48, 48n; Adams, *Diary and Autobiography*, vol. 1, 233, 309; *Sibley's Harvard Graduates*, vol. 10, 231–232.

57. Silvester Gardiner's account with Kilby, Barnard & Parker, 11 May 1758, Silvester Gardiner Papers, MeHS; *A Calendar of the Inner Temple Records*, ed. R. A. Roberts (London, 1936), vol. 5, 99; John A. Schutz, *William Shirley: King's Governor of Massachusetts* (Chapel Hill: University of North Carolina Press, 1961), 4; E. Alfred Jones, *American Members of the Inns of Court* (London: Saint Catherine Press, 1924), 10–11; *Sibley's Harvard Graduates*, vol. 10, 228.

58. J. H. Baker, *The Third University of England: The inns of court and the common-law tradition* (London: Selden Society, 1990); David Lemmings, *Gentlemen and Barristers: The Inns of Court and the English Bar, 1680–1730* (Oxford: Clarendon Press, 1990).

59. Lemmings, *Gentlemen and Barristers*, 11; Baker, *The Third University*, 16–21; William Blackstone, *Commentaries on the Laws of England*, 4 vols. (Oxford, 1765–69), vol. 1, 25–26.

60. David Lemmings, "Blackstone and Law Reform by Education: Preparation for the Bar and Lawyerly Culture in Eighteenth-Century England," *Law and History Review* 16 (Summer 1998), 211–255; Lemmings, *Gentlemen and Barristers*, 67; Baker, *The Third University*, 21; Paul Lucas, "A Collective Biography of Students and Barristers of Lincoln's Inn, 1680–1804: A Study in the 'Aristocratic Resurgence' of the Eighteenth Century," *Journal of Modern History* 46 (June 1974), 227–261. For more on what Lemmings calls the "litigious recession," see C. W. Brooks, "Interpersonal conflict and social tension: civil litigation in England, 1640–1830," in *The First Modern Society: Essays in English History in Honour of Lawrence Stone*, ed. A. L. Beier, David Cannadine and James M. Rosenheim (Cambridge: Cambridge University Press, 1989), 357–399.

61. Lemmings, *Gentlemen and Barristers*, 164.

62. Daniel Duman, "The English Bar in the Georgian Era," in *Lawyers in Early Modern Europe and America*, ed. Wilfrid Prest (New York: Holmes & Meier, 1981), 93–95; Lawrence Stone and Jeanne C. Fawtier Stone, *An Open Elite? England, 1540–1880* (Oxford: Clarendon Press, 1984), 23–24, 225, 403, 408; Lemmings, *Gentlemen and Barristers*, 173; Robert Robson, *The Attorney in Eighteenth-Century England* (Cambridge: Cambridge University Press, 1959), 58, 82–85, 111–112; M. Miles, "'Eminent Practitioners': The New Visage of Country Attorneys, c. 1750–1800," in *Law, Economy and Society, 1750–1914:*

Essays in the History of English Law, ed. G. R. Rubin and David Sugarman (Abingdon: Professional Books, 1984), 476–477. This last essay suggests that the success of provincial attorneys circumscribed that of barristers, but it supports the notion that the Georgian bar, though reduced in size and in the scope of its privileges, was also a beneficiary of the century's developments. On p. 499, Miles explains the decline in litigation in a way that dissociates caseload (down at Westminster) from fees (up for attorneys and barristers alike, due to new advisory services and agencies).

63. Lewis Namier, *The Structure of Politics at the Accession of George III* (London: Macmillan, 1961), 42–44; Duman, "The English Bar in the Georgian Era," 89–90, 99–100. The "Early Struggles of Eminent Lawyers" became a commonplace tale: see Archer Polson's *Law and Lawyers: A Sketch Book of Legal Biography, Gossip, and Anecdote* (London, 1858), 5–20.

64. Charles Carroll to Charles Carroll, 7 January 1763, in Kate Mason Rowland, *The Life of Charles Carroll of Carrollton, 1737–1832*, 2 vols. (New York, 1898), vol. 1, 53–54; John Rutledge to Edward Rutledge, 30 July 1769, in Jones, *American Members of the Inns*, 190–191; Robson, *The Attorney in Eighteenth-Century England*, 58–59; Lemmings, "Blackstone and Law Reform," 245–246.

65. Quoted in James Oldham, *The Mansfield Manuscripts and the Growth of English Law in the Eighteenth Century*, 2 vols. (Chapel Hill: University of North Carolina Press, 1992), vol. 1, 6.

66. Eric R. Watson, "John Wilkes and the 'Essay on Woman,'" *Notes and Queries*, 11th series, 9 (14 March 1914), 204. Family legend has it that Gardiner was a Mansfield favorite, but there is no hard evidence of a relationship. See R. H. Gardiner, *Early Recollections*, 18.

67. John Lord Campbell, *The Lives of the Chief Justices of England*, 2 vols. (London, 1849), vol. 2, 302–312; C. H. S. Fifoot, *Lord Mansfield* (Oxford: Clarendon Press, 1936), 27; Oldham, *Mansfield Manuscripts*, vol. 1, 27.

68. Quoted in John Almon, *Biographical, Literary, and Political Anecdotes of Several of the Most Eminent Persons of the Present Age*, 3 vols. (London, 1797), vol. 1, 222–223—the critical blast is quoted on 211–212; Oldham, *Mansfield Manuscripts*, vol. 1, 11.

69. Oldham, *Mansfield Manuscripts*, vol. 1, 12; Campbell, *Lives of the Chief Justices*, vol. 2, 359–364, 372–375.

70. Quoted in Campbell, *Lives of the Chief Justices*, vol. 2, 443.

71. BL Add. Mss. 15488, ff. 99–128; Oldham, *Mansfield Manuscripts*, vol. 1, 11–12.

72. Oldham, *Mansfield Manuscripts*, vol. 1, 15, 196–198.

73. Blackstone, *Commentaries*, vol. 1, 31.

74. Charles Carroll to Charles Carroll, 7 January 1763, *Life of Charles Carroll*, vol. 1, 53–54.

75. Lance Bertelsen, *The Nonsense Club: Literature and Popular Culture, 1749–1764* (Oxford: Clarendon Press, 1986), 29; Bryant Lillywhite, *London Coffee Houses* (London: George Allen & Unwin, 1963), 713–714.

76. Lillywhite, *London Coffee Houses*, 190–192, 234–235, 442; Walter Besant, *London* (London, 1892), 350–352.

77. Gardiner's acquaintance, the Welsh magnate Sir John Philipps, gave his son fifty pounds a quarter when the junior Philipps attended Pembroke College in 1763. See David W. Howell, *Patriarchs and Parasites: The Gentry of South-West Wales in the Eighteenth Century* (Cardiff: University of Wales Press, 1986), 172. On the relative costs of university and legal educations, see Lemmings, *Gentlemen and Barristers*, 24. John Gardiner's quarterly allowance was originally £37.10, but this increased to £45 by the second half of 1760. See Silvester Gardiner's account with Kilby, Barnard & Parker, GWA; *Calendar of the Inner Temple Records*, vol. 5, 185, 197.

78. James Boswell, *Boswell's London Journal, 1762–1763*, ed. Frederick A. Pottle (New York: McGraw-Hill, 1950), 1, 5, 9–10, 89–90, 234, 267, 306; *Calendar of the Inner Temple Records*, vol. 5, 133, 477.

79. *Boswell's London Journal*, 176, 227, 266, 306.

80. See John Gardiner's 1768 affidavit in John Almon, *The Correspondence of the Late John Wilkes*, 5 vols. (London, 1805), vol. 1, 141–147. BL Add. Mss. 22131, ff. 58–59, and 22132, ff. 47–48, also mention Gardiner's role in this episode.

81. *Correspondence of the Late John Wilkes*, vol. 1, 147–151; BL Add. Mss. 22131, ff. 63, 74–75, 80; George Rude, *Wilkes and Liberty: A Social Study of 1763 to 1774* (Oxford: Clarendon Press, 1962), 22–27; On Beardmore, refer to Bertelsen, *Nonsense Club*, 173.

82. BL Add. Mss. 22131, f. 133, and 22132, f. 179; a copy of the general warrant can be found at BL Add. Mss. 22131, f. 37.

83. BL Add. Mss. 22131, ff. 133–142, 179–180, and 22132, f. 179.

84. BL Add. Mss. 22132, ff. 195–202. See the *Massachusetts Centinel*, 17 March 1790, p. 3, where Gardiner described the waiter and advertised its disappearance. The barrister might have been the victim of robbers; he might also have been publicizing his legal crusade. The waiter rematerialized; see the photograph of this heirloom in Charles Edwin Allen's *History of Dresden, Maine* (Augusta, Maine, 1931), 415.

85. BL Add. Mss. 22132, ff. 197–198; Rude, *Wilkes and Liberty*, 26–27 and passim.

86. John Wilkes to the Earls of Egremont and Halifax, 9 May 1763, BL Add. Mss. 30867, f. 207; Eric R. Watson, "Wilkes and the 'Essay on Woman,'" *Notes and Queries* 9 (28 March 1914), 241.

87. BL Add. Mss. 22132, ff. 120–121; Watson, "Wilkes and the 'Essay on Woman,'" *Notes and Queries*, 9 (14 March 1914), 204. Early in Wilkes's exile, Gardiner may have purchased books on his behalf; their association was often concerned with the printed word. See Wilkes to [Humphrey Cotes], 5 April 1764, BL Add. Mss. 30868, f. 66.

88. "To the Author of the Gratulatory Address," *Independent Chronicle*, 9 September 1790, p. 1; "Legislature of Massachusetts," *Herald of Freedom*, 3 May

1791, p. 1. See the postscript to Gardiner's letter to John Wilkes, 2 October 1763, BL Add. Mss. 30867, f. 220. The best study of Churchill and his contemporaries is Bertelsen's *Nonsense Club*.

89. John Brewer, *Party ideology and popular politics at the accession of George III* (Cambridge: Cambridge University Press, 1976), 174, 180, 197–200. Also Bertelsen, *Nonsense Club*, 260–261, and Rude, *Wilkes and Liberty*.

90. Donald W. Livingston, "Hume, English Barbarism and American Independence," in *Scotland and America in the Age of Enlightenment*, 137–141.

91. John Gardiner to John Wilkes, 2 October 1763, BL Add. Mss. 30867, f. 220; Brewer, *Party ideology*, 180, 186; Linda Colley, *In Defiance of Oligarchy: The Tory Party, 1714–60* (Cambridge: Cambridge University Press, 1982), 172–173; Colley, *Britons: Forging the Nation, 1707–1837* (New Haven: Yale University Press, 1992), 106–108.

92. Horace Bleackley, *Life of John Wilkes* (London, 1917), 4–7, 32–34, 43, 94–95; Rude, *Wilkes and Liberty*, 17–20; Colley, *Britons*, 120–121.

93. James Chitterbuck [?] to John Wilkes, 25 October 1763, BL Add. Mss. 30867, f. 224; Brewer, *Party ideology*, 190, 197, 200.

94. Rude, *Wilkes and Liberty*, 171, 191–192.

The Revolution of Opportunities (pages 70–108)

1. Lemmings, *Gentlemen and Barristers*, 120; John Gardiner to Richard Derby, 13 February 1761, Derby Family Papers, Peabody Essex Museum, Salem (hereafter DFP); Silvester Gardiner's account with Kilby, Barnard & Co, 15 April and 21 October 1760, GWA.

2. James Duncan Phillips, *The Life and Times of Richard Derby, Merchant of Salem, 1712 to 1783* (Cambridge, Mass.: 1929), 27–29. Phillips errs when he states that the *Ranger* loaded its sugar in Martinique; see John Gardiner to Richard Derby, 19 March 1762, and Derby to Gardiner [draft copy], 3 July 1762, DFP. Also Cadwallader Colden to William Pitt, 27 December 1760, *Collections of the New-York Historical Society* (1876), 51. On Shirley, see John A. Schutz, *William Shirley: King's Governor of Massachusetts* (Chapel Hill: University of North Carolina Press, 1961), 84–85, 230–233. Schutz thinks highly of Shirley's service and contradicts Richard Derby's charges of rapacity: Schutz, *William Shirley*, 259–260; Richard Derby to John Gardiner, 9 October 1762, DFP.

3. John Gardiner to Richard Derby, 13 February 1761 and 11 September 1762, DFP.

4. John Gardiner to Richard Derby, 13 February 1761, DFP.

5. Richard Derby to John Gardiner, 3 July 1762 [copy] and 9 October 1762, DFP; Phillips, *Richard Derby*, 27–29.

6. John Gardiner to Richard Derby, 13 February 1761, 19 March and 23 April 1762, DFP; *Journal of the Commissioners for Trade and Plantations from January 1759 to December 1763* (London, 1935), 349–350, 352.

7. Richard Derby to John Gardiner, 26 December 1763 and 31 July 1764; Gardiner to Derby, 11 June 1765; Lane & Booth to Derby, 27 November 1765; Lane, Son & Fraser to Derby, 30 March 1767 and 23 January 1768; George Crowninshield to Lane, Son & Fraser, 28 March 1769. All letters in DFP.

8. *Susquehannah Company Papers,* ed. Julian P. Boyd and Robert J. Taylor, 11 vols. (Ithaca: Cornell University Press, 1962), vol. 1, lviii–lxix.

9. *Susquehannah Company Papers,* vol. 2, xli, 37–38n, 292, 304–310, 321–322, vol. 3, xxxi, 5–6, 90–91.

10. John Gardiner to Richard Derby, 23 April 1762, DFP; Duman, "The English Bar in the Georgian Era," *Lawyers in Early Modern Europe and America,* 96–99; Lemmings, *Gentlemen and Barristers,* 119–120; J. S. Cockburn, *A History of English Assizes, 1558–1714* (Cambridge: Cambridge University Press, 1972), x–xi, 23, 143.

11. Quoted in Cockburn, *English Assizes,* 153.

12. Cockburn, *English Assizes,* 6–8, 65–66, 153–162, 187.

13. Ibid., 86–150.

14. John Brown, J. W. Phillips, and Fred J. Warren, *The History of Haverfordwest* (Haverfordwest, 1914), 125–129; Cockburn, *English Assizes,* 3, 65. The two accounts are remarkably similar.

15. Quoted in G. R. Elton, *England under the Tudors* (London: Methuen, 1955), 160–161.

16. Elton, *England under the Tudors,* 160–161, 175–178; William Rees, "The Union of England and Wales," *Transactions of the Honourable Society of Cymmrodorion* (1937), 44–45; J. Gwynfor Jones, *Early Modern Wales, c. 1525–1640* (New York: St. Martin's Press, 1994), 48–49.

17. Rees, "Union of England and Wales," 27, 30, 35; Elton, *England under the Tudors,* 177–178; Jones, *Early Modern Wales,* 67.

18. Rees, "Union of England and Wales," 32, 57–58, 81; Elton, *England under the Tudors,* 177–178; Glyn Parry, *A Guide to the Records of Great Sessions in Wales* (Aberystwyth: National Library of Wales, 1995), iv–v; W. Llewelyn Williams, *An Account of the King's Court of Great Sessions in Wales* (London, 1916), 1–5; Jones, *Early Modern Wales,* 81–90. Jones wants to emphasize the continuities of the Welsh legal system but concedes that English structures were successfully imposed.

19. Cockburn, *English Assizes,* 187; William Russell Oldnall, *The Practice of the Court of Great Sessions on the Carmarthen Circuit* (London, 1814), 6–7, 7n; Brown, Phillips, and Warren, *History of Haverfordwest,* 93.

20. Rees, "Union of England and Wales," 79.

21. Lemmings, *Gentlemen and Barristers,* 251; W. L. Williams, *Account of the King's Court,* 38–42; W. R. Williams, *The History of the Great Sessions in Wales,*

1542–1830 (Brecknock, 1899), 19–24. The latter Williams defends the Welsh judges, but very few of his "great names"—judges later elevated to high justiceships—practiced in the eighteenth century, and fewer still around the time Gardiner rode the sessions. The two judges who presided over his circuit were typical: they were born outside Wales, attended Oxford and the Inns, and were men of influence in their counties. Both men were MPs. See Williams, *History of the Great Sessions*, 182, 184.

22. Parry, *Guide to the Records of Great Sessions*, v–vi, ix–xii; W. H. D. Winder, "Equity in the Courts of Great Sessions," *Law Quarterly Review* 55 (January 1939), 112–118; Oldnall, *Practice of the Court of Great Sessions*, 526.

23. Parry, *Guide to the Records of Great Sessions*, xvii–xxi.

24. Oldnall, *Practice of the Court of Great Sessions*, 24; Jones, *Early Modern Wales*, 81; David W. Howell, *Patriarchs and Parasites: The Gentry of South-West Wales in the Eighteenth Century* (Cardiff: University of Wales Press, 1986), 155.

25. M. Miles, "The Money Market in the Early Industrial Revolution: The Evidence from West Riding Attorneys, c. 1750–1800," *Business History* 23 (July 1981), 129–130; Cecil Price, *The English Theatre in Wales in the Eighteenth and Early Nineteenth Centuries* (Cardiff: University of Wales Press, 1948), 2–8.

26. Price, *English Theatre in Wales*, 2–13, 28; Price, "Polite Life in Eighteenth-Century Wales," *Welsh Anvil* 5 (July 1953), 95; Brown, Phillips, and Warren, *History of Haverfordwest*, 116.

27. David Howell, "Landed Society in Pembrokeshire, circa 1680–1830," *Pembrokeshire Historian* 3 (1971), 34; Cockburn, *English Assizes*, 8.

28. Gardiner also rode the Oxford circuit in the summer of 1762, as did Lord Mansfield: here is oblique support for the antiquarian theory of friendship between them. See John Gardiner to Richard Derby, 11 September 1762, DFP, and Oldham, *Mansfield Manuscripts*, vol. 2, 1488. However, the South Welsh and Oxford circuits ran on cooperative schedules, and many barristers rode both in the same season (Williams, *An Account of the King's Court*, 45).

29. John Gardiner to Richard Derby, 11 September 1762, DFP; Mary M. Drummond, "Rice, George," in *The House of Commons, 1754–1790*, ed. Sir Lewis Namier and John Brooke, 3 vols. (London: Secker & Warburg, 1985), vol. 3, 351–352.

30. John Gardiner to John Wilkes, 2 October 1763, BL Add. Mss. 30867, f. 220.

31. Peter D. G. Thomas, "Jacobitism in Wales," *Welsh History Review* 1 (1962), 287–289, 295–299; Colley, *In Defiance of Oligarchy*, 33–34, 76–77; Lewis Namier, *Crossroads of Power: Essays on Eighteenth-Century England* (London: Hamish Hamilton, 1962), 35.

32. Francis Jones, "The Society of Sea Serjeants," *Trans. Hon. Soc. Cymm.* (1967), 57–91; Thomas, "Jacobitism in Wales," 290–291; Howell, *Patriarchs and Parasites*, 117; Colley, *In Defiance of Oligarchy*, 69, 86; Namier, *Crossroads of Power*, 35–42; J. A. Cannon, "Philipps, Sir John," in *The House of Commons, 1754–1790*, vol. 3, 274–275.

33. Howell, "Landed Society in Pembrokeshire," 34; Richard Fenton, *A Historical Tour through Pembrokeshire* (London, 1810), 463–464; Jones, "Society of Sea Serjeants," 61–63, 72–75, 89–90; John Gardiner, *The Widowed Mourner* (Boston, 1791), 4n; Thomas, "Jacobitism in Wales," 292.

34. J. P. Jenkins, "Jacobites and Freemasons in Eighteenth-Century Wales," *Welsh History Review* 9 (December 1979), 391–406; Colley, *In Defiance of Oligarchy*, 34, 172–173, 337n; Philip Jenkins, *The making of a ruling class: The Glamorgan gentry, 1640–1790* (Cambridge: Cambridge University Press, 1983), 184; Howell, *Patriarchs and Parasites*, 120, 126.

35. John Gardiner to John Wilkes, 2 October 1763, BL Add. Mss. 30867, f. 220.

36. In fact, Philipps negotiated a deal by which John Symmons, Margaret's uncle, held the borough seat until another legacy Sea-Serjeant reached his majority and became the shire's representative (Howell, *Patriarchs and Parasites*, 126). To read of Harries's popularity, see Jones, "Society of Sea Serjeants," 89–90 (and, for more on Symmons, 87); John Gardiner, *Widowed Mourner*, 3n; Fenton, *Historical Tour*, 217–218. On her family, see Thomas Nicholas, *Annals and Antiquities of the Counties and County Families of Wales*, 2 vols. (London, 1872), vol. 2, 901, under John Henry Harries's "Lineage"; F. Jones, "Harries of Tregwynt," *Trans. Hon. Soc. Cymm.* (1943 and 1944), 108–119.

37. Francis Jones, "Disaffection and Dissent in Pembrokeshire," *Trans. Hon. Soc. Cymm.* (1946–47), 222; Nicholas discusses Harries's connections to the marchlords (*Annals*, vol. 2, 874–876) as does Edward Laws, in *The History of Little England beyond Wales* (Haverfordwest, [1888] 1995), 94–95, 99, 107–108, 119.

38. Gardiner, *Widowed Mourner*, 1–3n; Jones, "Society of Sea Serjeants," 89–90; Fenton, *Historical Tour*, 217–218, 466–467. Fenton claims that Margaret's brother, John Harries of Priskilly, was the last living Sea-Serjeant. John Gardiner would later allude to the "Fortune" that Margaret brought into their marriage, but, whatever its size, the dowry was not what it might have been. See W2, no. 10867, 27 March 1783, Deeds & Records, St. Kitts & Nevis Archives, Basseterre.

39. Lane, Son & Fraser to Richard Derby, 23 January 1768, DFP.

40. Cadwallader Colden to John Pownall, 12 January 1762 (Thomas Pownall had facilitated Colden's recent elevation to the lieutenant governorship: Colden to Thomas Pownall, 12 August 1761), *Collections of the New-York Historical Society* (1876), 109, 154; *Sibley's Harvard Graduates*, vol. 10, 226–239; Bailyn, *Ordeal of Thomas Hutchinson*, 30–31, 47–54. Read on for evidence of Prat's reluctance. I am grateful to Daniel J. Hulsebosch for his advice on New York's issues and sources.

41. Cadwallader Colden, "State of the Province of New York," 6 December 1765, *NYHS Colls.* (1877), 70; Patricia U. Bonomi, *A Factious People: Politics and Society in Colonial New York* (New York: Columbia University Press, 1971), 210–211, 227; *Dictionary of American Biography*, vol. 4, 286–287.

42. Colden to the Earl of Halifax, 22 February 1765; Colden to the Lords Commissioners for Trade and Plantations, 22 February 1765; Colden to the Earl of Egremont, 14 September 1763: *NYHS Colls.* (1876), 231, 468, 470.

43. Colden to the Lords Commissioners for Trade and Plantations, 7 April 1762, *NYHS Colls.* (1876), 187; Bonomi, *Factious People*, 177, 232–233; William Livingston et al., *The Independent Reflector*, ed. Milton M. Klein (Cambridge, Mass.: Harvard University Press, 1963), 1–50.

44. Colden to the Lords Commissioners for Trade and Plantations, 11 January and 7 April 1762, 8 July 1763; Colden to John Pownall, 6 February 1762; Colden to Halifax, 22 February 1765: *NYHS Colls.* (1876), 148–150, 162, 187, 191, 217 218, 470, Colden, "State of the Province of New York," 6 December 1765, *NYHS Colls.* (1877), 73.

45. Benjamin Prat to the Lords of Trade, 24 May 1762, *Documents Relative to the Colonial History of the State of New-York*, ed. E. B. O'Callaghan, 11 vols. (Albany, 1856–61), vol. 7, 501.

46. Prat to Cadwallader Colden, 3 October 1761, and Prat to Thomas Pownall, 7 January 1762, *NYHS Colls.* (1922), 81–82, 113–116; *Rural Household Inventories*, ed. Abbott Lowell Cummings (Boston: Society for the Preservation of New England Antiquities, 1964), 198–206.

47. Colden to the Lords Commissioners for Trade and Plantations, 11 January 1762, *NYHS Colls.* (1876), 148–150; Prat to Colden, 22 August and 3 October 1761, and Prat to Thomas Pownall, 7 January 1762, *NYHS Colls.* (1922), 68–69, 81–82, 113–116; Daniel J. Hulsebosch, "*Imperia in Imperio:* The Multiple Constitutions of Empire in New York, 1750–1777," *Law and History Review* 16 (Summer 1998), 372–376.

48. The quoted phrase is Cadwallader Colden's: Colden to the Lords Commissioners for Trade and Plantations, 22 February 1765, *NYHS Colls.* (1876), 468.

49. Prat to Colden, 14 September 1761, *NYHS Colls.* (1922), 76–78.

50. Adams, *Diary and Autobiography*, vol. 1, 241; *Sibley's Harvard Graduates*, vol. 10, 238.

51. "By the late Benjamin Prat, Esquire, Chief Justice of New-York, Written in Sickness," *St. James's Magazine* 2 (May 1763), 153–156; on this journal, see Bertelsen, *Nonsense Club*, 163–166, 184–186.

52. Prat to Thomas Pownall, 7 January 1762, *NYHS Colls.* (1922), 116; John Gardiner to Richard Derby, 19 March 1762 and 16 July 176[?], DFP; Schutz, *William Shirley*, 8–9, 12, 232–233; William Samuel Johnson to Samuel Johnson, 18 May 1767, and Nathaniel Rogers to William Samuel Johnson, 20 February 1769, William Samuel Johnson Papers, Connecticut Historical Society.

53. In researching and writing this section, I benefited greatly from the work of Andrew J. O'Shaughnessy. See, for example, O'Shaughnessy, "The Politics of the Leeward Islands, 1763–1783" (D.Phil. diss., Oxford University, 1987),

76—this dissertation became the basis of O'Shaughnessy's *An Empire Divided: The American Revolution and the British Caribbean* (Philadelphia: University of Pennsylvania Press, 2000); Lane, Son & Fraser to Richard Derby, 17 March 1769, DFP; Florentius Vassall to Silvester Gardiner, 14 [Dec?] 1768, GWA; Foote, *Annals*, vol. 2, 224, 315, 315n, 588; Sir Lewis Namier, "Trecothick, Barlow," *House of Commons 1754–1790*, vol. 3, 557–560.

54. Anthony Stokes, *A Narrative of the Official Conduct of Anthony Stokes* (London, 1784), 3–4; Stokes, *Desultory Observations, on the Situation, Extent, Climate, Population, Religion, &c. of Great Britain* (London, 1792), 4n; Rees L. Lloyd, "Welsh Masters of the Bench of the Inner Temple," *Trans. Hon. Soc. Cymm.* (1938), 230–232; Minutes of the Assembly of St. Christopher, 7 April 1769, C.O. 241/11.

55. Samuel Quincy to Ebenezer and Hannah Storer, 21 June 1780, Samuel Quincy Papers, MHS; *Sibley's Harvard Graduates*, vol. 13, 478–488.

56. Samuel Quincy to Hannah Quincy, 15–20 November 1780, Samuel Quincy to Henry Hill, 15–30 November 1780, MHS.

57. William Woodley to the Earl of Hillsborough, 22 April 1768, C.O. 152/48 (7–8). For social conditions on St. Kitts, see C.O. 152/50 (15, 17) and 152/54 (66); James Ramsay, *An Essay on the Treatment and Conversion of African Slaves in the British Sugar Colonies* (London, 1784), 80n, 111, 122; O'Shaughnessy, "Politics of the Leeward Islands," 55; Elsa V. Goveia, *Slave Society in the British Leeward Islands at the End of the Eighteenth Century* (New Haven: Yale University Press, 1965), 89, 107–110, 122; J. R. Ward, *British West Indian Slavery, 1750–1834: The Process of Amelioration* (Oxford: Clarendon Press, 1988), 74–77.

58. Ramsay, *Essay on the Treatment and Conversion of African Slaves*, 67–68, 83–86, 86n, 239.

59. Goveia, *Slave Society*, 87–91, 107–108.

60. *Calendar of the Inner Temple Records*, vol. 5, 99, 112, 131, 136, 215; *Caribbeana* 3 (October 1914), 362–364. I discuss Bryan's connections below.

61. "The Humble Petition of John Mahon, William Roscrow and William Burroughs," 10 October 1766, C.O. 152/30 (113–114); "The Humble Petition of John Garnett and William Burroughs," Minutes of the Assembly of St. Christopher's, 2 March 1770, C.O. 241/14; Stokes, *A View of the Constitution of the British Colonies, in North-America and the West Indies* (London, [1783] 1969), 269–270; Miles, "Eminent Practitioners," 486–487.

62. Stokes, *View of the Constitution*, 270; O'Shaughnessy, "Politics of the Leeward Islands," 36–39.

63. Samuel Quincy to Henry Hill, 15–30 November 1780, Samuel Quincy Papers, MHS; Stokes, *View of the Constitution*, 191; John Gardiner, "Precedents in Chancery," Rare Book Room, Langdell Library, Harvard Law School.

64. He was, in fact, one of the busiest solicitors in Chancery. See the Chancery Records, B3–3, St. Kitts & Nevis Archives, Basseterre; Gardiner, "Precedents in Chancery," 1–4, 29–30, 54.

65. For Gardiner's lands and chattels, see these items from Deeds & Records, St. Kitts Archives: H2, no. 8299, 30 November 1769, and no. 8387, 21 June 1770; I2, no. 8627, 31 August 1771; K2, no. 8724, 28 February 1772; L2, nos. 8780 and 8821, 11 and 23 June 1772; S2, no. 9914, 19 March 1778, and no. 9936, 2 December 1775; W2, no. 10699, 7 April 1783, and no. 10867, 27 March 1783. On the hurricane of 1772, see *An Account of the Late Dreadful Hurricane* (St. Christopher, 1772), 7, 42.

66. Jonathan Flemming, Appellant, 7 June 1770, Chancery Records, B3–3, St. Kitts Archives. Gardiner's brief is dated 2 December 1769.

67. Frank Wesley Pitman, "Slavery on British West India Plantations in the Eighteenth Century," *Journal of Negro History* 11 (October 1926), 666.

68. William Mathew Burt to Lord George Germain, 1 November 1777, C.O. 152/57 (75, 81–82). Burt mandated a more sensible docket of fees; see Burt to Germain, 16 June 1778, C.O. 152/34. Gardiner felt slighted by the new arrangement; after Burt's departure, he sought redress in Chancery (Gardiner, "Precedents," 93–95). When Gardiner returned to Boston, rumors of his past conduct circulated, but the full story never emerged. Take, for example, the debate recorded in the *Herald of Freedom*, 3 May 1791, p. 1.

69. John Pinney to Mills & Swanston, 3 May 1777 and 18 June 1778, Pinney Letterbook 4, University of Bristol.

70. Sir Ralph Payne to Dartmouth, 6 October 1773, C.O. 152/54 (1–4).

71. "The Humble Petition of George Taylor," from the Assembly Minutes, 27 September 1768, C.O. 241/11; see the census enclosed in William Woodley to Hillsborough, 24 January 1770, C.O. 152/50 (15, 17).

72. Assembly Minutes, 27 December 1768–10 January 1769, 7 April 1773, C.O. 241/11; Hillsborough to William Woodley, 21 April and 31 July 1770, C.O. 152/50 (13, 33).

73. Assembly Minutes, 24 October 1769, C.O. 241/14; "Answer of the Assembly of St. Christopher's to the Remonstrance and Petition and Petition of William Wharton, Esq. and others," 28 June 1770, C.O. 152/31 (145–147).

74. James Ramsay, *A Reply to the Personal Invectives and Objections* (London, 1785), 26; Assembly Minutes, 2 March 1770, C.O. 241/14; John Gardiner to John Pownall, 21 March 1771, C.O. 152/31 (66–68); O'Shaughnessy, "Politics of the Leeward Islands," 104–110.

75. John Gardiner, *The Argument or Speech of John Gardiner, Esquire* (Basseterre, St. Christopher, 1770), iv; Edwin Thomas's Memorial to the Court of King's Bench and Common Pleas, 29 June 1769, Edwin Thomas to Bishop Terrick, 26 December 1770, "The humble remonstrance and petition of James Ramsey" (to Lt. Gov. Richard Hawkshaw Losack): all to be found among the Fulham Papers, Lambeth Palace Library; [Edwin Thomas,] "Publicola," *Charribbean and General Gazette*, 31 October 1770, pp. 2–3.

76. Gardiner to John Pownall, 21 March 1771, C.O. 152/31 (66–68); O'Shaughnessy, "Politics of the Leeward Islands," 127. Shortly after arriving

on St. Kitts, Gardiner wrote to Wilkes of a subscription that had raised funds for the libertine's support (Gardiner to John Wilkes, 26 March 1769, Add. Mss. 30870, f. 133).

77. Assembly Minutes, 24 October 1769, C.O. 241/14; Executors of John Humphreys v. Edward Gillard, Samuel Crooke v. Edward Gillard, August Court 1770, King's Bench Records, B4–28, St. Kitts Archives. Throughout this period, Gardiner and Stanley were opposing advocates in many cases. See, for example, the King's Bench records for July 1770 and the Chancery proceedings (B3–3) for 12 December 1770 and 25 March 1771. Stanley's rate of success was high.

78. Assembly Minutes, 4 November 1769, C.O. 241/14.

79. Ibid. The assembly, with the hope of keeping the barrister in line, compelled him to attend its meetings between late November and March of the following year, at which time his lawsuits provoked the legislators to take punitive measures. See Gardiner, *Argument or Speech*, 30n.

80. Aretas Akers to James Ramsay [two undated examples, undoubtedly from 1769], Akers Letters; Assembly Minutes, 14 April 1770, C.O. 241/14; O'Shaughnessy, "Politics of the Leeward Islands," 106; Gardiner, *Argument or Speech*, 31n. The St. Mary Cayon parish register attributes Bryan's death on 23 November to "gaol fever" (*Caribbeana* 3 [July 1913], 101).

81. Assembly Minutes, 30 March 1770, C.O. 241/14; William Wharton v. James St. John, Henry Seaton v. Henry Berkeley, April Court 1770, King's Bench Records, B4–28, St. Kitts Archives; Gardiner, *Argument or Speech*, v–x. Gardiner would later complain of rough usage during his arrest: Gardiner v. John Fahie, August Court 1770, King's Bench. Jack Greene examines the imperial constitution at length in *Peripheries and Center: Constitutional Development in the Extended Politics of the British Empire and the United States, 1607–1788* (Athens: University of Georgia Press, 1986). See pp. 31–32, 94–95.

82. Gardiner, *Argument or Speech*, 1, 4–5, 12, 20.

83. Ibid., 31. The quoted phrase was the assembly's language; see its minutes, 4 November 1769, C.O. 241/14.

84. Gardiner, *Argument or Speech*, 13–15.

85. Ibid., 8–9.

86. Greene, *Peripheries and Center*, 98–103, 113–123.

87. Gardiner, *Argument or Speech*, 37–39.

88. Ibid., iv.

89. William Woodley to the Earl of Hillsborough, 20 April 1770, C.O. 152/31 (38–39); on the easy confusion of public and private animosities among whites, see Richard Hawkshaw Losack to Hillsborough, 11 December 1770, C.O. 152/31 (115), and Sir Ralph Payne to Dartmouth, 6 October 1773, C.O. 152/54 (1–4).

90. Ramsay, *A Reply to the Personal Invectives*, 26 (Woodley and Stanley were cousins; see *Caribbeana* 2 [July 1912], 295); Assembly Minutes, 9 November 1769, C.O. 241/14; Hillsborough to William Woodley, 21 April and 31 July

1770, C.O. 152/50 (13, 33); *The Speeches of His Excellency General Woodley* (1770), C.O. 152/50 (76–80); "To the Honorable Richard Hawkshaw Losack," C.O. 152/31 (43–44) and C.O. 152/50 (75); Richard Hawkshaw Losack to Hillsborough, 11 December 1770, 11 May and 6 August 1771, C.O. 152/31 (115, 124, 129); O'Shaughnessy, "Politics of the Leeward Islands," 122–123; Mary M. Drummond, "Payne, Ralph," *House of Commons 1754–1790*, vol. 3, 253–254.

91. Aretas Akers to James Ramsay, 20 February 1775, Akers Letters; "Representation of the Lords of Trade," 6 June 1771, C.O. 152/51 (97–100); *Acts of the Privy Council of England: Colonial Series*, 6 vols. (London, 1908–12), vol. 5, 277–280; O'Shaughnessy, "Politics of the Leeward Islands," 133–134.

92. Gardiner, *Argument or Speech*, 16–19.

93. [Edwin Thomas,] "Publicola," *Charribbean and General Gazette*, 24 November 1770, pp. 3–4.

94. Assembly Minutes, 28 June and 10 December 1770, 23 January 1771, 26 March 1773–13 September 1775, C.O. 241/11; Assembly Minutes, 6 June 1771, 20 January 1772, C.O. 241/14; Minutes of the Council of St. Christopher, 6 January 1772, 2 May 1774, C.O. 241/12.

95. O'Shaughnessy, "Politics of the Leeward Islands," 124, 127, 129; *Caribbeana* 3 (October 1914), 355, 362; J. M. Collinge, "Stanley, John," *The House of Commons 1790–1820*, ed. R. G. Thorne, 5 vols. (London: Secker & Warburg, 1986), vol. 5, 252–253.

96. Ramsay, *Essay on the Treatment and Conversion of African Slaves*, 68; Ward, *British West Indian Slavery*, 12–13; Goveia, *Slave Society*, 101–102.

97. Aretas Akers to James Ramsay, 5 December 1774, 20 February 1775, Akers to Alexander Douglas, 20 February 1782, Akers Letters; Akers to George Akers, 26 October 1783, cited in Anthony Wigan, "The Akers Letters," 44; Arthur P. Watts, *Nevis and St. Christopher's, 1782–1784* (Paris, 1925), 46, 51. Like Aretas Akers, John Pinney of Nevis at first favored reconciliation with America. He knew West Indian planters would suffer greatly in any conflict. During the war, Pinney acted as a British agent but was also on good terms with the French occupiers. See John Pinney to George Warry, 26 July 1775, to Simon Pretor, 26 July 1775 and 12 June 1777, to John Gaspard Ringmacher, 10 February 1776, Pinney Letterbook 4; Pinney to Thomas Coates, 22 July 1782, to William Manning, 19 September 1782, Pinney Letterbook 5; Richard Pares, *A West-India Fortune* (London: Longmans, Green, 1950), 98.

98. Aretas Akers to James Ramsay, 5 December 1774, to Alexander Douglas, 20 February 1782, James Akers to Aretas Akers, 21 March, 10 and 26 May, 1783, Akers Letters; Wigan, "Akers Letters," 35, 44. A descendant, Aretas Akers-Douglas, was a Home Secretary; see Eric Alexander, 3rd Viscount Chilston, *Chief Whip: The Political Life and Times of Aretas Akers-Douglas, 1st Viscount Chilston* (London: Routledge & Kegan Paul, 1961), 1–3.

99. Aretas Akers to James Ramsay, 5 December 1774, Akers Letters.

100. John Pinney to William Manning, 19 September 1782, Pinney to Edward Brazier, 21 September 1782, Pinney Letterbook 5; Pares, *West-India Fortune*, 100. After the peace, John Stanley—ever Gardiner's companion opposite—demanded the money from Pinney on behalf of the reinstated government. See Pinney to John Stanley, 13 July 1784, to Joseph Gill, 13 July 1784, to William Coker, 20 September 1786, Pinney Letterbook 6. For Clifton, see O'Shaughnessy, *An Empire Divided*, 183, and John Gardiner to Silvester Gardiner, 18 January and 19 July 1783, GWA. John describes his French service in the first of these letters and in his *Memorial and Petition of John Gardiner, Esq.* (Boston, 1783). Family legend erroneously made John Gardiner an attorney general (serving King George) upon his arrival in St. Kitts—see R. H. Gardiner, *Early Recollections*, 18.

101. Gardiner, *Memorial and Petition*; Gardiner, "Precedents in Chancery," 108. Gardiner's last transactions are found in folio W2, Deeds & Records, St. Kitts Archives: no. 10655, 11 March 1783; nos. 10697–98, 6–8 April 1783; no. 10777, 8 April 1783; no. 10867, 27 March 1783. On creole disaffection, see John Gardiner to Silvester Gardiner, 18 January and 14 July 1783, GWA; John Pinney to Mills's & Swanston, 28 September 1778, Pinney Letterbook 5; Pares, *West-India Fortune*, 98.

102. John Gardiner to Silvester Gardiner, 18 January and 14 July 1783, GWA.

103. William Gardiner to Silvester Gardiner, 2 July 1783, John Gardiner to Silvester Gardiner, 14 and 19 July 1783, 22 April and 4 May 1784, Oliver Whipple to Silvester Gardiner, 24 November 1783, Bartholomew Sullivan to Silvester Gardiner, 8 December 1783, GWA.

104. "The Petition of John Gardiner," a manuscript accompanying "An Act to remove all possibility of Doubt touching or concerning the free Citizenship of John Gardiner, Esq." [dated 12 February 1784, passed 13 February], *Acts and Resolves*, chap. 28, Massachusetts Archives.

105. Gardiner, *Memorial and Petition*; Samuel Parker to Jacob Bailey, 22 December 1783, quoted in Charles E. Allen, *History of Dresden, Maine* (Augusta, Maine, 1931), 419.

106. Oliver Whipple to Silvester Gardiner, 24 November 1783, GWA.

107. John Gardiner to Silvester Gardiner, 4 May 1784, John Haskins to Silvester Gardiner, 6 July 1783 and 18 April 1784, GWA; Meeting of the Proprietors, 16 January 1785, King's Chapel Archives, MHS. At a similar meeting on 28 March of that year, John Gardiner joined the vestry.

108. Silvester Gardiner to [the wardens of the Stone Chapel] (typescript copy), 7 April 1786, RHG; Thomas Bulfinch and Shrimpton Huchinson (wardens) to Silvester Gardiner, 29 March 1786, King's Chapel Archives, MHS.

109. Silvester Gardiner to [the wardens], 7 April 1786, RHG.

110. "One of the Majority," *Independent Chronicle*, 27 December 1792, p. 2; Carl Scovel and Charles C. Forman, *Journey Toward Independence: King's Chapel's Transition to Unitarianism* (Boston: Skinner House Books, 1993), 23.

111. Meetings of the proprietors, 20 February and 19 June 1785, King's Chapel Archives, MHS; "Theatre," *Independent Chronicle*, 19 January 1792, p. 3; "Remonstrance," *Independent Chronicle*, 27 December 1792, p. 1.

112. Foote, *Annals*, vol. 2, 378–380; Samuel Parker to Samuel Seabury, 28 January 1788, quoted in E. Edwards Beardsley, *Life and Correspondence of the Right Reverend Samuel Seabury* (Boston, 1881), 321–324.

113. *A Liturgy, collected principally from the Book of Common Prayer, for the use of the First Episcopal Church in Boston* (Boston, 1785). This edition is unpaginated; all quotations are from the preface. Clifford Shipton, in *Sibley's Harvard Graduates*, vol. 13, 598, names John Gardiner as the author of this preface. His source was an annotated family prayer book; I could not corroborate this attribution. A Houghton Library edition, presented to William Bentley by James Freeman, pushes the honor in Freeman's direction.

114. Foote, *Annals*, vol. 2, 383–386; Meeting of the Proprietors, 4 November 1787, King's Chapel Archives, MHS; "Novel Ordination," *Massachusetts Centinel*, 24 November 1787, pp. 2–3.

115. Meeting of the Proprietors, 11 November 1787, King's Chapel Archives, MHS.

116. "A Spectator," *Massachusetts Centinel*, 24 November 1787, p. 2.

117. [John Gardiner,] "A Rowland for your Oliver," *Massachusetts Centinel*, 28 November 1787, p. 2.

118. Samuel Seabury to Silvester Gardiner, 15 March 1785, GWA; the genealogy can be reconstructed from Updike, *History of the Episcopal Church*, 134. And see "Episcopacy," *Independent Chronicle*, 7 April 1786, p. 2 ("Barebones" is John Gardiner).

119. "No Episcopalian" [John Gardiner], "Episcopacy!" *American Herald*, 6 and 13 March 1786, pp. 3 and 1 respectively. Of the several lampoons published at this time, this piece best illustrates the Gardiner style. His authorship is confirmed by "Episcopacy," *Independent Chronicle*, 7 April 1786, p. 2, and intimated by a notice in the *Columbian Centinel*, 11 June 1791, p. 3. Also see "Episcopacy," *American Herald*, 27 March 1786, p. 3; "The North-About Bishop," *Massachusetts Centinel*, 1 April 1786, p. 2, and "To the Right Runagate . . . Bishop Whipper," *Massachusetts Centinel*, 15 April 1786, p. 2.

120. "Dr. Sylvester Gardiner's Last Will," 25 April 1786, GWA.

121. John Gardiner, *An Oration, Delivered July 4, 1785, at the Request of the Inhabitants of the Town of Boston in Celebration of the Anniversary of American Independence* (Boston, 1785), 10, 21, appendix iv, x.

122. John Gardiner, *An Oration*, 10.

123. Ibid., 14.

124. Ibid., 14, appendix ii–iv. Gardiner nods to Hume in his appendix; in the body of his speech, the discussion of Hastings and its consequences lifts lines verbatim from Hume's *History:* David Hume, *History of England*, vol. 1, 177, 217, 458. While Gardiner called William a bastard, Hume (vol. 1, 203n) reported the king's sense of humor.

125. John Gardiner, *An Oration*, 33–36, appendix xxi–xxii.
126. "Episcopacy," *Independent Chronicle*, 7 April 1786, p. 2.

Lawyers and Leadership (pages 109–133)

1. Murrin, "The Legal Transformation"; Richard D. Brown, *Knowledge Is Power: The Diffusion of Information in Early America, 1700–1865* (New York: Oxford University Press, 1989), 82–109; *Legal Papers of John Adams*, vol. 1, xcv–cxiv; Charles R. McKirdy, "Lawyers in Crisis: The Massachusetts Legal Profession, 1760–1790" (Ph.D. diss., Northwestern University, 1969), 89–107.
2. "Senex," *Herald of Freedom*, 25 September 1788, p. 1.
3. "Americanus," *Herald of Freedom*, 25 September 1788, p. 2. James Sullivan probably authored this piece—a fact that becomes significant below, where I suggest that the liberal sensibility arched over specific controversies and partisan affiliations. See Thomas C. Amory, *Life of James Sullivan, with Selections from His Writings*, 2 vols. (Boston, 1859), vol. 1, 397.
4. [Jonathan Jackson,] *Thoughts upon the Political Situation of the United States of America, in which that of Massachusetts, is more particularly considered* (Worcester, 1788). For a contrary reading, see David Hackett Fischer, *The Revolution of American Conservatism: The Federalist Party in the Era of Jeffersonian Democracy* (New York: Harper & Row, 1965), 3, 3n, 250; Fischer, "The Myth of the Essex Junto," *William and Mary Quarterly* 21 (April 1964), 191–235.
5. [Jackson,] *Thoughts upon the Political Situation*, 25–26, 54–55, 69.
6. Ibid., 89–92. One of the first scholars to see Hume's influence in American government was Douglass Adair (see "'That Politics May Be Reduced to a Science'").
7. [Jackson,] *Thoughts upon the Political Situation*, 22–23.
8. Ibid., 24–25, 86.
9. Ibid., 57. On 57–58n, Jackson quotes from Adams, *A Defence of the Constitutions of Government of the United States of America*, 3 vols., vol. 1, 116. Jackson would have been using a 1787 edition; the Philadelphia text of 1797 to which I refer is similarly paginated. Adams famously employed his ideas about managed risk to argue for a senate (vol. 1, vii). Like John Gardiner and other writers, Adams began his work by noting a general reformation of manners. He cited Hume early and often on matters of history (vol. 1, i-ii) and government (vol. 1, iv–v, xxi–xxii, 7). Along with Gardiner and Hume before him, Adams had little use for Gothic atavism. Unicameral assemblies were "the institutions of Woden and of Thor" (vol. 1, xix–xxi).
10. [Jackson,] *Thoughts upon the Political Situation*, 6, 155.
11. *Independent Chronicle*, 9 September 1790, p. 3.
12. "Number I," *Independent Chronicle*, 2 December 1790, p. 1.
13. Ibid.

14. Gerald W. Gawalt, *The Promise of Power: The Emergence of the Legal Profession in Massachusetts, 1760–1840* (Westport, Conn.: Greenwood Press, 1979), 48–66; Frederic Grant Jr., "Benjamin Austin Jr.'s Struggle with the Lawyers," *Boston Bar Journal* 25 (September 1981), 19–29.

15. "Honestus," *Independent Chronicle,* 23 March 1786, p. 1.

16. "Honestus," *Independent Chronicle,* 9 March 1786, p. 2, 23 March 1786, p. 1, and 11 January 1787, p. 2. Austin was a leading member of the Massachusetts Constitutional (or Democratic-Republican) Society, as noted in J. S. J. Gardiner's *Remarks on the Jacobiniad* (Boston, 1795).

17. "Honest Short," *Massachusetts Centinel,* 29 March 1786, p. 2; "Suffolk," *Independent Chronicle,* 18 January 1787, p. 1.

18. "Mentor," *Independent Chronicle,* 25 January 1787, p. 1.

19. "Lawyer," *Massachusetts Centinel,* 26 April 1786, p. 1; "Twig of the Branch," *Independent Chronicle,* 4 May 1786, p. 1. And notice the entrepreneurial view of electioneering.

20. "Free Republican," No. 5, *Independent Chronicle,* 22 December 1785, p. 1; Grant Jr., "Benjamin Austin Jr.'s Struggle," 22.

21. "Free Republican," No. 5, *Independent Chronicle,* 22 December 1785, p. 1.

22. "Barebones," *American Herald,* 26 June 1786, p. 3.

23. R. H. Gardiner, *Early Recollections,* 18.

24. "Barebones," *American Herald,* 26 June 1786, p. 3; "Record-Book of the Suffolk Bar," ed. George Dexter, *Proceedings of the Massachusetts Historical Society* 19 (1881–82), 159–161. Gardiner discussed the episode in one of his reforming speeches: *Massachusetts Centinel,* 30 January 1790, p. 1.

25. James Bridge to John Quincy Adams, 28 September 1787, "Diary of John Quincy Adams," *Proceedings of the Massachusetts Historical Society* 36 (1902), 434n.

26. John Gardiner to Samuel Adams, 8 September 1786 and 4 October 1787, Samuel Adams Papers, New York Public Library (hereafter NYPL); *Sibley's Harvard Graduates,* vol. 13, 601.

27. William D. Patterson, "Record of Marriages in Pownalborough, 1787–1794," *Maine Historical Magazine* 9 (January–February–March 1894), 44; Fannie S. Chase, *Wiscasset in Pownalborough* (Wiscasset: Southworth-Anthoensen Press, 1941), 128; Charles E. Allen, *History of Dresden,* 406–409. Some sources (R. H. Gardiner's *Early Recollections,* 19; Coolidge's *Colonial Entrepreneur,* 255) list 1786 as Margaret's terminal year, but this is an error: see John Gardiner to Samuel Adams, 4 October 1787, Samuel Adams Papers, NYPL; "Parish Registers of St. Kitts," in *Caribbeana* 3 (July 1913), 108; "Mr. Freeman's Trial for a Libel," *Independent Chronicle,* 10 March 1791, p. 1.

28. John Gardiner to Samuel Adams, 1 November 1789, Samuel Adams Papers, NYPL.

29. *Massachusetts Centinel,* 16 January 1790, p. 2; "The Law and its Practitioners," *Massachusetts Centinel,* 20 January 1790, p. 2, and continued in the *Massachusetts Centinel:* 23 January 1790, p. 2; 27 January 1790, p. 2; 30 January 1790, p. 1.

30. "Extract of a letter from a gentleman in Boston," *Western Star* (Stockbridge), 2 March 1790, p. 3.

31. "Buccinator," "The Law-Reformer's Object, or, the Cat Let Out of the Bag," *Massachusetts Centinel*, 17 February 1790, p. 1; "Extract of a letter from a gentleman in Boston," *Western Star*, 2 March 1790, p. 3; "Junius," *Independent Chronicle*, 11 February 1790, p. 2.

32. "A Correspondent Hopes . . . ," *Massachusetts Centinel*, 16 January 1790, p. 3. Gardiner responded with similar malice in the *Centinel*, 23 January 1790, p. 3 (signed "G.J"). And see "Proceedings in the General Court," *Massachusetts Centinel*, 6 February 1790, p. 2.

33. "The Law and its Practitioners," *Massachusetts Centinel*, 20 January 1790, p. 2.

34. "The Law and its Practitioners," *Massachusetts Centinel*, 30 January 1790, p. 1.

35. *Massachusetts Centinel*, 27 January 1790, p. 2.

36. "The Law and its Practitioners," *Massachusetts Centinel*, 30 January 1790, p. 1; Buel Jr., *Securing the Revolution*, 99–104. Gardiner had to reach to paint lawyers as old-fashioned. Their professional awareness, of which the bar association was indicative, partially arose from a resentment of Hutchinson and the other laymen who controlled the bench in the colonial period (Gawalt, *The Promise of Power*, 15–16).

37. *Massachusetts Centinel*, 27 January 1790, p. 2.

38. William E. Nelson, *Americanization of the Common Law: The Impact of Legal Change on Massachusetts Society, 1760–1830* (Athens: University of Georgia Press, 1994), xii, 21–23, 69–88.

39. Morton J. Horwitz, *The Transformation of American Law, 1780–1860* (Cambridge, Mass.: Harvard University Press, 1977), 1–9, 140–159. Horwitz perhaps goes a bit far when he describes the common law, in its eighteenth-century conception, as "found" or natural. He is willing to name Lord Mansfield as a pioneer of legal instrumentality (*Transformation*, 143–144). John Gardiner's exposure to Mansfield may help put the barrister's reforms in perspective.

40. *Massachusetts Centinel*, 27 January 1790, p. 2. On early national bankruptcy law, see Bruce H. Mann, *Republic of Debtors: Bankruptcy in the Age of American Independence* (Cambridge, Mass.: Harvard University Press, 2002).

41. *Massachusetts Centinel*, 27 January 1790, p. 2; Stanley N. Katz, "Republicanism and the Law of Inheritance in the American Revolutionary Era," *Michigan Law Review* 76 (November 1977), 1–29.

42. "A learned Law Lecture," *Columbian Centinel*, 12 February 1791, pp. 1–2.

43. Ibid.

44. Ibid.; "Mr. Gardiner's learned law lecture. Continued," *Columbian Centinel*, 16 February 1791, pp. 1–2.

45. "A learned Law Lecture," *Columbian Centinel*, 12 February 1791, pp. 1–2; "Mr. Gardiner's learned law lecture. Continued," *Columbian Centinel*, 16 February 1791, pp. 1–2. Gardiner's method had long been the norm in the Leeward Islands.

46. Hume, *History of England*, vol. 1, 161.

47. John Gardiner, *An Oration*, app. x. On pages xiii–xv of the same appendix, Gardiner anticipated his 1791 speech on entails. He quoted Hume on the "general revolution" on app. iv.

48. *Massachusetts Centinel*, 23 January 1790, p. 2.

49. "Extract of a letter from Boston," *Western Star*, 9 March 1790, p. 3. "An Act providing a more easy and simple Method . . . of barring Estates Tail" passed on 8 May 1792. Two other laws may have taken their lead from Gardiner's reform bill. These were "An Act authorizing particular Persons in certain Cases, to prosecute and defend Suits at Law" (passed 6 March 1790) and "An act in addition to . . . 'An Act for rendering Processes in Law less Expensive'" (which passed on 24 June 1790). See *Acts and Laws, Passed by the General Court of Massachusetts* for the years 1790 and 1792. For a kind view of Gardiner's efforts, see the Honorable Herbert T. Silsby, "John Gardiner: Law Prophet," *Supreme Judicial Court Historical Society Journal* 2 (1996), 75–94.

50. *Massachusetts Centinel*, 27 February 1790, p. 3.

51. "Reform of the Law," *Massachusetts Centinel*, 10 March 1790, p. 1.

52. Ibid.

53. He also had a gift for sliding between arguments. In this performance, he trumped an opponent with his knowledge of Latin. Less than a month before, Gardiner had objected to a bill on the Saco River fishery because it included a phrase from the same language ("Reform of the Law," *Massachusetts Centinel*, 10 February 1790, p. 2).

54. John Gardiner, "To the Author of the Gratulatory Address," *Independent Chronicle*, 2 September 1790, p. 1; Gardiner was most influenced by Aedanus Burke's *Considerations on the Society or Order of Cincinnati* (Philadelphia, 1783).

55. "Old Whackum," *Columbian Centinel*, 5 January 1791, p. 2; "Protest," *Columbian Centinel*, 29 December 1790, p. 2.

56. If not the same writer, then two critics were writing under the same signature: "A Card," *Columbian Centinel*, 4 September 1790, p. 2; "A Card," *Columbian Centinel*, 8 January 1791, p. 2. Gardiner admitted ("The Last Time," *Columbian Centinel*, 8 September 1790, p. 3) that he had promised money to the society, which he had understood to be a purely charitable organization. Note that he had just returned to America; he might have still been in Washington's company. Count Dillon, an Irish soldier with a French title, helped arrange Gardiner's audience with the commander-in-chief. Apparently, this favor did not incline Gardiner to a kinder treatment of "supercilious Nobles."

57. "To the Author of the Gratulatory Address," *Independent Chronicle*, 9 September 1790, p. 1.

58. Ibid.

59. The vote that prompted Gore's resignation is recorded after Gardiner's speech: "Legislature of Massachusetts," *Massachusetts Centinel*, 23 January

1790, pp. 2–3; "Mr. Gore's Resignation," *Massachusetts Centinel*, 30 January 1790, p. 2.

60. *Boston Gazette*, 31 January 1791, pp. 1–2.

61. "Debate on the Ineligibility of Federal Judges," *Columbian Centinel*, 5 February 1791, pp. 1–2; "Legislature of Massachusetts," *Columbian Centinel*, 2 February 1791, pp. 1–2.

62. "Debate on the Ineligibility of Federal Judges," *Columbian Centinel*, 5 February 1791, pp. 1–2.

63. Katz, "Republicanism and the Law of Inheritance," 13–14, 26; *Massachusetts Centinel*, 23 January 1790, 2; "Junius," *Independent Chronicle*, 11 February 1790, p. 2; Horwitz, *The Transformation of American Law*, 6–7.

64. "Theophilus," *Boston Gazette*, 8 February 1790, p. 2; A Correspondent Hopes . . . ," *Massachusetts Centinel*, 16 January 1790, p. 3; "Extract of a letter from a gentleman in Boston," *Western Star*, 2 March 1790, p. 3.

65. "G.J.," *Massachusetts Centinel*, 23 January 1790, p. 3.

66. "Junius," *Independent Chronicle*, 11 February 1790, p. 2; "Extract of a letter from a gentleman in Boston," *Western Star*, 2 March 1790, p. 3; "Extract of a letter from Boston," *Western Star*, 9 March 1790, p. 3.

67. "Y.," *Western Star*, 30 March 1790, p. 3.

68. "From a Correspondent," *Herald of Freedom*, 2 February 1790, p. 3.

69. Ibid. To find a "rosy-gilled" Gardiner, see "A Correspondent Hopes . . . ," *Massachusetts Centinel*, 16 January 1790, p. 3.

70. "From a Correspondent," *Herald of Freedom*, 2 February 1790, p. 3. That this phrase was particularly obnoxious to Gardiner is made clear in "Proceedings on the Examination of the Printer of the Herald," *Massachusetts Centinel*, 10 February 1790, pp. 1–2.

71. "Proceedings on the Examination of the Printer of the Herald," *Massachusetts Centinel*, 10 February 1790, pp. 1–2.

72. Ibid.

73. Ibid.; "Extract of a letter from Boston," *Western Star*, 9 March 1790, p. 3; "Trial for a Libel," *Independent Chronicle*, 24 February 1791, pp. 2–3.

74. "Trial for a Libel," *Independent Chronicle*, 24 February 1791, pp. 2–3.

75. Leonard W. Levy, *Legacy of Suppression: Freedom of Speech and Press in Early American History* (Cambridge, Mass.: Harvard University Press, 1960), 207–209. To his frustration, Levy finds that the Freeman case in no way advanced the modern notion of free speech. Also see Clyde A. Duniway, *The Development of Freedom of the Press in Massachusetts* (New York, 1906), 142–143.

76. "Mr. Freeman's Trial for a Libel," *Independent Chronicle*, 10 March 1791, p. 1.

77. "Trial for a Libel," *Independent Chronicle*, 24 February 1791, pp. 2–3.

78. "Mr. Freeman's Trial for a Libel," *Independent Chronicle*, 3 March 1791, p. 2; 17 March 1791, p. 2.

79. "Trial for a Libel," *Independent Chronicle*, 24 February 1791, pp. 2–3.

80. Ibid.
81. Ibid.
82. "Mr. Freeman's Trial for a Libel," *Independent Chronicle*, 10 March 1791, p. 1; Samuel Eliot Morison, *The Life and Letters of Harrison Gray Otis, Federalist, 1765–1848*, 2 vols. (Boston, 1913), vol. 1, 115–120.
83. "Mr. Freeman's Trial for a Libel," *Independent Chronicle*, 10 March 1791, p. 1.
84. Ibid.
85. "Proceedings on the Examination of the Printer of the Herald," *Massachusetts Centinel*, 10 February 1790, pp. 1–2.
86. "Mr. Freeman's Trial for a Libel," *Independent Chronicle*, 10 March 1791, p. 1.
87. "From a Correspondent," *Herald of Freedom*, 2 February 1790, p. 3.
88. "Mr. Freeman's Trial for a Libel," *Independent Chronicle*, 3 March 1791, p. 2; the pertinent episode is recorded in "The Law and its Practitioners," *Massachusetts Centinel*, 30 January 1790, p. 1. The phrase roughly means "concerning the dead, say nothing but good things."
89. "Mr. Freeman's Trial for a Libel," *Independent Chronicle*, 10 March 1791, p. 1.
90. "Mr. Freeman's Trial for a Libel," *Independent Chronicle*, 3 March 1791, p. 2.
91. "Mr. Freeman's Trial for a Libel," *Independent Chronicle*, 10 March 1791, p. 1.
92. "Junius," *Independent Chronicle*, 11 February 1790, p. 2. The article also despises Gardiner for bringing a libel suit after he had defamed lawyers as frauds and schemers. For attribution, see Amory, *Life of James Sullivan*, vol. 1, 397.
93. "Mr. Freeman's Trial for a Libel," *Independent Chronicle*, 10 March 1791, p. 1.
94. Ibid.
95. "Mr. Freeman's Trial for a Libel," *Independent Chronicle*, 17 March 1791, p. 2.
96. "Trial for a Libel," *Independent Chronicle*, 24 February 1791, pp. 2–3.

The Independent Province (pages 134–171)

1. Robert A. East, "The Business Entrepreneur in a Changing Colonial Economy, 1763–1795," *Journal of Economic History* 6 (May 1946), 16–27.
2. While both houses passed acts of repeal, the measure never became law. Governor John Hancock was not a friend to the theater, and he probably refused his signature. Nevertheless, the legislature's action was a decisive shift of political will. The ban expired in 1797, as per the conditions of its last renewal ("An Act for reviving and continuing sundry laws" [passed 2 July 1785], *Acts and Laws of the Commonwealth of Massachusetts* (Boston, 1785), chapter 19). By then, the Federal Street Theatre was in full swing. See "Theatre-Bill," *Independent Chronicle*, 28 March 1793, p. 3; *A Journal of the Honourable House of Representatives at a General Court of the Commonwealth of Massachusetts* (May 1792-March 1793), 443, 451–452; William W. Clapp Jr., *A Record of the Boston Stage* (Boston and Cambridge, 1853), 19.

3. Gardiner, *Speech of John Gardiner, Esquire,* 92–93; "An Act for Preventing Stage-plays and other Theatrical Entertainments" [passed 11 April 1750], *The Acts and Resolves, Public and Private, of the Province of the Massachusetts Bay,* 21 vols. (Boston, 1869–1922), vol. 3, 500–501; Kenneth Silverman, *A Cultural History of the American Revolution* (New York: Thomas Y. Crowell, 1976), 59–69; Jonas Barish, *The Antitheatrical Prejudice* (Berkeley: University of California Press, 1981), 5–65, 80–131, 155–190. For a record of private and collegiate theatricals, see *The Diary of Dr. Nathaniel Ames of Dedham, Massachusetts, 1758–1822,* ed. Robert Brand Hanson (Camden, Maine: Picton Press, 1998), 28–31, 41, 79.

4. Jean-Jacques Rousseau, *Politics and the Arts: Letter to M. D'Alembert on the Theatre,* trans. Allan Bloom (Glencoe, Ill.: Free Press, 1960), 11n, 17.

5. Ibid., 64–65.

6. Ibid. Also see pages 19 and 57.

7. Ibid,, 20, 22.

8. John Witherspoon, *A Serious Enquiry into the Nature and Effects of the Stage, in Essays on Important Subjects,* 2 vols. (London, 1765), vol. 2, 35–36, 72, 81, 107; Varnum L. Collins, *President Witherspoon,* 2 vols. in 1 (New York: Arno Press, 1969), vol. 2, 240.

9. "Philo Dramatis," *The Rights of the Drama: or, An Inquiry into the Origin, Principles, and Consequences of Theatrical Entertainments* (Boston, 1792), 19; "A.B.," *Boston Gazette,* 31 August 1789, p. 1.

10. The Harvard Divinity School copy of Witherspoon's essays, from which I cite the *Serious Enquiry,* was in 1790 the property of Abiel Holmes. The following year, Holmes was ordained as the minister of First Church, Cambridge.

11. Henry W. Bowden, *Dictionary of American Religious Biography* (Westport, Conn.: Greenwood Press, 1993), 620–621; Henry F. May, *The Enlightenment in America* (New York: Oxford University Press, 1976), 62–64, 96–97; Douglass Adair, "That Politics May Be Reduced to a Science," 343–360.

12. Silverman, *Cultural History of the American Revolution,* 271.

13. Ibid., 291–292.

14. "The Observer" [Samuel Adams], No. 7, *Massachusetts Centinel,* 15 January 1785, pp. 1–2; Charles Warren, "Samuel Adams and the Sans Souci Club in 1785," *Proceedings of the Massachusetts Historical Society* 60 (May 1927), 318–344; "Son of Candour," *Massachusetts Centinel,* 26 January 1785, p. 1.

15. "Sans Souci" [Harrison Gray Otis], *Massachusetts Centinel,* 19 January 1785, pp. 1–2.

16. "One of a Number," *Massachusetts Centinel,* 19 January 1785, p. 2.

17. Silverman, *Cultural History of the American Revolution,* 537, 542–545, 556–558, 592.

18. "A Bostonian," *Massachusetts Centinel,* 11 January 1786, pp. 1–2; "Cosmopolite," *Herald of Freedom,* 18 September 1788, p. 1; "Boston," *Herald of Freedom,* 2 October 1788, p. 3.

19. "To the Honourable the Senate, and to the Honourable the House of Representatives . . . Messrs. Hallam and Henry most respectfully represent," *Massachusetts Centinel*, 12 June 1790, p. 1.

20. "Boston, Thursday, October 27: Town Meeting—Faneuil Hall," *Independent Chronicle*, 27 October 1791, p. 3; Gardiner, *Speech of John Gardiner, Esquire*, p. 13; "Theatre," *Independent Chronicle*, 19 January 1792, p. 3.

21. "Theatre," *Independent Chronicle*, 19 January 1792, p. 3; "Sketch of the Proceedings in the General Court," *Independent Chronicle*, 2 February 1792, p. 3.

22. "A Ploughjogger," *Independent Chronicle*, 23 August 1792, p. 3; "Ramsey," *Independent Chronicle*, 24 November 1791, p. 2. These shows were well advertised: see p. 3 of the *Centinel* on 11 and 15 August 1792.

23. "Nestor," *Independent Chronicle*, 3 January 1793, p. 1; "Jacob," *Independent Chronicle*, 18 October 1792, p. 2; "Alfred," *Independent Chronicle*, 5 April 1792, p. 3.

24. "Ramsey," *Independent Chronicle*, 24 November 1791, p. 2; "A Mechanick and Voter," *Columbian Centinel*, 7 January 1792, p. 2; "Citizen," *Columbian Centinel*, 2 November 1791, p. 2. For one critic's appeal to the mechanics, see "A Bostonian," *Independent Chronicle*, 1 December 1791, p. 2.

25. Amory, *Life of James Sullivan*, vol. 1, 274; "A Friend to Peace," *Independent Chronicle*, 13 December 1792, p. 2.

26. "A Friend to Peace," *Independent Chronicle*, 13 December 1792, p. 2.

27. John Quincy Adams to John Adams, 16 December 1792, in J. Q. Adams, *Writings of John Quincy Adams*, ed. Worthington Chauncey Ford, 7 vols. (New York: Macmillan, 1913–17), vol. 1, 123–127; Robert A. East, *John Quincy Adams: The Critical Years, 1785–1794* (New York: Bookman, 1962), 55, 59–60, 64–65, 148–152.

28. "Menander," No. 1, *Columbian Centinel*, 19 December 1792, p. 1. A crack like that was not unusual for the times (Harrison Gray Otis's "wild Irish" speech has not yet been forgotten), and young Adams might have meant it casually, though Sullivan's father was born in Ireland.

29. "Menander," No. 1, *Columbian Centinel*, 19 December 1792, p. 1; "Menander," No. 2, *Columbian Centinel*, 22 December 1792, p. 1; Gordon S. Wood, *The Creation of the American Republic, 1776–1787* (Chapel Hill: University of North Carolina Press, 1969), 532–564.

30. "Z.," *Columbian Centinel*, 20 October 1792, p. 2 (the capitals are original to the text); "Theatre," *Columbian Centinel*, 26 October 1791, p. 2.

31. "One of a Majority," *Independent Chronicle*, 27 December 1792, p. 2; "Ramsey," *Independent Chronicle*, 24 November 1791, p. 2.

32. "One of a Majority," *Independent Chronicle*, 27 December 1792, p. 2.

33. "Candidus," *Columbian Centinel*, 8 September 1792, p. 1; "Rights of Man," *Columbian Centinel*, 5 September 1792, p. 2; "Theatrical," *Columbian Centinel*, 3 December 1791, p. 3.

34. "Philo Dramatis," *Rights of the Drama*, 8–9, 46–48; J. Q. Adams, *Writings*, vol. 1, 122n.

35. Gardiner, *Speech of John Gardiner, Esquire*, vii.

36. Ibid., 46, 92–93.

37. William Dunlap, *History of the American Theatre*, 2 vols. (London, 1833), vol. 1, 409–410; Gardiner, *Speech of John Gardiner, Esquire*, 46.

38. While a critic of the theater wrote jokingly of a similar enterprise, the "well regulated Brothel" (*Independent Chronicle*, 1 November 1792, p. 2), one wonders if some in the "Playhouse party" might not have seriously considered the idea. However, most advocates approached the issue of regulation conventionally. See the first three numbers in a series on "The expediency of a repeal of the Statute . . . against Stage Plays," *Columbian Centinel*: 10 November 1792, p. 1; 14 November 1792, p. 2; 17 November 1792, p. 1. The author was confident that moral purity could be achieved on the stage. Hallam and Henry were careful to mention state censorship in their petition, too. Not everyone agreed: "Philo Dramatis" disapproved of any attempt to frustrate creativity (*Rights of the Drama*, 41).

39. Gardiner, *Speech of John Gardiner, Esquire*, 49, 49n. I am quoting from the edition that the author donated to Harvard. It contains his emendations, of which there are two in this excerpt. Most noticeably, "Brutish" has been substituted for "British."

40. Also see "A Correspondent," *Columbian Centinel*, 26 October 1791, p. 3, and "Philo Dramatis," *Rights of the Drama*, 35.

41. "A Bostonian" [William Haliburton], *Effects of the Stage on the Manners of a People* (Boston, 1792); "A brief account of the Author of the Manuscripts in this Volumn. William Haliburton, Esquire, of Windsor, Nova Scotia," William Haliburton Papers, SB / Hal 1, New England Historic-Genealogical Society, Boston [hereafter NEHGS]. For hints of a childhood meeting, see *Materials for a Catalogue of . . . the Public Latin School*, 15–16.

42. [Haliburton,] *Effects of the Stage*, 8–9.

43. Adam Smith, *The Theory of Moral Sentiments*, ed. D. D. Raphael and A. L. Macfie (Oxford: Clarendon Press, 1976), 19, 153–154.

44. William Haliburton to Abigail Haliburton, 16 June 1792, William Haliburton Papers, NEHGS.

45. [Haliburton,] *Effects of the Stage*, 8–9.

46. William Haliburton to Abigail Haliburton, 16 June 1792. Thus an older language of place blended easily with the new; see my sketch of Charles Chauncy's social thought in the first narrative chapter.

47. "A Seeker after Happiness," *Columbian Centinel*, 5 September 1792, pp. 1–2.

48. [Haliburton,] *Effects of the Stage*, 25–26; Gardiner, *Speech of John Gardiner, Esquire*, 14–15; Elbridge Gerry to Samuel Adams, 17 July 1789, *MHS Procs.* 62 (1928–29), 58–61.

49. "No. IV," *Columbian Centinel*, 1 December 1792, p. 1; [Haliburton,] *Effects of the Stage*, 12.

50. [Haliburton,] *Effects of the Stage*, 6; "On Theatrical Amusements," *Independent Chronicle*, 10 January 1793, p. 1; "Junius," *Columbian Centinel*, 25 August

1792, p. 2; Fisher Ames to William Tudor, 24 November 1791, *Collections of the Massachusetts Historical Society*, 2nd series, vol. 7 (1826), 323–325.

51. Nathaniel Cutting, "Extracts from a Journal of a Gentleman visiting Boston in 1792," *Proceedings of the Massachusetts Historical Society* 12 (1871–73), 60–67.

52. *Independent Chronicle*, 4 November 1793, p. 1; Van Carl Kussrow Jr., "On with the Show: A study of public arguments in favor of theatre in America during the eighteenth century" (Ph.D. diss., Indiana University, 1959), 285; Blake, *Public Health*, 135–140; "By His Excellency John Hancock, Esq. Governor of the Commonwealth of Massachusetts. A Proclamation, For removing the General Court from the town of Boston to Concord," *Independent Chronicle*, 1 November 1792, p. 1. The day after the legislature convened in Concord, Hancock spoke to both houses about breaches in the theater ban (*Independent Chronicle*, 15 November 1792, p. 2).

53. "No. VI," *Columbian Centinel*, 8 December 1792, p. 1; "Junius," *Columbian Centinel*, 25 August 1792, p. 2; [Haliburton,] *Effects of the Stage*, 8.

54. [Haliburton,] *Effects of the Stage*, 31.

55. Ibid., 29; *Return of the Whole Number of Persons Within the Several Districts of the United States* (Philadelphia, 1791), 23.

56. "Theatre!" *Columbian Centinel*, 26 November 1791, p. 3.

57. "Theatre," *Columbian Centinel*, 26 October 1791, p. 2; "American Intelligence," *Independent Chronicle*, 14 February 1793, p. 2; Gardiner, *Speech of John Gardiner, Esquire*, 15–16.

58. Cutting, "Extracts from a Journal of a Gentleman," 63; Clapp, *Record of the Boston Stage*, 5–6.

59. Samuel Breck, *Recollections of Samuel Breck*, ed. H. E. Scudder (Philadelphia, 1877), 182–183.

60. "A New Theatrical," *Columbian Centinel*, 8 December 1792, p. 3; J. Q. Adams to John Adams, 8 and 16 December 1792, J. Q. Adams, *Writings*, vol. 1, 120–127; "Menander," No. 2, *Columbian Centinel*, 22 December 1792, p. 1; Clapp, *Record of the Boston Stage*, 12. Strangely, Otis opposed the town-meeting repeal petition of October 1791 ("Boston, Thursday, October 27: Town Meeting—Faneuil Hall," *Independent Chronicle*, 27 October 1791, p. 3). His signature graced the remonstrance of December 1792. See the following note and also J. Q. Adams to John Adams, 22 December 1792, J. Q. Adams, *Writings*, vol. 1, 130–133.

61. "Remonstrance, To the Honourable the Senate, and House of Representatives in General Court Assembled," *Independent Chronicle*, 27 December 1792, p. 1; Cutting, "Extracts from a Journal of a Gentleman," 66; Harold Kirker and James Kirker, *Bulfinch's Boston, 1787–1817* (New York: Oxford University Press, 1964).

62. "One of the Majority," *Independent Chronicle*, 27 December 1792, p. 2.

63. James M. Bugbee, "Boston under the Mayors, 1822–1880," *Memorial History of Boston*, vol. 3, 218–221.

64. Kirker and Kirker, *Bulfinch's Boston*, 125; Clapp, *Record of the Boston Stage*, 5–6; "Boston. Faneuil-Hall, May 11, 1784," *Massachusetts Centinel*, 15 May 1784, p. 3.

65. "Boston. Faneuil-Hall, May 11, 1784," *Massachusetts Centinel*, 15 May 1784, p. 3; Pauline Maier, *The Old Revolutionaries: Political Lives in the Age of Samuel Adams* (New York: Alfred A. Knopf, 1980), 33.

66. "Boston. Faneuil-Hall, May 11, 1784," *Massachusetts Centinel*, 15 May 1784, p. 3.

67. "A Mechanick," *Massachusetts Centinel*, 29 October 1785, p. 1; "A Bostonian," *Massachusetts Centinel*, 30 November 1785, p. 2.

68. "Publicola," *Massachusetts Centinel*, 9 November 1785, p. 2.

69. "Boreas," *Massachusetts Centinel*, 9 November 1785, p. 2; "Anti-Aristocratick," *Massachusetts Centinel*, 29 October 1785, p. 2; "Thwackum," *Massachusetts Centinel*, 23 November 1785, p. 1; "Boston. Faneuil-Hall, May 11, 1784," *Massachusetts Centinel*, 15 May 1784, p. 3; also see *Columbian Centinel*, 18 January 1792, p. 3.

70. "Anti-Aristocratick," *Massachusetts Centinel*, 29 October 1785, p. 2; "Thwackum," *Massachusetts Centinel*, 30 November 1785, p. 2. On Boston's market—or lack thereof—see G. B. Warden, *Boston, 1689–1776* (Boston: Little, Brown, 1970), 77–78, 117–118, 151; Barbara Clark Smith, "Markets, Streets, and Stores: Contested Terrain in Pre-Industrial Boston," in *Autre temps, Autre espace: Etudes su l'Amerique pre-industrielle*, ed. Elise Marienstras and Barbara Karsky (Nancy: Presses Universitaires de Nancy, 1986), 181–197.

71. *Independent Chronicle*, 17 June 1784, p. 3; "Don't Like It," *Massachusetts Centinel*, 19 June 1784, p. 2; "A Mechanick," *Massachusetts Centinel*, 29 October 1785, p. 1.

72. "Boston . . . Faneuil-Hall, June 17, 1784," *Massachusetts Centinel*, 19 June 1784, p. 3.

73. "Incorporation," *American Herald*, 7 November 1785, p. 2.

74. "An American," *Massachusetts Centinel*, 16 June 1784, pp. 1–2.

75. "Old Whackum," *Massachusetts Centinel*, 26 October 1785, p. 2; *Massachusetts Centinel*, 19 November 1785, pp. 1–2; *American Herald*, 28 November 1785, p. 3.

76. "Old Whackum," *Massachusetts Centinel*, 19 November 1785, pp. 1–2; *American Herald*, 28 November 1785, p. 3.

77. "Old Whackum," *Massachusetts Centinel*, 26 October 1785, p. 2; Adams's "Dissertation on the Canon and Feudal Law" first appeared in the *Boston Gazette* in August of 1765. See Charles Francis Adams, *The Works of John Adams*, 10 vols. (Boston, 1851), vol. 3, 445–464.

78. "Old Whackum," *Columbian Centinel*, 7 January 1792, p. 2; "John Paul Martin" [Abraham Bishop], *The Triumph of Truth: History and Visions of Clio* (Boston, 1791). According to an unfriendly account in the *Connecticut Courant*, which was then picked up by the Boston press, Bishop ran a sort of theatrical academy around the time of his visit to Massachusetts: "Abraham Bishop," *The Mercury*

and *New-England Palladium*, 24 November 1802, p. 2. See David Wald-streicher and Stephen R. Grossbart, "Abraham Bishop's Vocation; Or, The Mediation of Jeffersonian Politics," *Journal of the Early Republic* 18 (Winter 1998), 617–657.

79. "Old Whackum," *Columbian Centinel*, 7 January 1792, p. 2. As far as I can discern, Bishop and Webster were not cousins. They were classmates at Yale and, in later years, fierce political opponents (Harry R. Warfel, *Noah Webster: Schoolmaster to America* [New York: Octagon Books, 1966], 267–270). See their exchange of 1800, which began when Bishop attacked President Adams and his Federalist allies: Bishop, *An Oration on the Extent and Power of Political Delusion* (Newark, 1800; this was the second edition: Bishop delivered the oration in New Haven at the time of Yale commencement); [Webster,] *A Rod for the Fool's Back* (New Haven, 1800).

80. "Town Police," *Independent Chronicle*, 2 February 1792, p. 3; "Town Meeting," *Independent Chronicle*, 19 January 1792, pp. 2–3. In his study of the incorporation controversies, Edward Lewis Ballantyne identifies the advocates as the same men whom Henry Cabot Lodge distinguished as the postwar elites: the "gentry" from the surrounding counties, and Essex County especially (Ballantyne, "The Incorporation of Boston, 1784–1822" [senior honors essay, Harvard University, 1955], 47–48). At least one contemporary, a critic of the reforms, saw the controversy in similar terms: "A Mechanick," *Massachusetts Centinel*, 29 October 1785, p. 1. The following analysis broadens this interpretation.

81. "A Town-Born Child," *Columbian Centinel*, 4 February 1792, p. 1. John Quincy Adams reports that Benjamin Austin Jr. was the only dissenting member of the committee (J. Q. Adams to Thomas Boylston Adams, 1 February 1792, J. Q. Adams, *Writings*, vol. 1, 110–115).

82. Oscar and Mary F. Handlin, "Radicals and Conservatives in Massachusetts after Independence," *New England Quarterly* 17 (September 1944), 343–355; Paul Goodman, *The Democratic-Republicans of Massachusetts: Politics in a Young Republic* (Cambridge, Mass.: Harvard University Press, 1964), 50–52.

83. "Town Meeting," *Independent Chronicle*, 19 January 1792, pp. 2–3; "Town Police," *Independent Chronicle*, 19 January 1792, p. 3; Samuel Eliot Morison, *The Life and Letters of Harrison Gray Otis, Federalist, 1765–1848*, 2 vols. (Boston: Houghton Mifflin, 1913). Morison later condensed the biography into one volume: *Harrison Gray Otis, 1765–1848: The Urbane Federalist* (Boston: Houghton Mifflin, 1969).

84. *Sibley's Harvard Graduates*, vol. 16, 376–383; Breck, *Recollections*, 182–183; Morison, *Harrison Gray Otis* (1969), 96–97. In this context, it is worth noting that Jarvis studied abroad, in the London hospitals of the late 1760s.

85. "Town Police," *Independent Chronicle*, 2 February 1792, p. 3; J. Q. Adams to Thomas Boylston Adams, 1 February 1792, J. Q. Adams, *Writings*, vol. 1, 110–115.

86. Meetings of the Proprietors, 20 February 1785, 4 and 11 November 1787, King's Chapel Archives, MHS. For his views on municipal reform, see "Town Meeting," *Independent Chronicle*, 19 January 1792, pp. 2–3.

87. *Sibley's Harvard Graduates*, vol. 17, 555–561; *Pubs. Col. Soc. Mass.* 5 (March 1898), 282–293; Foote, *Annals*, vol. 2, 142–147; Kershaw, *Kennebeck Proprietors*, 81–84.

88. Warren, "Samuel Adams and the Sans Souci Club," 335; "Remonstrance," *Independent Chronicle*, 27 December 1792, p. 1; Clapp, *Record of the Boston Stage*, 15; "One of the Majority," *Independent Chronicle*, 27 December 1792, p. 2; Emily Pendleton and Milton Ellis, *Philenia: The Life and Works of Sarah Wentworth Morton, 1759–1846* (Orono, Maine: University of Maine Press [University of Maine Studies, 2nd series, no. 20], 1931), 32–39; *Sibley's Harvard Graduates*, vol. 17, 555–561; Kirker and Kirker, *Bulfinch's Boston*, 116, 139.

89. Pendleton and Ellis, *Philenia*, 24, 58–60; [J. S. J. Gardiner,] *Remarks on the Jacobiniad* (Boston, 1795), 4; John Cary, *Joseph Warren: Physician, Politician, Patriot* (Urbana: University of Illinois Press, 1961), 56, 59; James S. Loring, *The Hundred Boston Orators* (Boston, 1853), 129–130; Eugene P. Link, *Democratic-Republican Societies, 1790–1800* (New York: Columbia University Press, 1942), 86, 98.

90. The best studies of this phenomenon in Massachusetts are Oscar and Mary F. Handlin's *Commonwealth: A Study of the Role of Government in the American Economy: Massachusetts, 1774–1861* (Cambridge, Mass.: Harvard University Press, 1969) and Pauline Maier's article "The Debate over Incorporations: Massachusetts in the Early Republic," in *Massachusetts and the New Nation*, ed. Conrad Edick Wright (Boston: Massachusetts Historical Society, 1992), 73–117. Also see Bray Hammond, *Banks and Politics in America from the Revolution to the Civil War* (Princeton: Princeton University Press, 1957), 72, and, on Hamilton and the state debts, Stanley Elkins and Eric McKitrick, *The Age of Federalism* (New York: Oxford University Press, 1993), 114–123.

91. J. Q. Adams to John Adams, 21 September 1790, J. Q. Adams, *Writings*, vol. 1, 56–59.

92. "From New York," *Columbian Centinel*, 4 February 1785, p. 3; "A Freeman," *Independent Chronicle*, 23 February 1792, p. 2.

93. "General Court of Massachusetts," *Independent Chronicle*, 19 January 1792, p. 3; "Sketch of the Proceedings in the General Court," *Independent Chronicle*, 26 January 1792, p. 3; *The Constitution of the Boston Tontine Association* (Boston, 1791). "Z.S." unfavorably compares theaters and tontines in "The Theatre: A Dialogue: Between Sylvanus and Philander," *Massachusetts Magazine* 4 (November 1792), 688–690. On Europe, see David R. Weir, "Tontines, Public Finance, and Revolution in France and England, 1688–1789," *Journal of Economic History* 49 (March 1989), 95–124.

94. "A Landholder," *Independent Chronicle*, 2 February 1792, p. 2.

95. "A Spectator," *Independent Chronicle*, 26 January 1792, p. 1; "Candour," *Columbian Centinel*, 28 January 1792, p. 3. Also see "A Citizen," *Columbian Centinel*, 11 January 1792, p. 1.

96. *The Constitution of the Boston Tontine Association*, 19; *Sibley's Harvard Graduates*, vol. 16, 92–94, vol. 18, 27–29; *Dictionary of American Biography*, vol. 9, 15–16, vol. 14, 548; "A Spectator," *Independent Chronicle*, 26 January 1792, p. 1. Also see "A Citizen," *Columbian Centinel*, 11 January 1792, p. 1, "Candour," *Columbian Centinel*, 28 January 1792, p. 3, and "A Landholder," *Independent Chronicle*, 2 February 1792, p. 2. This last article proclaims the tontine's "republican" credentials.

97. N. S. B. Gras, *The Massachusetts First National Bank of Boston, 1784–1934* (Cambridge, Mass.: Harvard University Press, 1937), 17–18, 26, 53–55, 221, 538–540. Also see Hammond, *Banks and Politics*, 72.

98. James Sullivan, *The Path to Riches: An Inquiry into the Origins and Use of Money; and into the Principles of Stocks and Banks* (Boston, 1792), reprinted in *The Magazine of History* 46, extra no. 184 (1933), 173–174. Gras speculates that Sullivan dealt with the Massachusetts Bank in the mid-1780s and then bridled at its demands for payment (*Massachusetts First National Bank*, 58).

99. Sullivan, *The Path to Riches*, in *Magazine of History* (1933), 201, 207.

100. Amory, *Life of James Sullivan*, vol. 1, 131–132, 365, vol. 2, 191–192; Maier, "Debate over Incorporations," 105.

101. Sullivan, *The Path to Riches*, in *Magazine of History* (1933), 205–206; "Observer," *Columbian Centinel*, 29 February 1792, pp. 2–3; for allegations of bribery, see the January 1792 entry in the Journal of George Richards Minot, MHS; "Boston tontine dissolved," *Columbian Centinel*, 4 July 1792, p. 3; "An Act to incorporate sundry Persons by the Name of the President and Directors of the Union Bank," *Acts and Laws, Passed by the General Court of Massachusetts* (Boston, 1792), 199; *A Condensed Record of the National Union Bank of Boston, Massachusetts* (Boston, 1904?), 3; *Sibley's Harvard Graduates*, vol. 17, 555–561; Handlin and Handlin, *Commonwealth*, 115; *Journal of the Honourable House* (May 1792—March 1793), 92–93, 293–294.

102. John Avery to George Thatcher, 19 March 1792, George Thatcher Letters, BPL. Also see "Extract of a letter from the county of Cumberland" (*Independent Chronicle*, 19 January 1786, p. 3), which describes the "mighty balloon of separation."

103. Handlin and Handlin, *Commonwealth*, 82; Kershaw, *Kennebeck Proprietors*, 100–104.

104. "William Bingham's Maine Lands 1790–1820," ed. Frederick S. Allis Jr., *Publications of the Colonial Society of Massachusetts* 36 (1954), 79–81, 175, 175n.See Margaret L. Brown's three articles in vol. 61 (1937) of the *Pennsylvania Magazine of History and Biography:* in January, "William Bingham, Agent of the Continental Congress in Martinique," 54–87; in July, "Mr. and Mrs. William Bingham of Philadelphia: Rulers of the Republican Court," 286–324; in October, "William Bingham, Eighteenth Century Magnate," 387–434.

105. Brown, "William Bingham, Eighteenth Century Magnate," 418–432; "William Bingham's Maine Lands," 37 (1954), 913–914, 1175–1177, 1212–1223, 1252–1255.

106. R. H. Gardiner, *Early Recollections*, 62–73; "Legislature of Massachusetts," *Massachusetts Centinel*, 27 January 1790, p. 2—see "Chap. XIV"; Handlin and Handlin, *Commonwealth*, 85.

107. Dudley Hubbard to George Thatcher, 28 November 1790, Thatcher Family Papers II, MHS.

108. *Dictionary of American Biography*, vol. 18, 386–387; Daniel Cony to George Thatcher, 24 April 1790, George Thatcher Letters, BPL; Dudley Hubbard to George Thatcher, 28 November 1790, Thatcher Family Papers II, MHS; "Lincolnshire," *Columbian Centinel:* 24 November 1790, p. 1; 15 January 1791, p. 2; 19 January 1791, p. 2; 9 March 1791, p. 4; "Agumenticus," *Columbian Centinel:* 12 January 1791, p. 1; 12 February 1791, p. 1; "Extract of a letter from one of the Representatives in Congress," *Columbian Centinel,* 2 March 1791, p. 2.

109. *Independent Chronicle*, 24 February 1791, p. 3; "Sketch of the Proceedings in the State Legislature," *Columbian Centinel,* 26 February 1791, p. 2.

110. "An Address to the Numerous and Respectable Inhabitants of the Great and Extensive District of Maine," *Cumberland Gazette*, 21 March 1791, p. 1. Gardiner admits his authorship in "The Chairman of the late Meeting of Eastern Senators and Representatives," *Gazette of Maine*, 20 May 1791, p. 3.

111. "Alcibiades," No. 2, *Cumberland Gazette*, 4 April 1791, p. 1. Ronald F. Banks, the historian of Maine independence, identifies Symmes as "Alcibiades" in *Maine Becomes a State: The Movement to Separate Maine from Massachusetts, 1785–1820* (Middletown, Conn.: Wesleyan University Press, 1970), 27–28. "Orientalis" misidentified Gardiner with the same signature (*Cumberland Gazette*, 11 April 1791, p. 1). Symmes corrected this critic ("Alcibiades," *Cumberland Gazette*, 18 April 1791, p. 1), and "Orientalis" apologized to Gardiner "for attributing to him the writings of a man, who really appears to be much worse than himself" (*Cumberland Gazette*, 25 April 1791, p. 1).

112. "Alcibiades," No. 2, *Cumberland Gazette*, 4 April 1791, p. 1.

113. Banks, *Maine Becomes a State*, 28; the word "economize" is Symmes's ("Alcibiades," No. 2, *Cumberland Gazette*, 4 April 1791, p. 1).

114. James Freeman to Lois Freeman, 24 December 1782; Daniel Davis to James Freeman, 25 June 1785: both printed in *Minot Family Letters, 1773–1871*, ed. Katherine Minot Channing (Sherborn, Mass.: privately printed, 1957), 7, 26; William Willis, *A History of the Law, the Courts, and the Lawyers of Maine* (Portland, Maine, 1863), 110–116.

115. Willis, *History of the Law . . . and the Lawyers of Maine*, 110–116; James Freeman to George Thatcher, 30 May 1789, King's Chapel Archives (at the Parish House); Daniel Davis, *An Oration , Delivered at Portland, July 4th, 1796* (Portland, Maine, 1796), 16–17.

116. [Daniel Davis,] *An Address to the Inhabitants of the District of Maine, Upon the*

Subject of Their Separation from the Present Government of Massachusetts (Portland, Maine, 1791), 22.

117. [Davis,] *An Address to the Inhabitants of the District of Maine*, 8–9, 12–13, 25.

118. "Alcibiades," *Cumberland Gazette*, 28 March 1791, p. 2.

119. William Symmes, *An Oration, Delivered in the Meeting House of the First Parish in Portland, June 24th, 5796. At the Request and in the Presence of the Lodge of Free and Accepted Masons* (Portland, Maine, 1796), 4. Symmes borrowed the poetry from Alexander Pope's *Essay on Man;* Pope was a notable Freemason. On Masonic philosophy, see Margaret C. Jacob, *The Radical Enlightenment: Pantheists, Freemasons and Republicans* (London: George Allen & Unwin, 1981).

120. *Independent Chronicle*, 17 March 1791, p. 3.

121. "A White Bird," *Columbian Centinel*, 13 April 1791, p. 1; Gardiner responded in "The Bald Eagle of the East," *Gazette of Maine*, 12 May 1791, p. 3. As if the language of this piece weren't indicative enough, the *Columbian Centinel* (18 May 1791, p. 3) names Gardiner as its author.

122. "The Skulker," No. 5, *Herald of Freedom*, 24 May 1791, p. 2.

123. Ibid. John Gardiner pushed for the incorporation of a college in Maine, but he "hoped proper persons would be nominated to compose the Corporation." A previous bill included the names of some, who "were as improper to direct, govern or oversee a seminary of polite and general learning (more especially of the Latin and Greek languages, the characters of the latter of which . . . they could not even read) as it would be ridiculously improper in him to attempt the command of an army, or the management of an elephant" ("Legislature of Massachusetts," *Columbian Centinel*, 11 June 1791, p. 2). For the gaseous quality of Gardiner's projects, see "A Correspondent" (*Massachusetts Centinel*, 10 February 1790, p. 3) and "The Sachem Silent!!" (*Columbian Centinel*, 30 June 1792, p. 3).

124. "Silenus,—a Character," *Independent Chronicle*, 16 March 1786, p. 2.

125. "Jack the Giant-Killer's Third Phillipick," *Massachusetts Centinel*, 24 February 1790, p. 2. "Calls" is a play upon Gardiner's criticism of the bar-call. Also see "The Law-Reformer's Object, or the Cat Let out of the Bag," *Massachusetts Centinel*, 17 February 1790, p. 1; "Y.," *Western Star*, 30 March 1790, p. 3; "On Seeing Mr. Gardiner's Speech Advertised to be Sold at a Grocer's Shop," *Columbian Centinel*, 27 June 1792, p. 3.

126. "The Respite," *Columbian Centinel*, 11 June 1791, p. 3; "A Correspondent," *Massachusetts Centinel*, 10 February 1790, p. 3. Gardiner called himself the "Eastern Sachem" in a letter to the *Centinel* ("G.J.," *Massachusetts Centinel*, 23 January 1790, p. 3). One can only guess that he adopted the name out of pride for his Kennebeck connections. Indian guises and monikers were not unknown among early white Americans. Witness the Tea Party Mohawks and the white Indians of the Maine land revolts (for the latter, see Taylor, *Liberty Men and Great Proprietors*). In addition, "Sachem" was a title used in the Tammany Society of New York, a fact of which Bostonians were aware (*Herald of Freedom*, 24 May 1791, p. 2).

127. "The Sachem Silent!!," *Columbian Centinel,* 30 June 1792, 3 and, in the same vein, "Y.," *Western Star,* 30 March 1790, p. 3; "Legislature of Massachusetts," *Herald of Freedom,* 3 May 1791, p. 1; Edward Bangs to George Thatcher, 13 February 1790, George Thatcher Letters, BPL. For news of the "infamous" and "celebrated" Burroughs, see the *Independent Chronicle,* 5 May 1791, p. 3, and "The Bouquet," *Massachusetts Magazine* 3 (January 1791), 49. On the popularity and significance of the memoirs, refer to Philip Gura's preface to the *Memoirs of Stephen Burroughs* (Boston: Northeastern University Press, 1988).

128. "Advertisement of the Eastern Sachem, to the Western Beauties," *Columbian Centinel,* 13 June 1792, p. 1. Around this time, Gardiner was indeed courting a lady in Boston, and, as he remarked to a friend, "The Bellows heaved on both sides, not a little" (John Gardiner to ———, 11 November 1791, GWA). "The Excise Bill," *Massachusetts Centinel,* 20 February 1790, p. 3; "Food for the Humorist," *Independent Chronicle,* 17 February 1791, p. 3; "Anecdote," *Herald of Freedom,* 22 April 1791, p. 3.

129. Nathaniel Barrell to John Gardiner, 20 January 1791, copied in Barrell to George Thatcher, 15 February 1791, George Thatcher Letters, BPL.

130. Charles Churchill, *The Poetical Works of Charles Churchill,* ed. Douglas Grant (Oxford: Clarendon Press, 1956), xiv, 58, 58n. I've reproduced lines 293 to 296. See Bertelsen, *Nonsense Club,* 121–128.

131. "Legislature of Massachusetts," *Herald of Freedom,* 3 May 1791, p. 1; Gardiner repeats line 302 of "Night." See these "Old Whackum" pieces: *Massachusetts Centinel,* 26 October 1785, p. 2; *American Herald,* 28 November 1785, p. 3; *Columbian Centinel,* 5 January 1791. He alludes to Churchill in his open letter "To the Author of the Gratulatory Address" (*Independent Chronicle,* 9 September 1790, p. 1—he explains the allusion in a footnote) and quotes "The Rosciad" in his theater speech (*Speech of John Gardiner, Esquire,* 93–94n). In at least one case, Gardiner got a taste of his own medicine. "Agumenticus" quoted Churchill and, by so doing, mocked Churchill's admirer and acquaintance (*Columbian Centinel,* 12 February 1791, p. 1).

132. "To the celebrated Law-Reformer," *Massachusetts Centinel,* 20 February 1790, p. 4; *Sibley's Harvard Graduates,* vol. 13, 602; William Bentley, *The Diary of William Bentley, D.D.,* 4 vols. (Salem, Mass., 1907), vol 2, 71–73.

Letters and Distinction (pages 175–216)

1. John Gardiner, *The Widowed Mourner* (Boston, 1791), 1: lines 5–8; Bentley, *Diary,* vol. 2, 72–73.

2. Gardiner, *Widowed Mourner,* 2–3: lines 37–53, 3n.

3. Ibid., 1–2n.

4. Ibid., 3–4: lines 54–69, 3–4n; Francis Jones, "The Society of Sea Serjeants," 57–91.

5. Ibid., 4–5: lines 75–76.

6. Ibid., 5–6n, 8.

7. The author was William Jones, Parr's classmate and an acclaimed Orientalist whom Gardiner deeply admired (Arthur Maynard Walter to William Smith Shaw, 24 May 1800, in Joseph B. Felt's *Memorials of William Smith Shaw* [Boston, 1852], 111). This quotation is reprinted in Warren Derry, *Dr. Parr: A Portrait of the Whig Dr. Johnson* (Oxford: Clarendon Press, 1966), 50. For a record of Gardiner's education and Parr's influence, see John Gardiner's account with Samuel Parr, RHG (the account begins in September of 1776); Josiah Quincy, *The History of the Boston Athenaeum* (Cambridge, Mass., 1851), 6; George Ticknor, *Life of William Hickling Prescott* (Boston, 1864), 8. Also see the *Dictionary of American Biography*, vol. 7, 137–138.

8. John Gardiner to Silvester Gardiner, 19 July 1783, GWA; Derry, *Dr. Parr*, 12, 37–38, 137; A. M. Walter to W. S. Shaw, 24 May 1800, *Memorials of William Smith Shaw*, 111.

9. This note was appended to his father's letter of 19 July 1783, GWA.

10. "Record-Book of the Suffolk Bar," 159–160.

11. R. H. Gardiner, *Early Recollections*, 19; *Dictionary of American Biography*, vol. 7, 137–138; Extract of a letter from the Rev. Samuel Parker, GWA; *The Records of Trinity Church, Boston, 1728–1830*, ed. Andrew Oliver and James Bishop Peabody, *Publications of the Colonial Society of Massachusetts* 55 (1980), 232.

12. George Cabot to Theophilus Parsons, 12 August 1794, in Henry Cabot Lodge, *Life and Letters of George Cabot* (Boston, 1878), 79. On how another major Federalist understood the collective will, see Cecelia M. Kenyon, "Alexander Hamilton: Rousseau of the Right," *Political Science Quarterly* 73 (June 1958), 161–178.

13. These matters are taken up in James M. Banner Jr.'s *To the Hartford Convention: The Federalists and the Origins of Party Politics in Massachusetts, 1789–1815* (New York: Alfred A. Knopf, 1970) and in Linda Kerber's *Federalists in Dissent: Imagery and Ideology in Jeffersonian America* (Ithaca: Cornell University Press, 1980).

14. J. S. J. Gardiner, *A Sermon Delivered Before the Humane Society of the Commonwealth of Massachusetts* (Boston, 1803), 5, 9–10.

15. Gardiner, *A Sermon Delivered Before the Convention of the Protestant Episcopal Church, in the Commonwealth of Massachusetts* (Boston, 1802), 15.

16. Gardiner, *An Address Delivered Before the Members of the Massachusetts Charitable Fire Society* (Boston, 1803), 9, 20.

17. Gardiner, *A Discourse Delivered At Trinity Church, Boston, April 9, 1812, on the Day of Publick Fast* (Boston, 1812), 3, 10, 12–13, 15, 18–19.

18. Gardiner, *A Discourse Delivered at Trinity Church, Boston . . . upon the Declaration of War against Great-Britain* (Boston, 1812), 3, 6.

19. Gardiner, *Discourse Delivered . . . upon the Declaration of War*, 8–9. On John Randolph and Timothy Pickering as unpopular tellers of truth, see p. 10.

20. Ibid., 4–5, 9, 13–16.

21. Ibid., 15–19.

22. This is the argument of Banner's *To the Hartford Convention.*

23. Gardiner, *A Preservative against Unitarianism* (Boston, 1811), 22; Conrad Wright, *The Beginnings of Unitarianism in America* (Boston: Beacon Press, 1955), 252–280.

24. Gardiner, *A Sermon, Preached at Trinity-Church, Before the Trustees of the Society of Donations, and the Episcopal Convention of the State of Massachusetts* (Boston, 1813), 15. On Unitarian hubris, see *Preservative*, 5.

25. Gardiner, *Preservative*, 12, 15, 19.

26. Gardiner, *A Sermon Preached at Trinity-Church, Boston, before the Prayer-Book and Religious Tract Association* (Boston, 1816), 7; Gardiner, *Address Delivered Before the . . . Charitable Fire Society*, 16.

27. J. S. J. Gardiner to Silvester Gardiner, 10 March 1784, John Gardiner to Silvester Gardiner, 22 April 1784, Silvester Gardiner to Oliver Whipple, 27 July 1784, Oliver Whipple to Silvester Gardiner [copy], 8 November 1784, GWA; Amory, *Life of James Sullivan*, vol. 1, 138, 189–190; Bertram E. Packard, "John Gardiner, Barrister," *Sprague's Journal of Maine History* 9 (April–May–June 1921), 52.

28. "Pompus—A Character," *Continental Journal*, 27 April 1786, p. 2; "Pompus—A Character"; "Severus—A Character," *Continental Journal*, 4 May 1786, p. 2.

29. [J. S. J. Gardiner,] *An Epistle to Zenas* (Boston, 1786), 6–7: lines 27–28, 71–72.

30. Ibid., 13: lines 181–182.

31. Ibid., 6: line 26, 8n; R. H. Gardiner, *Early Recollections*, 95; "A High Churchman," *Boston Gazette*, 19 January 1795, p. 2. When young Gardiner returned from South Carolina, a correspondent to the *Centinel* (8 June 1791, p. 3)—probably John—hailed the arrival of "the second edition of Charles Churchill."

32. See Charles Prentiss's biography of Paine in *The Works in Verse and Prose, of the Late Robert Treat Paine, Jun. Esq.*, ed. Charles Prentiss (Boston, 1812), xvii; Joseph T. Buckingham, *Specimens of Newspaper Literature*, 2 vols. (Boston, 1850), vol. 2, 250; *Dictionary of American Biography*, vol. 14, 157–158.

33. [Gardiner,] *Epistle to Zenas*, 13: lines 191–192; Maas, *Return of the Massachusetts Loyalists*, 291, 294, 303, 523; "Legislature of Massachusetts," *Independent Chronicle*, 3–17 March 1791; *Dictionary of American Biography*, vol. 14, 156–157.

34. "Impartial Neutrality," *Mercury*, 9–13 January 1795, p. 2; "A Card," *Federal Orrery*, 15 January 1795, p. 3; [Gardiner,] *Epistle to Zenas*, 16–17; Paine, *Works in Verse and Prose*, xxxix; *Dictionary of American Biography*, vol. 14, 157.

35. See Prentiss's biography in Paine, *Works in Verse and Prose; Dictionary of American Biography*, vol. 14, 157.

36. Gardiner, *Speech of John Gardiner, Esquire*, 14–15: Gardiner alludes to Austin's opposition with his remark about "rope-makers."

37. Throughout this section, I will be quoting the whole printed versions of this text, though it first appeared in the *Federal Orrery*. See [J.S.J. Gardiner,] *Remarks on the Jacobiniad*, Part I (Boston, 1795), 26.

38. "One whom you have attempted to injure," *Independent Chronicle*, 23 April 1795, p. 2. See "Honestus, or one whom you have attempted to injure" and two other "Honestus" articles, all on the second page of the *Chronicle* on these dates in 1795: 30 April, 11 May, 18 May. It is quite likely that Austin also wrote "A Card," *Boston Gazette*, 5 January 1795, p. 3.

39. "An Episcopalian," *Independent Chronicle*, 18 May 1795, p. 2; "Trinity," *Boston Gazette*, 11 May 1795, p. 3; "Stentor," *Independent Chronicle*, 12 January 1795, p. 1; "High Churchman," *Boston Gazette*, 19 January 1795, p. 2. Goats were closely associated with Wales in that day: see "A Card," *Boston Gazette*, 5 January 1795, p. 3.

40. "Virtuoso," *Boston Gazette*, 27 April 1795, p. 3; "High Churchman," *Boston Gazette*, 19 January 1795, p. 2; "An Episcopalian," *Mercury*, 2–6 January 1795, p. 2; "Stentor," *Independent Chronicle*, 12 January 1795, p. 1.

41. Richard Buel Jr., *Securing the Revolution: Ideology in American Politics, 1789–1815* (Ithaca: Cornell University Press, 1972), x.

42. [Gardiner,] *Jacobiniad*, I, 44; Elkins and McKitrick, *Age of Federalism*, 456–459, 484–487.

43. [Gardiner,] *Jacobiniad*, I, 31–32.

44. Ibid., I, 37–38, 39.

45. "Argumentum Ad Hominem," *Independent Chronicle*, 25 May 1795, p. 2; "Thomas-A-Kempis," *Independent Chronicle*, 25 May 1795, p. 3.

46. [Gardiner,] *Remarks on the Jacobiniad*, Part II (Boston, 1798), 53–56, 56n.

47. [Gardiner,] *Jacobiniad*, I, 11–12.

48. "Boston . . . From Washington, Dec. 11, 1800," *Massachusetts Mercury*, 23 December 1800, p. 2.

49. "Address to the Public," *The Mercury and New-England Palladium*, 2 January 1801, p. 1.

50. Ibid.

51. "Literary Notice," *New-England Palladium*, 20 January 1801, p. 3; "Observations on the Corruptions of Literature," *New-England Palladium*, 6 January 1801, p. 1; "Address to the Public," *New-England Palladium*, 2 January 1801, p. 1.

52. The best study of Joseph Dennie remains Harold Milton Ellis's *Joseph Dennie and His Circle: A Study in American Literature from 1792 to 1812* (Austin: *Bulletin of the University of Texas* [Studies in English, no. 3], 1915). I am heavily indebted to this source. See pages iii, 149, 173, 208. Hawthorne's estimate appears in his sketch of Thomas Green Fessenden, in the *American Monthly Magazine* 5 (January 1838), 31.

53. Ellis, *Joseph Dennie*, 11–12, 16–18, 19, 25.

54. Howard C. Rice, "James Swan: Agent of the French Republic, 1794–1796," *New England Quarterly* 10 (September 1937), 465, 469; Francis S. Drake, *The*

Town of Roxbury: Its Memorable Persons and Places (Roxbury, Mass., 1878), 137; [James Swan,] *National Arithmetick: or, Observations on the Finances of the Commonwealth of Massachusetts* (Boston, 1786), 16, 16n, 22, 79n; *Resolves of the General Court of the Commonwealth of Massachusetts* (January session, 1785), 145; "William Bingham's Maine Lands," 495; Gras, *Massachusetts First National Bank*, 57, 65n, 281–283, 639, 646.

55. Drake, *Town of Roxbury*, 137–138; Foote, *Annals of King's Chapel*, vol. 2, 608. In fact, Gardiner's and Swan's pews were situated directly across the center aisle from each other: see Foote, *Annals*, vol. 2, 589, 597, and the plate between 310 and 311.

56. Ellis, *Joseph Dennie*, 27, 31–32; Joseph Dennie to Mary and Joseph Dennie, 16 July 1785, *The Letters of Joseph Dennie, 1768–1812*, ed. Laura Green Pedder (Orono: University of Maine Press, 1936), 6.

57. G. Thomas Tanselle, *Royall Tyler* (Cambridge, Mass.: Harvard University Press, 1967), 6–8.

58. Josiah Quincy, *The History of Harvard University*, 2 vols. (New York: Arno Press, 1977), vol. 2, 277; Samuel Eliot Morison, *Three Centuries of Harvard, 1636–1936* (Cambridge, Mass.: Harvard University Press, 1936), 175, 176. For a contemporary notice of such hijinks, see "History of a College Rake," *Monthly Anthology* 1 (February 1804), 152–156. The author was John Pierce, a former Harvard tutor. He briefly refers to a watermelon raid, an offense either common among New England's scholars or else easily ascribed to them after the publication of Stephen Burroughs's narrative (Burroughs, *Memoirs*, 24–25).

59. Ellis, *Joseph Dennie*, 34–35; Joseph Dennie to Roger Vose, 24 February and 11 March 1790, *Letters of Joseph Dennie*, 13–14. Dennie's report of this episode is worth repeating: "In this village resided a female favorite [Sarah ("Sally") Minot, whose portrait is in Boston's Museum of Fine Arts], whom it was necessary to kiss prior to my departure. I hastened to the mansion of this rural charmer, received a lesson on the *celestial globes*, bid her a most tender passionate adieu, and went on my way sorrowing."

60. John Callender to Joseph Dennie, 18 March 1790, Joseph Dennie Papers, Houghton Library, Harvard University.

61. "Farrago," no. 2, *Tablet*, 26 May 1795, p. 5—originally published in the *Morning Ray* (Windsor, Vermont) on 21 February 1792 (Ellis, *Joseph Dennie*, 238); L. G. Mitchell, *Charles James Fox* (New York: Oxford University Press, 1992), 1–3, 10–20, 43–45. Republicans and Federalists alike thought Fox appealing: see the *Federal Orrery*, 23 February 1795, p. 2, and the *Independent Chronicle*, 23 March 1795, p. 2.

62. College notes and exercises, Joseph Dennie Papers; "Farrago," no. 2, *Tablet*, 26 May 1795, p. 5.

63. Roger Vose to Joseph Dennie, 12 May 1790, Joseph Dennie Papers; Dennie to Vose, 29 April 1790, *Letters of Joseph Dennie*, 45.

64. Jeremiah Mason, *Memoir and Correspondence of Jeremiah Mason* (Cambridge, Mass., 1873), 30; Ellis, *Joseph Dennie*, 62.

65. Robert Ferguson, *Law and Letters in American Culture* (Cambridge, Mass.: Harvard University Press, 1984); see 150–182 in particular.

66. I will be quoting from the series's second appearance in the *Tablet*—in this instance, "Farrago," no. 1, *Tablet*, 19 May 1795, p. 1. For provenance, see Ellis, *Joseph Dennie*, 238.

67. "Farrago," no. 2, *Tablet*, 26 May 1795, p. 5.

68. Ibid., p. 6. The original no. 2 appeared in February 1792, the month after Gardiner's speech. "Meander" recites lines 83–84 of "Night," as reprinted in Grant's *Churchill*, 53.

69. "Farrago," no. 3, *Tablet*, 2 June 1795, p. 9; Joseph Dennie to Roger Vose, 16 May 1790, *Letters of Joseph Dennie*, 52.

70. "Farrago," no. 5, *Tablet*, 16 June 1795, p. 18; on the "polite scholar," see no. 3.

71. Joseph T. Buckingham, *Specimens of Newspaper Literature*, 2 vols. (Boston, 1850), vol. 2, 195–220. Buckingham was this very devil, and this particular anecdote is found in vol. 2, 197. Also see Mason, *Memoir and Correspondence*, 28; George Aldrich, *Walpole as It Was and as It Is* (Claremont, N.H., 1880), 79–83.

72. Joseph Dennie to Mary and Joseph Dennie, January 1794, *Letters of Joseph Dennie*, 132–141; Brown, *Knowledge is Power*, 82–109.

73. Joseph Dennie to Mary and Joseph Dennie, January 1794, *Letters of Joseph Dennie*, 132–141; "Farrago," no. 8, *Tablet*, 7 July 1795, p. 29.

74. "Biography," *Tablet*, 26 May 1795, pp. 6–7; 2 June, pp. 10–11; 28 July, pp. 42–43; "Original Criticism," *Tablet*, 9 June 1795, p. 14; 23 June, pp. 21–22; 30 June, pp. 25–26; 7 July, p. 30; 14 July, pp. 34–35; "Colon & Spondee," *Tablet*, 4 August 1795, pp. 46–47; Joseph Dennie to Mary Dennie, 24 April 1795, *Letters of Joseph Dennie*, 144–148.

75. Joseph Dennic to Mary Dennie, 24 April 1795, *Letters of Joseph Dennie*, 144–148; Joseph Dennie to Royall Tyler, 2 October 1795, *Letters of Joseph Dennie*, 151.

76. Joseph Dennie to Mary Dennie and Harriot Green, 29 August 1796, *Letters of Joseph Dennie*, 153–154; Buckingham, *Specimens*, vol. 2, 174–179. I suspect that, in this century, the circulation of the *Village Voice* has surpassed that of the *Museum* in its day.

77. Joseph Dennie, "Go thy way, eat thy bread with joy," *The Lay Preacher; or Short Sermons, for Idle Readers* (Walpole, N.H., 1796), reprinted in a facsimile edition, edited by Milton Ellis (New York, 1943), 35. This essay first appeared in the *Farmer's Weekly Museum* on 9 February 1796. For original attributions made here and in notes below, see Ellis, *Joseph Dennie*, 240–244. "What aileth thee?" *Lay Preacher*, 6 [*Museum*, 17 November 1795].

78. "Come, my beloved, let us go forth into the field," *Lay Preacher*, 29–30 [*Museum*, 14 June 1796]. Also see "How long wilt thou sleep O sluggard?" *Lay*

Preacher, 7–9 [*Museum*, 1 March 1796]; "Hate not Laborious Work, neither Husbandry," *Lay Preacher*, 36–38 [*Museum*, 15 March 1796].

79. "Drink waters out of thine own cistern," *Lay Preacher*, 23–24 [*Museum*, 8 March 1796]; "Hate not Laborious Work," *Lay Preacher*, 36–38.

80. "Favor is deceitful," *Lay Preacher*, 13 [*Museum*, 27 October 1795].

81. "Little children, keep yourselves from idols," *Lay Preacher*, 22 [*Museum*, 23 February 1796]; "The fashion of this world passeth away," *Lay Preacher*, 48 [*Museum*, 26 April 1796].

82. "In those days there was no king in Israel," *Lay Preacher*, 18–19 [*Museum*, 1 December 1795]; on the author's dandyism, see Buckingham, *Specimens*, vol. 2, 196.

83. "They made me the keeper of the vineyards," *Lay Preacher*, 57 [*Museum*, 12 April 1796]; "What aileth thee?" *Lay Preacher*, 27–28. Dennie's health was a persistent concern: see Joseph Dennie to Mary and Joseph Dennie, 6 February 1791, *Letters of Joseph Dennie*, 74).

84. "By this craft we have our wealth," *Lay Preacher*, 16–17 [*Museum*, 15 December 1795]; "Come, my beloved, let us go forth into the field," *Lay Preacher*, 29–30; Joseph Dennie to Mary Dennie and Harriot Green, 2 June 1795, *Letters of Joseph Dennie*, 149. For other references to Mandeville, see "From the Shop of Messrs. Colon & Spondee," *Federal Orrery*, 5 March 1795, p. 2, and *Farmer's Weekly Museum*, 17 May 1796, p. 1.

85. Joseph Dennie to Mary Dennie, 26 April 1797, Joseph Dennie to Mary Dennie and Harriot Green, 6 September 1799, Joseph Dennie to Mary and Joseph Dennie, 20 May 1800, *Letters of Joseph Dennie*, 159, 171, 182.

86. "Lay Preacher," *Gazette of the United States*, 12 December 1799, p. 3; "Was ye not that such a man as I can certainly divine?" *Farmer's Museum*, 15 July 1799, p. 4.

87. Ellis, *Joseph Dennie*, 108–112, 243; for the "Versatility" essays, see the *Museum*, 19 and 26 August 1799.

88. Thomas Boylston Adams to William Smith Shaw, 14 July 1799, 8 September 1799, 27 April 1801, 20 September 1801, *Proceedings of the American Antiquarian Society* 27 (April 1917), 97, 110, 152, 159. And see Linda Kerber and Walter John Morris, "Politics and Literature: The Adams Family and the *Port Folio*," *William and Mary Quarterly* 23 (July 1966), 450–476.

89. "Lay Preacher," *Gazette of the United States*, 11 January 1800, p. 3.

90. William Cobbett to Joseph Dennie, 7 May 1800, Joseph Dennie Papers (and also see Dennie's annotations of this letter); Joseph Dennie to Mary and Joseph Dennie, 20 May 1800, *Letters of Joseph Dennie*, 181.

91. The prospectus was printed as a preface to the *Port Folio* 1 (3 January 1801), see the note on p. i, and p. ii.

92. "I will rise now and go about the city," *Lay Preacher*, 97–99 [first appeared in the *Port Folio* on 17 January 1801].

93. "New Prospectus of the Port Folio," *Port Folio*, 2nd ser., vol. 1 (1806), 2–4; "Biography," *Port Folio*, 2nd ser., vol. 3 (25 April 1807), 259–260; "Political Paragraphs," *Port Folio*, 2nd ser., vol. 3 (27 June 1807), 413n.

94. "Law Intelligence," *Port Folio*, 2nd ser., vol. 2 (18 October 1806), 227–228. And see, in the same volume, similar reports on pp. 259–261, 275–276, and 411.

95. "Farrago," no. 11, *Tablet*, 28 July 1795, p. 41; Ellis, *Joseph Dennie*, 201, 211–212.

96. Ellis, *Joseph Dennie*, 197–198, 221.

97. Arthur Maynard Walter to William Smith Shaw, 26 September 1799, in Felt, *Memorials of William Smith Shaw*, 72–73; "Original Criticism," *Tablet*, 9 June 1795, p. 14; 23 June 1795, pp. 21–22; 30 June 1795, pp. 25–26; 7 July 1795, p. 30; 14 July 1795, pp. 34–35.

98. "Restorator," no. 1, *New-England Palladium*, 27 March 1801, p. 1.

99. Ibid.; "Fraternal Feast," *Independent Chronicle*, 9 April 1795, p. 3; "Boston Restorator," *Independent Chronicle*, 23 April 1795, p. 3; "Restorator," *American Apollo*, 1 November 1793, p. 4.

100. "Restorator," no. 2, *New-England Palladium*, 7 April 1801, p. 1; no. 5, 23 June 1801, p. 1; see Gardiner's review of *The Miscellaneous Works of David Humphreys* in the Monthly Anthology, vol. 1 (September 1804), 507.

101. Review of Humphreys, *Monthly Anthology*, vol. 1, 508; "Restorator," no. 8, *New-England Palladium*, 21 July 1801, p. 1; no. 10, 21 August 1801, p. 1.

102. "Restorator," no. 8, *New-England Palladium*, 21 July 1801, p. 1.

103. "Restorator," no. 15, *New-England Palladium*, 2 October 1801, p. 1; no. 19, 16 November 1801, p. 1: this number consists of a letter to the "Restorator" from "Aristarchus," but Joseph Dennie confirmed that Gardiner was on both ends of the dialogue ("To Readers and Correspondents," *Port Folio*, vol. 1 [21 November 1801], 375).

104. "Restorator," no. 2, *New-England Palladium*, 7 April 1801, p. 1.

105. "Restorator," no. 2, *New-England Palladium*, 7 April 1801, p. 1.

106. "Restorator," no. 20, *New-England Palladium*, 13 November 1801, p. 1; no. 4, 29 May 1801, p. 1.

107. *The Federalist Literary Mind: Selections from the Monthly Anthology and Boston Review*, ed. Lewis P. Simpson (Baton Rouge: Louisiana State University Press, 1962), 10–11, 229–233; *Journal of the Proceedings of the Society which Conducts The Monthly Anthology & Boston Review*, ed. Mark A. DeWolfe Howe (Boston, 1910), 298–299.

108. Joseph Stevens Buckminster, "On the Dangers and Duties of Men of Letters," *Monthly Anthology*, vol. 7 (September 1809), 146; Daniel Walker Howe, *The Unitarian Conscience: Harvard Moral Philosophy, 1805–1861* (Cambridge, Mass.: Harvard University Press, 1970), 310; Lawrence Buell, "Joseph Stevens Buckminster: The Making of a New England Saint," *Canadian Review of American Studies* 10 (spring 1979), 1–29. Buell describes Buckminster as "the apotheosis of the needs and hopes of cultivated Boston in the early 1800's . . . As the work of his successors became more specialized, they looked back upon him as almost a universal genius, an ideal to which he probably did aspire" (7–8, 23–24).

109. Buckminster, "On the Dangers and Duties," *Monthly Anthology*, vol. 7, 148–149, 156.

110. Ibid., vol. 7, 146, 155.

111. Ibid., vol. 7, 145.

112. *Federalist Literary Mind*, 11, 24.

113. Ibid., 3; *Journal of the Proceedings of the Society*, 10, 35.

114. *Journal of the Proceedings of the Society*, 67, 76, 83, 101, 103, 121, 152.

115. "Silva," no. 11: "Education," *Monthly Anthology*, vol. 3 (January 1806), 18–19.

116. "Education," *Monthly Anthology*, vol. 3, 18–19.

117. "To 'Harvardiensis,'" *Monthly Anthology*, vol. 2 (January 1805), 44; on New World puffery, see "The Remarker," no. 4, *Monthly Anthology*, vol. 2 (December 1805), 630, 632.

118. "Art. 31," *Monthly Anthology*, vol. 2 (May 1805), 265.

119. "Art. 26," *Monthly Anthology*, vol. 4 (May 1807), 274–275; "Silva," no. 13: "Imitation of Hudibras," *Monthly Anthology*, vol. 3 (March 1806), 129.

120. "Art. 13," *Monthly Anthology*, vol. 6 (March 1809), 185–187.

121. Ibid.

122. "Silva," no. 11: "Pope," *Monthly Anthology*, vol. 3 (January 1806), 15–16.

123. Edmund Burke, *A Philosophical Enquiry into the Origin of our Ideas of the Sublime and Beautiful*, ed. J. T. Boulton (London: Routledge, 1958), 57–87; William Charvat, *The Origins of American Critical Thought, 1810–1835* (New York: A. S. Barnes, 1961), 27–58; "Remarker," no. 35, *Monthly Anthology*, vol. 5 (August 1808), 416–417; "Silva," no. 43: "More of Gray," *Monthly Anthology*, vol. 5 (September 1808), 495; "Silva," no. 46: "More of Gray," *Monthly Anthology*, vol. 5 (December 1808), 654–655; "Art. 37," *Monthly Anthology*, vol. 4 (June 1807), 335–336. Benjamin Welles, in a piece that anticipated Emerson, wrote of the sublimities of nature and of the mind's intercourse with it. The essay ends, "Let him then, whose soul is pure and holy with the love of nature, take his position in the midst of creation, and commence the mighty work of the eternal perfection of thought" (*Monthly Anthology*, vol. 3 [June 1806], 285–288). Gardiner thought the piece "the most contemptible thing" to have ever appeared in the magazine. See Arthur Maynard Walter to Joseph Stevens Buckminster, 7 August 1806, Joseph Stevens Buckminster Papers, Boston Athenaeum.

124. "Remarker," no. 34, *Monthly Anthology*, vol. 5 (July 1808), 367–370; *Dictionary of National Biography*, vol. 8, 465–471.

125. "Remarker," no. 35, *Monthly Anthology*, vol. 5, 416–419; "Silva," no. 43: "More of Gray," *Monthly Anthology*, vol. 5, 495.

126. "Silva," no. 36: "Gray" and "Ode to Winter," *Monthly Anthology*, vol. 5 (February 1808), 100–101; "Silva," no. 41: "Ode on Summer," *Monthly Anthology*, vol. 5 (July 1808), 357; Bentley, *Diary*, vol. 3, 229.

127. *Journal of the Proceedings of the Society*, 158–159; Eliza Buckminster Lee, *Memoirs of Rev. Joseph Buckminster, D.D., and of his son, Rev. Joseph Stevens Buckminster* (Boston, 1851), 238.

128. *Federalist Literary Mind*, 25–28.

129. *Journal of the Proceedings of the Society*, 41; Felt, *Memorials of William Smith Shaw*, 213; "Art. 73," *Monthly Anthology*, vol. 2 (November 1805), 595–599; "Silva," no. 25: "Armstrong," *Monthly Anthology*, vol. 4 (March 1807), 135; Ronald Story, "Class and Culture in Boston: The Athenaeum, 1807–1860," *American Quarterly* 27 (May 1975), 178–199.

130. "Silva," no. 13: "Burns and Bloomfield," *Monthly Anthology*, vol. 3 (March 1806), 127–128.

131. "Journal," *Monthly Anthology*, vol. 3 (January 1806), 13–14; *Journal of the Proceedings of the Society*, 43.

132. David G. Dickason, "The Nineteenth-Century Indo-American Ice Trade: An Hyperborean Epic," *Modern Asian Studies* 25 (February 1991), 53–89. See also Gavin Weightman, *The Frozen-Water Trade* (New York: Hyperion, 2003).

133. "Art. 20," *Monthly Anthology*, vol. 5 (June 1808), 339–340; *Dictionary of American Biography*, vol. 3, 200–205.

134. *Journal of the Proceedings of the Society*, 231; Quincy, *History of the Boston Athenaeum*, 6; David B. Tyack, *George Ticknor and the Boston Brahmins* (Cambridge, Mass.: Harvard University Press, 1967); Ticknor, *Life of William Hickling Prescott*, 7–8. See also Ronald Story, "Harvard Students, the Boston Elite, and the New England Preparatory System, 1800–1876," *History of Education Quarterly* 15 (Autumn 1975), 287.

135. Lewis P. Simpson, "Federalism and the Crisis of Literary Order," *American Literature* 32 (November 1960), 265–266. Lawrence Buell enjoins us to be wary of the "alienation" thesis in *New England Literary Culture from Revolution through Renaissance* (New York: Cambridge University Press, 1986), 391.

136. [Benjamin Welles,] "Silva," no. 32: "Politicks," *Monthly Anthology*, vol. 4 (October 1807), 542–543; [Robert Hallowell Gardiner,] "An Essay upon the Multiplicity of our Literary Institutions," *Monthly Anthology*, vol. 4 (March 1807), 113–116.

137. [William Tudor,] "The Address of the Editors," *Monthly Anthology*, vol. 8 (January 1810), 3–5.

138. [Gardiner,] "An Essay upon the Multiplicity of our Literary Institutions," *Monthly Anthology*, vol. 4, 116.

139. Lawrence Park, *Gilbert Stuart*, 4 vols. (New York, 1926), vol. 1, 337–338, vol. 3, 185–186.

140. Laurel Thatcher Ulrich, *A Midwife's Tale: The Life of Martha Ballard, Based on her Diary, 1785–1812* (New York: Vintage, 1990), 67, 95.

141. Mary Gardiner to William Howard Gardiner, 15 September 1820, RHG.

142. William Dunlap, *The Life of George Fred. Cooke*, 2 vols. (London, 1815), vol. 2, 212–213.

143. Arthur Maynard Walter to Joseph Stevens Buckminster, 29 September–2 October 1806, and Buckminster to Walter, 20 December 1806, Joseph Stevens Buckminster Papers, Boston Athenaeum.

144. Lee, *Memoirs of Rev. Joseph Buckminster*, 123–124, 447; Bridenbaugh, *Mitre and Sceptre*, 211–229.

145. Gardiner, *The Christian Soldier: A Sermon Delivered before the Ancient and Honourable Artillery Company* (Boston, 1823), 11–14.

146. Gardiner, *Life a Journey, and Man a Traveller: A New-Year's Sermon* (Boston, 1825), 9, 15–16.

147. *Dictionary of American Biography*, vol. 7, 137–138.

Retrospect *(pages 217–222)*

1. J. S. J. Gardiner to William H. Gardiner, 15 January 1822, RHG.

2. Royall Tyler, "The Contrast," in *Early American Drama*, ed. Jeffrey H. Richards (New York: Penguin, 1997), 56–57.

3. Ferris Greenslet, *The Lowells and Their Seven Worlds* (Boston: Houghton Mifflin, 1946), 63–64, 72–74; "Record-Book of the Suffolk Bar," *MHS Procs.* (1881–82), 159–160.

4. Robert F. Dalzell Jr., *Enterprising Elite: The Boston Associates and the World They Made* (Cambridge, Mass.: Harvard University Press, 1987), 5–6; *Dictionary of American Biography*, vol. 11, 456–457.

5. Dalzell, *Enterprising Elite*, especially 7–25. In addition, see Ronald D. Story, "Class Development and Cultural Institutions in Boston, 1800–1870: Harvard, the Athenaeum, and the Lowell Institute," (Ph.D. diss., SUNY–Stony Brook, 1972), 4, 8; Peter Dobkin Hall, "Family Structure and Class Consolidation among the Boston Brahmins," (Ph.D. diss., SUNY–Stony Brook, 1973), 88–89, 92, 194, 467. Their main points are recapitulated in Story, *The Forging of an Aristocracy: Harvard and the Boston Upper Class, 1800–1870* (Middletown, Conn.: Wesleyan University Press, 1980), and in Hall, *The Organization of American Culture, 1700–1900* (New York: New York University Press, 1982).

6. Dalzell, *Enterprising Elite*, 164–224; G. B. Warden, "Inequality and Instability in Eighteenth-Century Boston," *Journal of Interdisciplinary History* 6 (Spring 1976), 611n; Van Beck Hall, *Politics without Parties: Massachusetts, 1780–1791* (Pittsburgh: University of Pittsburgh Press, 1972), 69–71.

7. Henry Cabot Lodge, "The Last Forty Years of Town Government, 1782–1822," *Memorial History of Boston*, vol. 3, 191.

8. John W. Tyler, "Persistence and Change within the Boston Business Community"; Waters, *Otis Family*, 126, 196–203; Hamilton Hill, "William Phillips and William Phillips, Father and Son, 1722–1827," *New England Historical and Genealogical Register* 39 (April 1885), 109–117; Maas, *Return of the Massachusetts Loyalists*, 306.

9. Phillipson, "Scottish Enlightenment," 22–31; Hancock, *Citizens of the World*.

10. Brown, *Knowledge is Power*, 82–109. Note how Brown's work reflects the pattern begun in Lodge: a nascent establishment gathers itself in the country and eventually supplants a competing group that once held the advantage—the most business, the best offices—in town.

11. Haliburton, *Effects of the Stage*, 8; "Number 1," *Independent Chronicle*, 2 December 1790, p. 1.

12. Thomas Jefferson to John Adams, 28 October 1813, in *The Adams-Jefferson Letters: The Complete Correspondence between Thomas Jefferson and Abigail and John Adams*, ed. Lester J. Cappon, 2 vols. (Chapel Hill: University of North Carolina Press, 1959), vol. 2, 388; [Jackson,] *Thoughts on the Political Situation*, 25–26, 69.

13. On this topic, see Linda Kerber, *Federalists in Dissent: Imagery and Ideology in Jeffersonian America* (Ithaca: Cornell University Press, 1980).

BIBLIOGRAPHY

Manuscripts

Additional Manuscripts, British Library

Akers Letters and Papers, privately held by C. M. Wigan at Downham House, Downham, Billericay, Essex (UK)

American Loyalist Claims and Colonial Office Papers, Public Record Office (UK)

Joseph Stevens Buckminster Papers, Boston Athenaeum

Henry Caner Letters, University of Bristol (UK)

Joseph Dennie Papers, Houghton Library, Harvard University

Derby Family Papers, Peabody Essex Museum, Salem

Gardiner-Whipple-Allen Papers, Massachusetts Historical Society

John Gardiner, "Precedents in Chancery," Rare Books, Langdell Law Library, Harvard University

John Gardiner, "The Petition of John Gardiner," Massachusetts Archives

Robert Hallowell Gardiner Papers, privately held at Oaklands, Gardiner, Maine

Silvester Gardiner Papers, Maine Historical Society

William Haliburton Papers, New England Historic-Genealogical Society

William Jepson Diary, New England Historic-Genealogical Society

William Samuel Johnson Papers, Connecticut Historical Society

King's Chapel Archives, at the King's Chapel Parish House, Boston

King's Chapel Archives, Massachusetts Historical Society

John Pinney Letterbooks, University of Bristol (UK)

Samuel Quincy Papers, Massachusetts Historical Society

James M. Robbins Papers, Massachusetts Historical Society

St. Kitts & Nevis Archives, Basseterre

George Thatcher Letters, Boston Public Library

Thatcher Family Papers II, Massachusetts Historical Society

Newspapers and Magazines

Unless noted otherwise, the following periodicals were published in Boston.

American Herald

Boston Gazette

Boston Weekly News-Letter

Charribbean and General Gazette

Continental Journal

Cumberland Gazette (Falmouth, Maine)
Farmer's Weekly Museum (Walpole, New Hampshire)
Federal Orrery
Gazette of Maine (Portland, Maine)
Gazette of the United States (Philadelphia)
The Guardian (London)
Herald of Freedom
Independent Chronicle
Massachusetts (later *Columbian*) *Centinel*
Massachusetts Magazine
Massachusetts Mercury (later *The Mercury and New-England Palladium*)
Monthly Anthology and Boston Review
Newport Mercury
Port Folio (Philadelphia)
St. James's Magazine (London)
The Tablet
Western Star (Stockbridge, Massachusetts)

Other Published Primary Sources

An Account of the Late Dreadful Hurricane. St. Christopher, 1772.

Acts and Laws of the Commonwealth of Massachusetts. Boston, 1785.

Acts and Laws, Passed by the General Court of Massachusetts. Boston, 1790 and 1792.

The Acts and Resolves, Public and Private, of the Province of the Massachusetts Bay. 21 vols. Boston, 1869–1922.

Acts of the Privy Council of England. Colonial Series. 6 vols. London, 1908–12.

Adams, John. *A Defence of the Constitutions of Government of the United States of America.* 3 vols. Philadelphia, 1797.

———. *Diary and Autobiography of John Adams.* Ed. L. H. Butterfield. 4 vols. Cambridge, Mass.: Harvard University Press, 1961.

Adams, John Quincy. *Writings of John Quincy Adams.* Ed. Worthington Chauncey Ford. 7 vols. New York: Macmillan, 1913–17.

Adams, Thomas Boylston, to William Smith Shaw. 14 July 1799. *Proceedings of the American Antiquarian Society* 27 (April 1917), 97.

The Adams-Jefferson Letters: The Complete Correspondence between Thomas Jefferson and Abigail and John Adams. Ed. Lester J. Cappon. 2 vols. Chapel Hill: University of North Carolina Press, 1959.

Almon, John. *The Correspondence of the Late John Wilkes.* 5 vols. London, 1805.

Ames, Fisher, to William Tudor. 24 November 1791. *Collections of the Massachusetts Historical Society,* 2nd series, vol. 7 (1826), 323–325.

Articles of Incorporation of the Society for encouraging Industry and employing the Poor. Boston, 1754.

Bentley, William. *The Diary of William Bentley, D.D.* 4 vols. Salem, Mass., 1907.

[Bishop, Abraham.] *The Triumph of Truth: History and Visions of Clio.* Boston, 1791.

Blackstone, William. *Commentaries on the Laws of England.* 4 vols. Oxford, 1765–69.

Boswell, James. *Boswell's London, Journal, 1762–1763.* Ed. Frederick A. Pottle. New York: McGraw-Hill, 1950.

Breck, Samuel. *Recollections of Samuel Breck.* Ed. H. E. Scudder. Philadelphia, 1877.

Bridge, James, to John Quincy Adams. 28 September 1787. "Diary of John Quincy Adams." *Proceedings of the Massachusetts Historical Society* 36 (1902), 434n.

Burke, Edmund. *A Philosophical Enquiry into the Origin of our Ideas of the Sublime and Beautiful.* Ed. J. T. Boulton. London: Routledge, 1958.

Burroughs, Stephen. *Memoirs of Stephen Burroughs.* Boston: Northeastern University Press, 1988.

Butler, Joseph. *Five Sermons Preached at the Rolls Chapel and A Dissertation Upon the Nature of Virtue.* Ed. Stuart M. Brown Jr. New York: Liberal Arts Press, 1950.

Chauncy, Charles. *The Idle-Poor secluded from the Bread of Charity by the Christian Law.* Boston, 1752.

———. *Benevolence of the Deity.* Boston, 1784.

Churchill, Charles. *The Poetical Works of Charles Churchill.* Ed. Douglas Grant. Oxford: Clarendon Press, 1956.

Cadwallader Colden Papers. *Collections of the New York Historical Society* (1876–77, 1922).

The Constitution of the Boston Tontine Association. Boston, 1791.

Cooper, Samuel. *A Sermon Preached in Boston, New-England, Before the Society for Encouraging Industry, and Employing the Poor.* Boston, 1753.

Cutting, Nathaniel. "Extracts from a Journal of a Gentleman visiting Boston in 1792." *Proceedings of the Massachusetts Historical Society* 12 (1871–73), 60–67.

[Davis, Daniel.] *An Address to the Inhabitants of the District of Maine, Upon the Subject of Their Separation from the Present Government of Massachusetts.* Portland, Maine, 1791.

———. *An Oration , Delivered at Portland, July 4th, 1796.* Portland, Maine, 1796.

Dennie, Joseph. *The Lay Preacher; or Short Sermons, for Idle Readers.* Ed. Milton Ellis. New York, 1943 [Walpole, N.H., 1796].

The Diary and Letters of Benjamin Pickman. Ed. George Francis Dow. Newport, 1928.

The Diary of Dr. Nathaniel Ames of Dedham, Massachusetts, 1758–1822. Ed. Robert Brand Hanson. Camden, Maine: Picton Press, 1998.

Documents Relative to the Colonial History of the State of New-York. Ed. E. B. O'Callaghan. 11 vols. Albany, 1856–61.

Dr. Gardiner versus James Flagg, Merchant. Boston, 1767.

[Flagg, James?] *A Strange Account of the Rising and Breaking of a Great Bubble.* "[O]n Sagadahock-River," 1767.

A full Answer to the Pamphlet intitled "a short Vindication." Boston, 1768[?].

Gardiner, Anne Gibbons. *Mrs. Gardiner's Family Receipts from 1763.* Ed. Gail Weesner. Boston: Rowan Tree Press, 1989.

Gardiner, John. *The Argument or Speech of John Gardiner, Esquire.* Basseterre, St. Christopher, 1770.

———. *An Oration, Delivered July 4, 1785, at the Request of the Inhabitants of the Town of Boston in Celebration of the Anniversary of American Independence.* Boston, 1785.

———. *The Memorial and Petition of John Gardiner, Esq.* Boston, 1783.

———. *The Speech of John Gardiner, Esquire. Delivered in the House of Representatives. On Thursday, the 26th of January, 1792.* Boston, 1792.

———. *The Widowed Mourner.* Boston, 1791.

Gardiner, J. S. J. *An Address Delivered Before the Members of the Massachusetts Charitable Fire Society.* Boston, 1803.

———. *The Christian Soldier: A Sermon Delivered before the Ancient and Honourable Artillery Company.* Boston, 1823.

———. *A Discourse Delivered at Trinity Church, Boston, April 9, 1812, on the Day of Publick Fast.* Boston, 1812.

———. *A Discourse Delivered at Trinity Church, Boston . . . upon the Declaration of War against Great-Britain.* Boston, 1812.

———. *An Epistle to Zenas.* Boston, 1786.

———. *Life a Journey, and Man a Traveller: A New-Year's Sermon.* Boston, 1825.

———. *A Preservative against Unitarianism.* Boston, 1811.

———. *Remarks on the Jacobiniad.* Parts I, II. Boston, 1795, 1798.

———. *A Sermon Delivered Before the Convention of the Protestant Episcopal Church, in the Commonwealth of Massachusetts.* Boston, 1802.

———. *A Sermon Delivered Before the Humane Society of the Commonwealth of Massachusetts.* Boston, 1803.

———. *A Sermon Preached at Trinity-Church, Boston, before the Prayer-Book and Religious Tract Association.* Boston, 1816.

———. *A Sermon, Preached at Trinity-Church, Before the Trustees of the Society of Donations, and the Episcopal Convention of the State of Massachusetts.* Boston, 1813.

[Gardiner, Silvester.] "To the Freeholders and other Inhabitants of the Town of Boston." Boston, 1761.

[Haliburton, William.] "A Bostonian." *Effects of the Stage on the Manners of a People.* Boston, 1792.

Hume, David. *Essays Moral, Political, and Literary.* Ed. Eugene F. Miller. Indianapolis: Liberty Fund, 1987.

———. *The History of England from the Invasion of Julius Caesar to the Abdication of James the Second, 1688.* 6 vols. Boston, 1854, 1856.

[Jackson, Jonathan.] *Thoughts upon the Political Situation of the United States of America, in which that of Massachusetts, is more particularly considered.* Worcester, 1788.

Journal of the Commissioners for Trade and Plantations from January 1759 to December 1763. London, 1935.

A Journal of the Honourable House of Representatives At a General Court of the Commonwealth of Massachusetts. Boston, May 1792-March 1793.

Journal of the Proceedings of the Society which Conducts The Monthly Anthology & Boston Review. Ed. Mark A. DeWolfe Howe. Boston, 1910.

Legal Papers of John Adams. Ed. L. Kinvin Wroth and Hiller B. Zobel. 3 vols. Cambridge, Mass.: Harvard University Press, 1965.

A Letter from Sir Richard Cox, Bart. to Thomas Prior, Esq; Shewing from Experience, A sure Method to establish the Linnen-Manufacture. Boston, 1750.

The Letters of Joseph Dennie, 1768–1812. Ed. Laura Green Pedder. Orono: University of Maine Press, 1936.

A Liturgy, collected principally from the Book of Common Prayer, for the use of the First Episcopal Church in Boston. Boston, 1785.

McDaniel II, W. B. "A Letter from Dr. Williams Smibert, of Boston, to his Former Fellow Student at Edinburgh, Dr. John Morgan, of Philadelphia, written February 14, 1769." *Annals of Medical History*, 3rd series, vol. 1 (March 1939), 194–196.

MacSparran, James. *A Letter Book and Abstract of Out Services, Written during the Years 1743–1751.* Boston, 1899.

Mandeville, Bernard. *The Fable of the Bees: or, Private Vices, Publick Benefits.* Ed. F. B. Kaye. 2 vols. Oxford: Clarendon Press, 1924.

Minot Family Letters, 1773–1871. Ed. Katherine Minot Channing. Sherborn, Mass.: privately printed, 1957.

Paine, Robert Treat, Jr. *The Works in Verse and Prose, of the Late Robert Treat Paine, Jun. Esq.* Ed. Charles Prentiss. Boston, 1812.

"Philo Dramatis." *The Rights of the Drama: or, An Inquiry into the Origin, Principles, and Consequences of Theatrical Entertainments.* Boston, 1792.

Prat, Benjamin, to the Lords of Trade. 24 May 1762. In *Documents Relative to the Colonial History of the State of New-York.* Ed. E. B. O'Callaghan. 11 vols. Albany, 1856–61, vol. 7, 501.

Ramsay, James. *An Essay on the Treatment and Conversion of African Slaves in the British Sugar Colonies.* London, 1784.

————. *A Reply to the Personal Invectives and Objections.* London, 1785.

"Record-Book of the Suffolk Bar." Ed. George Dexter. *Proceedings of the Massachusetts Historical Society* 19 (1881–82), 159–161.

The Records of Trinity Church, Boston, 1728–1830. Ed. Andrew Oliver and James Bishop Peabody. *Publications of the Colonial Society of Massachusetts* 55 (1980).

The Report of the Committee to the Society for encouraging Industry. Boston, 1752.

Resolves of the General Court of the Commonwealth of Massachusetts. Boston, 1785.

Return of the Whole Number of Persons Within the Several Districts of the United States. Philadelphia, 1791.

Robertson, William. *The History of the Reign of Charles the Fifth . . . to which is prefixed, A View of the Progress of Society in Europe.* 3 vols. Philadelphia, 1770.

Rousseau, Jean-Jacques. *Politics and the Arts: Letter to M. D'Alembert on the Theatre.* Trans. Allan Bloom. Glencoe, Ill.: Free Press, 1960.

Rowe, John. *Letters and Diary of John Rowe*, Ed. Anne Rowe Cunningham. Boston, 1903.

Rural Household Inventories. Ed. Abbott Lowell Cummings. Boston: Society for the Preservation of New England Antiquities, 1964.

Shaftesbury, Anthony Ashley Cooper, 3rd Earl. *An Inquiry Concerning Virtue, or Merit.* Manchester: Manchester University Press, 1977.

A short Vindication of the Conduct of the Referees in the Case of Gardiner versus Flagg. Boston, 1767.

Smith, Adam. *An Inquiry into the Nature and Causes of the Wealth of Nations.* Ed. R. H. Campbell and A. S. Skinner. 2 vols. Indianapolis: Liberty Fund, 1981.

———. *Lectures on Jurisprudence.* Ed. R. L. Meek, D. D. Raphael, and P. G. Stein. Oxford: Clarendon Press, 1978.

———. *The Theory of Moral Sentiments.* Ed. D. D. Raphael and A. L. Macfie. Oxford: Clarendon Press, 1976.

Stokes, Anthony. *Desultory Observations, on the Situation, Extent, Climate, Population, Religion, &c. of Great Britain.* London, 1792.

———. *A Narrative of the Official Conduct of Anthony Stokes.* London, 1784.

———. *A View of the Constitution of the British Colonies, in North-America and the West Indies.* London, 1783.

Sullivan, James. *The Path to Riches: An Inquiry into the Origins and Use of Money; and into the Principles of Stocks and Banks.* Boston, 1792.

Susquehannah Company Papers. Ed. Julian P. Boyd and Robert J. Taylor. 11 vols. Ithaca: Cornell University Press, 1962.

[Swan, James.] *National Arithmetick: or, Observations on the Finances of the Commonwealth of Massachusetts.* Boston, 1786.

Symmes, William. *An Oration, Delivered in the Meeting House of the First Parish in Portland, June 24th, 5796. At the Request and in the Presence of the Lodge of Free and Accepted Masons.* Portland, Maine, 1796.

Thacher, Oxenbridge, to Benjamin Prat [1762]. *Proceedings of the Massachusetts Historical Society* 20 (December 1882), 48.

Thayer, John, et al. *Controversy between the Rev. John Thayer, Catholic Missionary, of Boston, and the Rev. George Lesslie . . . to which are added, several other pieces.* Newburyport, Mass., 1793.

"The Theatre: A Dialogue: Between Sylvanus and Philander." *Massachusetts Magazine* 4 (November 1792), 688–690.

"To the Public." *Supplement to the Boston Evening-Post*, 20 July 1767, pp. 1–2.

Witherspoon, John. *A Serious Enquiry into the Nature and Effects of the Stage.* In *Essays on Important Subjects.* 2 vols. London, 1765.

Secondary Sources, Books and Theses

Addison, W. Innes. *The Matriculation Albums of the University of Glasgow, From 1728 to 1858.* Glasgow, 1913.

————. *A Roll of Graduates of the University of Glasgow.* Glasgow, 1898.

Aldrich, George. *Walpole as It Was and as It Is.* Claremont, N.H., 1880.

Allen, Charles Edwin. *History of Dresden, Maine.* Augusta, Maine, 1931.

Almon, John. *Biographical, Literary, and Political Anecdotes of Several of the Most Eminent Persons of the Present Age.* 3 vols. London, 1797.

Amory, Thomas C. *Life of James Sullivan, with Selections from His Writings.* 2 vols. Boston, 1859.

Appleby, Joyce. *Liberalism and Republicanism in the Historical Imagination.* Cambridge, Mass.: Harvard University Press, 1992.

Bagnall, William R. *The Textile Industries of the United States.* Cambridge, Mass.: Riverside Press, 1893.

Bahlman, Dudley W. R. *The Moral Revolution of 1688.* New Haven: Yale University Press, 1957.

Bailyn, Bernard. *The Ordeal of Thomas Hutchinson.* Cambridge, Mass.: Harvard University Press, 1974.

Baker, J. H. *The Third University of England: The inns of court and the common-law tradition.* London: Selden Society, 1990.

Ballantyne, Edward Lewis. "The Incorporation of Boston, 1784–1822." Senior honors essay, Harvard University, 1955.

Banks, Ronald F. *Maine Becomes a State: The Movement to Separate Maine from Massachusetts, 1785–1820.* Middletown, Conn.: Wesleyan University Press, 1970.

Banner, James M., Jr. *To the Hartford Convention: The Federalists and the Origins of Party Politics in Massachusetts, 1789–1815.* New York: Alfred A. Knopf, 1970.

Barish, Jonas. *The Antitheatrical Prejudice.* Berkeley: University of California Press, 1981.

Bartlet, William S. *The Frontier Missionary: A Memoir of the Life of Jacob Bailey.* Boston, 1853.

Bayly, C. A. *Imperial Meridian: The British Empire and the World, 1780–1830.* London: Longman, 1989.

Baynham, Walter. *The Glasgow Stage.* Glasgow, 1892.

Beardsley, E. Edwards. *Life and Correspondence of the Right Reverend Samuel Seabury.* Boston, 1881.

Bertelsen, Lance. *The Nonsense Club: Literature and Popular Culture, 1749–1764.* Oxford: Clarendon Press, 1986.

Besant, Walter. *London.* London, 1892.

Blake, John B. *Public Health in the Town of Boston, 1620–1822.* Cambridge, Mass.: Harvard University Press, 1959.

Bleackley, Horace. *Life of John Wilkes.* London, 1917.

Bonomi, Patricia U. *A Factious People: Politics and Society in Colonial New York.* New York: Columbia University Press, 1971.

Brewer, John. *Party ideology and popular politics at the accession of George III.* Cambridge: Cambridge University Press, 1976.

Bridenbaugh, Carl. *Cities in Revolt: Urban Life in America, 1743–1776.* New York: Capricorn Books, 1964.

Brown, John, J. W. Phillips, and Fred J. Warren. *The History of Haverfordwest.* Haverfordwest, 1914.

Brown, Richard D. *Knowledge is Power: The Diffusion of Information in Early America, 1700–1865.* New York: Oxford University Press, 1989.

Bryson, Gladys. *Man and Society: The Scottish Inquiry of the Eighteenth Century.* New York: Augustus M. Kelley, 1968.

Buckingham, Joseph T. *Specimens of Newspaper Literature.* 2 vols. Boston, 1850.

Buel, Richard, Jr. *Securing the Revolution: Ideology in American Politics, 1789–1815.* Ithaca: Cornell University Press, 1972.

Buell, Lawrence. *New England Literary Culture from Revolution through Renaissance.* New York: Cambridge University Press, 1986.

A Calendar of the Inner Temple Records. Ed. R. A. Roberts. London, 1936.

Campbell, John Lord. *The Lives of the Chief Justices of England.* 2 vols. London, 1849.

Caribbeana. Ed. Vere Langford Oliver. 6 vols. London, 1909–19.

Carpenter, Esther B. *South County Studies of Some Eighteenth Century Persons, Places & Conditions.* Boston, 1924.

Cary, John. *Joseph Warren: Physician, Politician, Patriot.* Urbana: University of Illinois Press, 1961.

Charvat, William. *The Origins of American Critical Thought, 1810–1835.* New York: A. S. Barnes, 1961.

Chase, Fannie S. *Wiscasset in Pownalborough.* Wiscasset, Maine: Southworth-Anthaensen Press, 1941.

Clapp, William W., Jr. *A Record of the Boston Stage.* Boston and Cambridge, 1853.

Clarke, W. K. Lowther. *Eighteenth Century Piety.* London: Macmillan, 1944.

Cockburn, J. S. *A History of English Assizes, 1558–1714.* Cambridge: Cambridge University Press, 1972.

Colley, Linda. *Britons: Forging the Nation, 1707–1837.* New Haven: Yale University Press, 1992.

———. *In Defiance of Oligarchy: The Tory Party, 1714–60.* Cambridge: Cambridge University Press, 1982.

Collins, Varnum L. *President Witherspoon.* 2 vols. in 1. New York: Arno Press, 1969.

Colonial America: Essays in Politics and Social Development. Ed. Stanley N. Katz. Boston: Little, Brown, 1971.

A Condensed Record of the National Union Bank of Boston, Massachusetts. Boston, 1904[?].

Coolidge, Olivia E. *Colonial Entrepreneur: Dr. Silvester Gardiner and the Settlement of Maine's Kennebec Valley.* Gardiner, Maine: Tilbury House, 1999.

Corrigan, John. *The hidden balance: Religion and the social theories of Charles Chauncy and Jonathan Mayhew.* New York: Cambridge University Press, 1987.

Dalzell, Robert F., Jr. *Enterprising Elite: The Boston Associates and the World They Made.* Cambridge, Mass.: Harvard University Press, 1987.

Derry, Warren. *Dr. Parr: A Portrait of the Whig Dr. Johnson.* Oxford: Clarendon Press, 1966.

Dibdin, James C. *The Annals of the Edinburgh Stage.* Edinburgh, 1888.

Dictionary of American Biography. Ed. Allen Johnson and Dumas Malone. 20 vols. New York, 1928–36.

Dictionary of National Biography. Ed. Sir Leslie Stephen and Sir Sidney Lee. 22 vols. Oxford: Oxford University Press, 1885–1901.

Drake, Francis S. *The Town of Roxbury: Its Memorable Persons and Places.* Roxbury, Mass., 1878.

Duniway, Clyde A. *The Development of Freedom of the Press in Massachusetts.* New York, 1906.

Dunlap, William. *History of the American Theatre.* 2 vols. London, 1833.

———. *The Life of George Fred. Cooke.* 2 vols. London, 1815.

Early American Drama. Ed. Jeffrey H. Richards. New York: Penguin, 1997.

East, Robert A. *John Quincy Adams: The Critical Years, 1785–1794.* New York: Bookman, 1962.

Elias, Norbert. *The Civilizing Process: The History of Manners.* Trans. Edmund Jephcott. New York: Urizen Books, 1978.

Elkins, Stanley, and Eric McKitrick. *The Age of Federalism.* New York: Oxford University Press, 1993.

Ellis, Harold Milton. *Joseph Dennie and His Circle: A Study in American Literature from 1792 to 1812.* Austin: *Bulletin of the University of Texas* [Studies in English, no. 3], 1915.

Elton, G. R. *England under the Tudors.* London: Methuen, 1955.

The Enlightenment in National Context. Ed. Roy Porter and Mikulas Teich. Cambridge: Cambridge University Press, 1981.

The Federalist Literary Mind: Selections from the Monthly Anthology and Boston Review. Ed. Lewis P. Simpson. Baton Rouge: Louisiana State University Press, 1962.

Felt, Joseph B. *Memorials of William Smith Shaw.* Boston, 1852.

Fenn, Elizabeth A. *Pox Americana: The Great Smallpox Epidemic of 1775–82.* New York: Hill & Wang, 2001.

Ferguson, Robert. *Law and Letters in American Culture.* Cambridge, Mass.: Harvard University Press, 1984.

Fiering, Norman. *Moral Philosophy at Seventeenth-Century Harvard: A Discipline in Transition.* Chapel Hill: University of North Carolina Press, 1981.

Fifoot, C. H. S. *Lord Mansfield.* Oxford: Clarendon Press, 1936.

The First Modern Society: Essays in English History in Honour of Lawrence Stone. Ed. A. L. Beier, David Cannadine, and James M. Rosenheim. Cambridge: Cambridge University Press, 1989.

Fischer, David Hackett. *The Revolution of American Conservatism: The Federalist Party in the Era of Jeffersonian Democracy.* New York: Harper & Row, 1965.

Folsom, George. *History of Saco and Biddeford.* Saco, Maine, 1830.

Foote, Henry Wilder. *Annals of King's Chapel.* 2 vols. Boston, 1896.

———. *John Smibert, Painter.* Cambridge, Mass.: Harvard University Press, 1950.

Forbes, Duncan. *Hume's Philosophical Politics.* Cambridge: Cambridge University Press, 1975.

Gardiner, Robert Hallowell. *Early Recollections of Robert Hallowell Gardiner, 1782–1864.* Hallowell, Maine, 1936.

Gaustad, Edwin S. *George Berkeley in America.* New Haven: Yale University Press, 1979.

Gawalt, Gerald W. *The Promise of Power: The Emergence of the Legal Profession in Massachusetts, 1760–1840.* Westport, Conn.: Greenwood Press, 1979.

The Glasgow Enlightenment. Ed. Andrew Hook and Richard B. Sher. East Lothian. U.K.: Tuckwell Press, 1995.

Glasgow, Volume I: Beginnings to 1830. Ed. T. M. Devine and Gordon Jackson. Manchester: Manchester University Press, 1995.

Goldthwaite, Charlotte. *Goldthwaite Genealogy.* Hartford, 1899.

Goodman, Paul. *The Democratic-Republicans of Massachusetts: Politics in a Young Republic.* Cambridge, Mass.: Harvard University Press, 1964.

Goveia, Elsa V. *Slave Society in the British Leeward Islands at the End of the Eighteenth Century.* New Haven: Yale University Press, 1965.

Gras, N. S. B. *The Massachusetts First National Bank of Boston, 1784–1934.* Cambridge, Mass.: Harvard University Press, 1937.

Greene, Jack. *Peripheries and Center: Constitutional Development in the Extended Politics of the British Empire and the United States, 1607–1788.* Athens: University of Georgia Press, 1986.

Greenslet, Ferris. *The Lowells and Their Seven Worlds.* Boston: Houghton Mifflin, 1946.

Griffin, Edward M. *Old Brick: Charles Chauncy of Boston, 1705–1787.* Minneapolis: University of Minnesota Press, 1980.

Hall, Peter Dobkin. "Family Structure and Class Consolidation among the Boston Brahmins." Ph.D. diss., SUNY-Stony Brook, 1973.

———. *The Organization of American Culture, 1700–1900.* New York: New York University Press, 1982.

Hall, Van Beck. *Politics without Parties: Massachusetts, 1780–1791.* Pittsburgh: University of Pittsburgh Press, 1972.

Hammond, Bray. *Banks and Politics in America from the Revolution to the Civil War.* Princeton: Princeton University Press, 1957.

Hancock, David. *Citizens of the World: London Merchants and the Integration of the British Atlantic Community, 1735–1785.* New York: Cambridge University Press, 1995.

Handlin, Oscar, and Mary Flug Handlin. *Commonwealth: A Study of the Role of Government in the American Economy: Massachusetts, 1774–1861.* Cambridge, Mass.: Harvard University Press, 1969.

Head, C. Grant. *Eighteenth Century Newfoundland: A Geographer's Perspective.* Toronto: McClelland and Stewart, 1976.

Hempton, David. *Religion and Political Culture in Britain and Ireland: From the Glorious Revolution to the Decline of Empire.* New York: Cambridge University Press, 1996.

Hirschman, Albert O. *The Passions and the Interests: Political Arguments for Capitalism before Its Triumph.* Princeton: Princeton University Press, 1977.

Horne, Thomas A. *The Social Thought of Bernard Mandeville: Virtue and Commerce in Early Eighteenth-Century England.* New York: Columbia University Press, 1978.

Horwitz, Morton J. *The Transformation of American Law, 1780–1860.* Cambridge, Mass.: Harvard University Press, 1977.

The House of Commons, 1754–1790. Ed. Sir Lewis Namier and John Brooke. 3 vols. London: Secker & Warburg, 1985.

The House of Commons, 1790–1820. Ed. R. G. Thorne. 5 vols. London: Secker & Warburg, 1986.

Howe, Daniel Walker. *The Unitarian Conscience: Harvard Moral Philosophy, 1805–1861.* Cambridge, Mass.: Harvard University Press, 1970.

Howell, David W. *Patriarchs and Parasites: The Gentry of South-West Wales in the Eighteenth Century.* Cardiff: University of Wales Press, 1986.

Jenkins, Philip. *The making of a ruling class: The Glamorgan gentry, 1640–1790.* Cambridge: Cambridge University Press, 1983.

Johnson, Richard R. *Adjustment to Empire: The New England Colonies, 1675–1715.* Brunswick, N.J.: Rutgers University Press, 1981.

Jones, E. Alfred. *American Members of the Inns of Court.* London: Saint Catherine Press, 1924.

Jones, J. Gwynfor. *Early Modern Wales, c. 1525–1640.* New York: St. Martin's Press, 1994.

Kerber, Linda. *Federalists in Dissent: Imagery and Ideology in Jeffersonian America.* Ithaca: Cornell University Press, 1980.

Kershaw, Gordon E. *The Kennebeck Proprietors, 1749–1775.* Somersworth, N.H.: New Hampshire Publishing Company, 1975.

Kirker, Harold, and James Kirker. *Bulfinch's Boston, 1787–1817.* New York: Oxford University Press, 1964.

Kremers, Edward, and George Urdang. *History of Pharmacy: A Guide and a Survey.* Philadelphia: J. B. Lippincott, 1940.

Kussrow, Van Carl, Jr. "On with the Show: A study of public arguments in favor of theatre in America during the eighteenth century." Ph.D. diss., Indiana University, 1959.

Langford, Paul. *A Polite and Commercial People: England, 1727–1783*. Oxford: Clarendon Press, 1989.

Law, Economy and Society, 1750–1914: Essays in the History of English Law. Ed. G. R. Rubin and David Sugarman. Abingdon: Professional Books, 1984.

Laws, Edward. *The History of Little England beyond Wales*. Haverfordwest, [1888] 1995.

Lawyers in Early Modern Europe and America. Ed. Wilfrid Prest. New York: Holmes & Meier, 1981.

Lee, Eliza Buckminster. *Memoirs of Rev. Joseph Buckminster, D.D., and of his son, Rev. Joseph Stevens Buckminster*. Boston, 1851.

Lemmings, David. *Gentlemen and Barristers: The Inns of Court and the English Bar 1680–1730*. Oxford: Clarendon Press, 1990.

Levy, Leonard W. *Legacy of Suppression: Freedom of Speech and Press in Early American History*. Cambridge, Mass.: Harvard University Press, 1960.

Lillywhite, Bryant. *London Coffee Houses*. London: George Allen & Unwin, 1963.

Link, Eugene P. *Democratic-Republican Societies, 1790–1800*. New York: Columbia University Press, 1942.

Lodge, Henry Cabot. *Life and Letters of George Cabot*. Boston, 1878.

Loring, James S. *The Hundred Boston Orators*. Boston, 1853.

Lovejoy, Arthur O. *The Great Chain of Being: A Study of the History of an Idea*. Cambridge, Mass.: Harvard University Press, 1964.

Maas, David Edward. *The Return of the Massachusetts Loyalists*. New York: Garland, 1989.

Maier, Pauline. *The Old Revolutionaries: Political Lives in the Age of Samuel Adams*. New York: Alfred A. Knopf, 1980.

Mann, Bruce H. *Republic of Debtors: Bankruptcy in the Age of American Independence*. Cambridge, Mass.: Harvard University Press, 2002.

Mason, Jeremiah. *Memoir and Correspondence of Jeremiah Mason*. Cambridge, Mass., 1873.

Massachusetts and the New Nation. Ed. Conrad Edick Wright. Boston: Massachusetts Historical Society, 1992.

Materials for a Catalogue of the Masters and Scholars who have belonged to the Public Latin School. Boston, 1847.

Maurer, Shawn Lisa. *Proposing Men: Dialectics of Gender and Class in the Eighteenth-Century Periodical*. Stanford: Stanford University Press, 1998.

May, Henry F. *The Enlightenment in America*. New York: Oxford University Press, 1976.

Meek, Ronald L. *Social science and the ignoble savage*. Cambridge: Cambridge University Press, 1976.

The Memorial History of Boston. Ed. Justin Winsor. 4 vols. Boston, 1882.

Mitchell, L. G. *Charles James Fox.* New York: Oxford University Press, 1992.

Morgan, Edmund S., and Helen M. Morgan. *The Stamp Act Crisis: Prologue to Revolution.* New York: Collier, 1963.

Morison, Samuel Eliot. *The Life and Letters of Harrison Gray Otis, Federalist, 1765–1848.* 2 vols. Boston, 1913.

————. *Three Centuries of Harvard, 1636–1936.* Cambridge, Mass.: Harvard University Press, 1936.

Namier, Lewis. *Crossroads of Power: Essays on Eighteenth-Century England.* London: Hamish Hamilton, 1962.

————. *The Structure of Politics at the Accession of George III.* London: Macmillan, 1961.

Nelson, William E. *Americanization of the Common Law: The Impact of Legal Change on Massachusetts Society, 1760–1830.* Athens: University of Georgia Press, 1994.

Newell, Margaret Ellen. *From Dependency to Independence: Economic Revolution in Colonial New England.* Ithaca: Cornell University Press, 1998.

Nicholas, Thomas. *Annals and Antiquities of the Counties and County Families of Wales.* 2 vols. London, 1872.

Norton, Mary Beth. *The British-Americans: The Loyalist Exiles in England, 1774–1789.* Boston: Little, Brown, 1972.

Oldham, James. *The Mansfield Manuscripts and the Growth of English Law in the Eighteenth Century.* 2 vols. Chapel Hill: University of North Carolina Press, 1992.

Oldnall, William Russell. *The Practice of the Court of Great Sessions on the Carmarthen Circuit.* London, 1814.

O'Shaughnessy, Andrew J. *An Empire Divided: The American Revolution and the British Caribbean.* Philadelphia: University of Pennsylvania Press, 2000.

————. "The Politics of the Leeward Islands, 1763–1783." D.Phil. diss., Oxford University, 1987.

Pares, Richard. *A West-India Fortune.* London: Longmans, Green, 1950.

Park, Lawrence. *Gilbert Stuart.* 4 vols. New York, 1926.

Parker, Barbara Neville. *John Singleton Copley.* Boston: Museum of Fine Arts, 1938.

Parkman, Francis. *Montcalm and Wolfe.* 2 vols. Boston, 1909.

Parry, Glyn. *A Guide to the Records of Great Sessions in Wales.* Aberystwyth: National Library of Wales, 1995.

Pendleton, Emily, and Milton Ellis. *Philenia: The Life and Works of Sarah Wentworth Morton, 1759–1846.* Orono, Maine: University of Maine Press [University of Maine Studies, 2nd ser., no. 20], 1931.

Phillips, James Duncan. *The Life and Times of Richard Derby, Merchant of Salem, 1712 to 1783.* Cambridge, Mass., 1929.

Phillipson, Nicholas. *Hume.* London: Weidenfeld & Nicolson, 1989.

Polson, Archer. *Law and Lawyers: A Sketch Book of Legal Biography, Gossip, and Anecdote.* London, 1858.

Porter, Roy, and G. S. Rousseau. *Gout: The Patrician Malady.* New Haven: Yale University Press, 1998.

The Press & the American Revolution. Ed. Bernard Bailyn and John Hench. Worcester: American Antiquarian Society, 1980.

Price, Cecil. *The English Theatre in Wales in the Eighteenth and Early Nineteenth Centuries.* Cardiff: University of Wales Press, 1948.

Prown, Jules David. *John Singleton Copley.* 2 vols. Cambridge, Mass.: Harvard University Press, 1966.

Quincy, Josiah. *The History of the Boston Athenaeum.* Cambridge, Mass., 1851.

————. *The History of Harvard University.* 2 vols. New York: Arno Press, 1977.

Rebora, Carrie, et al. *John Singleton Copley in America.* New York: Metropolitan Museum of Art, 1995.

Robinson, Caroline E. *The Gardiners of Narragansett.* Providence, 1919.

Robson, Robert. *The Attorney in Eighteenth-Century England.* Cambridge: Cambridge University Press, 1959.

Rowland, Kate Mason. *The Life of Charles Carroll of Carrollton, 1737–1832.* 2 vols. New York, 1898.

Rude, George. *Wilkes and Liberty: A Social Study of 1763 to 1774.* Oxford: Clarendon Press, 1962.

Saunders, Richard H. *John Smibert, Colonial America's First Portrait Painter.* New Haven: Yale University Press, 1995.

Schutz, John A. *William Shirley: King's Governor of Massachusetts.* Chapel Hill: University of North Carolina Press, 1961.

Scotland and America in the Age of Enlightenment. Ed. Richard B. Sher and Jeffrey R. Smitten. Edinburgh: Edinburgh University Press, 1990.

Scotland in the Age of Improvement: Essays in Scottish History in the Eighteenth Century. Ed. N. T. Phillipson and Rosalind Mitchison. Edinburgh: Edinburgh University Press, 1970.

Scott, Walter Robert. *Adam Smith as Student and Professor.* Glasgow, 1937.

Scovel, Carl, and Charles C. Forman. *Journey toward Independence: King's Chapel's Transition to Unitarianism.* Boston: Skinner House Books, 1993.

Shipton, Clifford K. *Sibley's Harvard Graduates*, vols. 4–17. Boston: Harvard University Press, 1933–75.

Silverman, Kenneth. *A Cultural History of the American Revolution.* New York: Thomas Y. Crowell, 1976.

Sociability and Society in Eighteenth-Century Scotland. Ed. John Dwyer and Richard B. Sher. Edinburgh: Mercat Press, 1993.

Stone, Lawrence, and Jeanne C. Fawtier Stone. *An Open Elite? England, 1540–1880.* Oxford: Clarendon Press, 1984.

Story, Ronald D. "Class Development and Cultural Institutions in Boston, 1800–1870: Harvard, the Athenaeum, and the Lowell Institute." Ph.D. diss., SUNY–Stony Brook, 1972.

————. *The Forging of an Aristocracy: Harvard and the Boston Upper Class, 1800–1870*. Middletown, Conn.: Wesleyan University Press, 1980.

Strang, John. *Glasgow and its Clubs*. London and Glasgow, 1857.

[Sullivan, William.] *Familiar Letters on Public Characters, and Public Events*. Boston, 1834.

Tanselle, G. Thomas. *Royall Tyler*. Cambridge, Mass.: Harvard University Press, 1967.

Taylor, Alan. *Liberty Men and Great Proprietors: The Revolutionary Settlement on the Maine Frontier, 1760–1820*. Chapel Hill: University of North Carolina Press, 1990.

[Thatcher, Benjamin B.] *Traits of the Tea Party; being a Memoir of George R. T. Hewes*. New York, 1835.

Ticknor, George. *Life of William Hickling Prescott*. Boston, 1864.

Townsend, Annette. *The Auchmuty Family of Scotland and America*. New York: Grafton Press, 1932.

Tyack, David B. *George Ticknor and the Boston Brahmins*. Cambridge, Mass.: Harvard University Press, 1967.

Ulrich, Laurel Thatcher. *A Midwife's Tale: The Life of Martha Ballard, Based on Her Diary, 1785–1812*. New York: Vintage, 1990.

A Union for Empire: Political Thought and the British Union of 1707. Ed. John Robertson. New York: Cambridge University Press, 1995.

Updike, Wilkins. *History of the Episcopal Church, in Narragansett, Rhode Island*. New York, 1947.

Viets, Henry R. *A Brief History of Medicine in Massachusetts*. Boston and New York, 1930.

Ward, J. R. *British West Indian Slavery, 1750–1834: The Process of Amelioration*. Oxford: Clarendon Press, 1988.

Warden, G. B. *Boston, 1689–1776*. Boston: Little, Brown, 1970.

Warfel, Harry R. *Noah Webster: Schoolmaster to America*. New York: Octagon Books, 1966.

Waters, John J., Jr. *The Otis Family in Provincial and Revolutionary Massachusetts*. Chapel Hill: University of North Carolina Press, 1968.

Watts, Arthur P. *Nevis and St. Christopher's, 1782–1784*. Paris, 1925.

Weightman, Gavin. *The Frozen-Water Trade*. New York: Hyperion, 2003.

William Robertson and the Expansion of Empire. Ed. Stewart J. Brown. New York: Cambridge University Press, 1997.

Williams, Raymond. *Culture and Society, 1780–1950*. New York: Columbia University Press, 1958.

Williams, W. Llewelyn. *An Account of the King's Court of Great Sessions in Wales*. London, 1916.

Williams, W. R. *The History of the Great Sessions in Wales, 1542–1830*. Brecknock, 1899.

Willis, William. *A History of the Law, the Courts, and the Lawyers of Maine.* Portland, Maine, 1863.

Wood, Gordon S. *The Creation of the American Republic, 1776–1787.* Chapel Hill: University of North Carolina Press, 1969.

———. *The Radicalism of the American Revolution.* New York: Alfred A. Knopf, 1992.

Wright, Conrad. *The Beginnings of Unitarianism in America.* Boston: Beacon Press, 1955.

Secondary Sources, Articles and Chapters

Adair, Douglass. "'That Politics May Be Reduced to a Science': David Hume, James Madison, and the Tenth *Federalist.*" *Huntington Library Quarterly* 20 (August 1957), 343–360.

Armitage, David. "Greater Britain: A Useful Category of Historical Analysis?" *American Historical Review* 104 (April 1999), 427–445.

Breen, T. H. "Ideology and Nationalism on the Eve of the American Revolution: Revisions Once More in Need of Revising." *Journal of American History* 84 (June 1997), 13–39.

Breskin, Isabel. "'On the Periphery of a Greater World': John Singleton Copley's *Turquerie* Portraits." *Winterthur Portfolio* 36 (Summer–Autumn 2001), 97–123.

Brooks, C. W. "Interpersonal conflict and social tension: civil litigation in England, 1640–1830." In *The First Modern Society,* 357–399.

Brown, Margaret L. "William Bingham, Agent of the Continental Congress in Martinique." *Pennsylvania Magazine of History and Biography* 61 (January 1937), 54–87.

———. "Mr. and Mrs. William Bingham of Philadelphia: Rulers of the Republican Court." *Pennsylvania Magazine of History and Biography* 61 (July 1937), 286–324.

———. "William Bingham, Eighteenth Century Magnate." *Pennsylvania Magazine of History and Biography* 61 (October 1937), 387–434.

Brown, Stewart J. "William Robertson (1721–1793) and the Scottish Enlightenment." In *William Robertson and the Expansion of Empire,* 7–35.

Buell, Lawrence. "Joseph Stevens Buckminster: The Making of a New England Saint." *Canadian Review of American Studies* 10 (Spring 1979), 1–29.

Christianson, Eric H. "The Colonial Surgeon's Rise to Prominence: Dr. Silvester Gardiner (1707–1786) and the Practice of Lithotomy in New England." *New England Historical and Genealogical Register* 136 (April 1982), 104–114.

Clive, John. "The Social Background of the Scottish Renaissance." In *Scotland in the Age of Improvement,* 224–244.

Clive, John, and Bernard Bailyn. "England's Cultural Provinces: Scotland and America." *William and Mary Quarterly* 11 (April 1954), 200–213.

Coats, A. W. "Changing Attitudes to Labour in the Mid-Eighteenth Century." *Economic History Review* 11 (August 1958), 35–51.

Colley, Linda. "Whose Nation? Class and National Consciousness in Britain, 1750–1830." *Past & Present* 113 (November 1986), 97–117

Dawson, Deidre. "Is Sympathy so Surprising?: Adam Smith and French Fictions of Sympathy." In *Sociability and Society*, 147–162.

Devine, T. M. "The Golden Age of Tobacco." In *Glasgow, Volume I: Beginnings to 1830*, 139–183.

Dickason, David G. "The Nineteenth-Century Indo-American Ice Trade: An Hyperborean Epic." *Modern Asian Studies* 25 (February 1991), 53–89.

Duffy, Eamon. "*Correspondence Fraternelle:* The SPCK, the SPG, and the Churches of Switzerland in the War of the Spanish Succession." In *Reform and Reformation: England and the Continent c. 1500–c. 1750*, Ed. Derek Baker. Oxford: Basil Blackwell, 1979, 251–280.

Duman, Daniel. "The English Bar in the Georgian Era." In *Lawyers in Early Modern Europe and America*, 86–107.

East, Robert A. "The Business Entrepreneur in a Changing Colonial Economy, 1763- 1795." *Journal of Economic History* 6 (May 1946), 16–27.

Elkins, Stanley, and Eric McKitrick. "The Founding Fathers: Young Men of the Revolution." *Political Science Quarterly* 76 (June 1961), 181–216.

Emerson, Roger L. "Politics and the Glasgow Professors, 1690–1800." In *The Glasgow Enlightenment*, 21–39.

Fischer, David Hackett. "The Myth of the Essex Junto." *William and Mary Quarterly* 21 (April 1964), 191–235.

Forbes, Duncan. "'Scientific' Whiggism: Adam Smith and John Millar." *Cambridge Journal* 7 (August 1954), 643–670.

Gould, Eliga H. "American Independence and Britain's Counter-Revolution." *Past & Present* 154 (February 1997), 107–141.

———. "A Virtual Nation: Greater Britain and the Imperial Legacy of the American Revolution." *American Historical Review* 104 (April 1999), 476–489.

Grant, Frederic, Jr. "Benjamin Austin, Jr.'s Struggle with the Lawyers." *Boston Bar Journal* 25 (September 1981), 19–29.

Handlin, Oscar, and Mary F. Handlin. "Radicals and Conservatives in Massachusetts after Independence." *New England Quarterly* 17 (September 1944), 343–355.

Hill, Hamilton. "William Phillips and William Phillips, Father and Son, 1722–1827." *New England Historical and Genealogical Register* 39 (April 1885), 109–117.

Howell, David. "Landed Society in Pembrokeshire, circa 1680–1830." *Pembrokeshire Historian* 3 (1971), 28–41.

Hulsebosch, Daniel J. "*Imperia in Imperio:* The Multiple Constitutions of Empire in New York, 1750–1777." *Law and History Review* 16 (Summer 1998), 319–379.

Jenkins, J. P. "Jacobites and Freemasons in Eighteenth-Century Wales." *Welsh History Review* 9 (December 1979), 391–406.

Jones, Francis. "Disaffection and Dissent in Pembrokeshire." *Trans. Hon. Soc. Cymm.* (1946–47), 206–231.

———. "Harries of Tregwynt." *Trans. Hon. Soc. Cymm.* (1943 and 1944), 108–119.

———. "The Society of Sea Serjeants." *Trans. Hon. Soc. Cymm.* (1967), 57–91.

Katz, Stanley N. "Republicanism and the Law of Inheritance in the American Revolutionary Era." *Michigan Law Review* 76 (November 1977), 1–29.

Kenyon, Cecelia M. "Alexander Hamilton: Rousseau of the Right." *Political Science Quarterly* 73 (June 1958), 161–178.

Kerber, Linda, and Walter John Morris. "Politics and Literature: The Adams Family and the *Port Folio*." *William and Mary Quarterly* 23 (July 1966), 450–476.

Kidd, Colin. "North Britishness and the Nature of Eighteenth-Century British Patriotisms." *Historical Journal* 39 (June 1996), 361–382.

Landsman, Ned. "The legacy of British Union for the North American colonies: provincial elites and the problem of Imperial Union." In *A Union for Empire,* 297–317.

Langford, Paul. "British Correspondence in the Colonial Press, 1763–1775: A Study in Anglo-American Misunderstanding before the American Revolution." In *The Press & the American Revolution,* 273–313.

Lemmings, David. "Blackstone and Law Reform by Education: Preparation for the Bar and Lawyerly Culture in Eighteenth-Century England." *Law and History Review* 16 (Summer 1998), 211–255.

Livingston, Donald W. "Hume, English Barbarism and American Independence." In *Scotland and America in the Age of Enlightenment,* 133–147.

Lloyd, Rees L. "Welsh Masters of the Bench of the Inner Temple." *Trans. Hon. Soc. Cymm.* (1938), 155–245.

Lucas, Paul. "A Collective Biography of Students and Barristers of Lincoln's Inn, 1680–1804: A Study in the 'Aristocratic Resurgence' of the Eighteenth Century." *Journal of Modern History* 46 (June 1974), 227–261.

Maier, Pauline. "The Debate over Incorporations: Massachusetts in the Early Republic." In *Massachusetts and the New Nation,* 73–117.

Marshall, P. J. "Empire and Authority in the later Eighteenth Century." *Journal of Imperial and Commonwealth History,* 15 (January 1987), 105–122.

Mathew, W. M. "The Origins and Occupations of Glasgow Students, 1740–1839." *Past & Present* 33 (April 1966), 74–94.

Meek, R. L. "New light on Adam Smith's Glasgow lectures on Jurisprudence." *History of Political Economy* 8 (Winter 1976), 439–477.

Miles, M. "'Eminent Practitioners': The New Visage of Country Attorneys, c. 1750–1800." In *Law, Economy and Society,* 470–503.

———. "The Money Market in the Early Industrial Revolution: The Evidence from West Riding Attorneys, c. 1750–1800." *Business History* 23 (July 1981), 127–146.

Miller, William Davis. "The Narragansett Planters." *Proceedings of the American Antiquarian Society* 43 (1933), 49–115.

Murrin, John M. "The Legal Transformation: The Bench and Bar of Eighteenth-Century Massachusetts." In *Colonial America*, 415–449.

Nash, Gary B. "The Failure of Female Factory Labor in Colonial Boston." *Labor History* 20 (Spring 1979), 165–188.

Nellis, Eric G. "Misreading the Signs: Industrial Imitation, Poverty, and the Social Order in Colonial Boston." *New England Quarterly* 59 (December 1986), 486–507.

Packard, Bertram E. "John Gardiner, Barrister." *Sprague's Journal of Maine History* 9 (April–May–June 1921), 49–59.

Packard, Francis R. "William Cheselden, Some of His Contemporaries, and Their American Pupils." *Annals of Medical History*, 2nd series, 9 (November 1937), 533–548.

Patterson, William D. "Record of Marriages in Pownalborough, 1787–1794." *Maine Historical Magazine* 9 (January–February–March 1894), 43–45.

Phillipson, Nicholas. "The Scottish Enlightenment." In *The Enlightenment in National Context*, 19–40.

Pitman, Frank Wesley. "Slavery on British West India Plantations in the Eighteenth Century." *Journal of Negro History* 11 (October 1926), 584–668.

Pocock, J. G. A. "Empire, State and Confederation: The War of American Independence as a Crisis in Multiple Monarchy." In *A Union for Empire*, 318–348.

Price, Cecil. "Polite Life in Eighteenth-Century Wales." *Welsh Anvil* 5 (July 1953), 89–98.

Price, Jacob M. "The Rise of Glasgow in the Chesapeake Tobacco Trade, 1707–1775." *William and Mary Quarterly* 11 (April 1954), 179–199.

Rees, William. "The Union of England and Wales." *Trans. Hon. Soc. Cymm.* (1937), 27–100.

Rice, Howard C. "James Swan: Agent of the French Republic, 1794–1796." *New England Quarterly* 10 (September 1937), 464–486.

Rosenberg, Nathan. "Mandeville and Laissez-Faire." *Journal of the History of Ideas* 24 (April–June 1963), 183–196.

Ross, Ian Simpson. "Adam Smith's 'Happiest' Years as a Glasgow Professor." In *Glasgow Enlightenment*, 73–94.

Seybolt, Robert Francis. "Lithotomies Performed by Dr. Gardiner, of Boston, 1738 and 1741." *New England Journal of Medicine* 202 (16 January 1930), 109.

Sher, Richard. "Commerce, Religion and the Enlightenment in Eighteenth-Century Glasgow." In *Glasgow, Volume I: Beginnings to 1830*, 312–359.

Silsby, Herbert T. "John Gardiner: Law Prophet." *Supreme Judicial Court Historical Society Journal* 2 (1996), 75–94.

Simpson, Lewis P. "Federalism and the Crisis of Literary Order." *American Literature* 32 (November 1960), 253–266.

Smith, Barbara Clark. "Markets, Streets, and Stores: Contested Terrain in Pre-Industrial Boston." In *Autre temps, autre espace: Etudes su l'Amerique pre-industrielle*. Ed. Elise Marienstras and Barbara Karsky. Nancy: Presses Universitaires de Nancy, 1986, 181–197.

Smith, Janet Adam. "Some Eighteenth-Century Ideas of Scotland." In *Scotland in the Age of Improvement*, 107–124.

Steele, I. K. "A London Trader and the Atlantic Empire: Joseph Cruttenden, Apothecary, 1710–1717." *William and Mary Quarterly* 34 (April 1977), 281–297.

Story, Ronald. "Class and Culture in Boston: The Athenaeum, 1807–1860." *American Quarterly* 27 (May 1975), 178–199.

Thomas, Peter D. G. "Jacobitism in Wales." *Welsh History Review* 1 (1962), 297–300.

Waldstreicher, David, and Stephen R. Grossbart. "Abraham Bishop's Vocation; or, The Mediation of Jeffersonian Politics." *Journal of the Early Republic* 18 (Winter 1998), 617–657.

Warden, G. B. "Inequality and Instability in Eighteenth-Century Boston." *Journal of Interdisciplinary History* 6 (Spring 1976), 585–620.

Warren, Charles. "Samuel Adams and the Sans Souci Club in 1785." *Proceedings of the Massachusetts Historical Society* 60 (May 1927), 318–344.

Watson, Eric R. "John Wilkes and the 'Essay on Woman.'" *Notes and Queries*, 11th series, vol. 9 (14 and 28 March 1914), 203–205, 241–242.

Weir, David R. "Tontines, Public Finance, and Revolution in France and England, 1688–1789." *Journal of Economic History* 49 (March 1989), 95–124.

"William Bingham's Maine Lands, 1790–1820." Ed. Frederick S. Allis Jr. *Publications of the Colonial Society of Massachusetts* 36 (1954).

Winder, W. H. D. "Equity in the Courts of Great Sessions." *Law Quarterly Review* 55 (January 1939), 106–121.

Wood, Gordon. "The Enemy is Us: Democratic Capitalism in the Early Republic." *Journal of the Early Republic* 16 (Summer 1996), 293–308.

Young, Alfred F. "George Robert Twelves Hewes (1742–1840): A Boston Shoemaker and the Memory of the American Revolution." *William and Mary Quarterly* 38 (October 1981), 561–623.

INDEX

Adams family, 5
Adams, Abigail, 143, 205
Adams, David Phineas, 204
Adams, John, 35, 58, 87, 111, 143, 154,
    167, 185, 201, 205, 250n9
Adams, John Quincy, 114, 143, 157, 159,
    205
Adams, Samuel, 47, 114–115, 139, 147,
    151, 157–158
Adams, Thomas Boylston, 200–201
Addison, Joseph, 25, 194, 202
Akers, Aretas, 94, 97, 99–100
America and Americans, 4–8, 17–18, 39,
    57, 70, 82, 84, 96, 108, 205; British
    connections, 2–4, 6, 20, 36, 41, 45,
    151–152, 163, 171, 177, 199, 201–203,
    214–216, 218, 222. *See also* Revolution,
    American; United States, their politics
American Company of Comedians, 139–
    140
Amherst, Sir Jeffrey, 38
Anglicans. *See* Church of England
Anne (queen of England and Scotland), 95
Anthology Society, 205–207, 210–211,
    213–214
Antigua, 88–89
Apthorp, Charles, 158
Apthorp, East, 215
Apthorp, Frances, 158
Assizes, 74–75, 77–80, 88. *See also* Great
    Sessions
Atterbury, Francis, 62, 81
Attucks, Crispus, 35
Auchmuty, Robert, 58–59
Auchmuty, Samuel, 84
Austin, Benjamin Jr., 113–114, 157, 160,
    185–186, 188

Bacon, Sir Francis, 50–51, 74, 76
Bahamas, 72, 87

Bailey, Jacob, 35, 37
Baring, Alexander, 164
Barrell, Joseph, 151–153
Basseterre, St. Kitts, 91, 94, 96, 100
Beardmore, Arthur, 65–66
Berkeley, George, 18, 45–46
Bermuda, 45
Bingham, Anne Willing, 164
Bingham, William, 163–164, 190
Bishop, Abraham, 155, 260n78
Blackstone, Sir William, 60, 64, 104,
    107, 116, 129
Board Alley Theatre, 142, 148, 150–151,
    156–157
Board of Trade, 32, 73, 80, 86–87, 90, 93
Boston, 1, 8–10, 12, 19, 21, 26, 29, 37,
    40, 46, 55, 57, 134, 139, 149–150,
    159–160, 187, 195, 204, 219; Massacre,
    35, 88; Medical Society of, 20; munici-
    pal reform, 136, 151–156; public
    health, 22–23, 148; town meeting, 22,
    27, 59, 141, 146, 151–153, 155–156
Boston Associates, 30, 218
Boston Athenaeum, 205, 211
Boston Latin School, 47, 146, 157
Boswell, James, 64–65
Bowdoin, James, 34, 46, 161, 219
Bradford, James, 73
Bradford, William, 30, 33
Breck, Samuel, 150
Bridge, James, 114
Brimstone Hill (St. Kitts), 99
Bristol, England, 37
Britain. *See* Great Britain
British America and British-Americans.
    See America and Americans
British Empire, 1, 3, 5, 7, 9–10, 12, 15–
    18, 27, 34, 45, 56, 84, 96, 136, 216,
    220, 222. *See also* Great Britain
Brown, William Hill, 158